GP0018/2015

# Advances in Organization Development

## Volume 1

edited by

Fred Massarik

 **ABLEX PUBLISHING CORPORATION**
**NORWOOD, NEW JERSEY**

Printed in the United States of America.

**Library of Congress Cataloging-in-Publication Data**

Advances in organization development / edited by Fred Massarik.
    p.  cm.
  Includes bibliographical references.
  ISBN 0–89391–242–5 (v. 1)
  1. Organizational change.  I. Massarik, Fred.
HD58.8.A38 1989
658.4'06—dc20                            89–17852
                                                CIP

Ablex Publishing Corporation
355 Chestnut St.
Norwood, NJ 07648

# Contents

## Part three    Explorations and Experiences in OD Practice

## Part four    Trends and Time Lines in the OD Profession

# Preface

This is the first in a series of volumes in Organization Development and related fields. It is the purpose of this series—and thereby of this initial contribution—to provide new perspectives and viewpoints, in concept and theory, as well as in application and practice. Trends and "weathervane" ideas, one hopes, may find their way into the pages of this and subsequent books, forthcoming in the years of this century's final decade.

Two basic premises underlie what's ahead. First, the nature and rates of change in organizations and in their external environments are vastly different now than they had been when Organization Development began to assume shape. Today, *rapid* change, complexity, crisis, transformation—even chaos—are common characteristics of organizations and their environments. And second, this is the age of globality and of interrelatedness. There is very little that stands alone or that can pursue a relatively quiescent path, with only an occasional "blip" to disturb its linear projections. It is hardly news these days to note, per the old saying, that "when Wall Street sneezes the World catches a cold," but also the correlates . . . that sneezes in Brussels, London, Tokyo, or Singapore may have significant effects on Lower Manhattan and on points north, south, east, and west, everywhere.

Given these circumstances, not surprisingly the contributors to this volume come to the field from a variety of international vantage points—Australia, Switzerland, Austria, Japan, and the U.S., among others. Nor do they adopt any single theoretic position, even if there were such—their papers vary considerably in focus and emphasis, though perhaps a fairly widely shared value position having to do with the importance of naturally unfolding processes in complex systems, a recognition of pervasive complexity, and a preference for a humanistic nontechnocratic style may link them.

The chapters are arranged by four major headings:

- VISIONS AND VIEWPOINTS
- STRATEGIES AND STYLES OF INTERVENTION
- EXPLORATIONS AND EXPERIENCES IN OD PRACTICE, and
- TRENDS AND TIME LINES IN THE OD PROFESSION.

No introduction can provide a "summary" of content without doing violence to most everything—the variegated substance of the contributions themselves, the authors' individual lines of thought, and the inevitable interrelationships among topics. Suffice it to say that the contents variously address core values and processes in OD, a selected set of direct approaches and strategies in rapid and evanescent change, several case illustrations drawn from contrasting cultural milieus, and evolving directions in concepts and in practitioner competencies.

As we look to the decade ahead, we note that the contributors to the field itself will become still more diverse, in backgrounds and in their orientations. Not much will remain stable and linear here either. New ideas sprouting from disparate intellectual roots will make the difference. If you have something that you believe meets the spirit of *Advances in Organization Development,* for possible publication in a future volume, please let us know.

May our shared Nineties be fun, productive, and exciting!

Fred Massarik
Anderson Graduate School
of Management
UCLA

# 1

# Chaos and Change: Examining the Aesthetics of Organization Development

**Fred Massarik**
*Anderson Graduate School of Management, UCLA*

. . . The board had a thousand sides, and surfaces and dimensions, the pieces were of unknown number, and nature and value, the rules were uncertain, often you did not know whom you played, or where they were, often the moves must be made in darkness, in ignorance of your opponents position, his pieces, his strengths, his skills, his moves . . .

(Norman, 1988, p. 188; regarding the game of Kaissa)

The concepts of *change* and *organization development* have come to be inextricably linked. The association is both semantic and substantive. It is semantic because the very term *development*, whatever its context, implies a succession of (well . . . how should we put it?) *changing* sets of conditions, presumably in some knowable and possibly ordered sequence. And it is substantive because a wide variety of definitions of organization development (OD) seize upon change—often *planned* change, as based on behavioral science principles—as the crux of the field.[1] Terms such as *change-agent* further underline this emphasis.[2]

There is, of course, vast and probably unmanageable literature on the *meaning* of change and its parameters in broad compass.[3] With-

---

[1] Early works, such as Bennis, Benne, and Chin (1961), Bennis (1966), and Schein and Bennis (1965) are characteristic. Textbooks, such as Huse (1980), reaffirm this theme, as do publications in other cultural settings (Chowdhury, 1970). Also, publications focused on particular intervention styles (Steele, 1975).

[2] Examples are many; see Schein and Bennis (1965, p. 370).

[3] For instance, on classical formulations of theories of culture and social change, works in anthropology and sociology are of importance (Malinowski, 1945, see especially, "Theories of Change," pp. 14–26, and "Scientific Principles and Instruments in the Study of Culture Change," pp. 73–83; Ogburn, 1922). Further, on theories of sociocultural change see a succinct summary in Ryan (1969, pp. 29–50).

out becoming enthralled by the resulting complexity, and recognizing that no "holy grail" of a single "correct" definition exists, it would seem particularly necessary at this time, for both pragmatic and conceptual reasons, to re-examine the nature and significance of *change* in the OD context. One reason for this asserted urgency is the recent rise of CHAOS.

"Hold on . . . hold on . . . ," we might hear from the wings, "what's all this business with *chaos?* Has this become the buzz word of the year? Or what?" Or else, does it speak to issues that matter for the longer term, in OD as a field of practice and inquiry? The jury likely is still out on this matter, but let's note quickly that *change* and *chaos* are brothers-under-the-skin—each is involved with events characterized by uncertainty and variability, as from Time A to Time B, and inevitably at the time points beyond. And in a practical sense, each necessarily challenges managers and OD consultants by ensuing turbulence and unpredictability, to *do* or be done *to,* and probably both. For this reason and others, let's take a second look at *change* as a concept, but first we need to put *chaos* in perspective.

## CHAOS

Chaos as an item in the popular management literature no doubt received its primary push to visibility from Tom Peters' book *Thriving on Chaos* (Peters, 1987), a volume widely at hand on manager's bookshelves, variously reviewed and vigorously discussed. In spite of its currency—and the appearance of the word "chaos" in its title—apparently Peters' book does not contain a specific definition of the term; indeed there is not even a reference to it in the index! One gets the impression, however, that Peters' usage relates mainly to the complexity and often-unpredictable competitiveness of the worldwide business scene.

More precise considerations and explicit treatments appear in publications such as Gleick's *Chaos—Making a New Science* (Gleick, 1987), in the works of Mandelbrot (1983)[4] and Feigenbaum (1981), and in current technical writings as in brief reports in *Science.*[5]

---

[4] See chapter 20 for a mathematical and highly conceptualized treatment.

[5] For example, Pool (1989), with application to epidemiology, and Pool (1988), with reference to fluid flows and barium ions, including brief, helpful comments on distinctions among simple, complex, and chaotic systems. See also Prigogine and Stengers (1984).

Given this context, we need to clarify the meaning of chaos and its relationship to change, as it relates to organization development. We suggest that there are (to oversimplify) at least three types of chaos.

1. *CHAOS I* (or *ultimate chaos*): this type involves *indeterminate* components in random array (i.e., disarray). Here it is altogether unclear what it is that we're dealing with, and equally we're in the dark over how that "what" (primordial or organizational goo?) is structured. This one is a total mess, literally and figuratively. It resembles the classic *tohu-va-bohu*.

   There being no information regarding the nature of the "stuff" that is before us, which in turn has no structure, no prediction is possible. We can hope for good luck or we can try to act randomly—to outwit, or flow with, the vortex of prevailing randomness. Or else we may simply appear paralyzed and impotent as we contemplate an all-enveloping powerful vagueness that, we suggest, constitutes the *ultimate chaos*, or CHAOS I.

2. *CHAOS II* (or *conventional chaos*): this type involves *determinate* components in unknown array, often in rapid flux. Here it is fairly clear what it is that we're dealing with—bunches of people in organizations; some kind of technology surrounded by poorly-understood environments; rapid bursts of complex and unclear effects, unpredictably generated and impacting all of the above. By way of example, we may think of a very large corporate entity in an uncertain economic and market environment and one individual person, such as a lone OD consultant, standing at its doorstep, trying to understand what's going on. Or then again there may be a group of effective line managers and OD generalists enmeshed in the web of a major merger whose organizational and practical implications remain largely uncertain. In each instance, what seems to be "out there" contains some determinate (i.e., specifiable) elements with which the observer(s) (e.g., that lone OD consultant or the manager-OD group) presumably have had some generic if not necessarily particular acquaintance. Beyond that, lots and lots of stuff is unknown and, significantly, in major flux—*successive states of unknown array*.

   Here life isn't easy, but there *is* hope. The present situation may be confusing and the future uncertain, but the pieces-and-their interconnections are available in some form and potentially can be sorted out. It becomes possible to conceptually rearrange, or perceive in different manner, the inchoate but determinate components.

   This process is, by its nature, *iterative*. The world of CHAOS

II is far from static. To use more conventional OD language, diagnosis needs to be continuous and environmental scanning ongoing. We might even speak of *aggressive diagnosis*, or *high-intensity diagnosis*, to underline the resolute, active, and continuing nature of the diagnostic process necessarily required in efforts to move from the chaotic to some kind of pattern, time and time again.

CHAOS II may be termed *conventional chaos*, representing, as is found more and more these days, conditions of rapid and erratic alteration in systems of interacting known components which, however, are poorly understood, in large measure, at a given time.

3. *CHAOS III* (or *patterned chaos*): this type involves determinate components (as those found in CHAOS II) *after* some successful aggressive or high-intensity diagnosis has taken place. Now some kind of pattern has emerged, but this pattern is unstable, may relapse into CHAOS II, fade and, at any rate, require continuous redefinition.

Resulting patterns are generally nonlinear, variable, and ephemeral; may be presented graphically, with or without the aid of computers; and exist in nature and in organizations (Mandelbrot, 1977).

CHAOS III may be illustrated in nature in terms of fractal geometries (Mandelbrot, 1983), or by conceptual means which impose or discover evolving patterning and regularity that had been previously unknown or misunderstood. DNA and evolution are of this sort, but such discoveries are, of course, in themselves never fixed. Successively new states supersede old as the high-intensity diagnosis of science—the process of research and "making science happen"—proceeds in its course (Hanson, 1958). In this sense, scientific inquiry and chaos relevant to OD share a common aesthetic.

We may wish to think of the delineation of a particular pattern as representing a diagnostic moment, rather than a steady state. As has been variously pointed out, K. Lewin's classic formulation of "unfreezing" and "re-freezing" force fields no longer holds as metaphor of choice, unless these processes are seen as following each other in rapid succession, with possible oscillations and field turbulence impacting both rate and character of the change process.

As an example of CHAOS III in OD, we may think of an organizational diagnosis of a large, rapidly changing system at a particular time point. We may visualize a conceptual map including a multidimensional organization chart (Massarik, 1980; Massarik, Tannenbaum, Kahane, & Weschler, 1961), taking account of formal (pre-scribed and/or perceived), informal, affective, and actual relationships, and appropriate and focused (but rarely exhaustive) descriptions of relevant technological and organizational–cultural variables. In addition, nested within this map, one may identify specific *strategically-placed* combinations of individuals and their intrapersonal dynamics and interpersonal processes, for instance, bearing on process consultation, team building, or some other pos-sible intervention program.

Yet, in spite of the hypothetical wealth of data, as may be gathered by interviews, observations, reviews, of published material, exam-inations of artifacts and symbols (such as buildings or spaces), etc., significant and massive changes may again rapidly burst upon the scene—removal of a CEO, the launching of a hostile takeover bid, the sale of established divisions, "downsizing" resulting in separa-tions of large numbers of employees (it's "lean and mean" time these days!), or the introduction of a revolutionary new technology—any one or several of these, occurring simultaneously, may cause regres-sion to CHAOS II. And then another diagnostic effort to recapture the revised and current form of "patterned chaos" appears in CHAOS III.

The types of Chaos considered, particularly II and III, are of im-portance to an understanding of the OD process under conditions of rapid change. The term "change" has been used only incidentally in the preceding pages, yet it is evident that chaos(es) as discussed constitutes a particular kind of change involving successive, uncer-tain shifts among states in variables of concern to OD implementa-tion. It also must be clear that such successive shifts may follow quickly on each other's heels—and they often do—but more gradual transformations also are possible.

In this context, the OD practitioner needs to *monitor, predict, and respond* to the relative speed of impending change, rather than *assuming* either chaos or constancy in the conditions are strategic for the OD effort. He or she needs to navigate, with professional skill, between the Scylla of quick (but possibly futile) response by high-intensity diagnosis, or the Charibdis of unconcern and complacent faith that everything has remained pretty much as it had been.

## GENERIC CHANGE

In practical terms, conditions confronted in OD surely involve *generic change*—here proposed as the encompassing concept subsuming both *chaos* and a more *gradual change.* We now return to the anatomy (or aesthetic?) of generic change.

OD consultants typically are concerned with the impact of their interventions. On the other hand, efforts to rigorously allocate a given outcome, be it positive or negative, to a specific intervention, or series of interventions, often are not terribly successful. Such efforts frequently are confined to consideration of a key client's opinion (e.g., client to OD consultant: "You guys sure did a nice job with that Hi-Tek Project Team . . . they seem to be working together better now than they used to"). Or else, it may be a matter of "no news is good news": the client permits OD to proceed on its course, and checks continue to be forthcoming. Or, new OD projects and contracts are negotiated and authorized. In some cases more precise allocations of impact are attempted.[6]

It is intuitively, but not always explicitly, clear that there is a very good reason why such allocation of OD impact is so difficult—it relates to the *multicausal* nature of generic change. OD activities are inevitably intertwined and comingled with other activities in the organization. These may include, importantly, managerial decisions, but may be affected by a virtually limitless agglomeration of other matters, all integrally and systemically interrelated. Accordingly to speak of *organization change* or for that matter of individual, interpersonal, or group change *brought about* by purposeful behavioral science interventions (as in various OD definitions) necessarily assumes some sort of uni-causality, while instead focus needs to be directed to complex cause/effect interactions.

The effects of OD, therefore, are embedded in such fields as cause/effect interaction and normally do not "pop out" explicitly as salient, clearly-silhouetted, free-standing phenomena. Rather, there may be some argument as just what led to what. This is the case especially in OD, with its frequent emphasis on participating modes and joint effort among managers, line employees, etc., which generates new interactions, that in turn interact with pre-existing circumstances. Indeed, positivistic, controlled research designs, while of interest, may not be as useful as phenomenal, deeply probing modes of inquiry seeking to understand, among client and practitioner, the position and impact of OD holistically within the unstable force field.

In light of the above, one notes that the typical OD intervention is lodged within, and complexly affects, a process of generic change. It is not engaged in a simple cause → effect nexus (such as, OD inter-

---

[6] See, for instance, Mirvis and Berg (1977), on the unfavorable side of the scale.

vention → results of this intervention), but is both child and parent of the force field's entanglements.

OD literature makes reference to "tolerance for ambiguity." Within the bounds of gradual change this concept has particular applicability. The external "organization" field, with its shifts, lacunae of information, and uncertainties, as well as the OD process in its own right, is replete with such ambiguity and makes it necessary to deal with it. As far as I know, no one has bothered to write an OD-oriented book on the *pleasures* of ambiguity (see Massarik, 1965), but *Thriving on Chaos* (Peters, 1987), does address the next rung on the change ladder: If you can *tolerate* ambiguity, can you *thrive* on chaos? Peters' reply, while affirmative, is itself paradoxic; he provides a *highly structured* set of 45 rules and principles, starting with C-1 and continuing through S-5, which suggest that to do this sort of thriving you must return to unambiguous, nonchaotic rules. We have thus come full circle to *horribile dictu:* classic organization theory,[7] which often deals with the vagaries of the world by constructing and proposing normative injunctions tied to erector-set-like frameworks of organization structure.

From another perspective, it is possible to devise a conceptual scheme to guide our thinking on the position of OD vis-á-vis generic change and its sub-sets. (Note: schemes of this kind resemble erector-like also, but such are unfortunate limitations of the linear page.)

In essence, we now face frequently, more so than even in the immediate past, that *point of discontinuity* where old rules—or even fairly-well learned approaches for dealing with conventional change—fail us. The "force field" once so neatly conceptualized by discrete and identifiable arrows, falls apart. Erratic turbulences embrace us, perhaps best thought of, instead of arrows, in terms of the kinds of "fractals" that have come to fascinate Mandelbrot and others (Mandelbrot, 1977, 1983). The task of high-intensity diagnosis, therefore, becomes one of finding the way—for OD and for other purposes—through the paradox of "regularity within chaos." Rather than by normally predictable stages, we will need to shift gears quickly; indeed we may need to design a new gear box while the vehicle is in motion!

Given these circumstances, the top-notch OD practitioner of the next decade will need to become rapidly and responsively adaptable to a world that will not hold still, not even long enough for tradi-

---

[7] Among other possible examples, see Sexton (1970, chapters 1–5) and Mooney (1947).

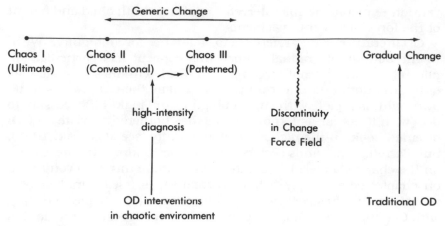

**FIGURE 1.** A conceptual scheme for thinking about chaos and change in OD.

tional diagnostic process and normal intervention design. High-speed heuristics, sometimes virtually on the spot, but rooted in a thorough understanding of underlying concepts, will become the order of the day. Versatility will count, in drawing from a suitable repertoire of intervention types; and team effort and networking among practitioners of varied fundamental styles will count to assure responsiveness to the demands of irregularity and chaotic transformation.

The above suggests that

1. Presently active OD practitioners will need to re-examine their styles—not *pro forma* but fundamentally—as a basis for retooling and relearning (indeed some may choose to leave the field);
2. New aspirants to OD practice will need to be trained differently—with increased emphasis on fundamental theory (internalized, not as mere "head trip")—theory from which flexible and adaptive practice may arise as needed;
3. OD practitioners, old and new, who wish to maintain an active position in the field, will need to become increasingly knowledgeable regarding the basic realities of the *broad* "external" environments (inside and outside the "target organization"), globality of business, the worldwide nature of markets, massive waves of mergers and acquisitions, "1992"—the practical elimination of boundaries in the European Economic Community, the impact of Asian economies, and numerous other issues.

The list is long and the stakes are high, going well beyond exclusive focus on team building, survey feedback, or even process consultation.

OD must assert itself as *both* "micro" *and* "macro" if it is to address appropriately the complexities of chaos in the world as it has become. Sometimes it may all seem overwhelming, but then perhaps there is some joy and satisfaction in distilling pattern from the chaotic, and in experiencing a newly emerging aesthetic of organization development as the field faces the century's final decade.

## REFERENCES

Bennis, W. G. (1966). *Changing organizations.* New York: McGraw-Hill.

Bennis, W. G., Benne, K. D., & Chin, R. (Eds.). (1961). *The planning of change.* New York: Holt, Rinehart and Winston.

Chowdhury, K. (1970). *Change-in-organizations.* Bombay: Lalvani Publishing.

Feigenbaum, M. (1981, Summer), Universal behavior in nonlinear systems. *Los Alamos Science, 1*(1).

Gleick, J. (1987). *Chaos: Making a new science.* New York: Viking.

Hanson, N. R. (1958). *Patterns of discovery: An inquiry into the conceptual foundations of science.* Cambridge: Cambridge University Press.

Huse, E. F. (1980). *Organizational development and change.* New York: West Publishing.

Malinowski, B. (1945). *The dynamics of culture change.* New Haven, CT: Yale University Press.

Mandelbrot, B. B. (1983). *The fractal geometry of nature.* San Francisco: W. H. Freeman.

Mandelbrot, B. B. (1977). *Fractals: Form, chance, and dimension.* San Francisco: W. H. Freeman.

Massarik, F. (1980). "Mental systems:" Towards a practical agenda for a phenomology of systems. In T. G. Cummings (Ed.), *Systems theory for organizational development.* New York: Wiley.

Massarik, F. (1965). *Functional ambiguity and the cushioning of organizational stress.* NASA Research Project Working Paper. Los Angeles: UCLA (GSBA).

Massarik, F., Tannenbaum, R., Kahane, M., & Weschler, I. R. (1961). Sociometric choice and organizational effectiveness. In R. Tannenbaum, I. R. Weschler, & F. Massarik (Eds.), *Leadership and organization.* New York: McGraw-Hill.

Mirvis, P. H., & Berg, D. N. (1977). *Failures in organizational development and change.* New York: Wiley.

Mooney, J. D. (1947). *The principles of organization.* New York: Harper & Row.

Ogburn, W. F. (1922). *Social change.* New York: Viking Press.

Peters, T. (1987). *Thriving on chaos.* New York: Knopf.

Pool, R. (1989, June 6). Is it chaos, or just noise. *Science, 243.*

Pool, R. (1988, August 12). Seeing chaos in a simple system. *Science, 241.*

Prigogine, I., & Stengers, I. (1977). *Failures in organizational development and change.* New York: Wiley.

Ryan, B. F. (1969). *Social and cultural change.* New York: Ronald Press.

Schein, E. H., & Bennis, W. G. (Eds.). (1965). *Personal and organizational change through group methods.* New York: Wiley.

Sexton, W. P. (Ed.). (1970). *Organization theories.* Columbus, OH: Charles E. Merrill.

Steele, F. (1975). *Consulting for organizational change.* Amherst, MA: University of Massachusetts.

part one

# Visions and Viewpoints

# 2

# Back to the Future: Recapturing the OD Vision*

**Edgar H. Schein**
*Sloan School of Management, MIT*

This chapter was motivated by two forces. The invitation to contribute to this volume was the initial one; the arrival of a questionnaire from a colleague wishing to do research on OD is the real one. To be more specific, a year or so ago I received a questionnaire from a colleague who wished to evaluate various aspects of OD. It was designed to make my task fairly simple in that I had only to check which of a number of "techniques" I used in my work as a consultant, and to evaluate what I thought the effectiveness of each of these techniques was.

I was invited to participate in the research because of my many years of experience and my previous writing about OD. The cover letter said that the amalgamated results from a number of such experienced practitioners would tell us what OD these days consists of and how it is doing.

I found myself very impatient with this questionnaire but until the invitation to write this chapter came, I did not really stop to analyze what my feelings were all about. What I then realized is that the source of my impatience and irritation was the very *format* of the questionnaire because it implied things about OD that I have never accepted and that reflect, in my view, a real corruption of what was originally a grand vision.

Specifically, the listing of approximately 50 different OD techniques such as "survey feedback," "managerial grid," "confrontation meeting," "sensing meeting," "team building," "process consultation," "organizational mirror," "open systems planning," "role analysis," "responsibility charting," and so on, made me realize that I did not see OD as a set of techniques at all, but as a *philosophy* or *attitude* toward how one can best work with organizations.

---

* I would like to thank Richard Beckhard, Michael Beer, Ed Nevis, and Fred Massarik for specific suggestions that enhanced this chapter.

By philosophy I mean a set of underlying assumptions about how things really work and how they ought to work. By an attitude I mean a predisposition to act in a certain way based on these assumptions. Such a philosophy or attitude toward working with human systems is explicitly articulated in my concept of "process consultation" (Schein, 1969, 1987a), and *it is the attitude that makes specific techniques such as team building or survey feedback effective, not the technique themselves.*

The focus on *process* rather than *content* reflects the assumption that how organizations work, how managers manage, how work is organized and carried out makes a crucial difference to the success of whatever it is that the organization or worker is doing. The great discovery underlying OD was that one could effectively intervene in work, group, and organizational processes without manipulating the content at all, and the group would become more effective.

The reason why this was so is that human systems develop not only their own beliefs, values, and ways of doing things that become entrenched and difficult to change, but that people have a need to solve their own problems. The great discovery of the early OD practitioners was that one of the best ways to intervene in human systems was to help them to help themselves, a concept that fitted well with other change theories, particularly those that emphasized "second-order changes," "double-loop learning," or "deutero-learning" (Argyris & Schon, 1978; Bateson, 1972).

In other words, the essence of OD was the underlying theory about the learning and change process, the philosophy and attitude that one had to figure out how to help the client system to help itself. The use of any given technique did not guarantee that it was being used with the right attitude or assumptions, hence the identification of OD with particular techniques implies from the outset a misunderstanding of what the "essence" of OD was, and, in my opinion should continue to be. This essence was for many of us a new vision of how one could work with and improve human systems, but my fear is that such a vision and the attitude that it generated is being lost in the mass of technologies that today connote OD.

In the remainder of this chapter I would like to: (1) spell out some of my assumptions underlying this conclusion, (2) speculate on why the field of OD has drifted away from its original vision, and (3) propose how we might go about recapturing or even evolving this vision.

## REFLECTIONS ON THE PAST

My first exposure to OD occurred in the Bethel Human Relations Training Workshops in the mid to late 1950s. What I remember most clearly is that we were involved in "leadership training," by which we meant that the training group's ultimate purpose, along with the lectures and large group exercises, was to teach leaders how to be better leaders, that is, how to manage human systems more effectively.

The most dramatic learning for me was the discovery of *group process*, and the insight that such process could not only be analyzed and understood, but that one could *intervene* in process, and, thereby, make groups more effective. I also remember the painful side of this learning, that "intervention" did *not* mean "direction." In fact, what most of us who learned how to become "trainers" discovered is that the methods used by therapists, particularly those influenced by Rogerian nondirective methods, were far more effective as interventions than suggestions, directions, and other forms of "active" leadership.

I remember vividly the universal question asked by every training group in the early stages of its life as a group: "Why don't you tell us what to do, Ed? You have run groups before and know what will work." I also remember that in most cases where I did make a suggestion or gave advice or directions that the group *did not follow it*. Our theory of how to intervene clearly needed to be modified, as therapists had already learned from their direct experience working with individuals or groups.

In my early consulting experiences the same kind of thing happened. I would be brought in to give advice and suggestions, only to find over and over again that the client did not really want that. If a group or larger system were involved, one could count on one part of the group to be dependent and wanting advice, while another part was counterdependent and would do everything in its power to subvert whatever suggestions were made, leading generally to a fruitless debate or conflict within the group. One also learned that if one allied oneself with the faction that was dependent, that wanted to take our advice, one would make matters worse because the client now was no longer the whole group or organization, but some faction within it.

We also learned how quickly groups and larger systems within organizations developed their own behavior patterns, norms, and basic underlying assumptions about themselves, about the world and about how to operate within it, what we called even then the group's "culture" (Schein, 1985). Thus training programs were deliberately placed in "cultural islands" in order to help trainees to gain perspective on their back home culture. But, because people get very committed to their cultural assumptions, we realized that real changes in such assumptions required a high degree of motivation and involvement on the part of the trainees. One could not impose new assumptions on individuals or groups.

The accumulated learning from such experiences constitutes for me the essence of OD: that *change in human systems will not come about without the active involvement of the members of the system who will undergo the change.* The client system has to come to terms with its own culture and political processes, its ambivalence, the factions within it, and its conflicts and power struggles. The role of the OD consultant is to help make this happen, not to take sides or line up with those who are willing to take advice.

Lewin had articulated this well as "action research," the involvement of the subject in the research process itself (Lewin, 1948). The so-called "laboratory method of training" was based on the fundamental assumption that learning and change could only result from learner involvement (Bradford, Gibb, & Benne, 1964; Schein & Bennis, 1965). The job of the trainer, teacher, leader was to create the conditions that would make such involvement optimally possible, and to act as a facilitator once the learning process was under way. This meant that one had to manage process, not content, and one had to learn how to be a catalyst in a field of forces that could not be predicted at the outset. Every group we ran was different and required different kinds of process innovations. In every group these innovations would result from the joint efforts of the trainer/consultant and the group members.

We all had to learn what we meant by "process," *how* groups worked on things instead of the content of what they worked on. Two groups might be solving the same assigned problem, but one group would choose a chairman and adopt parliamentary procedures, while another group decided on a free-form brainstorming session. One group developed norms of politely giving every one a turn to talk, while another developed norms that legitimized interruptions and confrontive arguments among members. One group would meet until it was finished, while another set very clear deadlines for each meetings. One group would develop a formal agenda and work its way through it, while another would bounce back and forth between periods of work and play.

The skill of the group trainer would be to "go with the flow," to observe processes carefully and to intervene facilitatively to make each group more effective in its own terms. We learned slowly that one could not impose "correct" processes on groups, but had to help each group to do its own best. If a group really needed to change its processes in a more fundamental way, the only way to accomplish that was to help the group to achieve this insight for itself. One could not force double-loop learning, one could only facilitate it.

Taking these insight into the organizational realm meant that (1) organizational processes had to be observed systematically, thus opening up new research areas, and (2) the assumption had to be made that *every client system and situation would be different and the crucial skill of the OD consultant would be his or her capacity to intervene innovatively and facilitatively around whatever issues might arise.*

For many readers I will undoubtedly have stated the obvious, and many OD practitioners agree and believe themselves to be operating precisely from such assumptions. But, unfortunately, for many others what OD has become today is a "technology of change" that consists of the application of specific tools and programs, that is imposed from the top with the help of consultants, and that pays only lip service to client involvement.

For example, in conducting a survey-feedback intervention how many OD practitioners today will actually go through the process of developing the questionnaire with the help of participants? How many such practitioners would actually abandon doing the survey if they discovered in their early interviews that it might not be the right intervention after all? Having convinced the client that a survey would be useful, would not many of them find it easier to take a previously standardized one off the shelf and assume that with all the research behind it, it probably would cover the right issues for most clients?

How many consultants who are hired to do team building will do a thorough investigation of whether team building is, in fact, relevant or timely? I will never forget a fateful lunch I had some years ago with a plant manager and his OD specialist where our task was to do the detailed design of the previously decided upon off-site team building exercise that was to take place 1 month hence.

I asked the routine question of how many participants were expected to attend the meeting. The plant manager, in order to make a count, reviewed the candidates, and as he did so, he suddenly became aware of the fact that he did not really believe in the competence of two of the potential attendees. I encouraged him to think out the consequences, and he realized that to have a team building session at this time would be dangerous and inappropriate. We both agreed that focusing on helping these two to succeed or else replacing them was the correct OD intervention, and canceled the team building meeting. My focus shifted to helping the plant manager figure out how to assess these two people fairly.

In reviewing this later, both the plant manager and I thought that my routine question turned out to be a critical "intervention" in that it focused squarely on an issue that had not been sufficiently thought through *by the client.* I have had this type of experience over and over again, that routine questions asked in complete innocence trigger thoughts and ideas in the client that take us into brand new and highly productive areas. In my view the OD philosophy requires that the consultant be sensitive to such new areas and pursue them as needed, even if that means giving up agreed upon programs or activities.

My vision of OD that grew out of experiences such as this was articulated as "process consultation," the effort to help a client system to become aware of its own processes and to become skilled enough to intervene in those processes so that its own immediate effectiveness increased, but, even more importantly, its ability to continue to solve its problems in the future increased.

The OD vision must include, in my view, a commitment to passing on one's skills in observing and intervening in process. An organization must be able to continue to help itself, not just to be able to benefit from an outside OD consultant's help. *This implies that the intervention skills must increasingly be learned by the management itself so that the development of the organization becomes increasingly a normal process of leadership and management implemented inside the organization by managers and internal consultants* (Beer & Walton, 1987; Schein, 1987a).

In order to provide such help the OD consultant must accept the client system wherever he or she finds it to be, must become enough involved in what is going on to be able to perceive what kind of intervention will be catalytic and facilitative, and above all, must learn not to trust any given technology as providing a ready made answer to any given problem. It is the commitment to managing *unpredictable contingencies* that is ultimately the essence of the attitude, and it is the acceptance of the theoretical assumption that all human systems are at some level unique and unpredictable that is the essence of the philosophical underpinning of OD.

## FORCES UNDERMINING THE VISION

I believe that there are four sets of forces that make it difficult to sustain the attitude and to maintain the philosophical assumption articulated above:

1. *Economic Forces.* Consultants who have to make a living from OD work must develop products that sell. OD practitioners who want to make a living in this new speciality have to have something to put into their brochures that distinguishes them from other professionals. Attitudes and philosophies are not as easily describable and salable as questionnaires, organized approaches to meetings, and predesigned programs.

    Clients who want to achieve changes also are subject to economic forces in that they want the "most change for the buck," and therefore collude with the sales-conscious consultant in looking for that technique which will promise the most for the least money.

2. *Technological Forces.* OD practitioners have invented some very powerful tools that do create client involvement, insight, and skill learning. As with any new technology, the temptation to use such tools across the board is overwhelming. Once the T-group as a method of learning had been invented, we applied it all over the place, including inside organizations where its use as an intervention was highly questionable, to give but one historical example. Today we see a similar indiscriminate use of survey-feedback and team building technologies, and in the area of organizational culture we see evolving new technologies for "quick and dirty" diagnoses of complex cultural issues even from practitioners who claim to eschew "quick fixes" (Kilmann, 1984).

3. *Cultural Forces.* Clients (in the United States in particular) are product- and activity-focused. They want to know what will be done to whom, and they are suspicious of silent consultants who mostly sit around and do very little, even though they will acknowledge that the few interventions that the consultant made were well timed and effective. Our culture values activity and productivity, putting the attitude and philosophy of OD

into a clearly countercultural position. In order to feel more at one culturally with their clients, many OD practitioners try to be active and try to prove how productive their technologies will be.

4.  *Research Forces.* Once OD programs began to be utilized, academic researchers moved in rapidly to determine whether or not the claims for improvement from T-groups and other OD technologies could be sustained with hard data. But the culture of research dictates that one must measure things, and, in order to measure them reliably, those things must be discrete entities that can be compared and contrasted. So we began to see research projects that compared the relative effectiveness of different OD techniques, never questioning whether *any* of these techniques were, in fact, being applied in terms of the OD philosophy and attitude.

The most absurd version of this corruption occurred when in a number of studies things such as survey research, team building, and process consultation were compared *with each other*, as if these were separable and discrete activities. As I argued before, the process consultation philosophy underlies many other techniques, so the research was measuring totally incomparable things.

Furthermore, the notion that OD projects could be characterized by the primary use of one technique flies in the face of most of my experience. If I think of companies I have worked with, over a period of time I will have used a whole variety of "techniques" in response to what was going on, and it would be impossible to describe the relationship in terms of any one of these techniques as being "primary."

The same research/measurement phenomenon has occurred in the field of therapy and education, where our obsession with different techniques has obscured the more important result that successful outcomes have more to do with general variables such as teacher or therapist attitude and client or student motivation (Frank, 1974). Attitudes and motivation are, of course, harder to measure than ratings of whether or not a given OD project involved primarily team building or survey research, but such measurement difficulties should not stand in the way of doing research appropriate to the phenomenon under consideration.

At the theoretical level another force has been the assumption coming from a number of change theories that one must make structural and behavioral interventions first, if one is ultimately to influence attitudes, values, and assumptions (Festinger, 1957; Haley, 1984). If one works from this assumption it is natural to look for incisive and clever ways to manipulate behavior change, particularly if one believes that such change will be "quicker" than the often drawn out therapeutic process of building awareness and working issues through.[1]

To the extent that the above forces have been working over the past several decades, we have corrupted and subverted the original OD vision, and, worse, possibly adopted technologies that are in fact less effective but easier to sell. This situation might be alright if we did not then label those technologies as being OD. But more and more I see the use of the OD label in a broad manner that suggests inclusion of everything from surveys to sensitivity training to behavior modification, with hardly a nod to the problem of developing the right attitude to facilitate client involvement, action research, and genuine contingency thinking around intervention.

## EVOLVING THE VISION: FUSION WITH THE CLINICAL PERSPECTIVE

The ultimate answer both to recapturing the vision and to evolving it lies in fusing the assumptions and attitudes of OD with the assumptions and attitudes of clinical work, particularly that part of clinical work that deals with individual and group therapy (Schein, 1987b).

Therapists have learned from decades of research that the attitudes and situational contingencies surrounding the therapeutic situation (e.g., how motivated the client is, how much trust or faith the client has in the therapist or the therapeutic process) are more predictive of outcomes than the particular techniques employed, and that with each client situation one must be prepared to adapt one's techniques to what one finds (Frank, 1974).

The OD consultant should take essentially the same perspective when he or she engages some segment of an organization and develops gradually a diagnostic sense of what may be going on, using exploratory rather than confrontive interventions (Schein, 1987a). In using the concept of "consultant" here, I am not limiting the discussion to the traditional outside consultant who can take a genuinely neutral stance toward any given problem. Increasingly I have found that part of any manager's job is to learn how to be a consultant to his or her own work group, to learn to make a neutral stance toward how the subordinates are conceptualizing the problem, and

---

[1] I am indebted to my colleague Ed Nevis for this observation.

ultimately to take the attitude that the most effective way to manage is to "help the subordinate to succeed" (Schein, 1987a).

Another area of potential fusion between OD and clinical philosophies lies in the use of conceptual models that involve us in thinking about pathology and health. Both clinicians and OD consultants must be concerned with what is health, and must be prepared to locate and enhance that part of a given system that is healthy and capable of learning. And, paradoxically, one will not know what the healthy parts are before one has attempted some interventions and observed the response. The ability to then shift gears and go in a different direction becomes an essential skill of both the good therapist and the OD practitioner. Here again the line manager in the organization becomes the ultimate purveyor of such skills and thus the true developer of organizations.

OD practitioners should also learn from their clinical colleagues to do the equivalent of "pathology conferences," systematic analyses of projects that are not working or that have gone wrong, with neutral colleagues who can provide perspective. During projects, OD practitioners should use training consultants or 'shadow' consultants to maintain a critical audience for what they are doing. Such activities would not only enhance the theories that underlie our notions of planned organizational change, but would force us to keep rearticulating our philosophies and to test our attitudes.

The equivalent activities for line managers practicing OD would be to develop helping relationships with their peers and bosses who could function as resources and "trainers" or shadow consultants *vis-à-vis* any given project that the manager is performing. One of my most successful interventions in organizations is to get groups of managers at the same level to get together to share problems they are having in supervising or managing their groups, and to develop an attitude that they can help each other with such problems.

Our models of organizational health must become broader and more comprehensive (Bennis, 1962). We cannot limit our thinking to narrow notions of power equalization, participation, openness, trust, full communication, teamwork, and all the other "motherhood" concepts that have come to pervade our field. As we have become more cross-cultural we have learned that many of these concepts are considered to be narrow American values, not general guides to organizational health.

In this regard one of the weaknesses of research on OD is that we do not yet have a clear enough concept of what we expect OD to accomplish. What do we mean when we say that organizational effectiveness has improved? When research on T-groups was first begun we ran into the paradox that training seemed to *reduce* self-insight, just the opposite of what had been predicted. The answer, of course, was that during training people came to realize how little they had understood themselves prior to training, so a comparison of before and after self-ratings of self-insight produced a lower score after training because people had a more accurate assessment of how little they knew about themselves.

The same kind of thing can happen when organizations are studied before and after OD interventions. It should also be pointed out that measures of effectiveness have to be judged against a trend, not in terms of a steady state. It has been my experience with some client organizations that they were on a steep downward trend with respect to some critical effectiveness variables, and what the OD interventions did was to slow down the decline. But the before-and-after measures would still show a decline from initial to final state.

## IMPLICATIONS FOR OD CONSULTING

If we pursue this vision, by which I mean that we take the assumptions underlying process consultation seriously and adopt the attitude I am advocating, what does this mean for our approach to actual OD projects? For example, does this mean that we abandon learning all of the many techniques that have become associated with OD? Not at all. Instead, I am advocating a concept of organization development that involves the consultant or manager in a more organic set of processes that can be characterized by a number of interrelated features:

1.  A full understanding of how each of the OD techniques would be applied if one took seriously the underlying assumption that one can only help the client to help himself or herself, and the assumption that every case is unique and requires its own particular pattern of interventions.

    For example, if we used the technique of survey-feedback, we would have to know how to develop, conduct, and feed back the results of a survey by means that are typically quite different from the frequently advocated top-down cascading approach. From an OD perspective one would work bottom up sharing with each level the data relevant to that level and getting that level to decide what should be passed upward to the next level.
2.  The development of the ability to work in "real time" or "on line"

without preconceptions of what elements of a change strategy would be most relevant as the project progressed.

The ability to observe the moment to moment interaction between the client and the consultant becomes a central skill, comparable with the analysis of transference and countertransference in psychoanalysis. This would imply as well the willingness to terminate at any time if the client did not feel ready to move forward. Contracts and agreements to pursue a whole series of steps would be avoided, so that each step could be evolved both by the consultant and the client of the moment. The OD consultant should always be sure that the client is owning responsibility for the interventions that are being made, which means that the client has to be involved on line as well.

3.  A commitment to contingent planning, implying a willingness to adjust to new data, a readiness to interpret client responses to interventions as further diagnostic indicators of what may be going on, a readiness to provide a number of options at every step of the process, and a suspension of judgment of what is the best way for the client to operate.

    This suspension of judgment implies that the OD consultant is committed to a set of values about process and helping, but is not committed to operational values for organizations such as power equalization or openness. In planning a major change program, one could lay out goals, a strategy, and a variety of options, but one should only plan the first step or two in detail, and that first step might be something minimal, such as a meeting with key members of the client system. At that meeting next steps could be discussed and committed to.

4.  A commitment to dynamic organizational theories that lead one to constructive concepts of organizational health and the fostering of self-correcting and self-managing processes (Bennis, 1962; Schein, 1980, 1985). Theories such as those of Argyris and Schon (1978) which emphasize double-loop learning, theories of organizational change that take culture seriously, and theories of learning and adaptation that take into account what has been learned anthropologically about change will serve us better than some of the traditional organization theories in use today.

## CONCLUDING COMMENT

In conclusion, as an OD consultant, I do not really know what I am going to do or what I should do until I am actually in the situation. I should share this insight with my contact client and encourage initial contacts that are only minimally structured. I offer to attend some meetings or continue to meet with the contact client to talk out what is needed. As I get a sense of the client organization's history, culture, and future aspirations it becomes much clearer what kinds of interventions might ultimately produce optimal results. If a client is not willing to engage at that level, the prognosis for the success of the project is low anyway.

Ultimately OD should be organizational therapy and the training of the OD practitioner should include enough clinical training to ensure that he or she will understand the tensions and anxieties that accompany changes in human systems. Treating OD as a technology that can be implemented by anyone who becomes competent to handle a few of the tools but who does not understand the philosophy or the helping attitude, is not only likely to be a waste of time but downright dangerous.

This assertion is paradoxical because I have also said that ultimately the practitioner of OD will have to be the line manager inside the organization. To be consistent, I would have to argue that line managers need more clinical training, and that is precisely the argument I wish to make. What line managers learn from consultants is to take a clinical perspective, and good line managers follow this up by learning more about the psychological dynamics of superior–subordinate relationships and group action. There is nothing more valuable for a line manager to learn than the psychology, sociology, and anthropology of interpersonal dynamics, and there is no more important skill for a manager to acquire than the clinical skill of handling people and groups.

If line managers, inside consultants, and outside consultants can recapture the OD vision and implement it, our organizations will have a chance to maximize their effectiveness over the long haul in this increasingly competitive world. Let us put OD back on the firm footing where it belongs and stop playing superficial games with organizations that have much too much at stake to be treated superficially or to be subjected to the latest technological fad.

## REFERENCES

Argyris, C., & Schon, D. A. (1978). *Organizational learning.* Reading, MA: Addison–Wesley.

Bateson, G. (1972). *Steps to an ecology of mind.* New York: Ballantine.

Beer, M., & Walton, A. E. (1987). Organization change and development. *Annual Review of Psychology, 38,* 339–367.

Bennis, W. G. (1962). Toward a truly scientific management: The concept of organizational health. *General Systems Yearbook, 7,* 269–282.

Bradford, L. P., Gibb, J. R., & Benne, K. D. (Eds.). (1964). *T-group theory and laboratory method.* New York: Wiley.

Festinger, L. (1957). *A theory of cognitive dissonance.* Evanston, IL: Row Peterson.

Frank, J. D. (1974). *Persuasion and healing* (rev. ed.). New York: Schocken.

Haley, J. (1984). *Ordeal therapy.* San Francisco: Jossey–Bass.

Kilmann, R. H. (1984). *Beyond the quick fix.* San Francisco: Jossey–Bass.

Lewin, K. (1948). *Resolving social conflicts.* New York: Harper & Row.

Schein, E. H. (1969). *Process consultation.* Reading, MA: Addison–Wesley.

Schein, E. H. (1980). *Organizational psychology* (3rd ed.). Englewood Cliffs, NJ: Prentice–Hall.

Schein, E. H. (1985). *Organizational culture and leadership.* San Francisco: Jossey–Bass.

Schein, E. H. (1987a). *Process consultation* (Vol. 2). Reading, MA: Addison–Wesley.

Schein, E. H. (1987b). *The clinical perspective in field work.* Newbury Park, CA: Sage.

Schein, E. H., & Bennis, W. G. (1965). *Personal and organizational change through group methods.* New York: Wiley.

# 3

# The Significance of Core Values on the Theory and Practice of Organizational Development

**Newton Margulies**
Graduate School of Management,
University of California, Irvine

**Anthony Raia**
Anderson Graduate School of
Management,
University of California, Los Angeles

There seems to be little question that values are powerful and yet invisible factors that guide research, theory building, and practice in the social sciences generally, and more specifically, in organizational development. Values are not only the outcomes of human choice, but are the underlying forces which guide and influence those choices. A value, according to Rokeach (1973), "is a belief that a specific mode of conduct or end state of existence is preferable, socially or personally, to an opposite or contrary end state or mode of conduct." The importance of values in the conduct of professional practice and in the meta-objectives of OD should be clear.

Discussing Laboratory Training, Schein and Bennis (1965) referred to values or "meta-goals" as important ingredients to learning in T-Group settings. They indicated that values, while highly generalized and sometimes vague, are undoubtedly "powerful and pervasive" in determining the course of Laboratory Training (its process) as well as its outcomes (its goals).

Some 15 years ago (Margulies & Raia, 1972), we argued that Organizational Development was not a value-free social science, and that indeed there is no such thing as a value-free social science. Consequently, in our definition and conceptualization of OD, we were obliged to try to identify the core values associated with the field. Tracing the historical foundations of the field, beginning with Lewin, Maslow, Argyris, MacGregor, and others, provides a perspective on the normative nature of the field and the underlying value base from which OD has emerged.

Based on the power and impact of these early writings, as well as our own sense of the developing field, we wrote that the values of the fully functioning organization might be stated as follows (Margulies & Raia, 1972, p. 3)

1.  Providing opportunities for people to function as human beings rather than as resources in the productive process.
2.  Providing opportunities for each organizational member, as well as the organization itself, to develop to full potential.
3.  Seeking to increase the effectiveness of the organization in terms of all its goals.
4.  Attempting to create an environment in which it is possible to find exciting and challenging work.
5.  Providing opportunities for people in organizations to influence the way in which they relate to work, the organization, and the environment.
6.  Treating each human being as a person with a complex set of needs, all of which are important in work and in life.

The notion of values in the theory and practice of organizational development is clearly a bilevel concept; a fact we might add that is often neglected by other analyses and descriptions. First, OD values provide a beacon or target which represents an "ideal" state toward which the design, structure and processes, of the organization is directed. The goals of Organizational Development, therefore, are not defined in simple terms; they are defined in terms of the organization's needs for effective goal achievement and in terms of the ideal organizational architecture implied by OD values. Second, values are implied by the very process of organizational development. The diagnostic process, for example, common to organizational development stresses participation, openness, and inquiry. These characteristics may be viewed as values in the process.

With regard to the first level, the above-stated values were a reasonable extrapolation from the historical literature. Later, in 1978, we discussed the important conceptual and philosophical antecedents which were the roots of OD values as they developed in the 1950s and 1960s (Margulies & Raia, 1978). Variations of course are possible. The essence, however, is what has often been labeled in the literature as a set of humanistically oriented values which are at the core of organizational development theory and practice. This desired end state cannot be ignored in spite of the simultaneous attention given to organizational effectiveness and efficiency.

At the second level, the practice of organizational development, and the implementation of the OD process, also reflects a powerful statement of values. Data collection and feedback, as well as joint diagnosis and action taking, imply values of participation, involvement, and the enfranchising of organizational members to act in the service of both organizational improvement and in the betterment of the quality of their working lives.

Tannenbaum and Davis (1967) also wrote about values and organizations. Their perspective, like ours, was that values represent "directions," rather than final goals. As they saw it, these directions were away from more traditional institutional and bureaucratic values and toward more personally relevant ones. They also use the "humanistic" label for what they observe as a general trend, slow to be sure, but nevertheless a trend on the part of management to move away from the debilitating aspects of the bureaucratic model toward a more individualistic and personalistic orientation. As we shall demonstrate later, these values are consonant with traditional American values of freedom, democracy, and human rights.

Tannenbaum and Davis also assert that these humanistically oriented values, which provide the basis for organizational development, are consonant with conceptual notions of organizational effectiveness and with the growing trend among the managers to accept and implement such values in their practice.

When we re-examined the conceptual foundations and revisited our notions of Organizational Development in 1978, we placed special emphasis on analyzing the value base and its impact on the field. We defined OD as "a value-based process and technology . . ." values which provide the ". . . underlying and guiding forces which reflect normative views about what is right, proper and appropriate for the design of organizations for the processes by which they are managed" (Margulies & Raia, 1978, pp. 136–137).

Our observations a decade ago reinforced our analysis and the views of other social scientists that there was a societal trend toward more humanism in organizations. Interest in Quality of Work Life projects, participative management techniques, quality circles, and other such mechanisms which sought to involve individuals in design and conduct of work, supported our contention.

Some writers criticize the field because of its duality in philosophical and value orientations (see, e.g., Conner, 1982). They assert that confusion exists because of OD's orientation to both the humanistic values and the values of organizational efficiency and effectiveness. This consistently linear view is representative of the lack of understanding and/or integration of the complex and multiple phenomena of organizational life. To criticize the underlying conceptual, theoretical, and value thrust of the field because of discrepancies in practice is similar to the criticisms of medical science which may result from faulty medical practice. Leaving the criticisms aside, our intention is to demonstrate that the core OD values are still central to theory and practice in the field. In fact, our analysis has led us to the conclusion that the values may be more important today than they were in the era of the 1950s and 1960s. We fear that

OD has become too technique-driven in nature and in application. We are concerned that in the service of being relevant, a plea heard from both theoreticians and practitioners, that the field has succumbed to the imperative of organizational efficiency and effectiveness, perhaps at any cost.

In the following sections we will review the Organizational Development literature of the past decade to examine the value themes present. We will demonstrate their enduring quality. We will also examine the underlying values of corporate America to determine whether or not they have changed. Finally, we will discuss the implications of value orientations for the theory and practice of Organizational Development.

## THE ENDURING QUALITY OF OD VALUES

Before embarking on a review of the literature, we would like to underscore some important implications concerning values and organizational development. Our perspective is best characterized by this lengthy quote:

> Most discussions of OD values focus on them as ends in themselves; that is, that the change process is directed toward creating a particular kind of organization. This "ideal" organization is frequently described as one in which participation and democracy are emphasized and where close interpersonal relationships and social need satisfaction are desired ends. Although these results may be desirable, and perhaps should be aimed for whenever possible, it must be noted that the kind of organization created by an OD effort may not have such ideal characteristics. The resulting organization may in fact be highly structured, may foster authoritarian management styles and practices, and may limit the degree of interaction among its members— and this may be quite appropriate given the mission or purpose of the organization! (Margulies & Raia, 1978, p. 145)

As we have already indicted, it is the *process*, guided by the core values, which is really at the heart of Organizational Development. The OD professional does not "sell" a value system, but instead incorporates the value system as a guiding beacon which directs the process of organizational analysis and development.

Values tend to have an enduring quality. As both Rokeach (1973) and Maslow (1954, 1965) have observed, there are higher-order and lower-order values. The higher order, or the broad categories of values, are probably more enduring and may not change radically over time. Umbrella terms such as "humanistic" and "democratic" convey a particular tendency or direction for the field which should remain stable. However, the lower-order values may be subject to change and should be reviewed. Equally as important, perhaps, their impact on management beliefs and practices should also be examined. We believe that the usefulness and effectiveness of OD is dependent upon the degree to which organizational values become consistent with the core values of organizational development.

A review of the literature which focuses on critiques, issues, and trends in the field reveals that the topics most commonly discussed include methodology, verifiability, theory versus practice, and quality control. An analysis may provide insights into future trends and issues, as well as the values which underlie OD.

It is evident that the core values have endured in spite of outside forces and pressures to change. This is due in part to the commonly held values of both theoreticians and practitioners and the consistency of internal communications of these values. In Burke and Goodstein (1980) and Spier, Sashkin, Jones, and Goodstein (1980) the treatment of trends, issues, and future directions are efforts to represent consensus on key aspects of the field. These are illustrations of continual reinforcements and communication of the OD value themes. The enduring nature of the values is demonstrated historically by other contributions to the literature. To begin with, McLean, Sims, Mangham, and Tuffield (1982) characterizes OD as being rooted in the assumptions of a more consensual and collaborative approach to decision making. This is clearly a statement of values.

Greiner (1980) gives a brief and yet comprehensive overview of how the values and goals of OD evolved from the 1950s to the late 1970s. According to his framework, the basic values of the 1950s were openness, feedback, and personal change. He indicates that those involved in the field were mostly academics trying to achieve the goals of self-awareness and social sensitivity. Greiner notes that there was a shift of emphasis to teamwork, integration, and organizational change in the early 1960s. Academics were joined by professional consultants whose goals were to market and sell new designs. In the early 1970s, the values were reinforced as the field became somewhat defensive in response to an increasing number of critics. Goals were modified to include a "bottom line" results orientation for OD interventions. Greiner also notes an increasing concern in the late 1970s about the quality-of-work-life, and identifies some new issues including turnover, absenteeism, morale and productivity.

Burke (1977) notes that the values of democracy still pervaded the field in the mid-1970s. He also describes change in the focus of OD efforts away from organizational climate, or value change, to changing the organizational structure. Harrison (1980) describes a major cultural shift away from hope, peace, and love, toward winning, power, and influence. Despite this observed shift, he concludes that the core values remained relatively intact since their inception. In fact, rather than changing, these values were actually strengthened and became even more reinforced with the passage of time. This point is also stressed by Rhinesmith (1970), Burke and Goodstein (1980), and Margulies and Raia (1978).

Despite the many different definitions and perspectives represented in the literature, we would conclude that the field is represented by a cohesive group of cohorts who share common values and norms which impact on the development of theory and which guide professional practice.

Many authors describe OD as a field in transition (Burke, 1977; Friedlander & Brown, 1977; Greiner, 1980; Harris, 1980; Harrison, 1980; Hornstein, 1980; Jones, 1980; Morely, 1980). Burke, for example describes as a field still in the process of becoming (1977). He notes a shift in the primary values of OD from primarily democracy and participation to include authenticity, and also that "genuine" behavior was emerging as a value equal to the participative credo. He maintains that there should not be a shift in OD values, but instead, the field must show the greater efficacy of its values to those of management. Burke goes on to say that the field has been largely responsive to organizational trends and needs and that OD should be cautioned about changing its own value system.

Herman (1977) also believes that although there have been some changes in the field, the core values remain unchanged. He describes OD as being biased toward "positive" emotions and attributes, which include logic and rationality, trust of and openness toward others, collaboration and participation, and affection and responsiveness. He also comments that OD appears to be biased against, or avoids, values such as authority and control, caution and reserve, autonomy and separateness, competition and aggressiveness, dislike and resistance, and self-interest. While Herman feels there is a need to acknowledge and validate such feelings, he does not suggest a change in core value. Instead he recommends that people in organizations need to learn to accept these feelings through the use of more directive consulting behavior.

These brief reviews clearly illustrate that OD values, derived from the culture of the 1950s and 1960s, have remained intact. It is doubtful that the same can be said for organizational values.

# THE CHANGING NATURE OF CORPORATE VALUES

We have tried to demonstrate that the core values of the field have remained intact over the last several decades. If OD were independent of organizations, perhaps there would be no need for further discussion about values. However, both the theory and practice of OD are symbiotically involved with them. If it is maintained that changes in the environment have led to major changes in organizations. Then one must ask if the values of OD are significantly different from the values of the organizations we propose to help change. And more importantly, one needs to ask questions regarding the consequent implications for the field? There are two different perspectives which seem to emerge in response to these questions. The first suggests an expansion of traditional concepts in order for the field to become more functional and effective. The second view warns against such change, seeing it as a dangerous modification of established standards, focus, and orientation which may alter the field's basic identity.

McLean et al. (1982) observe that OD is in a process of metamorphosis, due to the change from the stable environment of early days, to the more turbulent current times. They remind us that organizations appear to be more concerned with survival than with development, and that OD must respond to this change. Additionally, they note the diversity in style, ideas, and theories of most successful OD practitioners. The result, as they see it, is a more "mature" focus for OD, one which ultimately is ". . . relatively self-reliant, working more from an internal locus control, as compared with a predominantly external dependence on others for answers, techniques and ideas" (p. 122). Thus, while they acknowledge the fact that external changes have occurred, they still advocate remaining internally focused.

Hornstein (1980) believes that one result of the shifting of organizational values has been an increase in encountering "organizational nemeses" in his consulting endeavors. His nemeses are those individuals within an organization who hold grossly divergent values from OD. He sees a "counterreaction" by consultants to these nemeses resulting in ineffective behavior. One can see that as the values between OD and contemporary organizations become more divergent, the frequency of encountering an "organizational nemesis" is more likely to occur. Clearly, the potential result of the incompatibility between the core values of the field and organizational values is a less effective use of OD technology and interventions. This view often supports the idea that any changes from OD's original perspectives and values constitutes some sort of "selling out." There seems to be an underlying sanction against even the suggestion of a change in core OD values. The literature clearly demonstrates a growing diversity of perspectives, conceptual approaches, methodologies, and applications of techniques. Our own view, however, is that this trend does not in of itself indicate any divergence from the core values underlying the field.

McLean et al. (1982) see the traditional values of openness, honesty, clarity, consensus, and collaboration as a basis for the OD practitioners' repertoire, but they suspect that political values are also becoming prevalent. They elaborate that, especially among internal consultants, values are becoming less clear, and that there are increasing chances for the consultant to be caught in a web of organizational politics. They also indicate that instead of helping others to achieve their aspirations and values, many practitioners are trying to impose *their* own personal values and interpretations on the situation. Many OD practitioners describe themselves as neutral facilitators when in fact they are not totally objective. They are often unaware that they subtly control situations according to their own definitions. The authors do allow for the possibility that the existing framework of normative OD values may not be effective at facilitating change in organizations whose values differ.

Our review indicates that some practitioners do feel that the humanistic value structure of OD is somewhat narrow. However, most express concern at the thought of any change. They appear to feel that any change in core values would mean that they were not doing "organizational development." Similarly, there is the implication and a profound one at that, that somehow the values of management are corrupted by other motives, such as profit, competition, politics, and productivity. One result of this view, conscious or otherwise, is the belief that OD must convert organization values to the core values of the field and must be careful not to be contaminated with management's values in the process. The professional OD practitioner, in our view, cannot completely ignore the impact of organizational values on effective practice. It is our contention that most professionals attempt to integrate the organization's values with those of the field.

The authors also present a dichotomy between OD's *humanism* of the past, and its increasing *pragmatism* in the present as a response to organizational emphasis on survival. They note that appropriate OD theory and practice will be that which takes into account the values of both the organization and the field. They suggest that the need for the adaptation of values is better achieved through the application of broader OD theories, rather than by an examination of, or change in, organizational values.

Spier et al. (1980) also point to the increasing use of OD to improve organizational productivity and profitability. Many of their interviewees believe that there is an inherent conflict between "human" needs and "system" needs, and don't see any convergence between the two. If the emphasis on organizational survival is exacerbated by environmental conditions, it is possible that the needs of organizational members be of lower priority. This may result in an end to attempts to improve the quality of work life and other similar goal of OD interventions.

In an insightful argument, Lewis (1982) comments on the importance of society's values as an key factor in the performance of its enterprises. He notes that the belief in the right of every individual to equality and self-fulfillment, values which are central to OD and the American tradition, has created a basic distrust of authority and has instigated social conflicts within the enterprise. Such conflicts and adversarial relations, he argues, are more prevalent in our society than in most others where social hierarchies are accepted and managed. There is, therefore, this subtle adversarial relationship between OD and its value system and the inherent value system of organizations.

Finally, Greiner (1980) also describes the dilemma for the field as one which places the values of OD on one end of a spectrum and those of management on the other. Most OD practitioners are caught in the middle. He notes that while this compromise may be essential for the survival of the practitioner, it is not likely to facilitate the integration of divergent values between the field and organizations. He believes that OD may have become so involved in meeting organizational goals, that the question of values has been ignored. He also stressed that organizations must be the ones who change their values. While Greiner's analysis of the divergent values is accurate, his proposed solution does not allow for the possibility that they can be synergistically integrated.

## CONCLUSIONS AND IMPLICATIONS FOR THE FIELD

As we indicated earlier, OD values are deeply rooted in the traditional values of America. Central to this tradition is the assumption that individuals are better able to determine their interests and destinies than are collectivities. American values are based on individualism and enlightened self-interests, on achievement and success, on freedom and democracy, on moralism and humanitarianism, and on human and civil rights.

Modern organizations, on the other hand, seem to be transforming the traditional value system of America. Despite the warnings of Whyte's Organization Man of the 1950s, the campus unrest and civil rights turmoil of the 1960s, and the quality of work life projects of the 1970s, the transformation continues. Scott and Hart (1979) describe the shift as follows:

- From innate human nature to malleability; a belief that the individual is, by nature, nothing and has the potential to be made into anything. Since there is nothing in their nature to prevent them from adapting to whatever values and contingencies which are required, the organization is designed to shape and mold its members.
- From individualism to obedience; this is an essential ingredient in the chain of command since superiors depend on obedient subordinates to get the organization's work done.
- From indispensability to dispensability; necessary individuals cannot be tolerated lest the organization become dependent upon them.
- From community to specialization; dedication is not to the work group, where individuals are prized for their unique personal qualities, but to specialization which has utility for the organization. Loyalty is to the specialized function, the successful performance of which adds value to the collective whole.
- From spontaneity to planning; creativity and the "invisible hand" have been replaced by systematic planning and organizational controls. Spontaneity is unpredictable and, hence, uncontrollable.
- From voluntarism to paternalism; autonomy, free choice, and individual responsibility and accountability have been replaced by organizational paternalism and the attitude that "father knows best."

The authors conclude that the above shift is not a central part of a new, well-entrenched system of American values. Obedience is essential to organizational discipline; dispensability is necessary for adaptation and change; specialization is required for efficiency; planning is needed to reduce uncertainty; and paternalism justifies the organization's domination over its work force. According to them, the assault on the traditional value system has been led by a managerial elite and maintained by a cadre of professional managers.

While we do not agree that a total or radical transformation has taken place, or that managers are necessarily at fault, *our review of the literature leads us to believe that the values held by corporate America are regressing in a direction that is incompatible with the core values of the field of organizational development.* We ask ourselves why? How can this be, given the vast number of OD programs and activities over the years, the existence of professional internal staffs, the hordes of external consultants, and the countless number of interventions taking place on a daily basis? There appear to be several reasons.

To begin with, organizational life is no longer stable and predictable. The forces of change have stressed the ability to manage effectively organization structures, processes, and dynamics. Managers find themselves dealing with "double-bind" situations: productivity and efficiency versus the quality of working life, collaboration and teamwork versus competition and entrepreneurship, stability versus change, to name only a few. The emergence of a global economy and international competition, the technology explosion, the changing demographics and attitudes of the workforce, increasing government interventions, and the emergence of multiple stakeholders with conflicting interest and needs have combined to increase the pressures on managers. They must be pragmatic and expedient, think and act within short time frames, make quick decisions, and look for quick fixes. For most managers, management has become a predicament.

Responsibility, accountability, control, and stewardship are the hallmarks of the orthodox managerial outlook that still prevails today. The culture of an organization, including its reward system, reinforces the importance of identifying with organization values. Loyalty is to the organization, which often forces managers to "choose" between organization values and those which may be incompatible or in conflict with them. The more managers work in their organizations, the more these values tend to be reflected in their own personal values.

It is not our intention here to berate managers or to diminish the importance of organizations in our society. Both have served us well. It is also not our intention to discredit the field of organizational development. It too has served us well. We are concerned, however, that there has been an unwitting collusion between managers and OD practitioners along the following lines: the interventional technology has been (and continues to be) packaged and sold by OD practitioners and eagerly accepted by managers as a cure-all at best and as a quick fix at worst. More important, the techniques are accepted because (1) They seem to produce more effective employees, teams and/or systems, (2) They are seemingly more humane, (3) They promise to help people realize their potential and to cope with the pressures of organizational life, and (4) They are morally "good."

Professional managers are neither barbarians nor automatons. They are, in fact, people with decent and honorable intentions. OD technology provides them with an automatic, built-in conscience. The techniques in and of themselves are both "right" and "good." If it is believed that the application of "good" means will automatically produce good end results and "good" people, then the consideration of values becomes unnecessary and a waste of time. This assures managers that they need not engage in the time-consuming, intangible, and difficult business of clarifying and integrating incompatible values. They need look no further than the humaneness of the techniques. This simplifies the job because they can be confident that no one will be hurt in the normal course of things. On the contrary, the more they are involved with OD, the more humane they and their organizations become.

It is our belief that OD practitioners have become an integral part of this collusion. The field has been and continues to be technology-driven. Many practitioners have become routine in their applications; they have succumbed to management pressure for the quick fix, the emphasis on the bottom line, and the cure-all mentality; they have failed to maintain "marginality" in their roles as consultants and helpers to management—they are for all intents and purposes "in bed" with their client-systems; and more important perhaps, they seem to have lost sight of the core values of the field and the need to engage in the difficult and challenging process of integrating them into the organization's value systems as ends in and of themselves.

The implications for the field are reasonably obvious. We have examined the literature and concluded that OD core values have endured over the last several decades. Our analysis leads us to believe that these values are even more important today than they were during the formative stages of organizational development. First, because of the increasing divergence between OD values and those of corporate America, and second, because of what we have identified as an unwitting collusion between OD practitioners and management which appears to be eroding the values of the field. Consequently, if OD is to continue to develop as a discipline and as a profession, a number of changes appear to be in order. More specifically,

1.  The issue relating to the divergence or incompatibility of values is not a simple dialectic. That is, it is not an "either—or" proposition in which either the core values of the field or those of the organization must prevail. OD professionals are better advised to adopt a "Janusian" perspective, one which recognizes the legitimacy of *both* organizational needs for survival and efficiency and those of its members as reflected in the OD values.

2.  OD professionals need to reawaken the messianic spirit that pervaded the field in its formative years. The OD pioneers not only advocated, but applied the core values both as a desirable end state and as an integral part of the OD process. Present day practitioners need to rekindle the spirit and become more committed to and comfortable with the role of values advocate.

3.  OD professionals, both internal and external, need to maintain their marginality to the organization to keep from becoming co-opted by their client systems. There has been a trend to tie OD efforts to the organization's business goals. While this is certainly desirable, the result is often a capitulation of the core values in favor of the objectives of cost-effectiveness and efficiency. Maintaining marginality is one way of ensuring that this does not occur.

4.  A critical role can be played by helping managers better to understand the importance of and the need to integrate the traditional values of America, as described earlier, with the more recent concerns for competitive advantage, efficiency, and productivity. Providing this "conceptual therapy" for management is an important emerging dimension of the consultative role.

As we reflect on our review and analysis of the field, we find that our initial perspective remains unchanged. Organizational development *is* value-based, and more importantly its core values provide the guiding light for both the OD process and its technology. The very identity of the field is reflected in the existence and application of the values it advocates. Without them, OD represents nothing more than a set of techniques.

## REFERENCES

Adler, N. J. (1980). Cultural synergy: The management of cross-cultural organizations. In W. W. Burke & L. D. Goodstein (Eds.), *Trends and issues of OD: Current theory and practice.* San Diego: University Associates.

Burke, W. W., & Hornstein, H. A. (1972). *The social technology of OD.* La Jolla, CA: University Associates.

Burke, W. W. (1977). *Current issues and strategies in OD.* New York: Human Sciences Press.

Burke, W. W., & Goodstein, L. D. (1980). *Trends and issues in OD: Current theory and practice.* San Diego: University Associates.

Carlson, H. C. (1980). A model of quality of work life as a developmental process. In W. W. Burke & D. Goodstein (Eds.), *Trends and issues in OD: Current theory and practice.* San Diego: University Associates.

Chandler, A. D. (1977). *The visible hand.* Cambridge, MA: Harvard University Press.

Connor, P. E. (1982). A critical inquiry into some assumptions and values characterizing OD. In D. Robey & S. Altman (Eds.), *Organization Development* (pp. 57–64). New York: Macmillan.

Friedlander, F., & Brown, L. D. (1977). Research on organization development: A synthesis and some implications. In W. W. Burke (Ed.), *Current issues and strategies in OD.* New York: Human Sciences Press.

Greiner, L. E. (1980). OD values and the "bottom line." In W. W. Burke & L. D. Goodstein (Eds.), *Trends and issues in OD: Current theory and practice.* San Diego: University Associates.

Harris, R. T. (1980). Toward a technology of macrosystem interventions. In W. W. Burke & L. D. Goodstein (Eds.), *Trends and issues in OD: Current theory and practice.* San Diego: University Associates.

Harrison, R. (1980). Personal power and influence in organization development. In W. W. Burke & L. D. Goodstein (Eds.), *Trends and Issues in OD: Current theory and practice.* San Diego: University Associates.

Herman, S. M. (1977). The shadow of organization development. In W. W. Burke (Ed.), *Current Issues and Strategies in OD* (pp. 133–154). New York: Human Sciences Press.

Hornstein, H. A. (1980). Turning barriers into benefits: Searching for consultants' biases and their impact on relationships with clients. In W. W. Burke & L. D. Goodstein (Eds.), *Trends and issues in OD: Current theory and practice.* San Diego: University Associates.

Jones, J. E. (1980). Quality control of OD practitioners and practice. In W. W. Burke & L. D. Goodstein (Eds.), *Trends and issues in OD: Current theory and practice.* San Diego: University Associates.

Kanter, R. M. (1977). Women in organizations: Change agent skills. In W. W. Burke (Ed.), *Current issues and strategies in OD.* New York: Human Sciences Press.

Lewis, J. D. (1982). Technology, enterprise, and American economic growth. *Science, 215,* 1204–1211.

Margulies, N., & Raia, A. P. (1972). *Organizational development: Values, process, and technology.* New York: McGraw–Hill.

Margulies, N., & Raia, A. P. (1978). *Conceptual foundations of organizational development.* New York: McGraw–Hill.

Maslow, A. H. (1954). *Motivation and personality.* New York: Harper.

Maslow, A. H. (1965). *Eupschian management.* Homewood, IL: Irwin & Dorsey Press.

McLean, A. J., Sims, D. B. P., Mangham, I. L., & Tuffield, D. (1982). *Organization development in transition.* New York: Wiley.

Morely, E. (1980). Managing Integration. In W. W. Burke & L. D. Goodstein (Eds.), *Trends and issues in OD: Current theory and practice.* San Diego: University Associates.

OD Network Conference Brochure. (1985). *Foundations to futures.* San Francisco, October 13–October 17.

Peters, T. J., & Waterman, R. H. (1982). *In search of excellence.* New York: Harper & Row.

Rhinesmith, S. H. (1970). *Cultural-organizational analysis: The interrelationship of value orientations and managerial behavior.* Cambridge, MA: McBer.

Rokeach, M. (1973). *The nature of human values.* New York: Free Press.

Schein, E. H., & Bennis, W. G. (1965). *Personal and organizational change through group methods: The laboratory approach.* New York: Wiley.

Scott, W. G., & Hart, D. K. (1979). *Organizational America.* Boston: Houghton Mifflin.

Spier, M. S., Sashkin, M., Jones, J. E., & Goodstein, L. D. (1980). Predictions and projections for the decade: Trends and issues in Organization Development. In W. W. Burke & L. D. Goodstein (Eds.), *Trends and issues in OD: Current theory and practice.* San Diego: University Associates.

Srivastva, S. (1977). Some neglected issues in Organization Development. In W. W. Burke (Ed.), *Current issues and strategies in OD.* New York: Human Sciences Press.

Tannenbaum, R., & Davis, S. A. (1969). Values, man, and organizations. *Industrial Management Review, 10*(2), 67–86.

Woodcock, M., & Francis, D. (1980). Team building: Yes or no? In W. W. Burke & L. D. Goodstein (Eds.), *Trends and issues in OD: Current theory and practice.* San Diego: University Associates.

# 4

# Organizational Development as a Political Process*

**Karl Sandner**
*Wirtschaftsuniversität Wien,*
*Vienna*

Organizations are political entities. They are dominated by coalitions and allow the pursuit of goals and interests by individuals and groups from within and from outside the organization. They are multipurpose tools and have an instrumental value. Individuals and groups who compete through and also in organizations for scarce resources act politically.

The analysis of organizations in political terms is nothing new. Although "politics" is not considered to be a neglected area in the field, the literature presents itself particularized, fragmented, and limited. Usually some aspects are highlighted and, at the same time, one has the impression of seeing only a part of the picture. The literature on OD and politics appears even more specialized by concentrating mainly on participants, resources, and tactics in the power game (Borum, 1980; Cobb, 1986; Cobb & Margulies, 1981; Margulies & Raia, 1984; Pettigrew, 1975; Schein, 1977). This situation can be traced back to the underlying concepts of politics: for example, an explanation of politics via power (sometimes even as a tautology) generally leads to a discussion of power resources, an explanation via interests generally leads to a discussion of interest groups, coalitions, and networks. Such approaches do deal with important political aspects, but they are too narrow. Treating politics in organizations or political behavior as an additional variable, like many others in organizational theory, neglects its penetrating quality.

Therefore after a short review of existing concepts of politics, their implications for OD and the major problems accompanying these concepts are discussed. After that, instead of developing an

* This contribution is part of project J 0001. Funding for this project was made possible by a grant from the Fonds zur Förderung der Wissenschaftlichen Forschung, Vienna, Austria.

additional definition of politics, the return to two historical concepts of politics is suggested. The reinterpretation of these two concepts for organizational purposes then seems to be more productive and extensive than the existing concepts of politics in organizations are at present.

## CONCEPTS OF POLITICS AND IMPLICATIONS FOR OD: WHAT IS "POLITICS"?

Within organizational theory we find several competing concepts of politics. Traditionally every author presents his or her own concept and there are indeed only few contributions which rely on the same concept. Such a situation is symptomatic for either an immature state of the particular scientific field or for a paradigmatic transition in that field (Kuhn, 1979), whereby the former argument seems to carry more weight.

The existing definitions and concepts of politics in organizations emphasize one of four different aspects:

1. They center on the conditions of antecedence for political activities, which are interests, goals, or more generally self-serving behavior;
2. They outline the political process;
3. They concentrate on the main transformation variable, power; or
4. They highlight the organization as a political exchange system. Each of these approaches leads to its own priorities and carries different implications for OD.

### INTERESTS AND SELF-SERVING BEHAVIOR

Demands and interests arise from within the organization and from outside. Thus Narayanan and Fahey (1982, p. 26) view the organization as "loose structures of interests and demands, competing for organizational attention and resources." Political behavior is directed toward the attainment of interests and goals of individuals and groups. For Robbins (1976, p. 64) politics is "any behavior by an organizational member that is self-serving," and Porter, Allen, and Angle (1981, p. 112) define political behavior as discretionary influence attempts intended to "promote or protect the self-interests of individuals and groups."

Applied to OD processes, the uncovering and clarification of interests become especially important, as well as the disclosure of hidden agendas. Here the verbal and often alleged justifications of actions take second priority to the examination of the functionality of the actions in realization of interests. In addition the dependencies (Emerson, 1962) of the actors have to be discovered as they will play a strategical role in the process of balancing the various interests. Within this approach the behavior of the OD consultant has to be political too, an aspect which is usually neglected. If we assume that everybody engaged in the change process has interests, then the same view has to be applied to the OD consultant. He or she cannot remain the neutral catalyst any longer: rather, one asks: (a) Which individual or group interests in the organization benefit through the consultant's actions? Who gets what? and, (b) what are the consultants own interests? where are his or her open and hidden coalitions and compromises?

## Process

Another group of authors sees the characteristic element of politics embodied in the process. Burns (1961, p. 259) describes politics as "a mode of doing," a "particular mode of behavior"; for Tushman (1977, p. 211) "the political perspective focuses on decision making processes." Madison, Allen, Porter, Renwick, and Mayes (1980, p. 81) maintain organizational politics as "a process of influence," accompanied by Mayes and Allen (1977, p. 675) with "the management of influence." Lawler and Bacharach also generalize politics in their alignment model to "efforts of social actors to mobilize support" (1983, p. 85) and view "organizations as politically negotiated orders" (Bacharach & Lawler, 1980, p. 1). With the emphasis on the process, behavior strategies (Kakabadse & Parker, 1984) and tactics (e.g., Allen, Madison, Porter, Renwick, & Mayes, 1979) receive their strategical value. Mintzberg (1983) finally dissolves the political process in a number of political games.

As far as OD is concerned the following questions have to be asked: How are decisions made? Who is involved on which organizational levels, and how intensely is he or she engaged—directly or indirectly? Which institutionalized ways of conflict resolution exist? Which resources are necessary and who controls them? The dynamic aspect is stressed by shifting coalitions, negotiations, and bargaining. The main viewpoint changes from "who gets what" to "how does one get it?". This means looking out for successful influence behavior, for influence strategies, for rule systems which determine the status quo of the distribution of resources, and for indirect means of control. The OD consultant contributes to the dynamic of the process, but he or she is only one player in the field.

## Power

Those who concentrate on the crucial process variable, view "politics as power" (Simon, 1953, p. 500). For Cobb (1986, p. 483) "organizational politics simply refers to how power is used." Pettigrew (1975, p. 191) suggests that the ability of an internal consultant to influence clients will be "a function of his possession and tactical use of five power resources"; in a similar manner, Borum (1980, p. 123) promotes a "power-strategy alternative to organization development."

For OD a politics concept that centers around power means the investigation of so-called power holders, resources and dependencies, the exercise of power, the ways of organizing power like coalitions and networks, and legitimation processes. The viewpoint shifts to "how does one get power?", which also leads to another series of questions related to the theoretical and methodological problems of the power concept. The OD consultant becomes one of the power players. His or her success depends on the backing of powerful interest groups.

## The Organization as a Political Exchange System

This approach takes a broader view where "political rationality pertains to organizations as governance systems" (Scott, Mitchell, & Peery, 1981, p. 135). Power is used to "modify or protect an organization's exchange structure" (Cobb & Margulies, 1981, p. 50), political behavior influences "the distribution of advantages and disadvantages within the organization" (Farell & Petersen, 1982, p. 403) to "enhance or protect a share in an exchange" (Frost & Hayes, 1983, p. 374).

OD based on such an approach deals with organizational interest structures, the flow and distribution of power and resources. Sound systems for the allocation of positions, resources, and values have to be developed. Political behavior is examined as to its functionality for the system maintenance, or more accurately, its functionality for the regime maintenance. The OD consultant acts in a role similar to the political broker created by March (1962) and Cyert and March (1963). In such an approach OD helps to legitimize power.

Each of these four concepts of organizational politics focuses on different priorities. From a layperson's point of view, all four concepts relate positively to the idea of "politics," which might lead to the assumption that in the end every social behavior is "somehow political." Mangham (1979, p. 18) proposes such a view: "all behavior at all levels and in all circumstances may be regarded as political." With such a statement some theoretical and methodological problems arise. At least the concepts "politics" and "behavior" fall together and the idea of nonpolitical social behavior is gone. Probably one of the greatest problems with the traditional concepts of politics is the appropriate idea of nonpolitics. What is to be included in the concept seems to present less of a problem than what is to be excluded. This leads to the critical examination of the four presented concepts of politics in organizations.

## SOME PROBLEMS WITH "POLITICS"

### Reductionism

The goals—means approaches portray politics as a mode of competitive behavior. Goals or interests are connected with tactics and strategies, leading to conflict, which is then resolved through negotiation and bargaining and/or power. Here, politics is reduced to a technical enterprise. There is no real need to call such behavior "political"; the existing social science concepts will suffice. Placing the competitive (= "political") behavior within formal organizations, will not help much either. Then one manner of behavior is presented as legitimate whereas another as illegitimate (e.g., Mayes & Allen, 1977; Mintzberg, 1983; Vredenburgh & Maurer, 1984). But that is a differentiation in legitimation, mainly understood as legalization. In such a framework it is hard to see why everyday tactical encounters should qualify as political.

### Nonpolitical Behavior

The excluded behavior, the behavior that is nonpolitical, tells more about the concept of politics than the included behavior.

If politics is connected with conflict (e.g., Tushman, 1977) and resistance (e.g., Pettigrew, 1975), we are going to miss manipulation or ecological control. There the intended action neither aims at nor results in visible conflict or resistance. An issue may be loaded with onesided interests and potential conflicts and yet no sign of resistance may be found. The same holds true for the connection of politics with the use of power (e.g., Cobb, 1986). If an individual or group withdraws from its goals and does not use power (in fear of a likely defeat), there are no signs of resistance or conflict either. Of course, the essence of these examples leads rather to a *methodological* problem than a theoretical one. But as behaviorism usually doesn't deal with the concept of real and false interests the methodology directs the concept, thereby missing parts of reality. In a similar situation Frey (1971) pleaded rather for a weak measurement of important phenomena than for the excellent measurement of trivialities.

The traditional discussion of political behavior starts in a situation when essential organizational decisions have already been made. Decisions within the formal legitimate frame of the organization are declared nonpolitical, the "political behavior resides in informal structures" (Farell & Peterson, 1982, p. 405; see also Frost & Hayes, 1983; Porter et al., 1981; Schein, 1977). That means that the preconditions of organizational political behavior would then be nonpolitical. Thus by legalization, political behavior will become nonpolitical behavior, or, to put it the other way round, the more success political behavior has the less political it will be; successful politics dissolves in nonpolitics. This is a contradiction to itself. Such an approach also comes close to a pejorative treatment of politics. When nonpolitical behavior occurs within the formal, legitimate frame of the organization, the deviations will be disqualified as political. And at the same time through self-legitimation by the powerful every political behavior could be declared as being nonpolitical.

## Politics and Structures

The traditional literature on politics and OD has not yet found a way to deal with structural aspects of politics. If politics has something to do with the pursuit of interests and the exercise of power then the visible political behavior can only be the surface of the phenomenon. An apparent organizational smoothness could be a sign of successful politics: for domination as legitimized power (Weber, 1972). When power is regarded an essential element of politics, its *institutionalization* as the next logical step cannot be left out.

Therefore organizational politics should deal with its structural elements because organizational structures are at the same time the product and the medium of production of organizational politics.

## HISTORICAL CONCEPTUALIZATIONS OF POLITICS

Theoretical concepts are constructions about reality. As demonstrated, the existing concepts of OD and politics incorporate several theoretical and methodological problems. But instead of developing an additional concept of politics the return to *historical conceptualizations* might prove advantageous. Therefore with regard to their usefulness, some mainstreams of the historical politics discussion are examined. Their *reinterpretation* could render some more or less artificial neoconstructions superfluous, and what is more, the "old" concepts may even prove more modern and far-reaching than the existing "new" ones.

### Politics, Power, and Domination

The origins of our present politics concepts can be traced back to the constitution of the bourgeois societies, at the end of the Middle Ages in Europe (Lenk & Franke, 1987; Sellin, 1978). Especially in the Italian townships, a growing bourgeoisie made its first attempts to change the social order. Niccolo Machiavelli (1469–1527), oriented toward the rulers, elaborates a framework of power and domination. For him, politics is the total of means to become powerful and to stay in power to make the best use of it. Politics is the technique of acquiring and maintaining power. However, the fascination of power should not distract. What Machiavelli aims at is power as a tool, whereby *domination is the final goal*. As far as organizational theory quotes (and mostly misunderstands) Machiavelli, the domination aspects is usually left out (e.g., Pfeffer, 1981). But for Machiavelli, power is not the end in itself, for him power finds its completion in its institutionalization. Such a domination-oriented concept of politics offers its services to these individuals, groups, and institutions who constitute the rulers or the ruling systems.

Max Weber (1864–1920), some centuries later, follows a similar line of argumentation. For him, politics means the struggle for power. Political decisions always incorporate the distribution, the maintenance, or shifting of power. He does not stop at power either, in fact, he does not even like the concept. Explicitly he is aiming at domination. His three ways of legitimate domination are well known. When domination means the chance to find voluntary obedience, then in formal organizations legalization is the main form of legitimation. Thus in formal organizations all social relations which contribute to the attainment of the organizational goals have to be viewed as *dominance relations* and organizations are institutionalized systems of domination. Referring to this, Weber too was often misunderstood, including Parson's famous "translation" error.

## Politics and Interests

Another stream of political thinking evolved in England and France in the 17th and 18th century. Based on substantial economic and social changes, and later especially due to the industrialization of the 19th century, this concept of politics now deals with interests. The state was viewed as an arena of *individual and collective interests*. Politics then was the process of balancing the various interests. As far as public issues were concerned the participation of all who were affected was demanded. While the Marxist line of argumentation went toward the fight of social classes, the liberal line of argumentation still views politics as the sphere of interest-determined conflicts.

## ORGANIZATIONS AND POLITICS

Both the domination and the interests approach seem to have a high plausibility for politics in organizations. Yet, as far as domination is concerned, more often than not, organizational theories and, of course, theories about behavior in organizations show some "shyness." But the more one sees this bias the more obvious appears the heuristic value of both the domination and the interests approach for an utilitarian concept of politics in organizations. Traditionally, concepts of organizational politics have concentrated on a somehow reduced interests approach (micropolitics).

I believe that, to understand politics in organizations, we have to take into consideration both aspects: interests and domination. Organizations can be viewed as networks of dominance relations. Power (and those who command) strive for stabilization and institutionalization, which means to reach a level where the existing mode of social regulation is accepted as the existing organizational order by those dominated. This is also supported by efficiency considerations: complex organizations must have a certain amount of unquestioned rules and regulations, otherwise they would break down. But at the same time there runs another trend of action too. Individuals and groups try to reinterpret, change, instrumentalize the organization's rules and regulations in favor of their own goals and interests; they look for niches or simply violate the rules and regulations. They get organized to change the working conditions and the exchange structures. There are struggles about getting one's share; there are also strategies, tactics, and open or hidden conflicts. Thus the domination aspect of politics appears rather nonvisible, stabilizing, and solidly anchored, whereas the interests aspect of politics appears rather visible, destabilizing, and with a flux of issues and participants. Consequently, in both aspects of organizational politics their content is accompanied by different *patterns* of social relations.

I am not suggesting that politics in organizations therefore should be the sum of the domination and the interests aspect. I am only suggesting a possible organizational empirical validity of two historical lines of thinking about politics. I think both lines of politics can be found in modern organizations. There is, of course, a theoretical link between the two concepts: the institutionalization of interests.

## The Domination Aspect of Politics in Organizations

Referring to Machiavelli and Weber, the relevant questions are how to become powerful and how to stay in power. Both authors talk about the "art of power." Applied to organizations this suggests viewing them as systems of governance. According to the historical order of their development, four main modes of regulation of behavior in organizations can be distinguished (e.g., Edwards, 1979; Braverman, 1974): technological control, bureaucratic control, psychological control, and, recently, cultural control.

*Technological control.* Technological control tries to reduce the individual as a source of possible errors and uncertainties. The technological rationality prescribes the logic and course of action. As with all indirect controls, there is no visible controlling person. This contributes to the individual's unawareness of being controlled by the organization's technology.

However, recent research indicates that the use of modern information technology may lead to higher qualifications of the individuals and also to enlarged individual spheres of action in the production process (Kern & Schumann, 1985). As a consequence, the individual's impression of rather one-sided dependency could be substituted by the insight into the interdepencies of the labor process, thereby complicating the process of control.

**Bureaucratic control.** In order to reduce complexity, organizations must have standardized modes of interaction. Rules and regulations tell the individual what they are expected to do and thus bind their actions. The more these rules and regulations are based on myths (Meyer & Rowan, 1977; Westerlund & Sjoestrand, 1981) and not on evident economical or administrative rationality (which also may be based on myths) the more difficult it is for individuals to become aware of them, to get them out of the protected areas of nonreflection and to get them back into areas of discussion.

**Psychological control.** Psychological control had its forerunners in the early states of the Human Relations approach. Its second phase of instrumentality came with the combination of motivation theory and organizational tasks (e.g., Herzberg, 1966), which led finally to sophisticated models of work and job (re)design (e.g., Hackman & Oldham, 1980). On the surface, most of these models appear as psychological ones. In their relevant context, however, their criteria of being a success or of being failures are ultimately economical and not psychological—the economical rationality sets the frame for psychological opportunities (economic determination). Therefore these models address means of control (Sandner, 1984).

The reason why recent changes in technological control caused by new technologies may not go that far could be due to "psychological" means of control: the gained spheres of action could be bound again by "autonomy," "responsibility," or similarly "professional commitment."

**Cultural control.** From an utilitarian point of view, cultural control is a fascinating concept. If it is possible to get the parameters of organizational culture under control, one obtains an extensive and tendentiously totalitarian mode of control. Then the control of body movements, human relations, needs, or "critical psychological states" won't be necessary any longer. Cultural control will be the basis from which the members of an organization will then control themselves. Despite increased activities, fortunately or unfortunately (depending on one's point of view) the total cultural control of organizations does not seem to be at hand within the next years.

## The Interests Aspect of Politics in Organizations

The organization itself can be viewed as a political actor pursuing its interests in an normative environment. Within the organization political arenas develop around issues. Interests transform into dependencies and counterdependencies, and, through processes of negotiation and bargaining conditions of realization or nonacceptance are established.

Individual interests usually do not affect the system of domination. The realization of individual interests usually rearranges the distribution of values within structural limitations. When individuals change positions in the organization the domination system itself remains unchanged. Collective interests are also oriented toward the reorganization of the value distribution, but they affect—especially in their institutionalized forms—the system of domination. As one of the main tasks of domination is to protect itself, politics as domination limits politics as interests. Domination tries to set the patterns and borderlines within which politics as interests finds its place, for example, even if models of reorganization and job (re)design promise to be more efficient than the existing ones, politics as domination might limit their application because they might endanger the existing system of domination. Let us assume that the members of an organization demand to choose their superiors by themselves. Probably, and within certain economical limitations, the existing system of domination will treat efficiency considerations as though they were of secondary importance. They will see the demand as an attack on the existing organizational order and will rather accept less efficiency than resign from domination.

## POLITICS AND OD

Where does that leave OD? It has its place in both the domination and interest aspect of politics. And one way or the other: there is no nonpolitical OD; OD is a political enterprise.

From a politics-as-domination point of view, the functionality of OD programs is the main political problem. Does the program contribute to the stabilization and immunization of the system? If so, how? Does it make domination smoother? Usually and in correspondence with the predominant technical-economical rationality OD programs are oriented toward the effectiveness and the efficiency of the organization; structural and processual changes then are—whatever they may look like on the surface—instrumental for these purposes. Of course, some years ago humanization and quality of worklife programs were in great demand. But they too remained within the predominant rationality and were finally functional for the system of domination. OD programs provide excellent opportunities for the legitimation of calculated changes. The legitimatory value of symbolic participation in the change process cannot be overlooked (Edelman, 1971).

From a politics-as-interests point of view OD programs are instrumental for some organizational members; in other words, they serve somebody. And in the process of change they provide opportunities for the assertion of demands. In such processes of (re)distribution of values, opportunities, and resources the OD consultant is not neutral. Viewed in terms of functionality he or she is an agent in a political field, willingly or not, an agent for the interests of individuals or groups. But the OD consultant is also an agent for his or her own interests, which do not disappear when the OD consultant works for an organization. Even if the consultant tries to be nonpolitical or neutral, this neutrality and possible inaction are functional and therefore political for the interests of some organizational member(s), and/or directly or indirectly functional for the consultant's own interests. From the politics-as-interests point of view there are no neutral or nonpolitical activities of an OD consultant. To label an OD consultant's activities in such a way seems then to be either naïvité or ideology.

## METAPOLITICS

Both reinterpretations of historical views about politics cannot be reduced to open conflicts or "the management of politics" as an additional variable which managers or OD consultants have to take care of. At the same time it seems rather obvious that at least the domination aspect of politics generally is ignored, or even worse, stigmatized. On the other hand, there is no doubt that organizations can be viewed as systems of domination; maybe the domination aspect still is too political for organization theory. But that would also mean that the rise and fall of topics within organization theory incorporates political aspects itself.

I think we can find both the domination and the interests aspect of politics in modern organizations. OD then is not only a political process itself; the way it deals with politics is a political phenomenon in its own right.

## REFERENCES

Allen, R. W., Madison, D. L., Porter, L. W., Renwick, P. A., & Mayes, B. T. (1979). Organizational politics. Tactics and characteristics of its actors. *California Management Review, 22,* 77–83.

Bacharach, S. B., & Lawler, E. J. (1980). *Power and politics in organizations.* San Francisco: Jossey–Bass.

Borum, F. (1980). A power-strategy alternative to organization development. *Organization Studies, 1,* 123–146.

Braverman, H. (1974). *Labor and monopoly capital.* New York, London: Monthly Review Press.

Burns, T. (1961). Micropolitics: Mechanisms of institutional change. *Administrative Science Quarterly, 6,* 257–281.

Cobb, A. T. (1986). Political diagnosis: Applications in organizational development. *Academy of Management Review, 11,* 482–496.

Cobb, A. T., & Margulies, N. (1981). Organization development: A political perspective. *Academy of Management Review, 6,* 49–59.

Cyert, R. M., & March, J. G. (1963). *A behavioral theory of the firm.* Englewood Cliffs, NJ: Prentice–Hall.

Edelman, M. (1971). *Politics as symbolic action.* New York: Academic Press.

Edwards, R. (1979). *Contested terrain.* New York: Basic Books.

Emerson, R. M. (1962). Power-dependence relations. *American Sociological Review, 27,* 31–41.

Farell, D., & Petersen, J. C. (1982). Patterns of political behavior in organizations. *Academy of Management Review, 7,* 403–412.

Frey, F. W. (1971). Comment: On issues and nonissues in the study of power. *American Political Science Review, 65,* 1081–1101.

Frost, P. J., & Hayes, D. C. (1983). An exploration in two cultures of a model of political behavior in organizations. In R. W. Allen & L. M. Porter (Eds.), *Organizational influence processes* (pp. 369–392). Glenview, IL: Scott, Foresman.

Habermas, J. (1981). *Theorie des kommunikativen Handelns* (2 vols.). Frankfurt: Suhrkamp.

Hackman, J. R., & Oldham, G. R. (1980). *Work redesign.* Reading, MA: Addison–Wesley.

Hennis, W. (1963). *Politik und praktische Philosophie.* Neuwied, Berlin: Luchterhand.

Herzberg, F. (1966). *Work and the nature of man.* Cleveland: World.

Kakabadse, A., & Parker, C. (1984). Towards a theory of political behavior in organizations. In A. Kakabadse & C. Parker (Eds.), *Power, politics, and organizations* (pp. 87–108). Chichester, England: Wiley.

Kern, H., & Schumann, M. (1985). *Das Ende der Arbeitsteilung? Rationalisierung in der industriellen Produktion.* Munich: Beck.

Kuhn, T. S. (1979). *Die Struktur wissenschaftlicher Revolutionen.* Frankfurt: Suhrkamp. (originally, *The Structure of Scientific Revolutions.* University of Chicago, 1970.)

Lawler, E. J., & Bacharach, S. B. (1983). Political action and alignments in organizations. In S. B. Bacharach (Ed.), *Research in the sociology of organizations* (Vol. 2, pp. 83–107). Greenwich, CT: Jai Press.

Lenk, K., & Franke, B. (1987). *Theorie der Politik.* Frankfurt, New York: Campus.

Lukes, S. (1974). *Power. A radical view.* London: Macmillan.

Machiavelli, N. (1961). *Der Fürst* (*Il Principe*). Stuttgart: Reclam.

Madison, D. L., Allen, R. W., Porter, L. W., Renwick, P. A., & Mayes, B. T. (1980). Organizational politics: An exploration of managers' perceptions. *Human Relations, 33,* 79–100.

Mangham, I. (1979). *The Politics of organizational change.* London: Associated Business Press.

March, J. G. (1962). The business firm as a political coalition. *Journal of Politics, 24,* 662–678.

Margulies, N., & Raia, T. (1984). The politics of organization development. *Training and Development Journal, 38,* 20–23.

Mayes, B. T., & Allen, R. W. (1977). Toward a definition of organizational politics. *Academy of Management Review, 2,* 672–678.

Meyer, J. W., & Rowan, B. (1977). Institutionalized organizations. Formal structure as myth and ceremony. *American Journal of Sociology, 83,* 340–363.

Mintzberg, H. (1983). *Power in and around organizations.* Englewood Cliffs, NJ: Prentice–Hall.

Narayanan, U. K., & Fahey, L. (1982). The micro-politics of strategy formulation. *Academy of Management Review, 7,* 25–34.

Pettigrew, A. M. (1975). Towards a political theory of organizational intervention. *Human Relations, 28,* 191–208.

Pfeffer, J. (1981). *Power in organizations.* Boston: Pitman.

Porter, L. W., Allen, R. W., & Angle, H. L. (1981). The politics of upward influence in organizations. In L. L. Cummings & B. L. Staw (Eds.), *Research in organizational behavior* (Vol. 3, pp. 109–149). Greenwich, CT: Jai Press.

Robbins, S. P. (1976). *The administrative process.* Englewood Cliffs, NJ: Prentice–Hall.

Sandner, K. (1984). Lenkung und Kontrolle beruflicher Arbeit. *Journal für Betriebswirtschaft, 34,* 172–183.

Schein, U. (1977). Political strategies for implementing organizational change. *Group and Organization Studies, 2,* 42–48.

Scott, W. G., Mitchell, T. R., & Peery, N. S. (1981). Organizational governance. In P. C. Nystrom & W. H. Starbuck (Eds.), *Handbook of organizational design* (Vol. 2, pp. 135–151). London: Oxford University Press.

Sellin, V. (1978). Politik. In O. Brunner (Ed.), *Geschichtliche Grundbegriffe: Historisches Lexikon zur politisch—sozialen Sprache in Deutschland* (pp. 789–874). Stuttgart: Klett Cotta.

Simon, H. A. (1953). Notes on the observation and measurement of political power. *Journal of Politics, 15,* 500–516.

Steinmann, H. (Hg.) (1976). *Betriebswirtschaftslehre als normative Handlungswissenschaft.* Wiesbaden: Gabler.

Tushman, M. L. (1977). A political approach to organizations: A review and rationale. *Academy of Management Review, 2,* 206–216.

Ulrich, P. (1986). *Transformation der ökonomischen Vernunft.* Bern, Stuttgart: Haupt.

Vredenburgh, D. J., & Maurer, J. G. (1984). A process framework of organizational politics. *Human Relations, 37,* 47–66.

Weber, M. *Wirtschaft und Gesellschaft.* Tübingen: Mohr (orig. 1922).

Westerlund, G., & Sjoestrand, S. E. (1981). *Organisationsmythen.* Stuttgart: Klett.

# 5

# The Concept of Framing as a Basis for Understanding a Blind Spot in the Way Managers Wield Power

Samuel A. Culbert
John J. McDonough
University of California,
  Los Angeles

Managers have a significant blind spot when it comes to the wielding of power. It's not the result of their being naïve about power or particularly cynical about its use. In fact, most managers understand the general importance of power and track its presence in the ebb and flow of organization events. They watch how others use it and accept it as a commodity that is often necessary for getting things done. On the other hand, most managers are blind to the impact their power—seeking and power-wielding activities has on others. They do not comprehend that the way they naturally perceive and characterize organization events is covertly calculated to establishing and ensuring their own personal and organization power. They do not see that merely the way they characterize organization events wields power at the expense of someone else.

The pervasiveness of this managerial blind spot is partly explained by the way managers are conditioned to think about organization events. Most see themselves as the pawns of power-laden events, not as the masters of them. Their awareness focuses primarily on the forces of power above them in the hierarchy and on what has been thrust on them as a result of how a higher-up views a situation or the actions a higher up has thought to take. This skewed perception creates the illusion that the flow of organization power always comes from higher echelons and that no one possesses power independent of what trickles down from above.

We are concerned about this managerial blind spot because managers who fail to comprehend the active roles they play in seeking and wielding power cannot take responsibility for the power dynamics they initiate or for the system-wide problems that are created in the process. Managers who are unconscious of wielding power cannot consider the impact of their actions on others or comprehend what they might do differently in order to further managerial team-work and cooperation. The result is the widespread usage of a set of destructive power tactics which are steadily becoming the dominant problem-solving mode among contemporary managers.

Thus the goals of this chapter are to examine this power-wielding blind spot, to identify the destructive consequences associated with it, and to make suggestions for how present practices might, in the short run, be curtailed and, in the longer run, changed. Before this examination takes place, however, it is important to introduce a concept that helps make the wielding of power a more conscious managerial consideration. It is a concept that is quite helpful in reducing organization events to the level and scale where managers can more easily view their own involvements and their personal stakes in day-to-day power dynamics.

## THE CONCEPT OF "FRAMING"

We are living in a period in which skill and success in characterizing organizational events for self- and organizational empowerment— framing—has never been more crucial to people's success at work. "Framing" is the process by which managers at any level attempt to impose their preferred version of reality on situations. They may do this *explicitly* by aggressively arguing for a particular characteriza-tion of a specific situation or event. They may do this *implicitly* by behaving as if a situation were a certain way, perhaps by acting alarmed in relation to someone else's characterization of the facts. They may do this *indirectly* by supporting someone else who is argu-ing or acting in a way that favors one interpretation rather than another. They may do this *politically* by trading favors or by becom-ing so important, intimidating, or threatening to certain others that these intimidated individuals figure out ways to structure situa-tions to support and appease them without their ever having to voice an explicit opinion.

On a daily basis, virtually all managers are involved in the framing of organization events. Some more so, some less so, but all manag-ers get involved. Managers are ever looking to characterize organiza-tion events in ways that are basically good for their personal and professional objectives and for their work unit's and their organiza-tion's success. And while many managers are at least vaguely con-scious of what they are doing, most fail to recognize the gravity of the consequences associated with their involvements in the framing process. When events or one's contributions are viewed in the light of a friendly frame, then even a mediocre effort can be made to look strongly competent. And when events or one's contributions are viewed in the light of an unfriendly or hostile frame, then even a strong performance can appear weak or misdirected.

Success in getting one's preferred characterizations accepted as the dominant reality of an organization determines a manager's organizational power. "Assertive" managers get power by emphasizing the importance of their unit being able to move decisively in the face of changing market conditions and their own ability to direct and lead. "People-oriented" managers gain power by stressing the importance of work-unit cohesiveness and their own capacity to cultivate team-play. "Analytically oriented" managers gain power by highlighting the importance of their unit taking action based on long-term objectives and rational decision making and their capacity to exercise strategic direction. Regardless of style, skill and success in framing is achieved by calling attention to the special way one's commitments, and actions, and the circumstances of a situation hang together to produce effective organizational results. The objective is to show how one's actions and contributions link both to the formally acknowledged goals of the organization and to the thinking of those others who have a stake in how one performs his or her job.

## POWER FRAMING—A COMPETITIVE FORM OF FRAMING

As indicated earlier, we are very much concerned about the unconscious wielding of power in the way managers self-conveniently characterize and frame organization events, oftentimes at the expense of someone else's power. It's a dangerously flawed mode of operating that rapidly is becoming the dominant problem-solving mode of managers. In order to label it and segment it for scrutiny, we have coined the term "power framing."

"Power framing" is a special case of framing in which a manager casts his or her representation of a situation, performance, or point of view as an "objective" portrayal of reality, as if every rational thinking person would arrive at the same set of conclusions, when in fact the manager's representation is *not* objective. A manager's representation may lack objectivity because it does not fairly portray the circumstances, contexts, and objectives that others see operating in the situation that is being characterized, or it may lack objectivity because it does not adequately depict the self-empowering and subjective considerations that cause a manager to choose one "objective" characterization of events over another. The net result is that the so-called objective characterization turns out to be competitive. It empowers the person who is making the "objective" characterization while disempowering others whose empowerment needs can only be met by the situation being characterized differently.

In its essence, power framing is a competitive tactic. People with different needs for personal and organizational empowerment, with different organizational advocacies, and with different self-interests vie with one another by labeling situations, defining the organization's reality, in ways that establish the context that they think provides them the best chance for personal and organizational success. People don't necessarily set out to be competitive, and their manipulations are not necessarily conscious. In fact, in the majority of instances, managers actually see organization events a certain way and make their pronouncements accordingly.

Some managers who employ power framing are more successful than others in gaining acceptance for the characterizations they espouse. Some are quicker to recognize a competitive situation and more inclined toward swamping their competitors. Some are more articulate in their characterizations and more naturally persuasive in getting their story across. Some leverage their hierarchical status and make pronouncements without giving lower downs a chance to tell a different story. And of course there are also those who consistently miss opportunities to frame their stories in convincing terms, perhaps because they are relatively unconscious about the need to do so, or perhaps because of their desire to avoid conflict by not getting in the room with those who think and advocate differently.

In order to illustrate power framing and its potential to wreak organizational havoc we have a chosen a case from industry that we observed first-hand. We have chosen this particular case not because the person doing the power framing was power hungry or uncaring in his intentions but because in doing what so many managers naturally do he acted maliciously. The results created problems both for the manager and his company and were injurious to those people who became the targets of the manager's characterizations. The subject of this case is Fred, the vice-president for operations of a firm that manufactures electrical parts for the aerospace industry, which last year did about $60 million in sales.

It was hard to believe what Fred was telling us about his heretofore favorite division manager: "I'm going to remove Terry and bring in Roy Jefferson to manage the Sepulveda Division. Our sales are lagging and I'm afraid Terry will never turn things back around. Roy's reputation as a hatchet man may be somewhat deserved but after two successive quarters of disappointing sales I think a bit of shaking up is what's needed over there."

Having been close to Fred for a number of years, we had been privy to the thinking that had gone into the original search for a division manager and his recruitment of Terry. At the time, the Sepulveda Division had been plagued by labor disputes, low morale, and serious turnover problems to the point where management was committed to finding someone to run the division who had more than a fire-fighting orientation. Fred and his boss wanted someone with the skills and commitment necessary to provide immediate stability, and to build an effective team effort that would move the organization toward greater long-term efficiency.

When reminded that at one time Terry was thought to be the perfect choice and that style-wise Roy seemed to represent a return to the old days of quick fix, fire fighting, Fred responded: "I agree that Terry is bright and has good intentions but he just lacks that 'take charge' spirit that you need to keep the people at Sepulveda in line. Frankly, I find him ponderous, stubborn, and overly permissive with his managers. He insists on delegating and working through people in a situation that cries out for active leadership.

We were dismayed by Fred's turnaround to the extent that McDonough took on the challenge of confronting him. He said, "Fred, wouldn't you agree that one of your greatest strengths is that you are very good at providing strategic direction to the overall efforts of your (three) operating divisions? And isn't it also true that of all your division managers Terry is the best at following your direction and doing so in a way that is not only responsive to the spirit of your lead but adaptive to the circumstances facing his division?"

After pausing long enough to force a grudging nod, McDonough continued: "With this in mind, I want you to take a closer look at how you describe Terry. You say he is ponderous. I would put it differently. I see him as a very thoughtful person who takes his time in reaching important decisions. It's a mistake to confuse his deliberate style with an unwillingness to make the tough decisions. Once he makes up his mind, you know, as well as anyone, that he's nothing less than tenacious. And, you shouldn't confuse his readiness to follow your lead with an inability to formulate definitive action plans on his own. He simply acknowledges the strength of your leadership and is smart enough to follow it without losing himself in the process." McDonough also mentioned that he saw Terry playing the devil's advocate role in the service of testing the limits of the perspective that Fred was expecting him to make operational.

We wish we could report a happy ending. While acknowledging the cleverness of the points we made, Fred said he was too far along to change his mind. Perhaps as a way of signaling to Terry that he was on his way out, Fred began dealing directly with Terry's subordinate managers and asserting himself into business decisions which, of course, undermined Terry's authority. Terry quickly got the message and found another job, and Roy was brought in to restore order and turn this faltering division around.

In our view, Fred lost the best division manager he ever had and events eventually brought Fred around to this same view. Following Terry's departure and Roy's insertion into the division's leadership, the division returned to its old state of low morale, high turnover, and problems with quality. Roy soon failed and got the boot. A replacement manager was brought in from outside, at a substantial enhancement in pay, but he fared no better, to the point that Fred, in a moment of sheepish candor, asked us "Do you think we could find a way to lure Terry back?" McDonough couldn't resist this opening and replied, "Fred, at this point not even George Steinbrenner[1] could get Terry back.:

We choose this story in order to illustrate the nature and impact of power framing. The next section provides a detailed examination of power framing which is organized around six major propositions aimed at answering the following questions.

1.  Why is power framing so impactful and what makes the images and frameworks it establishes so difficult to dislodge?
2.  How does power framing disempower those who feel "framed" by the power-framing statements?
3.  What are the major motivations behind power framing and what are the payoffs for the so-called "framer."
4.  What systematic biases does power framing bring to the formulation of problems and to statements about the actions required to correct them?
5.  How does power framing influence those who are not direct parties to the events being characterized but whose opinions are

---

[1]The owner of the New York Yankees, who has a long history of hiring managers, publicly criticizing their decisions, summarily firing them, and then rehiring them.

necessary to uphold the validity of the reality that is being asserted?

6. What are the destructive effects of power framing and how do these effects get transmitted outward into the organization?

## 6 FRAMING PROPOSITIONS

The answer to the first question "Why is power framing so impactful and what makes the images and frameworks it establishes so difficult to dislodge?" is summarized by our first proposition:

1. Power framing derives its impact from the "framer's" ability to link several levels of reality together to formulate a compelling statement of the problem and an organizationally desirable course of action. The framer's statement swamps competing rationales and becomes the dominant organizational logic used in making decisions and justifying actions.

Effective power framing takes the facts of a situation and weaves them together to present a compelling version of reality that drives out the alternative explanations that others might use to explain the same facts. It reduces the baffling complexity of a situation to a linear account that crisply states the organizational problem, or the opportunity, the managerial actions that are required, and the results that are forthcoming. And in today's organizations the story is often expanded to specify the bottom-line indicators that might give clear and unequivocal evidence of whether or not desirable results were achieved.

In our case, Fred had created such a compelling story that even he himself could not open-mindedly contemplate a competing interpretation of the same facts. He linked together facts, taken from several levels of reality, to assert that Terry's lack of leadership had allowed sales to decline creating a near-crisis situation which could only be remedied by a strong-armed replacement. More specifically, here are the critical facts that got strung together.

### FRED'S FRAMING OF TERRY

*Fact 1:*   The Sepulveda Division's performance over the last two quarters has declined to create a near-crisis situation.

*Fact 2:*   Terry's laid-back leadership style is the principal cause of the sales decline. Terry has been too removed from day-to-day decisions, overly protective of his staff, and too reticent to demonstrate that he is the boss.

*Fact 3:*    The situation has declined to the point where Fred must recognize the crisis and change managers.

Fred's power framing links several levels of reality. It combines negative images of the division's performance with sharp images of Terry's central role in the decline leading to a crisis requiring decisive managerial action by Fred.

Power framing establishes the grounds for comprehending a situation and evaluating proposals for action. In place, it becomes a self-sealing framework with the capacity to absorb the refutation of any constituent fact or opposing view. While at the time we patted ourselves on the backs for articulateness in explaining Terry's strengths to Fred, what we said in our point-by-point refutation of the so-called facts was insufficient to overturn the framework that Fred had dropped on the situation and which was playing with his boss, peers, and Terry's subordinates at the Sepulveda Division. Subsequently we have learned that point-by-point refutations seldom prove persuasive. They only succeed in highlighting the very grounds that are the source of the deficiency or problem.

In attempting to refute the framework on a point-by-point basis we proceeded the way most managers proceed when they attempt to contest the validity of a power-framing characterization. In fact, as this chapter is being written, the *New York Times* is carrying a front page picture of Philippine President Corazon Aquino lifting her bedspread to show reporters that there is no place for her to crawl in an effort to refute the image political opponents have sought to create that during a recent coup attempt she hid under her bed. However, all her spirited defense accomplished was to give worldwide coverage to the very issue that her critics want circulated—that she is not "man enough" for the job. Likewise, in the case involving Fred and Terry. The underlying issue was the framework that Fred used that focused on *Terry's* inadequacies and not his (Fred's) own. The real problem was not Terry's inability to handle a crisis situation; it was Fred's inability to manage by any other means than crisis management.

Power framing derives a good deal of its durability from the fact that it forces those who are "framed," who have their actions placed in an alien context that differs significantly from the circumstances that produced those actions, to engage issues on two levels simultaneously. First, they must be capable of responding to the direct charges leveled at their performance; second, they need to be able to reframe a situation in which their own behavior has been cast as the problem, doing so with an air of objectivity and nondefensiveness.

On the other hand, the only effective way of dealing with power framing is to be able to characterize the facts within an alternative framework, one that holds plausibility for key onlookers. Then, even if the onlookers don't prefer the second framework to the first, they at least have a means of viewing the subjective roots behind the power-framer's ruse of impartial "objectivity."

The answer to the next question "How does power framing disempower those who feel 'framed' by the power-framing statements?" is summarized by our second proposition:

> 2. Power framing disempowers by disconnecting the "framed" individual's actions from the contexts—the mental sets and managerial frameworks—that generated these actions. Seen without contextual considerations, an individual is deprived of the frameworks that make the sensibilities and meaning of his or her actions apparent and visible. Actions that can not stand on their own visible merits will appear disoriented, even to the person who is being framed.

The full impact of power framing is seldom comprehended until an individual personally experiences what it is like being on the receiving end—*framed* by a power framer's pronouncements. Being framed is often a very emotional experience. An individual who is framed feels frustrated and often quite angry. One's emotions are further heightened when he or she has a close and trusting relationship with the power framer, for then that person is upset further by feelings of betrayal.

People feel framed when they are characterized differently than they view themselves; when different intentions are attributed to their actions than what they know in their hearts were their actual motivations; when the actions they took are placed in the wrong context, one that makes it impossible for observers to comprehend the constructiveness and instrumentality of the actions they took; and, when others fail to recognize the value of what they believe they accomplished.

When Fred's characterization of events finally caught up with him, Terry felt framed. As is typical, no single point in a power-framing characterization was all that false. However, when all the points of the characterization were put together the resulting story became skewed in a single, unflattering, direction. The three elements of Fred's story each had a grain of truth but were combined to produce a distorted and inaccurate picture of the situation, one that

Terry felt systematically slandered his talents, contributions, and accomplishments.

In Terry's judgment, Fred was technically correct in saying that sales were off two quarters in a row but was considerably off target in his attempt to characterize this as "a crisis." It was true that sales were "down" from the previous two quarters but in this company, and in this industry, sales had an annual pattern of being low in the first two quarters and then building up the last two quarters of the year. It was also not true that sales were down in relation to last year's. In fact they were up 6% in contrast to the same two quarters of the previous year. Sales were down in relation to the company's sales plan which had been based on the hope that a 15% increase could be sustained for the second year in a row. The way Terry saw things, the Sepulveda Division was off to a profitable year with a healthy sales increase; some deficiency in Fred either caused him not to recognize this or not to be able to sell this logic to higher-ups who were demanding evidence that the budgeted 15% increase would be achieved.

Likewise, Fred's characterization of Terry's style also had elements of the truth but, as we tried to counsel Fred, seemed to have significantly missed the mark. Yes, it was true that Terry's style was much less directive than Fred's. Terry was a self-professed delegator who would give on-the-spot lectures in which he claimed that effective delegation required that you show people that you have confidence in their judgment and that hovering over people undercuts their development. Fred may have been correct in thinking that Terry was not the best choice for a crisis situation. But since it was not at all clear that the situation was a *crisis,* the inference that Terry's handling of the division demonstrated a generic inability to handle crisis was not documentable.

Power framing frequently characterizes a situation in a way that disconnects people from the contexts that make it possible to judge accurately the validity of their actions. The resulting characterization can be overly positive or overly negative. Examples of the overly positive are readily recognizable in the rhetoric associated with a political campaign endorsement or perhaps a president's advocacy of a controversial cabinet or court nominee. An example of the negative is seen in Fred's characterization of Terry.

Fred either overlooked or forgot that Terry had been hired because his style was seen as a terrific match for the situation. In fact Terry says he was explicitly told, "We've hired you because we need someone who has the style, temperament, and skill to take the longer term view in the management of this division and who will be able to get the division beyond the fire-fighting mode that has dominated its operation up to now." But Fred disconnected Terry from the mandate he had been given and which was still providing the context from which Terry was proceeding. Fred switched contexts on Terry and, as much as any factor, this was responsible for Terry seeming like a failure. Instead of being viewed in the context of the progress made in building a solid team and the creation of well-functioning manufacturing and management systems, Terry was being evaluated in the context of how well he responded to a crisis he didn't perceive as if the other dimensions did not exist. In our field-work with companies, we can't count the number of times we've seen a sudden switch in context result in a yesterday's hero being turned into today's obsolescent manager.

In organizations, all people operate with distinctive styles. A "style" emphasizes one set of strengths, skills, and attributes and, by definition, de-emphasizes others. People also come with personal flaws. Styles compensate for flaws. What gets missed because some-one can't do something one way, either gets attended to or made less important because that person does it another way. When some element of the task is done poorly, or is omitted, it usually surfaces as a problem or symptom and the individual gets the change to amend his or her style to compensate. Most people have sufficient latitude to expand or refocus their styles once they understand that the expectations of others and the context they are working in has been switched. Few people have styles that can immediately with-stand a radical and sudden shift in context and framework.

The inevitable result of a sudden and radical shift in context is that an individual's strengths get measured within a framework that is different than what the individual had in mind when he or she took action and they show up as weaknesses. This is what hap-pened to Terry when Fred switched contexts on him. Terry's toler-ance and patience were viewed as a lack of aggressiveness. His in-terest in developing managers was seen as passivity and an inability to demonstrate his leadership and be the boss. His commitment to planning and longer-term development in the areas of reducing turnover and increasing the management skills of his line super-visors were seen as misguided priorities that directed attention away from bottom line sales and profits. His unflappable style was seen as lack of the emotional commitment and toughness needed to get the job done.

As much as anything, the existence of power framing illustrates a manager's vulnerability and the mutability of strengths and weak-nesses. In organizations, strengths and weaknesses are not absolutes but products of the situations in which one finds one's self and of the contexts in which one's energies are applied. Shifting frameworks and changing the context makes it possible for power framing to turn strengths into weaknesses. And of course the reverse alchemy is also possible. Although there are fewer instances of this in organizations, sometimes people who are thought to be obsolete are "born again." To some extent this is what Fred was doing when he characterized Roy Jefferson as the "hatchet" man who is just the person needed to turn the Sepulveda Division around.

The third question "What is the major motivation behind power framing and what are the payoffs for the person doing the framing" is dealt with in our next proposition:

3. Power framing substitutes the framer's self-empowering view of what is required for the organization to function effectively for the context that the "framed" individual had in mind when he or she thought and acted as he or she did. It advances images, frameworks, and imperatives for individual and organizational action that are linked to the framer's subjective interests and to his or her self-convenient perceptions of what will make the organization succeed.

Most power framing is instinctive, not conscious, and usually not the product of deliberate desire to be destructive and manipulate. Oftentimes power framing is merely the result of people straightforwardly expressing what they see and connecting a sequence of events that they think have an interlocking association with one another. However, needs and interests influence an individual's perceptions, and the mere reporting of one's perceptions can inadvertently cast others, whose needs are different and thus see things differently, in the wrong context making it more difficult for them to pursue their goals.

We have no reason to believe that Fred's framing of the Sepulveda Division's situation was intended to be a malicious act toward Terry. Fred was merely judging Terry in relation to the framework that, at that point in time, was guiding his own efforts and enabling him to operate empoweredly. As suggested earlier, the crucial issue was not Terry's inability to handle crisis situations but Fred's inability to manage by any means other than crisis management. Fred is an action-oriented hands-on manager who performs very well in crisis, so well that he falls prey to the danger of creating crises as a basis for taking charge and maintaining his preferred course of direction.

For Fred, personal empowerment comes from situations that are sharply defined almost to the point of being black and white. Fred gets very anxious when he doesn't know exactly what to do and when he senses the possibility of failure. If given a choice of assignments Fred would undoubtedly opt for those situations which were in the worse shape where he would have maximum leverage to dramatize the problems that need attention and to implement solutions that might eliminate them.

Over time Fred became apprehensive with the role of looking over Terry's shoulders. While his intentions in hiring Terry to build strength from within were quite positive, Fred was finding arms-length management a temperamentally difficult thing to do. He was finding it more and more difficult to check the feelings of powerlessness and impatience that welled up inside him while watching Terry's stolid way of operating. Increasingly he was measuring Terry against the standards that guided his own orientation and slowly his own subjective standards began to replace the different standards he had in mind when recruiting Terry. As a result Fred began to accumulate a list of concerns and grievances that eroded his confidence in Terry. And he found himself in the awkward position of not being able to keep his own boss convinced that he was sufficiently informed on what was happening at the Sepulveda Division.

Although power framing is an approach to organizational problem solving that produces domination over others, it seldom represents a conscious attempt to do so. In most instances its use represents less the intent to manipulate and more the intent to impose self-empowering standards on the wider situation. In fact, needs for self-empowerment are not a self-indulgent whim. All managers require personal and organizational power to get the job done. Most importantly, they need it to operate efficiently and decisively. There is nothing wrong per se with the criteria Fred used to evaluate Terry, and we would find little reprehensible about his flawed handling of the situation if only he had owned up to the real reasons why he needed to switch frames. The everpresent danger with power framing is that framers will confuse those criteria that make themselves comfortable with the ones that are exclusively "appropriate" to the situation. In terms of organizational effectiveness, power framing goes off track when framers get so caught up in getting power for themselves that they disempower others in the process.

The next question "What systematic biases does power framing bring to the formulation of problems and to statements about the actions required to correct them?" is addressed in our fourth proposition:

4. We have identified two systematic biases:

a. Power framing has the effect of making the framer's characterizations of events and problems appear to be "objective"—to be how any rational thinking individual would see them, think about them, and act upon them. What is subjective and empowering to the framer gets portrayed as organizationally "correct" and communicated to onlookers as the only valid orientation to use in viewing the actions and skills of the "framed" individual.

b. Portraying one's position as purely "objective" leads people who power-frame to a deficiency model that systematically imputes what other people are doing when those actions fail to fit with what the framer asserts is organizationally desirable. Such an orientation puts people on the defensive. They become preoccupied with justifying their efforts, on terms chosen for their appeal to the power framer, instead of open-mindedly thinking about what might be improved and developing the conditions and circumstances that maximize their output and proficiency.

The quest for empowerment leads managers who power-frame to judge events, and other people's performances in them, from a perspective that artificially "objectifies" their personal standards and points of view. Power framing enables people to portray perspectives based partly, or largely, on subjective considerations as if they were "objective fact" and, by doing so, gain maximum power and leverage for their points of view. Much of the time such objectified portrayals are perpetrated with no conscious intent to misrepresent or manipulate, they are straightforward representations of how someone who is focused on his or her own empowerment views the "facts."

Of course this is what Fred did to Terry. He self-conveniently seized on Terry's strengths, Terry's capacity to follow Fred's lead and to work through his managers, to construct a story of deficiency. The real problem was Fred's disorientation. Fred lost focus of the big picture and what had been his own strategic plan. He became preoccupied looking for ways to exercise his authority and to establish that his own moment-by-moment activities were making a contribution to the organization's effectiveness. Without the proper focus he didn't know how to answer his bosses' questions regarding the Sepulveda Division's performance and why they were falling short of budgeted goals. Of course the irony struck us that since Fred prides himself on being a skilled strategic planner, he needs the skills to stay focused more than most. No planner succeeds for long if the punch line for all "objective" analysis is that everyone has to do things the boss's way. Fred's power framing of the situation, and his portrayal of Terry as characterologically deficient, was a prototypical example of the self-defeating problems that power framing can create.

Reporting perceptions that have a large subjective component as totally rational and "objective" is part of the way people working in organizations have been conditioned to talk. In fact, explicitly acknowledging the subjective commitments that underlie one's orientation to organizational events makes an individual excessively vulnerable to discreditation by anyone whose subjective commitments leads him or her to support or emphasize a different "objective" point of view. Fred was particularly proficient at talking this way and this skill, coupled with his organizational stature, allowed him to convince everyone up and down the line that he was speaking the so-called "objective truth." To Fred's credit, with subsequent experience, he was quick to admit that he had been wrong.

When power framing, people take their own preferred "objective" orientation and impose it as the standard in evaluating others, oftentimes without realizing the presence of their biases themselves. From such a self-objectifying orientation it is very difficult for them to keep someone else's strengths in focus. Such an orientation leads them, in effect, to reason "How does this person's overall performance stand up against the frame of reference that I endorse?" which by "coincidence" happens to be maximally empowering to them. Thus, they focus on the areas of greatest gaps between their needs and the other person's style and intent, not on what the other person does particularly well or on how situations might be configured to provide others with a more optimal context for the types of contributions they can make uniquely well.

As a consequence, people who engage in power framing have a propensity for formulating performance problems in ways that feature another person's, or another unit's, limitations in working the way they would personally prefer them to work as skill problems and personal flaws. People whose style features rapport building and teamwork are called "soft-minded" and "conflict avoiders." Units that don't communicate are called "excessively territorial" and "overly competitive." Problems caused by another person or another unit not orienting as the power framer desires them to orient are externalized as negative traits with the implication that these traits are present in all situations, and that people or work units who possess them are "objectively" and irrefutably deficient.

The fifth question, "How does power framing influence those who are not direct parties to the events being characterized but whose opinions are necessary to uphold the validity of the reality that is being asserted?" is addressed in the next proposition:

5. Power framing misleads onlookers by masking the connection between the empowerment interests of the framer and the mental sets and managerial frameworks that are being advanced as "objective." Without directly seeing this connection, onlookers are in the position of unwittingly endorsing reality depictions that they might never endorse, or endorse only with reservation, if they knew how convenient these depictions were to the interests of the framer. Thus onlookers get manipulated into further "objectifying" the contextual needs of the framer and reifying modified, self-convenient portrayals of the dominant organizational reality.

No doubt by now readers have gotten the point that power framing has its roots in a manager's need to create a setting that enables him or her to function with empowerment. When managers engage in power framing they are seeking to establish standards, relationships, and organizational frameworks and logics that make it easy for them to accentuate their strengths and preferred orientations. They do so by framing problems to emphasize issues for which their preferred modes of operating are ideally suited and which lead to solutions that they know they can implement competently, and that others will acknowledge as organizationally effective.

Featured in any power-framed characterization is the connection between the problem, the actions required to solve it, and the organization's success. De-emphasized in any power-framed characterization are connections between the stated problem and actions to solve it and the power framer's subjective interests and personal needs for success. Most organizations possess a morality that censures self-serving actions. This is why all characterizations emphasize the objective value of what is asserted as if all the criteria for evaluating a problem statement and the actions for solving it reside externally in what the organization, not the problem framer, needs to function effectively.

Of course, as our example so clearly illustrates, some of the objective criteria for an organization's success rest in the empowerment and success of each individual who works for the organization. Any characterization of organization events that advances one person's empowerment needs at the expense of someone else's fails these criteria. This is why we have been so critical of Fred and why we see power framing as such a destructive force in organizations today. Masked and obscured was the fact that Fred's framing of the situation was self-convenient and in zero-sum opposition to Terry's needs to be empowered and to contribute to the organization and to succeed.

Onlookers play a critical role in sealing the fate of people who are the targets of a power-framing characterization. Their endorsement of what a power framer asserts endows that characterization with objectivity. And onlookers are easily persuaded. They usually lack first-hand knowledge of the situation and thus have no data-based way of disputing what has been portrayed as the facts. They usually lack insight into how what is being asserted as objective links to that which is self-convenient and subjective to the framer and thus have little cause or ability to dispute the veracity of what a power framer asserts. And, they usually react negatively to single point refutations made by a power-framing victim. They interpret coming to one's own defense as reeking with subjectivity and this creates a credibility gap that makes the framer's characterizations seem all the more objective. What's more, single-point refutations seldom are persuasive to an individual who has been introduced to an interlocking framework that persuasively advances the opposite point of view.

Even when their instincts tell them that something is off, onlookers have a difficult time making the connection between the self-interests of the power framer and what has been advanced as "objective" in sufficiently convincing terms to defend the framed individual without compromising their own credibility. Faced with such a situation most onlookers acquiesce and decide to go along publicly with the characterization rather than join a fight that, they reason, probably can not be won. However, in going along and not taking action, onlookers unwittingly add organizational validity to a process that has deeper implications. Power framing creates the circumstances whereby onlookers get manipulated into "objectifying" the contextual needs of the framer in ways that establish them as the organization's standard.

The answer to our last question "What are the destructive effects of power framing and how do these effects get transmitted outward into the organization?" is reflected in our sixth and final proposition:

6. Widespread usage of power framing has long-term destructive effects on the "health" and development of an organization. The most pronounced effect is on the loss of trust and the capacity of managers to build trusting relationships. A less obvious but equally serious effect is that it retards management learning and establishes the conditions whereby younger managers see it as a desirable mode of operation.

The rhetoric and results of power framing can appear very compelling, particularly to an outsider or interested onlooker who lacks access to independent information. The person performing the power framing appears self-confident and very clear in his or her perceptions. The story that is asserted appears coherent and logical and presents a solution for every problem that is referenced. And in each instance, the presented narrative explains how the organization's performance will increase when the other "less competent" people get moving in the logical directions asserted by the framer. Seldom, if ever, does the power framer describe a problem that portrays oneself as a primary cause or in any significant way deficient. Almost always the story presented features the framer as someone whose professional and personal resources will be useful in picking up the organization and moving it ahead.

The case involving Fred and Terry illustrates the above points. From our perspective both managers are competent and desire to live a moral organizational life. But the way the story of the organization's problems and the actions that might remedy them got told, only one manager was portrayed as competent. While we are not suggesting that this one incident ruined Terry's professional life, or doomed the organization to an epidemic of deceptive and distrusting relationships, we do believe that the costs were considerable.

Several destructive aspects of power framing are viewed in this incident. The most obvious are the lowering of Terry's, and his immediate cohorts', abilities to trust and the fact that Terry's departure deprives the corporation of a valuable resource. Less obvious, although no less a loss, is the diminishment of trust that occurred among managers at all levels of the Sepulveda Division.

Terry left the company resentful and threatening a lawsuit. In his mind he was betrayed. The mandate he had enthusiastically embraced had been, without notice, reversed on him. To leave the company, he literally accepted the first job offered to him. He told us, "I was looking for any reasonable way to get out from under a managerial situation in which I was being undermined, humiliated, and squeezed out." The experience he had is the type that too often builds cynicism and distrust. From talking with Terry, we got the impression that it's going to take him a while before he can again commit himself to an organization with anything like the wholeheartedness that characterized his involvements at the Sepulveda Division. Until then we expect him to watch political events vigilantly and work on becoming skilled in his new orientation which he calls "playing it safe."

As for Fred, the loss of trust takes a different form. For him, the loss of trust does not involve a breach within the system but a breach within himself. No longer is he going to put his organizational fate in the hands of people whose perspectives and modes of operating do not match up with his own action-oriented instincts. For a solution to the "problems" created by Terry, Fred preferred an action-oriented person like Roy, whose faults he knows well and whom he likens to a hatchet man. But Fred also knows better, and this is demonstrated by his quick disenchantment with Roy and his reattraction to Terry. Of course we can also conjecture that from Roy's perspective he got the same treatment as Terry. Fred brought him in for a set of attributes that Fred later categorized as managerial obsolescence and grounds for dismissal.

Although bewildered and disheartened by Fred's characterizations and behavior, it is not apparent that Terry took Fred's assessment to heart. Terry still values team play and sees himself as contributing to organizational excellence by empowering other managers and building on existing managerial strengths. On the other hand, many power-framing victims do buy into the characterizations that are levied at them. They accept that the responsibility for "failure" is theirs and in the process experience self-doubts about the adequacies of their most essential attributes. These are the situations in which power framing has its most perverse impact. Even if, for example, Terry had taken Fred's characterizations to heart, how could he have responded in a satisfactory manner? He would be in the position of being asked to display a "go-get-em, take charge" attitude that would undermine the very framework he was attempting to erect. And he would be asked to perform with maximum strength while disoriented by being in a situation that gave him no credit for what he had confidence that he could do.

At least Terry had the presence of mind to find another job and quit when the context was switched to one which deprived him of his integrity and strength. What happens to those who are not so fortunate, who take power-framing characterizations to heart and make strenuous efforts to instantly mend their ways? Many of these individuals also wind up leaving their companies but only after taking "rehabilitative" measures that haunt them for years. Many others never leave their organizations and will labor on, valiantly trying to succeed on terms imposed by others. They spend the rest of their organizational life thinking about what other people want before they consider their own beliefs about what the situations needs, with their security dependent on their ability to provide loyal support to their boss of the moment.

Of course, some people respond to power framing with a fight. They find themselves and their projects disempowered by what is being asserted and decide to stand their grounds. Only if the power framing is relatively weak do they have a chance of conducting their fight on constructive grounds, calmly espousing their alternative and preferred formulation of the organizational situation and the actions required to make the organization effective. However, most of the time people feel their survival, let alone their ultimate success, rests in exposing the subjectivity behind what the other person asserts. They don't want others to believe for a minute that the accusations regarding their alleged deficiencies are valid and decide to conduct their fight on every ground available to them. The natural conclusion is the type of vicious in-fighting that characterizes too many organizations today.

From a human resource perspective, the most discouraging aspect of power framing is the impact it has on those who fight back and the lessons they take away from their experiences of being on the firing line. The stronger people find ways of absorbing the punishments and console themselves by seeing these abuses as part of the organization game. They view power framing as a corrupt part of what goes on in organizations and something to defend against as best they can. They fight, they submit, they do whatever they can confident that one day they will rise sufficiently in the hierarchy to assume the "driver's seat." Thus, their ultimate response is to take power framing to a deeper political level by deferring gratification to a later period when they will be in positions to operate in an equally arbitrary fashion. This is the ultimate reason why we see power framing as being so perverse and destructive. It perpetuates a organizationally dysfunctional system using people who themselves shunned the abuses when they were on the receiving end.

## THE APPEAL OF POWER FRAMING

The appeal of power framing can be summarized in a single word: *power.* Power framing provides a ready way for an individual to advance his or her subjective interests while appearing exclusively involved in furthering the "objective" interests of the organization. Its use promises high organizational payoffs for the power framer with few, apparent, personal costs.

Power framing provides a way of getting others to think and participate within a framework that is empowering to the framer. A manager sees a problem, finds that another person or unit is to blame, comprehends a clear-cut solution, and brings this all into focus by simply making a linear, power-framing, statement of what the organization needs in the way of a remedy. And while, taken in isolation, the framework chosen for this "objective" pronouncement is usually functional to the organization's interests and needs, it is also tailored to the framer's subjective interests and needs for empowerment. The problem is that too often such linear statements prove disempowering to others whom the power framer holds responsible and blames but whom the organization is also counting on to function with empowerment and to succeed.

Inevitably the framework implied in the power framer's characterization of the problem and remedy makes the framer dominant, a position that is elevated further by the framer's stature in the organization's hierarchy. And the people who are characterized as key contributors to a problem inevitably wind up on the down side of an up-down relationship where: (1) They allow their style and ways of orienting to be critiqued as subjective and suboptimal; (2) They accept the framer's preferred style and ways of orienting as being, by definition, organizationally desirable; (3) They accept total responsibility for getting their preferences to mirror more completely the framework that the framer is calling "objective"; and (4) They take no initiative in critiquing the personal convenience of the images advanced by the power framer, thereby reinforcing the airs of objectivity implied by the way those images are advanced.

In the extreme case, power framing sets up a unilateral relationship where an individual who is having his or her performance framed is totally accountable to the reality of the power framer and where the power framer is only minimally accountable to that other person. We are not suggesting that power framing leads irreversibly to one-sided power relationships. We are merely pointing out that an important aspect of its appeal lies in the fact that every manager fantasizes about the "ideal" situation where the rest of the world pays laser-like attention to what he or she self-conveniently claims that the organization needs and has the time and energy, oneself, to advance on those objectives. The use of power framing pushes managerial relationships in this idealized direction.

Why would anyone on the receiving end of a power-framing relationship ever agree, even implicitly, to go along with this way of doing things? Many buy in because they are not aware of what they are doing. Others who do see the imbalance accept the terms by rationalizing that this is how they will eventually get themselves into a position of power taking, as contrasted to power acquiescing. They accept the conditions as an inevitable step on their way up the ladder and identify with the power-framing position as a future goal.

## THE ALTERNATIVE TO POWER FRAMING

Several insights are necessary before managers modify their dependence on power framing and reduce the role it plays in their thinking and domination of others. Above all, managers require a model of organization that gives them a more comprehensive understanding of the role of power in everyday organizational life and, in particular, of the role that framing plays in the distribution of power. They need a perspective which alerts them to the character and destructive nature of power framing and to the fact that the alternatives to power framing require a concern for other people's power as well as their own. They need a way of knowing when power framing is taking place, who is affected by it, and, most importantly, they need to find ways of framing situations that allow for their potential victim's empowerment along with their own.

Framing for mutual empowerment is the alternative to power framing. Such framing requires that managers explicitly do for others what they implicitly do, when power framing, for themselves. Power framers formulate problems based on what should happen given their interests in operating with empowerment. They conceptualize situations with their own strengths, resources, commitments, aspirations, and limitations as unstated givens, and critique other people's actions against a set of standards that are tailored to their own needs for empowerment. People who frame for mutual empowerment formulate problems based on what should happen given the other person's needs to be empowered as well as their own. They conceptualize situations from the perspective of what the organization needs given that the organization possesses the resources of themselves and the others who desire empowerment. They operate as if the organization succeeds to the extent that as many key people as possible are maximally energized and empowered.

Framing for another person's empowerment along with one's own is not an easy perspective to apply for it entails constantly searching outward to comprehend what other people are seeking and what resources they can contribute. It entails going beyond what one automatically sees by looking inward to scrutinize situations from the contexts of what other key participants are attempting to accomplish. It entails rethinking how problems are formulated to reflect the fact that satisfying one's own subjective interests is only one consideration in maximizing organizational output.

Of course framing for mutual empowerment is not what Fred was inclined to do. If you would have asked him, there is little doubt that he would have said that this is what he did and cited how well he and Terry used to get along and how well he and the other managers currently get along. But framing for mutual empowerment is not the same as two or more people buying into the same framework or agreeing to go along with the same dominant reality which, in organizations, can take place for a multitude of practical and political reasons. The way Fred dealt with Terry convinced us that his inclinations were more toward framing for his own empowerment, power framing, than to frame for mutual empowerment. We never thought his intentions were malicious, it's just that his skills were more attuned to power framing. Fred slipped into a way of conceptualizing the Sepulveda Division's situation that was consistent with his subjective interests and Terry's orientation was not well aligned.

What would Fred have done it he were looking to frame situations for his and Terry's mutual empowerment? What does anyone with such collaborative values need to do to frame situations for mutual empowerment? The answer is first to place the other person's thinking and actions in the context of that person's strengths, commitments, limitations, and perceptions of situational and political givens; second, to make this other person's empowerment needs a factor in all formulations of organizational situations and what one chooses to call "reality"; and third, to ensure that the organization's needs for product and market viability are not subordinated to the various empowerment needs that are being pursued.

Placing another person in the proper context, in the context of what that person sees as his or her strengths, commitments, limitations, and situational and political givens entails considerable research into the perceptions of that other person and a recognition of the fact that empowerment needs impact and bias each individual's perceptions including one's own. Elsewhere we have used the term *alignment* to characterize the distinctive lens through which people see organization events and formulate personal strategies for being effective (Culbert & McDonough, 1980, 1985). Viewed in the context of the alignment of the person taking action, that which formerly did not make sense often appears logical, even actions that still are judged not to be particularly effective. The same actions seldom make sense, however, when they are placed in the context of the viewer's alignment, rather than the alignment of the individual who took them. Then the standard criticism becomes (we editorialize) "How could this person be so stupid as to act as I never would have acted given my unique background and distinctive needs for empowerment."

Making other people's empowerment needs facts in all formulations of organizational situations and what one chooses to term "reality" requires discipline. An individual must go beyond inclinations to characterize situations impulsively in ways that lead to personal empowerment at a teammate's expense. An individual must transcend the tendency to respond defensively to actions that teammates take that initially seem to make it more difficult to function with self-empowerment. For many people such inclinations are natural and instinctive and are neither conscious nor caused by a desire to harm. But before people can check this natural tendency they must be aware of it. And of course they must possess the reality framing skills that allow them to find the organizational frames and frameworks that simultaneously empower a range of individuals including themselves and the political savvy to sell others on the merits of such collaborative formulations.

Ensuring that the organization's needs for product and market viability are not subordinated to the empowerment needs that its members pursue requires that people keep an outward focus at the same time that they think about internal teamwork and personal effectiveness. It entails not getting overly captured by the "objectified" realities that power framers assert and that onlookers reify when accepting those portrayals or that victims counter with when asserting "more" objective realities of their own. It entails avoiding the work unit equivalent of the market-insensitivity problem framed by the following caption appearing in a recent edition of the *Los Angeles Times:* "GM–Toyota Plant Produces Happy Workers, High-Quality Product—and a Glut of Unsold Chevrolet Novas." In short, market forces are essential variables to use in checking the human tendency to get taken in thinking that some well-phrased characterization, advanced with ardor, makes someone's depiction of the facts an organizational truth.

## CONCLUSION

In this chapter we have attempted to show how, in contemporary organizations, managerial power results most centrally from an individual's ability to influence and control the frames that are being used to view his or her accomplishments and those organizational situations that affect his or her image and daily functioning. We have also asserted that most people are confused about this and that's why we've called this a major blind spot in the way managers wield power. We see too many managers who go around nonchalantly saying what they think, giving self-conveniently "accurate" accounts what they see, without serious concern for three essential facts: (1) that what they see is greatly determined by their own needs for empowerment; (2) that others, with different needs for empowerment, will inevitably have different thoughts and perceptions which, in many or most instances, will be as valid as their own; and (3) that any conceptualization of the facts that favor their self-interested accounts while disregarding the thinking and perceptions of others creates internal competition, sometimes of organizational life and death proportions, that works against the overarching teamwork needs of the institution.

We have also made the point that disregard for any or all of the aforementioned facts leads a manager to wanton power framing. Yet this is exactly what is taking place in organizations today. We live in an era in which many of the managers who pride themselves most on valuing teamwork and internal collaboration are the biggest offenders. They frame situations consistently with their own empowerment interests. They deride others, with whom they are supposed to be teaming, for their mistaken logic and biased perceptions. And they rationalize that simply calling organizational events the way they see them, while giving lip-service legitimacy to the perceptions of those who see them differently, is in the best overall interests of their organization.

Life in an organization has never been that straightforward and perhaps it has never been more difficult and dangerous than it is today. It shouldn't have to be so dangerous and wouldn't be if people were more conscious of their capacity to wield power and the subjective inclinations that lead them to wield it when they do. This is why we emphasize the problems associated with power framing and the importance of people becoming more conscious of what they are doing and checking their inclinations simply to call things the way they see them without consideration and respect for the ways others, who also seek empowerment, would frame and structure situations in order to be effective themselves. Organizational existence has always involved a social contract. Now it's time to expand that contract to include exercising discretion in the frames and frameworks one uses when relating to the efforts of someone else and to framing situations so that many people can be empowered simultaneously.

## REFERENCES

Bateson, G. (1972). *Steps to an ecology of mind.* New York: Ballantine Books.

Culbert, S. A., & McDonough, J. J. (1985). *Radical management: Power, politics and the pursuit of trust.* New York: The Free Press.

Culbert, S. A., & McDonough, J. J. (1980). *The invisible war: Pursuing self-interests at work.* New York: Wiley.

Friere, P. (1970). *Pedagogy of the oppressed.* New York: Seabury Press.

Minsky, M. (1987). *The society of mind.* New York: Simon and Schuster.

Schoen, D. (1983). *The reflexive practitioner.* New York: Basic Books.

Watzlawick, P., Weakland, J., & Fisch, R. (1974). *Change.* New York: W. W. Norton.

# part two

# Strategies and Styles of Intervention

# 6

# Transformational and Coercive Strategies for Planned Organizational Change: Beyond the OD Model*

**Dexter C. Dunphy**
**Doug A. Stace**
*Australian Graduate School of Management,*
*University of New South Wales, Australia*

The literature on Organization Development (OD) represents a prolific contribution to theories of organizational change. On the whole the OD model presents an ideology of gradualism, for effective change is seen to proceed by small, incremental adjustments. Usually change is seen also as synonymous with growth, and the strategies for organizational change advocated typically involve widespread employee participation to ensure emergent consensus among the key parties affected.

By contrast what we can observe happening with increasing frequency in contemporary organizations is markedly different. We see the dramatic effect of takeovers, mergers, and closings, often involving large scale firing of employees, and massive, almost instantaneous restructuring. The strategies of change adopted in these situations are often top-down, and achieved coercively by dictates from outsiders, from newly imposed chief executives, or through the charismatic leadership of a single individual using substantial institutional and personal power, often combined with a hidden agenda of political maneuvers.

Advocates for these latter approaches are more often found among corporate strategists, financial experts, and senior managers than among behavioral scientists. In advocating rapid coercive restructuring, they often express impatience and contempt for OD approaches, which they regard as trivial and time consuming. It is becoming increasingly apparent that the models of change used by both behavioral scientists and other advocates are extremely limited

---

*Reprinted with permission from *Organization Studies*, Volume 9, Issue 3, 1988.

and value-based. A more encompassing descriptive model is needed, and also a normative model which offers broadly based assistance to organizations operating in the much more turbulent environment of postindustrial economies.

## THE THESIS OF INCREMENTALISM

The dominant model arising from the OD and related literature has been that of incrementalism, planned change and orderly transitioning. (Dunphy, 1981; Gagliardi, 1986; Golembiewski, 1979; Kanter, 1983; J. B. Quinn, 1977). For example, J. B. Quinn (1977, 1980) has argued forcibly for the incrementalist view and against radical change in strategic organizational directions, systems or central processes. Quinn's 1980 work in particular is a cogently presented version of the incrementalist thesis. Paraphrased, his argument is that the effective manager moves the organization forward in small, logical steps. This is achieved by ensuring that the organization collects and utilizes appropriate environmental information over a long time frame and, as information is shared, assimilated and internalized by employees, subsystems can be adjusted progressively rather than discontinuously. Quinn argues that incremental change increases confidence amongst employees, reducing organizational dependence on outsiders to provide the impetus and momentum for change.

J. B. Quinn's thesis is a prototype of the behavioral scientist's argument for incrementalism. It values evolutionary rather than revolutionary change, order rather than disorder, consensus and collaboration in preference to conflict and power, the use of expert authority and the persuasiveness of data rather than the dictates of positional authority or the emotionality of charismatic leadership. An associated model with similar emphasis is that of systems approaches to change and organization development (Beer, 1980).

## THE THESIS OF TRANSFORMATIVE CHANGE

While incrementalism has been well suited to environments producing stability and growth, increasingly since the mid- to late-1970s and into the 1980s these conditions have disappeared in whole sectors of Western industrial economies (Bell, 1976; Ferguson, 1980; Ginsberg & Vojta, 1981; Reich, 1983). The "age of discontinuity," as Drucker (1969) called it, created conditions in the 1970s and 1980s which were often antithetical to an incrementalist approach. In particular, the West's leading role in mass production was increasingly lost as East Asian nations (initially Japan) built more competitive industrial bases. This demanded widespread organizational and economic restructuring. The significance of these major environmental changes was at first ignored by the OD movement which, as Beer and Walton (1987) have noted "has focused too narrowly on planned, internal efforts and neglected the role of environmental factors" (p. 357).

However, these changed environmental conditions eventually led to a growing literature on large-scale organizational transitions, not just involving components of the organization, but total structures, management processes, and corporate cultures. (Beer & Walton, 1987; Harris, 1985; Kilmann et al., 1985; Kimberly & R. E. Quinn, 1984; Miller, 1984; Schein, 1985). Kimberly and R. E. Quinn's theme of Restructuring, Repositioning, and Revitalization, outlined in *Managing Organizational Transitions*, is representative of this literature.

Reliance on incrementalism as a preferred model of change for all situations carries some assumptions that can be challenged both conceptually and practically. First there is the assumption that senior managers have the capacity to anticipate fully the environmental forces and future conditions that represent opportunities and threats to further development. In stable times and in some organizations this assumption may be reasonable. However, an age of discontinuity presents an environment so complex and turbulent that it is sometimes impossible, even with the most competent managers and effective organization systems, to predict future conditions accurately.

Second, there is the assumption that organizations are run by intelligent, proactive managers. Societal selection processes for senior managerial ranks are such that many managers may be of only average intelligence, have limited experience (particularly outside their own industry) and be ill-equipped to judge the complex information generated by effective environmental scanning systems. In fact, many organizations do not have such systems, and so the relevant information may never become available for evaluation by managers.

Third, there is the assumption that large-scale organizational change can always be accomplished incrementally. This is questionable. Managers may have little, if any, control over economic fluctuations and discontinuities, political interventions, industry restructuring, market and price leaders in the industry, and new technological developments which may destroy whole markets or force a transformation of organizational processes and substructures. Such forces can exert powerful constraints on managerial action, particularly when they are unforeseen. We are not arguing that managers are completely powerless in a deterministic world. We see Johnson and Scholes's (1984) view as more descriptive of the reality faced by most managers. Johnson and Scholes argue that there are both determinate forces which a manager cannot affect, and scope for the exercise of managerial choice.

Thus discontinuities arise which are often beyond the capacity of managers to sense and act upon, particularly given that managers are members of a dominant coalition with an historically conditioned model of reality. To the extent that managers can be powerless to change external forces that may also be unforeseen, and can be trapped in a fixed mind-set, they will be forced into a reactive rather than proactive mode. When reality breaks in upon them, their reaction may have to be fast and transformative if the organization is to survive.

In such crises, the choice is between organizational extinction or immediate and radical transformation. However, no power elite currently in the organization may be motivated or equipped to attempt such a change. In such cases, externally imposed change may be the only way to bring the organization back into fit with its environment. It may also create enough conflict to release the trapped human energy in the organization which can provide the impetus for change. We will discuss the issue of coercion more fully below.

Several frequently occurring scenarios may create conditions which demand such large-scale organizational transformation rather than incrementalism:

**Environmental "creep".** The environment itself may be changing incrementally and in ways imperceptible to managers. The degree of change over time may be large and require major readjustment by the organization.

**Organizational 'creep'.** The organization itself may move out of strategic alignment with an environment which remains relatively stable.

**Diversification, acquisition, merger, shutdowns.** Diversification, for example, often involves a major structural shift from a functional to a divisional structure. Because the structures are radically different, incremental changeover is often not a realistic possibility. Similarly the large-scale additions to or subtractions from organizations involved in acquisition, merger, and shutdown may preclude the incrementalist approach.

**Industry reorganization.** An organization may be adjusting appropriately within an industry structure, but that structure itself may be dramatically altered. An example of this is the deregulation of the Australian banking system. No proactive manager in an individual bank could have avoided the discontinuity of deregulation. Changing ownership laws have had similarly dramatic effects on the Australian media industry.

***Major technological breakthroughs.*** An organization may become locked into its current form of technology, particularly when it is in a capital-intensive industry. A major new technological breakthrough may dramatically change production costs for potential competitors who have not yet invested in the older technology. An example of this is the introduction of minimills in the steel industry. To remain competitive, the organization originally involved in the industry may have to transform their sociotechnical systems radically and rapidly. In the above circumstances radical transformation rather than incremental change may be a more appropriate change strategy.

## INCREMENTALISM OR TRANSFORMATION—AN INTEGRATION

So we have within the organizational change and related literature arguments for incrementalism on the one hand, and on the other equally eloquent arguments for abrupt and radical organizational transformation. Which arguments have most credence?

Arguments for incremental change arose from environments characterized by unidirectional growth and relative environmental stability. They also arose during an era when organizations operated primarily within the bounds of national economies. By contrast, arguments for large-scale organizational transformation arose under conditions of widespread economic restructuring, recession, and discontinuity. The development of a global economy also radically challenged the existing operating assumptions of many organizations. Radical times may demand radical remedies.

A comprehensive change theory, with its set of intervention strategies, needs to include both approaches. The approaches are complementary rather than conflicting and, the issue is not whether but when to adopt an incrementalist or a transformational approach. Incrementalist strategies apply when the organization is basically in fit with its current and predicted future environmental conditions, but where some adjustments are needed in mission, strategy, structure, and/or internal processes. Alternatively incrementalist strategies are also appropriate where such fit no longer exists but there is sufficient time to make changes without endangering the organization's validity. Transformational strategies apply when the organization is markedly out of fit, or the environment changes dramatically and, for the organization to survive fit must be achieved by more discontinuous change processes.

Some writers have, in fact proposed models which allow for both incremental and transformative types of change, but see these types of change as applying at different stages in the organizational life cycle (Greiner, 1972; Miller, 1982; Miller & Friesen, 1984; Tushman, Newman, & Romanelli, 1986). The actual terms vary slightly from ours, some writers using the terms evolution and revolution (Greiner, 1972; Miller, 1982; Miller & Friesen, 1984), others convergence and frame-breaking change (Tushman et al., 1986). (A summary of related concepts from the literature is shown in Table 1.)

A major tenet of these writers is that revolutionary change is necessary when a relatively stable environment becomes turbulent, or when major elements of organizational functioning (strategy, structure, and process) are out of "fit" with the environment and require substantial realignment. These writers appear to place no negative value on "revolution" as do those from the incrementalist

## TABLE 1. SOME RELATED CONCEPTS IN THE ORGANIZATIONAL CHANGE LITERATURE

| | | |
|---|---|---|
| Dunphy & Stace (this volume) | • Incremental change<br>• Evolutionary change | • Transformative change<br>• Revolutionary change |
| Levy (1986) | • First-order change | • Second-order change |
| Tushman, Newman, & Romanelli (1986) | • Convergence<br>• Incrementalism<br>• Evolutionary change | • Frame breaking change<br>• Upheaval<br>• Transformational change |
| Pettigrew (1985) | • Evolutions (lower levels of change activity) | • Revolutions (higher levels of change activity) |
| Fiol and Lyles (1985) organizational learning | • Incremental change and "constant learning" at all organizational levels | • Transformative change and "periodic learning" occurring mainly in upper organizational levels |
| Miller & Friesen (1984) | • Incremental, piecemeal change | • Multifaceted, concerted change |
| Miller (1982) | • Evolutionary, incremental change | • Revolutionary change<br>• Quantum change |
| Greiner (1972) organizational life-cycle model | • Evolution, in times of stability | • Revolution, at different stages of organizational growth |

tradition, such as Golembiewski (1979), who writes: "Some would argue that only revolution offers any hope that our institutions will be renewed. . . . At the very least, however, massive efforts at renewal should precede that last resort, revolution."

Thus, writers such as Beer and Walton (1987), Greiner (1972), Miller and Friesen (1984), and Tushman et al. (1986) seem to have moved beyond value-laden assessments about one desirable change type to a more differentiated model centered on the organizational life-cycle, or based on the relative stability/turbulence of the environment. Yet revolutionary change is still seen as exceptional. Miller and Friesen, for example, write of "long periods of the maintenance of a given configuration, punctuated by brief periods of multifaceted and concerted transition" (1984, p. 23). Nicholson (1987) is an exception in arguing that "change, through the core mechanism of transition, is the norm and stable equilibrium the exception" (p. 168).

In our view, the essential difference between incremental and transformative change is not the difference between slow and rapid change, or normal and exceptional change. Rather the difference lies in whether organizations are effecting change on a continuous or on a discontinuous basis. Fiol and Lyles (1985) have characterized the former as organizations which undergo "constant learning" at all levels in the organization, and the latter as those which undergo "periodic learning" mainly within the upper echelons of the organization (op. cit., pp. 803–813). Organizations undergoing periodic learning often find or regain fit by a series of large-scale adjustments in strategy, structure, or process, or a combination of the three. It is this kind of change that is properly referred to as transformative. Closest to our own view of incremental and transformative change is Levy's "polar ideal type model" (Levy, 1986, p. 10) of first-order and second-order change. Levy defines first-order change as taking place by incremental adjustments that do not change the system's core. By contrast, second-order change involves alteration of the system's basic governing rules. Second-order change is multidimensional, multicomponent, and multilevel alteration that shifts the system irreversibly to a new and revolutionary paradigm. Levy argues that the model of change advanced by OD practitioners does not go deeply enough to create second-order change, for OD interventions do not attempt to change the "meta-rules" of the system. In our view, this is because OD practitioners (internal or external) have mainly been recruited and deployed by managers whose basic commitment has been to the dominant paradigm and who want assistance in managing change incrementally, that is, who seek evolution rather than revolution. In addition the ideological commitment to incrementalism of the majority of OD practitioners has led them to seek and select incrementalist situations and options, thus creating a self-reinforcing cycle.

## COLLABORATION OR COERCION? THE MEANS OF EFFECTING ORGANIZATIONAL CHANGE

So far we have examined arguments relating to the efficacy of two types of organizational change—evolution versus transformation. Now we turn to the equally controversial issue of the means of effecting organizational change. In the main, the organizational change literature has tended to support the general value position of OD writers. This position has argued for the collaborative approach of employee participation as the one universal way to effect organizational change. The major aim in adopting a collaborative approach has been to facilitate the development of a common organizational vision based on shared values (see, e.g., Schein, 1985).

Nevertheless, there are significant variations among organizational change theorists about the nature of participation and the rationale for it. A full review of the issue is beyond the scope of this chapter but some differences are germane to our argument and will therefore be reviewed here.

On the whole, OD writers argue for using participative methods as a means of overcoming resistance in the workforce to change initiated and planned management. Participation by the workforce is normally limited to determining subgoals of a larger change program designed for management, or to determining how management initiated goals are to be implemented. In the major (predominantly U.S.) OD tradition, there is often an implicit assumption of a harmony of interests among the organizational stakeholders and a downplaying of the value of conflicts of interest. The emphasis too is on creating a process of informal participative change rather than on creating enduring formal participative structures. The managerial prerogative is thus preserved, workforce participation being at the invitation of management and essentially limited to consultative processes. It is fair to point out that management can and does from time to time, withdraw the invitation to participate if participation appears to be "getting out of hand."

Another (predominantly European) tradition stands in contrast to the OD version of the participative change modes. This is the industrial democracy (ID) tradition, often associated with "sociotechnical systems analysis" as a change intervention strategy. The ID model stresses democratization rather than participation. Its adherents frequently emphasize the conflicting interests of stakeholder groups, specifically rejecting industrial harmony as a dangerous illusion. They stress the creation of enduring participative structures with legitimate (sometimes legally enforceable) powers which limit the managerial prerogative in some circumstances. This tradition has been formally incorporated into organizational life in Germany, Norway, and Sweden, for example (Elden, 1986).

The ID tradition of participation also emphasizes workforce participation in the setting of major organizational change goals as well as implementation strategies. Its apologists argue that those whose lives will be affected by organizational change programs should have a significant role in determining the direction of change. They also argue that the OD model does not envisage the possibility of participation transforming the existing power structure through generating more commitment to it. This is another powerful critique of the OD model, again suggesting that OD interventions may retard the process of transformation by limiting workforce criticism of mission and structure as well as creating deeper commitment to the established managerial elite. The elite's self-interests and/or circumscribed interpretive scheme may well be preventing the central paradigm shift needed to transform the organization and bring it into fit in a changed environment. In Elden's words: "Conventional OD tends to sustain rather than transform hierarchical authority" (Elden, 1986, p. 250).

There is evidence of a growing debate about the importance of participation in organizational change. There is not only controversy among the proponents of participation about the kind of participation that is appropriate, but also about whether participation can realistically be advocated as a universal approach to increasing organizational effectiveness. A major attack on the universalist approach was mounted by Locke, Schweiger, and Latham in 1986. Locke made a spirited attack on the general OD tradition of using participative methods of change in all circumstances, but particularly criticized an article by Sashkin (1984). Sashkin argued that employee participation is not only effective but that its use by management is an ethical imperative. Locke argued, as had Vroom and Yetton (1973) and Kanter (1982) before him, that participation is "simply a managerial technique that is appropriate in certain circumstances" (p. 65). Sashkin (1986) subsequently replied, reaffirming his position, and using the same body of studies referred to by

Locke to argue that "participative management improves performance when it is properly designed and implemented" (p. 71). Thus Sashkin continued to argue for the universal effectiveness of participation. More recently, however, Nord and Tucker (1987) concluded that participation "often does not lead to the best decision" (p. 35). Rubenstein and Washburn use agency theory to show how the OD emphasis on shared vision and values impedes or prevents the emergence of champions for new ideas that might challenge dominant organizational paradigms (1987).

In our view, another major limitation of the participative approach is that it has been limited to employee participation. Employees and managers are only two key stakeholders in a potentially wider range of organizational stakeholders who may have vital and legitimate interests in the direction and extent of organizational change. Other important stakeholders are customers/clients, and governments. Clearly however the ID tradition of participation presents a telling critique of traditional OD change strategies and significantly widens the debate about the universal applicability of OD methods, particularly in bringing about transformative change.

While the ID tradition accepts the reality of real conflicts of interest, it too fails to present a comprehensive model of the full range of organizational change modes. It goes beyond a simple collaborative mode to include the negotiation of change between two key stakeholder groups (managers and workforce, or their representatives) but does not include other key stakeholders. It also assumes that interests can eventually be reconciled through negotiated trade-offs. However, clearly there may be win/lose situations where the interests of the respective parties are incompatible, or where other stakeholders cannot or will not accept a negotiated settlement between management and labor which is not in their (i.e., the third stakeholder's) interests.

In such circumstances these significant conflicts of interest may only be resolved by authoritative directive (e.g., on the part of legally constituted authority), or by coercion (i.e., a solution imposed by a stronger party). There is an emerging recognition in the organizational change literature that the political dynamics of change are often shaped more directively or coercively than a traditional collaborative approach would recommend, and that this may be the only (or even best) way to bring the organization back into fit with changed environmental circumstances. So we posit a continuum of the means of bringing about change that includes participative means, authoritative direction and coercion. This theme is dealt with by Kotter and Schlesinger (1979) in their exploration of collaborative and coercive means of overcoming resistance to change. It is also covered to some extent by Nadler (1981) in his division of the requirements of organizational change into three parts, namely, motivating change, managing the transition, and shaping the political dynamics of change. The pluralist/power writers, such as Salancik and Pfeffer (1978), Mason and Mitroff (1981), and Bourgeois (1980, 1984) have also emphasized that the management task, and change programs, are heavily dependent on the exercise of power and characteristically take place in a milieu dominated by the interests of a plethora of stakeholders forming into influential coalitions. The use of coercive power is often seen by these writers as a legitimate means of achieving the aims of the executive or of a dominant coalition of interests.

This accords with our own observations of organizational functioning: managers, executives, and key stakeholders often abandon a collaborative approach to change if that approach is demonstrably unsuited to achieving the changes they value. In other cases, collaboration may be tried but fail, if there has not been a history or culture of collaboration within an organization.

This leads us to postulate that collaboration or coercion may be equally effective modes of bringing about change in different situations. Collaborative change involves participation by both managers and employees in important decisions about the organization's future (Heller & Wilpert, 1981, p. 47) and assumes a high degree of communication within the organization about organizational adjustment and change. It is an effective approach to change when managers and employees are both motivated to support the changes needed to bring the organization into fit. Directive change involves the use of legitimate authority to effect organizational change and may be effective where the authority is respected by key stakeholders. Coercive change involves the use of explicit or implicit force between managers and employees, and an autocratic process of decision making by management or other key stakeholders (Heller & Wilpert, op. cit.). It may be effective in bringing the organization into fit if the dominant coalition has sufficient power to gain control of the change process. No value judgments are attached to these constructs in proposing the model which follows. We are simply accepting the logical implications of Nicholas's review (1982) of the impact of 64 OD interventions on "hard criteria" such as costs, productivity, quality, and absenteeism. Nicholas concluded that "the single most apparent finding of this research is that no one change technique or class of techniques works well in all situations" (p. 540).

## PROCESS STRATEGIES FOR CHANGE—A MODEL

In developing an encompassing process model of change, we combine the two dimensions (type and mode of change) discussed above to create a matrix which can be used to classify organizational approaches to change (see Figure 1).

The *type* of organizational change and the *mode* of change involving the workforce will differ between organizations, and the matrix shows the propensity of organizations to effect change according to the typology shown in Fig. 1, namely, by:

- Incremental adjustment, achieved by collaborative means (Participative Evolution—Type 1);
- Large-scale discontinuous change, achieved by collaborative means (Charismatic Transformation—Type 2);
- Incremental adjustment, achieved by coercive means (Forced Evolution—Type 3);
- Large-scale discontinuous change, achieved by coercive means (Dictatorial Transformation—Type 4).

These change types are situational, and represent equally effective means of bringing organizations into environmental fit, the effectiveness of the strategy being mainly dependent on the volatility of the organization's strategic environment and workforce support for change. Change Types 1 to 4 as outlined in Figure 1 are based on the tradition of Weberian "ideal types" (Weber, in Henderson & Parsons, 1947, pp. 11–13).

These four types also define four major traditions of change consultancies. OD consultancy is clearly related to box 1, but it is increasingly adopting box 2 strategies (note Kanter's work in this regard). Box 3 is represented by consultancies frequently associated with large consulting firms who make change primarily through designing and installing control systems and managerial tech-

|  | Incremental change strategies | Transformative change strategies |
|---|---|---|
| Collaborative modes | Type 1<br>**Participative evolution** | Type 2<br>**Charismatic transformation** |
| Coercive modes | Type 3<br>**Forced evolution** | Type 4<br>**Dictatorial transformation** |

**FIGURE 1.** A typology of change strategies.

niques. There has been a recent trend for such firms to enlarge their activities to include box 1 methods. Finally there are many well-known corporate strategy consultants who operate mainly in box 4. Our view is that advocates of each of these approaches have much to learn about the situational specificity of their own particular consulting approach and can learn to widen the applicability of their consultancy, if they wish, by learning from the approaches of others or creating partnerships with other groups with divergent approaches. Several examples may assist in understanding the application of the model to organizational change.

Type 1: IBM worldwide appears to be reasonably representative of the "participative evolution" approach to organizational change whilst retaining "fit." IBM has changed mainly through incremental adjustive processes (although there have been some departures from this); a high degree of employee involvement in management process, and a comprehensive, systematized approach to human resource management policy and practice involving employees at all levels.

Type 2: In Australia, the Bank of NSW/Westpac Banking Corporation, during its major period of transformation from a regulated, domestic financial institution in the mid to late 1970s, to a deregulated financial intermediary with international aspirations, appears to typify the Type 2 organization. This bank appears until recently to have made major strategic, structural, and systems changes with a high degree of collaboration with its employees. The focus of human resource policy and practice during and after a change intervention designed by Canadian consultant Bill Reddin was on executives and managers (4,000 in a workforce of 43,000), most of whom were heavily involved in team-building, goal setting appraisal processes, and management development programs.

Recent organizational change has been more incremental in nature, and this has been associated with more systematic attention to human resource management practice for other sectors of the workforce. This suggests that Westpac may now be moving toward Type 1 on the change typology. The transformative change process at Honeywell Information Systems (Kanter, 1983; Renier, 1987) is also indicative of Type 2 change.

Type 3: Organizations within the electricity generation and supply industry in Australia typify the Type 3 organization. In a technically dominated, capital-intensive environment, change in this industry is normally effected by an incremental adjustive process. The relationship between management and the workforce is usually more directive (coercive) than collaborative. Major environmental turbulence could cause this type of organization to move to Type 4 in its change methodologies.

White-collar service organizations can also fit this type. In Australia, at least one major banking organization achieved improved performance by a predominantly coercive/change mode that involved large-scale severance of managers and other employees, substantial restructuring, and closing of branches. All this was undertaken on the advice of a major firm of international strategic consultants.

Type 4: In Australia the Hunter River and Sydney Water boards appear to fit the Type 4 category. They are Statutory Authorities established and controlled by government legislation. Major discontinuities in their environment led to political intervention, the appointment by government of new chief executives, changed Acts of Parliament, and a brief to provide a more cost-effective service to users. As a result both organizations underwent large-scale, transformative change. In the case of the Sydney Water Board, over a period of 24 months, staffing levels were reduced from 15,300 to 12,300; the organization structure was recast and changed from (in some cases) 14 levels between the chief executive and line workers to a maximum of 7; regional offices were established; many central functions (e.g., skills training) disbanded and a process of culture change begun. During this change process 17 internally appointed human resource consultants reporting directly to the director of reorganization had the brief to facilitate change, and to work actively to unsettle pockets of resistance to the change process. The major changes having been made, these organizations now appear to have moved to Type 3 in their process of ongoing change.

Internationally, the Rupert Murdoch change programs in the media and related industries changed once ailing, out-of-fit organizations into profitable enterprises (Harris, 1987). The price paid for these transformations was massive industrial conflict and loss of jobs. Less conflictful, perhaps, was Lee Iacocca's rescue of Chrysler, but the transformation was also accompanied by substantial reductions in the workforce at all levels.

Thus, the model of change we propose goes beyond the unidimensional models of Greiner (1972) and Tushman et al. (1986) which concentrate essentially on the type of change (evolutionary-revolutionary; convergent-frame breaking) to encompass also the mode by which change is effected. The model assumes no a priori value stance on change methodologies but is rather a contingency model of change in which the ultimate criterion is organizational effectiveness.

Lundberg, in his analysis of strategies for major organizational transitioning, has commented on the paucity of such processual models in the change management literature:

> Our knowledge and practice . . . focus on the internal fine-tuning of purposive organizations and their improved alignment to their relevant external environments. To raise questions about the management of those organizational changes we have termed transitions immediately pinpoints two notable omissions in the change literature—missing are change models concerning the dynamics and structures of major system shifts, that is, organizational transitions, and change strategies, that is, those macro models which guide major change endeavours. (1984, p. 61)

Lundberg's comments are focused on large-scale change in organizations. His analysis, however, could also be extended to writers in the classic incremental OD tradition; more often than not there is a concentration on stand-alone techniques for change (micro or macro), often only loosely linked to major systemic elements of organizational functioning (e.g., management methodologies and personnel systems). Microlevel techniques of this type include T-groups; team building; job design; training modules; while macrolevel techniques include employee attitude surveys, corporate culture programs, worker participation schemes and management-by-objectives approaches.

Writers such as Beer (1980), who concentrate on systems approaches to change, have provided a useful social systems framework for analyzing the major elements of change, but the classic OD literature still appears to lack holistic change models, or process strategies. Beer himself has concluded recently: "We need a theory of organizational adaptation that incorporates *all* types of interventions, applying them to the management of the numerous crises all organizations face" (Beer & Walton, 1987, p. 362). Pettigrew, too, has taken up this theme: ". . . there is a dearth of studies which can make statements about the how and why of change, about the processual dynamics of change . . . which go behind the analysis of change and begin to theorise about changing" (1985, p. 15).

A differentiated contingency model of change strategies such as that in Figure 1 allows managers and researchers to conceptualize the change management task in situational terms. What this paradigm of change strategies suggests is that much of the traditional OD literature has been concerned with box 1, "participative evolution," and that its prescriptions are valid for the conditions described in that box. These conditions are more prevalent in times of stability or steady economic growth. However, forced evolution (box 3) will also be used at such times in organizations where key internal interest groups oppose change. However as environmental discontinuity increases, charismatic transformation (box 2) becomes a more viable approach when there is an acceptance on the part of key organizational stakeholders of the need for large-scale transformation. This is usually the case where rewards are available to ensure sufficient support from within the organization and where there are not widely divergent views on how to bring the organization back into fit. Schein (1985, pp. 277–282) in a section on "How Cultures Change" outlines several alternative approaches to "collaborative/transformative" change.

Finally, dictatorial transformation (box 4) will become more common in turbulent recessionary times. At such times major organizational restructuring is needed, may run counter to the entrenched interests of key internal groups, and there may be few rewards to offer for change. In such circumstances, external force (authoritative direction or coercion) may become the only available means to ensure organizational survival. There are many current cases of the application of this strategy. In the public sector in Australia, governments have used commissions of inquiry, replacement of "permanent" heads of departments and statutory authorities, and efficiency audits to bring government organizations into line with changed definitions of function, and reductions in resources. In the private sector, boards of management have removed CEOs and executive staff, and individual entrepreneurs have used takeovers and mergers to initiate organization-wide transformation. Kanter (1983) cites many examples of this type of change in American corporations.

We emphasize, however, that the two dimensions on this change model are continua, not discrete positions. The above change types and examples are indicative rather than definitive as we would expect many organizations to "tend" more to one type of change than to another. However there could also be a melding of strategies for change, and different strategies for different workforce sectors, and for major product divisions within the one organization.

*Our point is that the selection of appropriate types of change depends entirely on a strategic analysis of the situation.* Figure 2 indicates the main bases on which this analysis can be made. Change agents (internal or external) should select the most effective strategy and mode of change, rather than reflexively relying on a change strategy and mode compatible with their own personal values. An implication is that most OD practitioners will need more

|  | Incremental Change Strategies | Transformative Change Strategies |
|---|---|---|
| Collaborative Modes | 1. PARTICIPATIVE EVOLUTION<br><br>Use when organization is in "fit" but needs minor adjustment, or is out of fit but time is available and key interest groups favor change. | 2. CHARISMATIC TRANSFORMATION<br><br>Use when organization is out of "fit," there is little time for extensive participation but there is support for radical change within the organization. |
| Coercive Modes | 3. FORCED EVOLUTION<br><br>Use when organization is in "fit" but needs minor adjustment, or is out of fit but time is available, but key interest groups oppose change. | 4. DICTATORIAL TRANSFORMATION<br><br>Use when organization is out of "fit" there is no time for extensive participation and no support within the organization for radical change, but radical change is vital to organizational survival and fulfilment of basic mission. |

FIGURE 2. A typology of change strategies & conditions for their use.

knowledge of charismatic and coercive strategies, more competence in using emotion and symbolism and in engaging in politically based interventions. Similarly, financial and strategic corporate consultants need to develop more appreciation of the role that participative methods of change can play, in some circumstances, in achieving the implementation of their recommendations as well as improving the quality of their recommendations. In most cases, also, they need to develop better skills of working with people to implement change.

## CONCLUSION

This chapter suggests a more comprehensive approach to organizational change management strategies which finds a place for trans-

102 Dunphy and Stace

formation as well as incrementalism and which accommodates the use of directive/coercive as well as collaborative means of achieving change. It reconciles the views of two major and often opposing theoretical traditions in the organization behavior area, as they apply to the management of organizational change. These are the "tender-minded" tradition of the "human relations/human resource" theorists whose theories underlie OD strategies, and the "tough-minded" tradition of the pluralistic power perspective (Marx to Mason and Mitroff). Rather than evolution and transformation being incompatible strategies, and collaboration and coercion being incompatible modes, they are in fact complementary, their usefulness depending on the particular circumstances. Thus the model described here is a contingency model for planned change strategies which allows managers and consultants to go beyond personal value preference as the major selection criterion for an organizational change strategy. The model replaces such preferences with a systematic analysis based on what is needed to maintain or establish organizational fit or effectiveness.

## REFERENCES

Argyris, C., & Schon, D. (1978). *Organizational learning.* Reading, MA: Addison—Wesley.
Bartunek, J. M. (1984). Changing interpretive schemes and organizational restructuring: The example of a religious order. *Administrative Sciences Quarterly, 29.*
Beer, M. (1980). *Organization change and development: A systems view.* Glenview, IL: Scott Foresman.
Beer, M., & Walton, A. E. (1987). Organization change and development. *Annual Review of Psychology, 38.*
Bell, D. (1976). *The post-industrial society.* New York: Harper & Row.
Bourgeois, L. J. (1980). Strategy and environment: A conceptual integration. *Academy of Management Review, 5*(1).
Bourgeois, L. J. (1984). Strategic management and determinism. *Academy of Management Review, 9*(4).
Drucker, P. (1969). *The age of discontinuity.* New York: Harper & Row.
Dunphy, D. C. (1981). *Organizational change by choice.* Sydney: McGraw—Hill.
Elden, M. (1986). Sociotechnical system ideas as public policy in Norway: Empowering participation through worker-managed change. *Journal of Applied Behavioral Science, 22*(3).
Ferguson, M. (1980). *The Aquarian conspiracy.* London: Paladin.
Fiol, C. M., & Lyles, M. A. (1985). Organizational learning. *Academy of Management Review, 10*(4).

Gagliardi, P. (1986). The creation and change of organizational cultures: A conceptual framework. *Organizational Studies, 7*(2).

Ginsberg, E., & Vojta, G. (1981). The service sector in the U.S. Economy. *Scientific American, 244,*(3).

Golembiewski, R. T. (1979). *Approaches to planned change* (Parts 1 & 2). New York: Marcel Dekker.

Greiner, L. E. (1972). Evolution and revolution as organizations grow. *Harvard Business Review,* July–August.

Harris, R. (1987, January 22). Rupert Murdoch: Media tycoon, strike breaker and citizen of the world. *The Listener.*

Harris, P. R. (1985). *Management in transition.* San Francisco: Jossey–Bass.

Harrison, R. (1965). Choosing the depth of an organizational intervention. *Journal of Applied Behavioral Science, 1.*

Heller, F. A., & Wilpert, B. (1981). *Competence and power in managerial decision-making.* New York: Wiley–Interscience.

Henderson, A. M., & Parson, T. (Eds. and trans.). (1947). *Max Weber: The theory of social and economic organization.* New York: Free Press.

Johnson, G., & Scholes, K. (1984). *Exploring corporate strategy.* Englewood Cliffs, NJ: Prentice–Hall.

Kanter, R. M. (1983). *The change masters: Innovation and entrepreneurship in the American corporation.* New York: Simon & Schuster.

Kanter, R. M. (1982, Summer). Dilemmas of managing participation. *Organizational Dynamics.*

Kilmann, R. H. (1985). *Gaining control of the corporate culture.* San Francisco: Jossey–Bass.

Kimberly, J., & Quinn, R. E. (Eds.). (1984). *Managing organizational transitions.* Homewood, IL: Irwin.

Kotter, J. P., & Schlesinger, L. A. (1979, March–April). Choosing strategies for change. *Harvard Business Review.*

Levy, A. (1986, Summer). Second-order planned change: Definition and conceptualization. *Organizational Dynamics,* Summer.

Lundberg, C. C. (1984). Strategies for Organizational Transitioning. In J. Kimberly & R. E. Quinn (Eds.), *Managing organizational transitions.* Homewood, IL: Irwin.

Mason, R. O., & Mitroff, I. I. (1981). *Challenging strategic planning assumptions.* New York: Wiley–Interscience.

Miller, D. (1982). Evolution and revolution: A Quantum view of structural change in organizations. *Journal of Management Studies, 19*(2).

Miller, D., & Friesen, P. H. (1984). *Organizations: A quantum view.* Englewood Cliffs, NJ: Prentice–Hall.

Nadler, D. A., (1981). Managing organizational change: An integrative perspective. *Journal of Applied Behavioural Science, 17*(2).

Nicholas, J. (1982). The comparative impact of organization development interventions on hard criteria measures. *Academy of Management Review, 9.*

Nicholson, M. (1987). The transition cycle: A conceptual framework for the analysis of change and human resource management. In K. M. Roland & G. R. Ferris (Eds.), *Research in personnel and human resource management.* Greenwich, CT: JAI Press.

Nord, W. R., & Tucker, S. (1987). *Implementing routine and radical innovations.* Lexington, MA: Lexington Books.

Pateman, C. (1970). *Participation and democratic theory.* London: Cambridge University Press.

Pettigrew, A. M. (1985). *The awakening giant: Continuity and change in Imperial Chemical Industries.* Oxford, England: Blackwell.

Pfeffer, J., & Salancik, G. R. (1978). *The external control of organizations.* New York: Harper & Row.

Quinn, J. B. (1980). *Strategies for change: Logical incrementalism.* New York: Irwin.

Quinn, J. B. (1977, Fall). Strategic goals: Process and politics. *Sloan Management Review.*

Reich, R. B. (1983). *The next American frontier.* New York: Times Books.

Renier, J. J. (1987, February). The turnaround of information systems at Honeywell. *Academy of Management Executive.*

Rubinstein, D., & Washburn, P. G. (1987). *Championship and change: Three mysteries and three theories.* Unpublished paper presented to the American Academy of Management Meetings, New Orleans.

Salancik, G. R., & Pfeffer, J. (1978). *The external control of organizations: A resource dependence perspective.* New York: Harper & Row.

Sashkin, M. (1984, Spring). Participative management is an ethical imperative. *Organizational Dynamics,* pp. 5–22.

Sashkin, M. (1986, Spring). Participative management remains an ethical imperative. *Organizational Dynamics,* pp. 62–75.

Schein, E. (1985). *Organizational culture and leadership: A dynamic view.* San Francisco: Jossey–Bass.

Tushman, M. L., Newman, W. H., & Romanelli, E. (1986). Convergence and upheaval: Managing the unsteady pace of organizational evolution. *California Management Review, 29.*

Vroom, V., & Yetton, P. (1973). *Leadership and decisionmaking.* Pittsburgh: University of Pittsburgh Press.

# 7

# Crisis Creation by Design

**Ian I. Mitroff**
University of Southern California

**Will McWhinney**
Fielding Institute,
Santa Barbara, CA

America's organizations and industries are experiencing unprecedented crises. The worst provide us with a whole new set of household words: Tylenol (product tampering), Bhopal (the worst industrial accident in history), Chernobyl (the worse accident in the world's nuclear industry), and the space shuttle Challenger. Others quietly drain away the lives of employees (asbestos, Johns–Manville) or poison the residents who have moved near industrial dumps (Love Canal). For every crisis that gets the attention of the media, countless more devastate private and public organizations every year; acts of sabotage (as in the recent San Juan hotel fire), executive kidnappings, recall of defective products (Audi), computer failures, hostile takeovers; the list goes on and on.

No organization, private or public, is immune. It is no longer a question of "if," only "when," and "how" a major crisis will strike this company or that community. With the ever-growing complexity of new technologies, the increasing instability in financial markets and world affairs, and high stress experienced by employees, no responsible management can operate today without a program of crisis management.

At first look, it seems that there is no way to respond to the incredible range of possible disasters. Some firms and governmental organizations act as though the best response is to bury their collective head in the sand so at least they don't have to know what is about to hit them. Others take a far more active stance learning how to: (1) identify the early warning signals of impending crisis, (2) initiate preventative measures, (3) formulate the implement coping plans for those crises which do occur, and (4) recover with minimal personal and economic losses.

However, given the unpredictability and the high cost of protection from crises, few organizations can prepare anywhere near adequate responses. Few firms deliberately or intentionally create crisis, yet most organizations nonetheless create crises for themselves, their employees, neighbors, and customers by the kind of management style they embody. There is a strong relation between the kinds of crises that an organization experiences and even brings about, and the underlying management style and organizational structure it possesses. A broader understanding of crises and their underlying causes thus allows management to be even better prepared.

## CRISES CAN COME FROM ANYWHERE

The variety of modern disasters is so large that it seems useless to plan for their occurrence. However, studies of modern crises shows that there actually are two simple dimensions which underlie them (Mitroff & Kilmann, 1984). Knowledge of these dimensions allows one to monitor signals that invariably announce disasters before their actual occurrence and thus limit their damage before they get out of control. Thus, it is critical to differentiate between those crises in which the signals come from inside an organization and those that arise from without. We can also differentiate between those signals that arise and hence are detectable from technical and economic data or sources, and those that are due to personal, social, and organizational issues (see Figure 1).

Data on both source and type are necessary because almost every major *technological* crisis has part of its source in *people* (or organizational) issues, and vice versa. For example, the technological failure of the O-Ring on the space shuttle was due to the prior breakdown and inadequacy of NASA's management. Indeed, prior to the accident, a long and repeated string of messages warning of the impending failure of the O-rings failed to make it through the organization to correct the problem.

## THE MANAGER'S RESPONSE

Once we see what the sources of crisis are, we have the basis of a strategy to prevent their occurrence. Figure 2 displays a variety of preventative actions, ranging from "do-nothing" to technical, quick-fix, short-term responses, to long-term, broadly focused, whole-systems planning. Ideally, one should choose that strategy that is called for objectively. But research shows that an organization's response is dictated more by its management style than by what is objectively needed (Ackoff, 1981; Mitroff & Kilmann, 1984).

For our purposes, management styles can be classified into four

Technical/economic

| Cell 1 | Cell 2 |
|---|---|
| Product/service defects<br>Plant defects/industrial<br>accidents<br>Computer breakdown<br>Defective, undisclosed<br>information<br>Bankruptcy | Widespread environmental<br>destruction/industrial<br>accidents<br>Large-scale systems failure<br>Natural disasters<br>Hostile takeovers<br>Governmental crises<br>International crises |

| *Internal* | SOURCE | *External* |
|---|---|---|

| Cell 3 | Cell 4 |
|---|---|
| Failure to adapt/change<br>Organizational breakdown<br>Miscommunication<br>Sabotage<br>On-site product tampering<br>Counterfeiting<br>Rumors, sick jokes, malicious<br>slander<br>Illegal activities<br>Sexual harassment<br>Occupational health diseases | Symbolic projection<br>Sabotage<br>Terrorism<br>Executive kidnapping<br>Off-site product tampering<br>Counterfeiting<br>False rumors, sick jokes,<br>malicious slander<br>Labor strikes<br>Boycotts |

*People/social/organizational*

**FIGURE 1.** Different types of corporate crises.

basic types. They range from organizations, in fact, whole industries, that are totally unresponsive to threats to those that interact with the sources of crises such as to "dissolve" or remove their causes before they ever result in a major disaster. Figure 2 exhibits the major characteristics of each of these four types.

## Inactive Organizations

Essentially, these are maintenance organizations. Their primary aim is survival alone and the preservation of capital with the mini-

| Planning philosophy/ organizational style | Attitude toward problems | Aspiration level | Managerial focus (concerns) | Type of crisis management practiced |
|---|---|---|---|---|
| INACTIVE | Absolve (avoid) | Survival | Financial exclusively | (Attend to no crises) |
| REACTIVE | Resolve (satisfice) | Viable | Financial + Organizational (i.e., infrastructure) | (Attend to past crises) |
| PREACTIVE | Solve (optimize) | Growth | Financial + Organizational + Technological | (Anticipate future crises) |
| INTERACTIVE | Dissolve (reevaluate) | Development | Financial + Organizational + Technological + Interpersonal | (Anticipate present, past, future crises) |

**FIGURE 2.** Four basic styles of organizations.

mal involvement of those who own or work for them. Such organizations can only exist in benign or protected environments; for example, property-based organizations in rural economies, traditional institutions, such as universities and welfare organizations, and great monopolies in dying industries (e.g., the U.S. railroads since 1950). Typically, their focus is maintenance of the status quo, usually measured in financial terms. Thus, they strive to do nothing for as long as they can get away with it. If they do respond, it is only after being hit repeatedly by those crises that will not go away; even then their major response is to achieve short-run cost minimization to ensure the survival of the institution.

### Reactive

A more important class of organizations is those which aim to minimize the disturbance to their operation and internal structure. Many of the so-called "smokestack" industries fell into this stance following the Great Depression. This stance is best characterized as following what has proved itself in the past. If they practice crisis management at all, they focus exclusively on known forms—for example, problems caused by labor initiatives, price wars, and inventory cycles. The heavy emphasis on the past (the "tried and true") leads them to reject the experience of other industries; thus they are not likely to learn from the experience of others because it's supposedly irrelevant to their situation given their narrow definition of the environment in which they exist.

Reactive organizations are risk-aversive. Thus, they are inclined to avoid more strenuously errors of commission (doing what they need not have done) than those of omission (not doing what they should have done). They put little effort into anticipating or preparing for new forms of crisis. Hence, a Bhopal, a Three Mile Island and a Chernobyl will have to hit them before they will design responses for preventing their reoccurrence. Typically, they do not move until legislation threatens their very survival if they fail to respond. They are not likely to generalize, to develop tactics to counter different but related events. For example, a reactive industrial company would not see product tampering with food or medicine as any warning for it to prepare against tampering with its products.

## Preactive

It is natural for high-technology companies to spend considerable parts of their efforts to predicting and to forecasting both positive and negative aspects of their environments, anticipating new products, market changes, and potential disasters. Such firms anticipate new problems and even regard them as opportunities, building strategies that will defend against destructive forces both within the firm and from the environment which would inhibit their future growth.

## Interactive

The strategies of each of the three types of organizations mentioned above take the environment as a given: overwhelming to the inactive institution, an old enemy to the reactive, and a challenge to the preactive. The interactive organization engages with its environment to *create* events that are favorable to its future well-being. It also engages in redesigning itself to convert crises from threats into opportunities. This is what principally differentiates it from the preactive organization which may not engage in redesign and because of its hi-tech orientation prepares mainly for technical crises but not for people, that is, human or organizationally caused, crises.

Interactive organizations are concerned with increasing the *quality* of life of its members and its surrounding community. The preactive firm, with its technical orientation, expresses its concern with maintaining the prevailing *standard* of living, measured in quantitative terms. The qualitative orientation of the interaction organization leads to a concern for *developing* the human potential of its members to foster creative responses to an unpredictable future, counting on ingenuity rather than size or growth alone to sustain them through the unending crises of everyday living.

Each of these types thus responds to crises in accordance with its underlying style. It is fruitless to insist that each use the most appropriate strategy for they will not. Rather each must find an approach that will effectively improve its response.

## MATCHING RESPONSE STRATEGIES TO CAPABILITIES

Every crisis is preceded by a complex chain of events, any one of which can block a crisis from happening, so that in effect there is no one unique *cause.* The investigation into the Challenger disaster showed a rich web of contributing factors, technological, managerial, and political, each of which was necessary to have prevented the explosion. Even a well-defined act of sabotage, such as the arson fire in the San Juan Hotel in January 1987, could have been prevented by actions taken in the hotel, that is, by installing sprinklers, by more effective union relations, by a different educational system on the island, or by a more involved management team. At which point the chain should have been broken is in part a function of the immediate situation, but it also should be chosen as part of an overall management strategy.

The prevention of all crises is impossible, and indeed complete or perfect prevention is not the fundamental point of crisis management or crisis planning. *The fundamental point is to anticipate as many crises as possible so that the process of organizational learning can be speeded up.* No crisis ever follows a plan. At the same time, it has been found that the organization that has anticipated the most is in the best position to be most adaptive in responding to any kind of crisis that actually hits it.

Figure 3 represents a catalog of actions that organizations can engage in prior to, during, and after a major crisis to blunt its effects. The actions vary greatly in the kind of impact they have, the way in which they are applied, and the cost to different organizations. They have been arranged in the figure to facilitate building a crisis management strategy for the different types of organizations in Figure 2 and the different sets of crises presented in Figure 1. They are differentiated once again by technical/economic versus

Technical/economic

|  | Cell 1 | | Cell 2 |
|---|---|---|---|
| | Preventive packaging | **CONTENT**   **FOCUS/CONCERN** | Expert monitoring systems; networks |
| | Better detection | | Hold "continual" planning workshops |
| | Tighten system security | | Bring in outside experts; form permanent |
| | Tighten internal operations | | networks |
| | Better operator/management controls | | Design stores of the future |
| | Tighten design of plants/equipment | | Systems-wide monitoring |
| | Chain of command | | Establish crises command centers |
| | Crisis management units | | Periodic, mandated reviews |

| *One-shot short-term* | | *Repeated long-term* |
|---|---|---|
| | T I M E and | |
| *Immediate environment limited-individual parts* | S P A C E | *Extended environment systemic* |

|  | Cell 3 | | Cell 4 |
|---|---|---|---|
| | Emotional preparation | | Develop profiles of psychopaths, terrorists, |
| | Psychological counseling for employees | | copycats, etc. |
| | Security training for all employees | | Establish preventative hot lines |
| | Detection training | | Sponsor community watch groups |
| | Social support groups | | Consumer education |
| | Media training | | Political action groups |
| | | | Sponsor mental-health programs |
| | | | Counseling groups |
| | | | Reexamine one's organizational culture |
| | | | Establish permanent crisis management units |
| | | | Organization redesign |
| | | | Ombudspersons, whistleblowers |
| | | | Outside auditing teams to inspect |
| | | | vulnerabilities |
| | | | Media programs/training for all executives |
| | | | Work with industry associations |
| | | | Work with research centers |
| | | | Establish programs on business ethics |

People/social/organizational

**FIGURE 3.** Preventative organizational actions.

people/organizational actions that organizations can use to limit or curtail crises. They range from specific, limited actions to deep structural changes within whole industries. The methods in Cell 1 operate *within* the organization using *technical* and administrative changes to block disasters or to improve information that can prevent them from developing. Cell 2 uses a different set of tools to achieve the same blockage of factors originating *outside* of an organization. Cells 3 and 4 list methods which deal with *people*, organizations, or communities. Cell 3 focuses on actions *within* the organization; cell 4, on the *surrounding* community or environment of the organization.

## STRATEGIES FOR DIFFERENT MANAGEMENT STYLES

### Inactive

The only interest of these organizations is with avoiding those crises that are likely to destroy their capital rapidly. It appears easy in theory to build such a strategy, but it proves difficult in practice, for it is the classic problem of protecting a "sitting duck." If there are no anticipatory processes built into an organization, the organization will have no way of knowing what the forces are, either within or without, that could destroy it. It simply has to depend on the world remaining as it has been: "If we're not dead yet, why should we worry?" A minimal tactic should lead all organizations no matter what their style to identify at least one significant crisis from each of the four quadrants in Figure 1, and systematically examine what would be necessary for it to survive in case it occurs. This is a kind of a quick, worst case analysis, that is, finding four deadly events, exploring their impact, then seeing what tool, as listed in Figure 3, might provide some chance of survival.

### Reactive

Reactive organizations are likely to *see* the cause of all crises as emanating from the first cell of Figure 1 since these are the ones that are most likely to have been faced by them in the past. Thus, no matter what the source of a crisis, the reactive organization sees as its source of control the first cell in Figure 3. Instead, firms which are reactive ought to think seriously about what other factors coming from the other cells could equally destroy them.

### Preactive

The natural approach of a preactive organization is to see all crises as having their source in the broader technical or economic environment. As a result, they look for preventative measures in Cell 2 of Figure 3. In a world of high-tech, this is understandable arrogance, but we have moved so fast and far in the development of new technologies that it is no longer reasonable to have confidence that we can predict the outcome of changes in large systems. *Prediction as a base for prevention is no longer a sufficient approach.*

A natural extension of predictive methods to move to an interactive stance. This requires management to move beyond normal scientific thinking which takes the environment as given. One way to do this is to build strategies of crisis management that are based in gaming, that is, thinking in terms of counteractions. Such is clearly a major method of dealing with terrorists, takeover artists, and boycotters. Gaming models stay within the quantitative tradition of the preactive style while giving access to the preventative actions of the third and fourth cells. In simple terms, the preactive must move from a strictly scientific way of thinking to a consideration of political and social factors if they and we are to gain an upper hand.

## Interactive

As emphasized earlier, interactive organizations do not make a simple division between themselves and the environment. Thus, in addition to the other tools of prevention based in technical and economic thinking, interactive strategies includes means of affecting the attitudes of others, adapting new values systems, developing coalitions to work through pending technical, social and political issues. Such strategies have been well developed for dealing with the attitudes of employees through such means as extending participation and ownership to employees, working with communities in setting up community councils and consumer panels, and using traditional methods of lobbying with governmental regulators. Perhaps the clearest examples of this mode are organizations that have been formed to revive cities hit by the loss of employment in major industries. An excellent example is Jamestown, N.Y., revived through the creation of an industry-wide labor council.

Most of these measures are in cell 4 of Figure 3. Preventative measures listed in the other cells typically would have already been built into the normal procedures of interactive organizations. Such a program covering all four cells ought to be enough; it would certainly be difficult to fault such an organization, that is, hold it legally liable for having undertaken such a program. But for the sake of completeness, we need take a look beyond the typical view of a crisis as a destructive event.

In periods of great unrest and traumatic change, some events first seen as crises are better viewed as symptoms or harbingers of new social arrangements, true acts of revolution, and therefore not simply to be viewed as terroristic or catastrophic. There comes a time when an organization should expand its focus beyond prevention, and have the courage to recognize and support emergent processes. But to do this truly requires that an organization think broadly. After all, the Chinese symbol for crisis is also that of opportunity. To know which is which truly requires vision; it also requires bravery, qualities which surely every crisis situation requires.

## REFERENCES

Ackoff, R. L. (1981). *Creating the corporate future, plan or be planned for.* New York: Wiley.

Mitroff, I. I., & Kilmann, R. (1984). *Corporate tragedies, product tampering, sabatoge, and other catastrophes.* New York: Praeger.

Perrow, C. (1984). *Normal accidents.* New York: Basic Books.

Raphael, B. (1986). *When disaster strikes, how individuals and communities cope with catastrophe.* New York: Basic Books.

*Report of the President's Commission on the Space Shuttle Challenger Accident.* Washington, DC: Government Printing Office.

Shrivastava, P. (1987). *Bhopal: Anatomy of a crisis.* Cambridge, MA: Ballinger.

# 8

# Personal Empowerment in Organization Development (OD)

**Richard J. Mayer**
Battelle Pacific NW Labs

This chapter is an attempt to share some perceptions, speculations, knowledge, and experience around the ramifications of a workshop aimed at personal growth as an OD facilitation. It is primarily intended to provoke thoughtful consideration of the neglected role of individual development or personal empowerment in OD. It is not intended as an argument for individual versus group development; rather, it is part of an advocacy for both in appropriate balance. The reader is urged to read for the "feel" or overall gestalt, rather than the details.

When I began my career in OD—not long after the field, itself, came into its own—our focus was on the *group.* We invented, worked in, and had dazzling times with group dynamics, team building, interpersonal communications and trust building. All are valid approaches to organizational effectiveness. However, in practice, they seldom fulfill their potential. In my experience, they fall short primarily because most individuals—particularly, most managers—will not *sustain* the commitment required to establish and maintain an effective group. Furthermore, they *cannot;* temporary highs are the most the majority can and will settle for.

They cannot because they have not yet matured enough individually to function effectively over the long term in groups requiring ongoing mutual adjustment and trust. They lack the awareness, the concomitant skills and are too dominated by ego. In other words, they are established too low on Maslow's hierarchy (or virtually any of the multistage consciousness models used during the past millennium).

This factor undoubtedly contributed to the experience of TRW Systems, Battelle Northwest (BNW) and others who originally sent large numbers of UCLA's Ojai Leadership Laboratory, essentially a T-group incorporated into an organic educational framework, believing that the awakening almost guaranteed by that marvelous and powerful experience would carry over into the workplace. However, it rarely translates directly. Most participants treat it as an anomalous and treasured event in their lives, apparently content with the glimpse of life beyond the golden doorway. Furthermore, the workplace, with its emphasis on performance measures, the hierarchy and politics will not support the open group life exposed to Ojai. (These organizations continue to send participants, primarily because of the impact on the individual which is believed to impact the organization positively.)

Other manifestations are the massive team-building programs carried out by a number of organizations which apparently failed to deliver the predicted results. These efforts have helped—there is no way to measure how much—yet the great expectations for "Theory Y" and "Theory Z" organizations have generally not materialized via OD programs. Such organizations do seem to flourish for fragile periods under appropriate leadership, only to fade in the face of the almost inevitable change to what Americans, at least, term "strong management" (i.e., management by weak, ego-driven managers).

So it has always been. Some 2600 years ago, Lao Tzu, in the *Tao Te Ching*, wrote of what it took to govern society effectively. His words obviously trigger responses in our souls—the tiny book has been translated and reprinted more often than any except the Bible. Interestingly, neither Lao Tzu nor the Yogis, students of human potential for thousands of years, used group methods to build groups/society. They focused on the development of the individual, knowing that effective functioning in society/groups is a *natural outcome* of self-discovery/realization. The "bottom line," in simple everyday words, is that self-realization brings greater confidence, less domination by ego, more giving, more unconditional love and acceptance, and greater knowledge of where one truly fits (role) within the big picture—so teamwork flows naturally.

At present, at least within American organizations, ego, power, and their symbols dominate. Contracting, skill building and other OD interventions are poor and fragile substitutes for higher-stage collaborative awareness. The hierarchy takes over readily—especially during adverse circumstances—when ego and fear are the *real* driving forces.

I've had the privilege of seeing short-term examples of team building by *individual* development rather than by group methods. For the past 8 years, I have conducted an unusual workshop as an OD intervention. The subject of the workshop, called "Insight," is personal empowerment. The workshop has been held 35 times to date, twice as a public offering in California under the sponsorship of San Jose State University and the rest for BNW management, staff, and family members. Top executives, managers, scientists, engineers, lawyers, secretaries, support system specialists, public relations professionals, and a wide variety of others have attended.

The workshop is consonant with the integrated learnings on human potential of the past few thousand years and resonant with the modern findings of humanistic and transpersonal psychologies. Participants come away from the workshop empowered in ways that enhance their personal growth and development, thus benefiting their organizations. Indications are that conducting this workshop with work groups prior to facilitating team-building exercises, as a first stage of the overall team-building process, accelerates and deepens the process.

As a personal empowerment workshop, it is as effective as others that are much more structured, intrusive, and confrontive. The "teaching" methodology appears to be the oldest known for the subject matter—namely, "simple" sharing.

Some bottom-line-oriented managers have sent more than their share because they have seen the results. The reported results cover an extraordinary range: increased job effectiveness, upgraded leadership, improved public speaking, greater assertiveness, improved work and family relationships, greater managerial effectiveness, a wide variety of personal growth experiences, spiritual development, healings, etc., etc., etc. Some small groups of participants attending this 3-day workshop—in which interpersonal interaction is not allowed during class sessions and unsponsored during breaks—emerge as close a family as from any 5-day T-group or team-building process I have led or experienced. (I have not observed this phenomenon with groups of more than 12 people, nor is it consistently true of all small groups.)

The workshop content can only be indicated within the scope of this brief article. It includes the following, in no particular order.

***The nature of knowledge and how we acquire it.*** The role of the senses *vis-á-vis* the role of previously stored information; how our stored models/ideas/constructs/stereotypes dominate what we call "reality," so that "reality" is often in fact mostly fantasy; thus we see and hear mainly what we expect and project rather than truly taking in what's "there." This is a basic source of so-called "communication problems."

***The self-image or ego.*** One of our major, determining, influential and dominating constructs is our idea of who we are—our self-image, self-concept, or "ego." For most of us, our sense of who we are is merely an *image* or *concept*, not a direct experience. Thus our true identities are hidden from our own awareness behind ideas which we continually develop and defend. We lack a direct, felt sense of self, a real sense of identity, the certain knowledge of "being somebody." We are urged and taught to take action to improve our personal self-image rather than to discover the true self. We look outward—to our deeds and into the eyes of others—rather than inward, in futile attempts to find ourselves.

**The mind.** Our mind has a will of its own (an ancient illustration being to attempt, for just 60 seconds, not to think of a pink monkey), generating thought after thought, mostly negative, often in the form of "disaster films." Disaster films generate commensurate feelings—unnecessary stress, frustration and anxiety.

Ego and mind, working together—some authors refer to the combination as "ego-mind"—breed and perpetuate our sense of inadequacy and limitation. The ego, typically including Karen Horney's "idealized self-image," cannot be satisfied and the mind generates comparisons, assumptions, "what if's" and "if-only's." We typically are lost in thought—in our own fantasy world—rather than here, now. So we tend to miss what's going on around us; this is particularly true of high achievers continuously involved in doing—in finding the next mountain and climbing it—rather than in being. It is also particularly true of all the love seekers looking to others in their secret, desperate, perpetual search for the treasure hidden within their own hearts.

**The true nature and roles of the future and the past.** The future and the past do not in fact exist except as individual and idiosyncratic mental constructs. Guilt arises predominantly from the avoidance of personal responsibility for previous choices and behaviors and/or from the desire for self-punishment as a means of expiating breaches of unowned values. The so-called "future" is merely a set of thoughts and fantasies (unless, of course, one is clairvoyant/omniscient, if, indeed, such abilities exist). Thus, planning, for most of us, is actually a here-and-now activity based on predictions—fantasies and judgments—of what is to come. Predictability depends largely on experience. Hence, an experienced and talented boat builder planning the process of building a new boat can be reasonably certain of the outcome. On the other hand, no one has experienced living his or her life before (or remembers doing so if one believes in reincarnation), so life planning is actually an exercise in uncertainty based on wants and fantasies. The key issue is how to tap the wisdom necessary to make the right choices. Wisdom ultimately must come from within, directly, although qualified guides can help point the way.

**The role of ego at work.** Each of us comes to the workplace with two—often competing, if not mutually exclusive—personal agendas. One is to attempt to satisfy the needs of the ego and the other has to do with getting a job done. Since ego agendas—unless appropriately harnessed—so often extract and divert energy from that available for getting the job done, ego needs have been institutionalized in the form of the familiar "status" and "recognition" rewards. The ego is, for many if not most, a master impossible to satisfy, an internal task master much more severe and unyielding than any supervisor or manager. Ego compares, looking for evidence of superiority or inferiority relative to some unconscious and idealized standard, thereby keeping the person inevitably and permanently vulnerable, watchful, and defensive. Body shape, age, publications, degrees, home, neighborhood, relationships, office size, position, pay, skills, dress, bank account, friends, alma mater, color, race, pets, tastes, etc., etc., etc., all become aspects of ego/identity/self-image/self-concept, or false self. Again, efforts to improve the self-image—adding to ego attributes—rather than to discover the true self or identity are analogous to adding to a house of cards.

***The development of relationships.*** Relationships are too often based on ego, a particular sense of dependency and deficiency, rather than on real communication or contact. Commensurately, and paradoxically to what is typically considered "normal," a degree of autonomy is required for a true relationship. Romantic love, considered in our culture to perhaps be the epitome of relationships, stems—speaking simplistically—from a sense of deficiency. Each person carries a sense of deficiency, inadequacy, or deprivation which is relieved by the other's "love." Manager–subordinate relationships are often similarly based. Another way of characterizing and illuminating such relationships is from the viewpoint of a parent–child archetype. Thus, virtually all of us are involved in relationships wherein we depend upon others to behave—to say or do things—in ways which maintain our sense of well being, our positive self-image. This is tantamount to saying that many of our relationships are, in fact, based on *addiction*. Personal growth, then, involves elevating addiction to preference. The awareness which eliminates such addiction is the basis of the powerful possibility of unilaterally improving a relationship; realizing one of the games or processes that we enter into because of our vulnerabilities releases us from further need to use the game to manipulate for our ends. As a result, choice arises along with acceptance leading to a new level of relating.

***The debilitating tendency to judge.*** The tendency to judge everything—particularly others—dulls our world. Judgment of others is a product of self-condemnation, of ego's need to feel superior. The phrase, "love thy neighbor *as thyself*" is an expression of a necessary condition. Regard for our fellows *requires* regard for ourselves. Furthermore, we typically have, in fact, no basis for judgments of others except ego's pathetic projections. Acceptance—or forgiveness in the true sense of the word—lifts the weight of the world off our shoulders. We seldom have any accurate basis for judging others—or events for that matter. Typically, judging an event—say a layoff—as good or bad would, in fact, require the ability to predict all of the future ramifications of the event. This is an impossibility for most of us most of the time for which, again, we usually have ego-mind to thank. Such judgments hinder or preclude true assessment based on data, for example, the performance of a worker by a supervisor.

**The nature of stress and the role of meditation.** Long-term stress or "malstress" and worry could be precluded or prevented by getting rid of ego and stopping thoughts. This is a practical impossibility for most of us, nevertheless it does indicate the direction necessary. Ego's incessant demands, manifested through desires (thoughts) and the mind's negative focus on the past and future, generate almost all ongoing stress. An indication of the potential of the egoless and thoughtless state is that experienced during effective work, hobby, or recreational activities. Any activity that commands or induces full attention and concentration produces the sense of alert, confident, appreciative, well-being associated with focus. Focus or concentration requires the absence of extraneous thought, in fact is almost definable as the absence of thought. Concentration on any activity is an act of meditation. Since we must concentrate to achieve our potential level of effectiveness in any endeavor, we all have been meditating all of our lives.

The cessation of thought increases the probability of peak experiences, glimpses, and glimmers of reality, clues to the true essence of life, if only for a moment imparting an oceanic sense of confidence, oneness, and wonder. Such experiences, plus the realization that emotions such as anger, happiness, and love arise from *within* and are at most triggered by outside events, led the ancient "inner research scientists" or yogis to explore and invent ways of directly contacting our positive inner states. They found, as modern humanistic and transpersonal psychologists have discovered, that our true identity—loving, compassionate, creative, and wise—emerges as ego dies and extraneous thought subsides. So, too, arise personal and professional effectiveness to the level of our respective potentials and training. The primary methodology developed thousands of years ago and adopted by modern psychology are various forms of sitting and/or active meditation. The workshop includes a session on meditation.

The nature of our true identity is indicated by reminding the participants that—as the ordinary way we speak of ourselves correctly indicates—we have thoughts, feelings, a mind, a body, and dreams. Hence, we are none of these. Who is the "I" that has the "my" when we speak of any of these "owned" parts of ourselves? This "I" must be experienced directly and cannot be figured out or explained. Like the taste of a mango, the only way to discover it is to taste it. Once we discover our true identity, we know we're okay/worthy regardless of external circumstances.

***Effective leadership.*** We all can be leaders, especially if we honor our own nature. To honor our own nature we must discover it—directly, from within. To exercise leadership we must learn to manage ourselves effectively. This calls for self-knowledge or realization. Placing ourselves in suitable positions for leadership in work and other key situations also calls for self-understanding. Optimal development as a leader in a particular role requires the choice of appropriate growth experiences—again, the product of critical self-awareness. In other words, the discovery and enhancement of one's leadership effectiveness is largely determined by one's level of awareness. (Thus the workshop can also be postured as a leadership development experience.)

A crucial feature of the workshop is its design—or lack of design. It was a product of an extraordinary insight of my own, flying in the face of anything I had ever done. The insight produced considerable inner turmoil until circumstances virtually forced me to implement it. I merely sit in front of the participants and share the material without rehearsal, without a lesson plan, without forethought or notes. Each sharing session lasts from 45 to about 90 minutes. There are seven such sessions during the 3-day schedule with long breaks between them. Questions and sharing by the participants are welcomed but not promoted; a participant is free to sit without speaking for the entire workshop, and many do. During class periods, communication between participants is rare to nonexistent. I tell them I will not argue (intellectual/philosophical understanding of the material wins the booby prize), and not to take my word for anything I say. I also point out with satisfaction that I did not originate the material and methodology I am attempting to pass on to them; I merely provide a particular way of viewing it and the means of appropriately sharing it within a professional/work/organizational context.

The basics are almost as old as time and as modern as tomorrow: self-observation by witnessing, watching or self-remembering; welcoming "ahas!" and, as I dubbed them after reading Peck, "Oh shit ahas!"; crises as opportunities for awakening/learning ("The Paradoxical Value of Crisis"); life, itself, as the great institute of learning—the acceptance and observation of everyday feelings and experiences as the key to growth ("The Paradoxical Theory of Change"); self-examination and questioning; journal keeping and other proven aids to growing awareness; the role of feedback and qualified "therapeutic friends"; the source of intuition, wisdom, and creativity; the fundamental nature of meditation; the true nature of identity; the mind as best friend and worst enemy (coupled with ego); the self-restrictions of the "comfort zone" and the role of ego-mind in its creation; the nature of peak or reality experiences; the essential role of self-awareness in achieving one's potential in any area of life; the role of choice and self-fulfilling prophecy; the fundamental requirement for personal responsibility and the prices to be paid for accepting it.

Perhaps most important, I illustrate everything I share with personal examples drawn from my own experience.

Another overarching message repeated and illustrated by examples is that *to change the world, I must change myself.* The directions for positive change or personal growth emerge with the discovery of the truth: "You shall know the truth and the truth will set you free." Thus the frequent admonition, "don't take my word for this; look for yourself."

After hearing me say this many times at Insight and experiencing a number of freeing "oh shit ahas," one participant sent me a poster that may sum up the workshop better than I have. The poster is a picture of a Raggedy Ann doll caught in the ringer of an old-fashioned washing machine. The doll is being squeezed across the chest and abdomen. Her face looks directly at the observer. The caption reads, "The truth will set you free—but first it will make you miserable."

The primary workshop leadership and facilitation is by knowing and *being.* Thus, the facilitator could not give away what he or she does not own. Being comes from personal growth/self-realization. For this, at various stages, teachers are necessary . . . and so the cycle continues.

## APPENDIX

This list of applicable references for the workshop—itself a holistic distillation—is almost arbitrarily long. A short list might include:

1. *Motivation and Personality,* Abraham H. Maslow, Harper and Row, 2nd Ed., 1970. A good introduction to stages of consciousness or personal growth by a pioneering psychologist.
2. *The Farther Reaches of Human Nature,* Abraham H. Maslow, Viking Press, 1971. An extension of Reference 1. Read, particularly, "Theory Z" which presents organizational variables. Introduces humanistic and transpersonal psychologies.
3. *The Tao of Leadership,* John Heider, Humanics Limited, 1985. Effectively adapts the *Tao Te Ching* to the issues of organization and leadership.
4. *Mystery of the Mind,* Swami Muktananda, SYDA Foundation, 1981. A very short work on the functions of the mind by a contemporary yogi and author of many books.
5. *Real Power,* Janet O. Hagberg, Winston Press, 1984. Elegantly portrays stages of consciousness within the context of modern, American organizations.
6. *The Road Less Traveled,* M. Scott Peck, M.D., Simon and Schuster, 1978. A best-seller describing personal and transpersonal growth through psychotherapy.
7. *Neurosis and Human Growth,* Karen Horney, M.D., Norton and Company, 1950. Describes neurosis as a process which hides the real self.
8. *The Relaxation Response,* Herbert Benson, M.D., William Morrow and Company, 1975. Presents meditation as a simple technique for stress reduction and the prevention of tension-related illness.
9. *Meditate,* Swami Muktananda, State University of New York Press, 1980. The practice of meditation from the viewpoint of its ancient roots as a means of self-realization.
10. *Psychotherapy, East and West,* Alan W. Watts, Pantheon Books, 1961. The common ground between Western psychiatry and Eastern philosophy by one of the outstanding interpreters of the latter.
11. *Sensory Awareness,* Charles V. W. Brooks, Viking, 1974. Methods for awakening to the here and now, and moving toward discovering the truth which sets us free.

# 9

# Experiential Learning in Organizations: Humanistic Education and Organization Development

**Gerhard Fatzer**
Zuerich, Switzerland

For a better understanding of present problems of Humanistic Education we need to consider briefly the origins. Humanistic Education is not a new invention, but can be traced back to German, French, and Italian beginnings, even to the Greeks. I should point out, however, that "humanism" or "humanistic" had slightly different meanings in different cultures and epochs.

A first line of development could be named Rational Humanism and starts with Plato, and Aristotle and proceeds via Descartes, Leibniz, and Spinoza to the American humanists such as Robert M. Hutchins (1962) and Mortimer Adler (1939). A second line of development may be called Wholistic Humanism and starts with Protagoras and develops via Rousseau, and Pestalozzi to the most prominent American educator, John Dewey (1938), to the present movement of Humanistic Education. It points out that the human being (or the learner) is a wholeness of mind, body, and soul. The goal of education or training is to enhance this wholeness. Very often this approach criticizes the fact that learning tends to overestimate the aspect of mind and cognition while neglecting affect and feelings.

Humanistic Education can offer a promising approach for management education because we can observe the analogous problems in most management education approaches as well (Kolb, 1976, 1983).

Humanistic Education of our era was formed under the influence of the Free School movement of the 1960s and school critics as Paul Goodman (1964), John Holt (1968), and Herbert Kohl (1969) and even more distinctively by the works of Humanistic Psychologists such as Carl Rogers (1969), Charlotte Buehler (1969), and Abraham Maslow (1968a,b, 1969).

The goals of Humanistic Education have often been described in broad and "fuzzy" terms. A more specific reformulation appears in a small booklet, published 1978 by the Association of Supervision and Curriculum Development (ASCD):

Humanistic Education:
1. Accepts the learner's needs and purposes and develops experiences and programs around the unique potentials of the learner.
2. Facilitates self-actualization and strives to develop in all persons a sense of personal adequacy.
3. Fosters acquisition of basic skills necessary for living in a multicultured society, including academic, personal, interpersonal, communicative and economic proficiency.
4. Personalizes educational decision and practices. To this end it includes students in the process of their own education.
5. Recognizes the primacy of human feelings and utilizes personal values and perceptions as integral factors in educational processes.
6. Develops a learning climate which nurtures growth through learning environments perceived by all involved as challenging, understanding, supportive, exciting, and free from threat.
7. Develops in learners genuine concern and respect for the worth of others and conflict resolution.

If we consider these goals for management education and training we can see how important their application would be (Kolb, 1983; Schein, 1987, (in this book)). The main characteristics of experiential learning compare strongly to Humanistic Education, as Kolb (1983, pp. 25–36) outlines:

Learning is the process whereby knowledge is created through the transformation of experience.
The characteristics of experiential learning are:
• Learning is best conceived as a process, not in terms of outcomes
• Learning is a continuous process grounded in experience
• The process of learning requires the resolution of conflicts between dialectically opposed modes of adaptation to the world
• Learning is an holistic process of adaptation to the world
• Learning involves transactions between the person and the environment
• Learning is the process of creating knowledge.

It also becomes clear that Lewin (1947), with his seminal discoveries of action research and laboratory training as the foundation of OD and organization learning, should be seen in this line of educational tradition.

The different programs of Humanistic Education and experiential learning have taken different formats. I will only mention a few:

- Confluent education (Brown, 1971);
- Theme centered interaction (Cohn, 1975), the best known approach in Europe;
- Humanistic teacher education (Combs, 1962, 1972, 1974);
- Self-science education (Weinstein, 1970, 1976);
- Affective education (Newberg, 1978).

We will consider some problems in application of illustrative humanistic learning/teaching modes which translate readily into management education and OD training.

## MISSING LINKS BETWEEN HUMANISTIC EDUCATION AND ORGANIZATIONAL CHANGE

The first problem, the limited awareness of organizational structures by most humanistic educators or programs was pointed out in an interview with Carl Rogers in 1981:

*Question:* I would like to ask you a question about the educational aspect of the topic (nondirective attitude). During the last months I was working very hard on the following problem: If you teach your teacher students one approach of humanistic education and then send them out to the schools to be teachers, one of the problems will be that there are great contradictions between the goals and values of schools and the goals of humanistic education. Could you discuss this topic from your point of view? I believe that one of the reasons why the movement of humanistic education seems to be fading in the U.S. might be, that their founders didn't develop enough consciousness for "organizational learning." Perhaps it would be better to develop a combination of the goals and values of humanistic education and those of the school, because there might be a danger to terminate association with the "school system," the value conflicts between kids, teachers, parents, and school board increase. And the school system can be characterized as hierarchical and competitive.

*Carl Rogers:* This is a good description of the present situation of humanistic education. My first comment: humanistic education must acknowledge that educational institutions like the public schools must be turned "upside down," if it wants to be successful. I made the experience with humanistic teachers who wanted to teach teacher students, that they had to adapt to the hierarchical institution or run the risk of being thrown out. Additionally I would agree with you that I and other humanistic educators haven't been sensitive to the problems of "organizational change." For example: I don't believe that I would be afraid of an individual or a group that seeks help. In this area I have the necessary self-confidence. But if I were to be confronted with the question how I should change a school or a whole school system, then I don't have as many ideas or as much confidence.

On the other side I should mention that some institutions have tried to deal with this problem. The St. Lawrence University in the state of New York has a humanistic teacher education program. They realized that the humanistic teachers would get into trouble as soon as they got into service. Because of that they built a program where the practice teachers are former members of the training program. And afterwards they also try to send the teacher students to humanistic schools.

These comments certainly illustrate a dramatic discrepancy between the "dominant organizational culture" of schools and the goals of humanistic education.

Relatively little is published about the nature of "schools as institutions or organizations" or about the processes of "planned educational change" (Goodlad, 1975b) in humanistic literature, although most educators know the importance of these considerations. This is the case, not because there isn't a vast body of general literature on these topics, but because in its specific implications, the problem has not been considered of sufficient importance by most humanistic educators of the 1960s (Bentzen & Tye, 1973; Blumberg, 1976; Coffey, 1971; Dalin, 1978; Dickenson, 1970; Herriott & Gross, 1979; Hoyle, 1970; Sergiovanni, 1979).

Humanistic education was more concerned with providing and creating a new paradigm of teacher–pupil relationships and of learning processes, as well as with the necessary instruments and methods. Organizational resistances against these goals and methods did not exist at that time, because the educational world and the public was then enthusiastic regarding the humanistic goals. Traditional education had failed, people were dissatisfied with the competitive and cognitive goals of public education and the negative consequences on the school climate. Much student protest was aimed directly at these issues.

Humanistic education and planned educational change (or organization development in schools) were developed—to use a metaphor—on different floors of the building called "education" or "pedagogics." The first one in the area of psychological-education processes at the microlevel (key words: image of humankind, teacher—pupil relationship, instructional philosophy, values, personal—interpersonal level); the latter in the area of sociological-political processes at the macrolevel (key words: roles, power, decision-making structures, innovation processes, educational sociology of schools, schools as systems, organizational structure, school system, function of school).

There now exist only a few approaches trying to link these two different levels. The most promising is certainly "Organizational Development in Schools" (Schmuck, 1971, 1974; Runkel, 1980; Miles, 1980) and the approach of "linkage agents" (Liebermann, 1977; Crandall, 1977).

OD was historically developed in the area of management and industry, including "humanization of the workplace," and grew initially from the works of Kurt Lewin (Margulies & Raia, 1978; Fatzer, 1980a,b). This specific historical origin of OD constitutes one of the main difficulties in linking OD to humanistic approaches in education. The basis and the methods of OD in current practice often are very technological in nature (together with much jargon), while humanistic education can be located at another end of the continuum, no doubt with a technique (and jargon) of its own.

Warren Bennis (1985) has noted, "What OD needs very badly is a spirit and a heart. On the other side, humanistic education and psychology need more technology."

Schmuck, Runkel, and Miles, with their vast work in OD, have demonstrated how combinations, as proposed by Bennis, may look like. Humanistic education and organization development, as two different sides of the same medal, both with implicit humanistic goals and values, put more emphasis on process than content, varying between the micro- and macrolevel. The result of such a combination of humanistic approaches and OD would be such that teachers and management trainers, not only will be trained in areas as "confluent education," "self science education," or "affective education," but also in simulations of "schools as organizations,"—in forms of situational role-plays, simulations, and through support groups. Newberg (1978) and Combs (1972, 1974) have tried to incorporate such approaches into their humanistic programs (Sergiovanni, 1979; Eiben & Milliren, 1976). One of the most important elements of experiential learning (or humanistic education) is the institutional frame. This phenomenon was described—in the early beginnings of the group dynamics movement—as the "backhome problem" (Fatzer, 1980b, p. 194). The participants experience intense experiential learning processes, for example, in a group training, but are unable to transfer these into their private or professional everyday life. Slowly they start to realize that this context (e.g. the organization or institution) is "constructed" differently than the ideal situation of the training, where participants try to be open, empathetic, and accepting. The key word here would be "organizational learning" (Argyris, 1978) or "experiential learning in organizations" (Fatzer, 1987).

Dailey (1984) provides a description of the two opposite organizational settings—namely traditional, hierarchical versus open organizations or systems. These two paradigms of learning have been called "pedagogy" versus "andragogy."

Figures 1 and 2 show "Learning in traditional organizations" and "Learning in open systems" and compare the basic assumptions of "pedagogy" and "andragogy" with those organizational structures (Dailey, 1984, pp. 65–66).

In traditional, hierarchical organizations, the most important components of organizational life, namely structure, culture, and leadership, need to be questioned, diagnosed, and eventually changed.

In traditional, bureaucratic organizations the members' motivation for self-improvement and learning is smaller than in open systems (Knowles, 1978, p. 113).

> In traditional settings, structure often dictates the social roles of employees, the distribution of power, the control systems, the reward systems and the communication process in general. The structure . . . is a pyramid modeled on military institutions and churches . . . is dominated by policies, rules and procedures that foment distrust and encourage mediocrity. (Dailey, 1984, p. 64)

The culture of the organization plays an eminent role in modern organizational life (Fatzer, 1983), because it has an enormous influence on long term behavior in organizations. Culture can be seen as "an integrated pattern of human behavior that includes thought, speech, action and artifacts." In organizational terms, culture is "the way we do things around here" (Dailey, 1984, p. 64). The organizational culture can be seen as diffusing the particular value system and organizational climate (Schein, 1985).

In addition to structure and culture, leadership has a great influ-

|  | Pedagogy | Traditional, hierarchical organizations |
|---|---|---|
| **Structure** | based on aging process | pyramid, bureaucratic, hierarchical |
|  | subject/curriculum-centered | rigid, static, ritualistic |
|  | rigid format | rules, procedures, laws |
|  | rules, procedures, laws |  |
| **Atmosphere** | authority-oriented | chain of command |
|  | formal, low trust | formal, aloof, low trust |
|  | competitive | competitive |
|  | win-lose | win-lose |
| **Leadership** | teacher dominant | seniority important |
|  | controlling | controlling |
|  | high task, low relationship | high task, low relationship |
|  | assumes student immaturity & | assumes worker immaturity & |
|  | dependency | dependency |
|  | low risk | low risk values seniority-related |
|  | does not value experience | experience |
| **Planning** | by administration and teacher | by top management |
|  | emphasizes rational, legal | emphasizes rational, legal |
|  | mechanisms | mechanisms |
|  | policies, plans and decisions | policy making and implementation |
|  | highly political | highly political (territoriality) |
| **Motivation** | by external rewards and | by external rewards and |
|  | punishments | punishments |
| **Communication** | one-way downward | one-way downward |
|  | transmittal techniques | hidden agendas |
|  | feelings repressed | feelings repressed |
| **Evaluation** | by teacher | by supervisor |
|  | norm-referenced (curve) | budget-referenced (average %) |
|  | grades | performance appraisals |
|  | subjective | subjective |

**FIGURE 1.** Learning in traditional organizations

ence on an organization's capability to change (Bennis, 1985). If in an organization the creative energies of the participants are to be set free, all three variables (structure, culture, and leadership) need to be changed towards the basic assumptions of andragogy (or experiential learning).

An *open system* is adaptive, flexible, and responsive to internal and external stimuli. Multichannel communications, networking, innovation, creativity, and risk taking are other elements. The transition from a traditional hierarchy to an open system is often accompanied by contradictions and paradoxes: for example, "organizational schizophrenia" (DeVries, 1980; DeVries & Miller, 1984). This condition is comparable with a certain form of an adolescent stage of human development (Dailey, 1984, p. 66). In organizational terms, teachers and pupils are sometimes treated as adults and sometimes

| | Andragogy | Open, future-oriented organizations |
|---|---|---|
| **Structure** | flexible, open, broad responsive interdisciplinary developmental | flexible, temporary (task forces, ad hoc) responsive networks holistic purposive |
| **Atmosphere** | relaxed, trusting mutually respectful informal, warm collaborative, supportive win-win | people-centered, caring informal, warm, intimate goal-oriented win-win |
| **Leadership** | innovative, creative high task, high relationship interdependent, mature relationship mentoring, modeling high risk, experiential | innovative, creative high task, high relationship interdependent, mature team work personnel development career planning high risk, experiential |
| **Planning** | by administration, faculty and students mutual assessment collaborative needs analysis mutual negotiation problem centered | relevant participation by all those affected collaborative policy making and implementation decision making by problem solving |
| **Motivation** | by internal incentives (curiosity) self-directed learning contracts | positive expectations intrinsic learning contracts |
| **Communication** | two-way mutually respectful feelings expressed supportive | multi-channel (upward, downward, laterally) feelings expressed (respectful) |
| **Evaluation** | criterion-based objective and subjective jointly chosen standards by students, peers, and teachers | goal-oriented objective and subjective |

**FIGURE 2.** Learning in open systems

as children. Leaders fluctuate between expecting members to be self-directed and responsible for their behavior, and directing them rigidly.

## WEAK LINKS BETWEEN HUMANISTIC EDUCATION AND POLITICAL STRUCTURES

In recent times, the U.S. seems to be significantly impacted by "back-to-basics" waves in education. This looks like a reaction to the openness, liberalism, and experiments prevalent in the years between 1967 to 1975. This confrontation of two coexisting modes of thought in education and training seems to arise and change in almost every decade. Goodlad provides a good description of this phenomenon:

> Anyone who has been in the education profession for twenty-five years or longer is aware that there are two seemingly irreconcilable modes of thought in American education. They stand side-by-side, one or the other at various times dominating the conduct of schooling. William James characterized them as "the hard and the tough" on one hand and "the soft and the tender" on the other. The hard and the tough usually means clearly defined and separated subject fields or disciplines. It is based on academic goals, textbooks, workbooks and teacher domination of instruction, marks and reports of marks, strong discipline from above, evaluation by norm-based achievement tests, tracking and achievement grouping, considerable adherence to the normal curve, and so on. . . For the soft and the tender, we could take each of these ideas and make quite different statements. A broad range of goals with emphasis on self-understanding and self-awareness is typical of the soft and tender. Preference for a wide array of instructional material, including a multimedia approach, is considered vital. Considerable emphasis is placed on student planning in learning and decision-making, inquiring methodology, pupil–teacher interaction and pupil–pupil interaction. (Goodlad, 1978, p. 1)

Of course, the soft and the tough teaching styles can rarely be seen in pure form; more often they are mixed. Yet, one of the main reasons for this "back-to-basics" movement can be found in the lack of confidence of the public toward humanistic schools. Back-to-basics advocates point to certain educators who have practiced humanistic education in the form of unsophisticated and chaotic experiments, with misunderstood labels and ideologies, discrediting and undermining other, more solid efforts.

A second or even more important reason lies in the eroded public support of public education. Public schools are drained because many parents who can afford to do so have on occasion chosen to take their children out of public schools to enroll them in private schools—not because private education is generally better (vast research shows the opposite), but because they do not wish to deal with ethnic and associated social problems.

Most of the humanistic schools also have had to deal with problems of financial support and resource constraints (Glass, 1981; Goodlad, 1978; Greening, 1981; Leer, 1981; Newberg, 1978). Combs (1972, 1974) and Aspy and Roebuck (1977) point out that there is not enough financial support for research and development of humanistic education. The entire issue of the *Journal of Humanistic Psychology* (1981) describes and illustrates these points. Weak links between humanistic education and political structures can be seen in the fact that there exist comparatively few university and teacher education programs on a distinctly humanistic basis.

> We have underestimated the challenges humanistic education has presented to established cultural values. Our culture is heavily results-oriented and the results of humanistic education are not only hard to evaluate, but often delayed in time. (Glass, 1981, p. 76)

Similar problems are observed for "confluent education,"

> The narrow theoretical base and the values confusion are also reflected in the minimal attention paid by confluent education to a broad societal perspective. The emphasis in CE has been placed upon psychology and individual development. The assumption is that if you make individuals healthier and contribute to their full development, you will eventually create a healthier, whole and more integrated society. . . However, society is also composed of complex webs of human relationships, long established norms and mores, powerful entrenched institutions. . . If we do not train the students to be change agents, help them acquire knowledge of institutions, develop leadership abilities, that likelihood of self and society will be minimal. (Phillips, 1974, p. 2)

## ABSTRACT AND CONTRADICTING GOALS OF SCHOOLS

It is characteristic for any organization to try to reach certain goals. Unlike most industrial organizations, schools are aiming at very different and contradictory goals at the same time. Such goals often tend to be abstract and not fully implemented by the teachers involved. Basically the organizational goals of schools can be grouped into two categories: (1) Technocratic goals, and (2) Humanistic (or educational) goals.

These goals are illustrated by Peter (1973, pp. 118–119):
1. To teach a certain standard of knowledge, capabilities and skills. A maximum of pupils should reach the class goals, pass the tests. Curricula should be implemented.

2.  Besides the pure teaching of knowledge, schools should provide education, i.e. teach social and personal norms outside of pure intellectuality.
3.  Through the outside financial support schools are materially dependent on the state, and therefore school also serves to teach the fundamental societal, religious and political attitudes which allow to maintain the system.

The main contradiction which is evident is the contradiction between personal development of pupils and a clear mandate for selection among the pupils through tests and grading.

As I already have pointed out, most of the organizational goals are rather abstract, so they rarely influence directly the real conduct of schooling. The teachers help themselves through the substitution of goals by means, that is, workbooks and textbooks structure instruction and interpersonal relationships.

For a better understanding of the organizational goals of schools—as one example of an organization which provides learning—and in order to examine the main contradictions, it would be useful to consider the different functions of schools. Mayntz (1972) makes the following distinctions:

*Pupil related functions*
- qualification
- personal development
- emancipation
- socialization
- selection and allocation
- integration into community life

*Societal functions*
- reproduction of social order
- protection
- power reproduction

*Organizational functions*
- disposition of material, energy, and resources
- support
- adaptation and innovation
- leadership.

Even this short list shows remarkable contradictions, for example:
- qualification versus selection;
- integration versus reproduction;
- emancipation versus stabilization of the system.

These contradicting goals and functions become evident in the form of serious role conflicts of the teacher or trainer (Fatzer, 1987).

A first role conflict can be observed between the teacher/trainer as a person who facilitates personal growth and the one who carries out hard selection which influences the school or professional career of the pupil/participant.

A second role conflict of the teacher/trainer lies in the fact that he or she occupies different contradicting roles at the same time: The teacher is not only a teacher, but also a father or a mother, an adult person and a former pupil/learner. The pupils/participants have not only the roles of pupils, but also those of children. The teacher/trainer can only separate the different emotional needs artificially. If the atmosphere in the classroom, or in the training, gets too "familiar," supervisors or parents/schoolboard tend to intervene. The teacher in the role of the former pupil/learner tends to react unconsciously in the same way his or her teacher reacted. If we look at the teaching/learning process from such a psychoanalytic perspective, the problems of transference/countertransference become obvious (DeVries, 1980; DeVries & Miller, 1984; Flamholtz & Randle, 1987). These conflicting roles create severe communication problems, heavily influencing the school/learning climate. Schmuck (1974), in an analysis of this situation, describes it as follows:

> Teachers have tended to underestimate the power of the school organization for helping or inhibiting the humanization of their own learning climates. We think that most efforts to make learning climates more humanistic collapse or are absorbed into the school's traditional processes without effect because too little attention is given to the organization in which the reforms are attempted. Since schools are human organizations, any major innovation in curriculum or teaching procedures implies a change in the school's culture. The relationships between teachers and administrators, for example, are bound to change, especially when the teacher shows a new way of allowing more freedom for the students. As a result authority structures, role definitions, communication networks, status grouping and even friendships are forced to change. During this arduous change process, the innovation itself often fails or is restricted to conform to the old, more impersonal way of doing things.

## HUMANISTIC EDUCATION, EXPERIENTIAL LEARNING AND ORGANIZATION DEVELOPMENT: A TRAINING PROGRAM

In the training program that I have attempted to develop for teacher students, adult educators, and managers, I have made an effort to incorporate different elements of Humanistic Education and OD.

Taking into account the several problems noted above, the following outline is illustrative.

### Humanistic/Confluent Education in Organizations
*Three levels:*

A.   Self-experience as teacher/student/learner/manager
B.   Humanistic and experiential teaching and learning
C.   Self-experience within your organization (school, university, corporation)

### A. Self-Experience as Teacher/Trainer
Goals:

* To look at own experiences and attitudes toward school/ organization
* To find out how this influences decision to teach and existence as teacher/trainer

Elements:

* Education of the self, "self-science" (Weinstein, 1976, 1970)
* Confluent education (Brown, 1971)
* Learning diary (Fatzer, 1987)
* Exercises centering on own learning experiences (Fatzer, 1987)

Example: See Fatzer (1987, pp. 137–143)

### B. Humanistic Teaching and Experiential Learning
*Part 1: Teacher/trainer–pupil/learner relationship*
Goals:

* To experience interdependency and interrelationship between teacher/trainer and pupil/learner
* To experience contact and boundaries as important dimensions of teaching and learning (Nevis, 1987)
* To try out change of roles between teacher–pupil and trainer–learner

Elements:

* Gestalt exercises
* Role plays
* Simulations of consulting or teaching

Example: *Gestalt exercise*—"Difficult client/learner"
Goal: To become aware of difficulties I have in dealing with a difficult
pupil/client/learner
Procedure:

1. Split into pairs.
2. Number one is teacher/manager/consultant, sits in one chair and puts the difficult pupil/client/learner into the second chair.
3. Number two is observer.
4. The teacher/manager/consultant imagines a pupil/ learner/client who was difficult to deal with.
5. Dialogue between the two, change of chairs/roles for several times.
6. Short exchange with observer: What kinds of feelings did I experience? What caused the difficulties I experienced with my partner? What did I appreciate? Observations?
7. Change of roles: Steps 2 to 6.
8. Processing, final exchange: What did I observe and experience? Was it difficult to emphasize the other role? Which connections do I see?
9. Comment of the chairman about the role of projections and interdependencies between teacher–pupil, manager–learner and consultant–client within the teaching–learning process.

This exercise can illustrate nicely and experientially how the difficulties I might experience often have a lot to do with my own experiences in the other role. Surprisingly enough, a lot of my teacher students find that they have difficulties with children who are very similar or very different from them, so that they often deal with them by way of projections instead of contact. The same thing often occurs between consultants and clients, or managers and subordinates.
*Part 2: Humanistic teaching and experiential learning*
Goals:

* To experience different teaching and learning styles (affective-cognitive learning styles) (Kolb, 1983)
* To see similarities and differences to other teaching methods as project learning
* To develop own teaching style
* To collect experiences as teacher/trainer in simulated teaching situations ("microteaching")

Elements:

- Methods of humanistic teaching and experiential learning like role plays, exercises, simulations, body/movement, and group interaction
- Demonstration units (Fatzer, 1987)

Example: See Fatzer (1987, pp. 124–135)

**C. Self-Experience Within Own Organization**

Goals:

- To become aware of potential role conflicts as teacher/trainer; manager/subordinate; client/consultant
- To compare personal values of teaching with teaching goals of school or corporation/training department
- To understand organizational frame of school or organization as a system
- To learn about possibilities of support groups among teachers/trainers, etc., with similar orientation
- To discuss potential value conflicts between teaching/learning and the organization (school, corporation)

Elements:

- Anticipatory role plays of conflict situations
- OD in schools: exercises and simulations
- Diagnostic exercises
- Networking and supervision in schools or organizations

Examples: Diagnostic OD exercise—"Me and My Organization" (Guided Fantasy)

Goals: This guided fantasy represents a projective diagnostic exercise and aims at creating the unconscious part of one's own organization and at tapping into the individual's mental map of the organization. Through this guided fantasy the "inner reconstruction" of the organization can be better understood. It can help one's "self-diagnosis" within an organization and provides emotional or subjective side. Missing parts and positive or negative relationships can be discovered.

Time: 2 to 3 hours

Procedure: After a phase of relaxation, the participant starts to imagine or picture a Wednesday morning, how he or she gets up, eats breakfast, goes to his or her organization. He or she arrives there, looks at the building, and walks slowly toward the entrance, opens the door and walks through the hall toward the office. Each movement and each feeling is experienced fully. On the way, he or she meets the colleague whom he or she likes best. What does one tell him and how do they deal with each other? What does he or she experience? After a certain time he or she walks on and meets the colleague that he or she dislikes most. What does participant experience?

Then he or she arrives at his or her office: How does the participant like it? What does one perceive? What kind of attitude or relationship does he or she have toward it? What kind of relationship does he or she have with work? After a working day, the participant leaves the organization.

(Guide the participants slowly back into the actual room, take enough time.)

Exchange and feedback. For comments see Fatzer, 1987, p. 213.

It is important to note the generality and power of the "systems perspective" in humanistic education and OD context. Shapiro (1983) observes:

The latest model in confluent education is based on integration of human systems with the general systems principles governing individuals, small groups and organizations. An important idea, however, is not to remain on the 1960's narrow, affective-experientially based concept of personal growth. . . Perhaps "development of the whole person in the world" is a better phrase. To do this effectively in the 1980's, we will need the following: A cultural-contextual orientation that moves beyond the "myself psychology" and "duty-to-fill-my-needs-morality," but one that does not replace the basic humanistic paradigm. This orientation will note the diversity and readiness of the clients. It will give much more attention to the economic, political, historical and organizational factors that profoundly influence individuals.

And as a concluding point, I see similar integrative processes in the field of OD itself, with the emergence of "organizational culture" (Schein, 1985; Sackmann, 1983; Fatzer, 1987) as an important topic and concept. OD practitioners increasingly realize that many OD projects do not produce long time changes because the understanding of organizational culture has been missing. *The very evolution and change of such culture hinges on the learning process,* with relevant implications to be drawn from humanistic/confluent education and experiential learning. A rapprochement between OD/management education and these fields in education may prove salutary.

# REFERENCES

Adler, M. (1939). The crisis in contemporary education. *The Social Frontier, 5,* 11–20.

Argyris, C. (1978). *Organizational learning.* Reading, MA: Addison-Wesley.

Aristotle. (1962). *The politics of Aristotle* (E. N. Barker, Trans. and Ed.). New York: Basic.

ASCD. (1978). *Humanistic education.* Washington, DC: Association for Supervision and Curriculum Development.

Aspy, D. N. (1972). *Towards a technology for humanizing education.* Champaign, IL: Research Press.

Aspy, D. N., & Roebuck, F. (1977). *Kids don't learn from teachers they don't like.* Amherst, MA: Mandala.

Bennis, W., & Nanus, B. (1985). *Leaders.* New York: McGraw-Hill.

Bentzen, M., & Tye, K. (1973). Change in elementary schools. In J. I. Goodlad (Ed.), *Yearbook of the National Society for the study of education.* Washington, DC: National Society for the Study of Education.

Bidwell, C. (1965). School as formal organization. In J. March & H. Simon (Eds.), *Handbook of organizations.* Chicago: University of Chicago Press.

Blumberg, A. (1976). OD's future in schools, or is there one? *Education and Urban Society, 8,* 213–226.

Bridges, W. (1973). The three factors of Humanistic Education. *Journal of Humanistic Psychology, 3,* 325–335.

Brown, G. I. (1971). *Human teaching for human learning.* New York: Praeger.

Buehler, C. (1969). Humanistic psychology as an educational program. *American Psychologist, 24,* 736–742.

Castillo, G. (1974). *Left handed teaching.* New York: Praeger.

Coffey, H. S. (1971). Psychology of change within an institution. In R. G. Havighurst (Ed.), *Yearbook of National Society for the study of education.* Chicago: National Society for the Study of Education.

Cohen, A., & Gadon, E. (1978). Changing the management culture in a public school system. *Journal of Applied Behavioral Science, 14,* 61–78.

Cohn, R. (1975). *Von der Psychoanalyse zur Themenzentrierten Interaktion.* Stuttgart: Klett.

Combs, A. W. (1962). Perceiving, behaving, becoming. In A. U. Combs (Ed.), *Yearbook of ASCD.* Washington, DC: Association for Supervision and Curriculum Development.

Combs, A. W. (1972). Some basic concepts for teacher education. *Journal of Teacher Education, 23,* 286–290.

Combs, A. W. (1974). *The professional education of teachers.* Boston: Allyn and Beacon.

Crandall, P. (1977). Supporting and training linkage agents. In N. Nash & P.

Culbertson (Eds.), *Linking processes in educational improvement.* Columbus, OH: Merrill.

Dailey, N. (1984, December). Adult learning and organizations. *Training and Development Journal*, 64–68.

Dalin, P. (1978). *Limits to educational change.* London: MacMillan.

Derr, B. (1976). Schools and OD. *Education and Urban Society, 8*, 227–241.

DeVries, K. (1980). *Organizational paradoxes.* London: Tavistock.

DeVries, K., & Miller, D. (1984). Neurotic organization. San Francisco, CA: Jossey-Bass.

Dewey, J. (1938). *Democracy and education.* New York: Basic.

Dickenson, W. (1970). A humanistic program for change in a large city school system. *Journal of Humanistic Psychology, 10*, 111–120.

Eiben, R., & Milliren, A. (1976). *Educational change.* San Diego, CA: University Associates.

Fatzer, G. (1980a). Transfer in der Arbeit mit Gruppen. *Gruppendynamik, 4*, 243–259.

Fatzer, G. (1980b). *Gruppe als Methode.* Weinheim: Beltz.

Fatzer, G. (1983). OD in den Vereinigten Staaten. *Gruppendynamik, 4*, 345–358.

Fatzer, G. (1985). Switzerland: Conflict and Integration. In J. Hawkins (Ed.), *Education and Intergroup Relations.* New York: Praeger.

Fatzer, G. (1987). *Ganzheitliches Lernen. Humanistische Paedagogik und Organisationsentwicklung.* Paderborn: Junfermann.

Fatzer, G. (1988). Evaluation von Psychotherapieausbildungen. *Jahrbuch fuer Humanistische Psychologie.*

Fatzer, G. (1989). *Supervision und Beratung.* Freiburg: Lambertus.

Fatzer, G. (in press). *Intercultural learning in organizations: OD in Africa.*

Flamholtz, E. G., & Randle, Y. (1987). *The inner game of management.* New York: Amacom.

Glass, J. (1968). Improving graduate education. *The Education Forum, 32*, 439–446.

Glass, J. (1981). Humanistic education: A tale of two professors. *Journal of Humanistic Psychology, 2*, 71–77.

Goodlad, J. I. (1967, March). The Humanistic Curriculum. *Music Educator Journal*, 91–95.

Goodlad, J. I. (1975a). *The conventional and the alternative in education.* Berkeley, CA: McCutchan.

Goodlad, J. I. (1975b). *The dynamics of educational change.* New York: McGraw-Hill.

Goodlad, J. I. (1978, January). The trouble with humanistic education. *Journal of Humanistic Education*, 8–29.

Goodlad, J. I. (1984). *A place called school.* New York: McGraw-Hill.

Goodman, P. (1964). *Compulsory miseducation.* New York: Vintage.

Greening, T. (1981). Power, decision making and coercion in experimental colleges. *Journal of Humanistic Psychology, 2*, 97–109.

Herriott, R., & Gross, N. (Eds.). (1979). *The dynamics of educational change*. Berkeley, CA: McCutchan.

Holt, J. (1968). *How children fail*. New York: Basic.

Hoyle, E. (1970). Planned educational change in education. *Research in Education, 3*, 1–22.

Hutchins, R. M. (1962). *Higher learning in America*. New Haven, CT: Yale University Press.

Jannone, R. (1971). Humanistic approach to teacher education. *Journal of Teacher Education, 11*, 429–433.

Kahn, M. (1981). The Kresge experiment. *Journal of Humanistic Psychology, 2*, 63–69.

Knowles, M. (1978). *The adult learner*. Houston, TX: Gulf.

Kohl, H. (1969). *Thirty six children*. New York: Basic.

Kolb, D. (1976). *Organizational psychology*. Englewood Cliffs, NJ: Prentice-Hall.

Kolb, D. (1983). *Experimental learning*. New York: McGraw-Hill.

Leer, N. (1981). Innovation and power struggle. *Journal of Humanistic Psychology, 2*, 15–24.

Lewin, K. (1947). Frontiers in group dynamics. *Human Relations, 1*, 142–153.

Liebermann, A. (1977). Linkage processes in educational change. In J. Nash & P. Culbertson (Eds.), *Linking processes in educational improvement*. Columbus, OH: Merrill.

Margulies, N., & Raia, T. (1978). *Conceptual foundations of OD*. New York: McGraw-Hill.

Maslow, A. (1968a). *Goals in humanistic education*. Esalen: Esalen Press.

Maslow, A. (1968b). Some educational implications of humanistic psychology. *Harvard Educational Review, 38*, 685–696.

Maslow, A. (1969). Humanistic education vs. professional education. *New Directions in Teaching, 2*, 6–8.

Mayntz, R. (1972). *Soziologie der Organisation*. Reinbek: Rowohlt.

Miles, M. B. (1980). OD in Schools. *Review of Educational Research, 2*, 121–183.

Nevis, E. (1987). *Organizational consulting: A Gestalt approach*. Cleveland, OH: Gestalt Institute Press.

Newberg, N. (1978). *Strategies for impacting urban school systems*. Unpublished dissertation, University of California, Santa Barbara, CA.

Pestalozzi, H. (1978). *Texte fuer die Gegenwart*. Balmer: Zug.

Peter, H. U. (1973). *Schule als soziale Organisation*. Beltz: Weinheim.

Phillips, M. (1974). *Confluent education in perspective*. Unpublished, University of California, Santa Barbara, CA.

Rogers, C. R. (1969). *Freedom to learn*. Columbus, OH: Merrill.

Rousseau, J. J. (1962). *Emile*. New York: Basic.

Runkel, P. (1980). *Organizational self renewal in a school district*. Eugene: CEPM.

Rust, V. (1975a). Humanistic Roots of Alternatives in Education. In J. I.

Goodlad (Ed.), *The conventional and the alternative in education.* Berkeley, CA: McCutchan.

Sackmann, S. (1983). Organisationskultur. *Gruppendynamik, 4,* 392–406.

Schein, E. (1985). *Leadership and organizational culture.* San Francisco, CA: Jossey-Bass.

Schein, E. (1987). *Process consultation: Vol. 2.* Reading, MA: Addison-Wesley.

Schmuck, R. (1971). *OD in schools.* San Diego, CA: University Associates.

Schmuck, R. (1974). *Humanistic psychology of education.* Palo Alto, CA: National Press.

Sergiovanni, T. (1979). The odyssey of organizational theory and implications for humanistic education. In R. Weller (Ed.), *Humanistic education.* Berkeley, CA: McCutchan.

Shapiro, S. (1983). Confluent education: Paradigm lost? *Journal of Humanistic Psychology, 2,* 85–96.

Walter, G. A. (1981). *Experiential learning and change.* New York: Wiley.

Weinstein, G. (1970). *Towards humanistic education.* New York: Praeger.

Weinstein, G. (1976). *Education of the self.* Amherst, MA: Mandala.

**part three**

# Explorations and Experiences in OD Practice

# 10

# Partnership for Development: Toward a Macro-approach in Organization Development

**Raghu Nath**
*Graduate School of Business, University of Pittsburgh*

We are living in an interdependent world wherein economies of various countries are interlinked. Thus, development cannot occur in isolation. For development to proceed at the needed pace, various countries have to work together.

A crucial issue facing the world today is the relationship between developed and developing countries. Most developed economies are in a mature state while *potential* demand in developing countries is enormous. Yet this potential demand is not likely to materialize if these countries are unable to raise the standard of living of their people. This can happen only through the development process which, in turn, requires help from developed nations.

In spite of some success stories, the gap between developed and developing nations has increased over the last few decades. In other words, the rich have become richer while the poor have become poorer. As a result, relationships between developed and developing countries have become strained. At international conferences, one hears much acrimony. The atmosphere is one of mistrust. At the same time, protectionist sentiments are on the rise in many developed nations. This set of circumstances can lead to nothing but deceleration in world development.

The major challenge confronting the world, therefore, is to find ways to develop an open dialogue between developed and developing nations so that this may lead to a program of action intended to strengthen the worldwide development process. The Partnerships for Development program was conceived to achieve this objective. Before we outline various aspects of the program, it will be useful to look at the framework which guided the program's design. The framework integrated several concepts and ideas which were drawn from a variety of fields such as international and comparative management, strategic planning, conflict management, organization and management theory, and organization development.

## THE FRAMEWORK

The core ideas for the program evolved from the field of Organization Development (OD). Basic to OD is the notion of planned change through collaborative planning involving all relevant parties in a given system.

### The International System and Relevant Parties

Productive relationship between developed and developing nations are seen as essential for sustained growth and development of the international system. In addition to developed and developing nations, other significant parties in the international system are international organizations and multinational corporations (MNCS). Primary and secondary interactions among these four major parties in the development process are depicted in Figure 1.

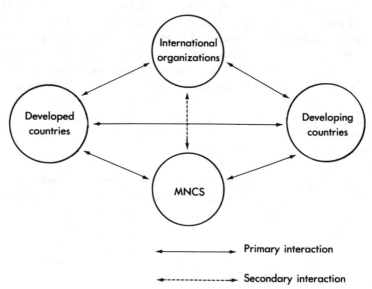

**FIGURE 1.** Interaction among major parties.

## Stakeholders within a Nation

One of the major contributions of the strategic planning field has been the concept of "stakeholders." According to Mitroff (1983), a corporation has many stakeholders, such as stockholders, consumers, unions, banks, suppliers, customers, community, and other national groups. For a given strategic issue, some of the stakeholders become especially significant and relevant; therefore, strategy for that issue must be planned considering interest, as well as position, of each of these relevant stakeholders.

Considering the strategic issue of development at the national level, it is necessary to identify relevant stakeholders who may have interests as well as positions relevant to this issue. Accordingly, a planning committee comprising of experts from international organizations and multinational corporations was established to identify relevant stakeholders from both developed and developing nations. After a year-long deliberation, the committee identified several types of stakeholders. These included leaders of business, labor, government, media, and academic institutions from both developed and developing countries.

## Leadership and Vision

Organization development literature has always stressed the importance of obtaining commitment of the top management of the organization. Empirical research has indicated that successful OD programs received greater support from top management, compared with unsuccessful programs (Franklin, 1976). There is an emergent consensus that bringing about effective change is beyond a quick fix (Kilmann, 1984). Thus, long-term commitment by top management is needed for a successful change effort.

In recent years, writings in the field of organizational theory and management have emphasized the visionary role of leadership, particularly for the creation of organizational culture of excellence and sustained development. In fact, many authors have emphasized that the malaise affecting American management is primarily due to the lack of visionary leaders (Bennis, 1984). Also, there is evidence from field research that visionary leadership is usually present in excellent companies (Peters & Waterman, 1982). Finally, Noel Tichy (Tichy & Devanna, 1986) has argued that visionary leadership is

necessary for the successful management of organization transformation.

It is obvious from the above that, for the development process to
be successful, it is essential to have commitment from the top management who must develop a vision of the future, convey this vision
to rest of the organization, and be committed to implement the
vision. Thus, visionary and committed leadership must play a very
active role in the organization development and transformational
change effort.

Most organizations have a well-defined hierarchy. Therefore,
identification of leadership role is clear. It is usually the CEO, or the
office of the CEO, that performs a key leadership role. For example,
in the case of Chrysler Corporation, it was Lee Iacocca who provided
the visionary leadership. At the level of the nation, however, development process requires collaboration among all relevant
stakeholders. Government alone can not do the job. Thus, a collaborative network of leaders is usually needed. This is also true for
regional development. For example, the Century 21 project in Penn-
sylvania has been built around this notion of collaboration among
business, government, and academic leaders. Though the concept
of networking has been in evidence for some time in both the organization and interorganization literature, this notion is particularly
applicable at the community, regional, national, and international
levels.

Having identified the four parties centrally involved in the development process, as well as various stakeholders within developed
and developing nations, it became clear that a program needs to be
developed so that leaders from each one of the four major parties
specified in the framework can be brought together to discuss issues of mutual concern in an open and family-like dialogue setting.
It was hoped that this dialogue would facilitate the development of a
committed network of leaders to forge a vision for the future and an
action plan to implement this vision.

## THE PROGRAM

Having identified the strategic issue of bringing together leaders of
government, business, labor, media, and academic institutions
from developed and developing countries for a dialogue on issues of
mutual interest and concern, and to devise an action plan to address
these issues, the primary intervention strategy selected focused on

organization of a series of "Partnerships for Development Dialogue Conferences."

The conference was conceived as *a goal-oriented team building session*. Therefore, content and process aspects were carefully planned. At the content level, the focus was to identify goals as well as to develop an action plan to implement these goals. At the process level, the major objective was to create a climate of collaboration and trust so that serious issues can be confronted and discussed. At the meta-level, it was expected that, if the conference achieved both content and process objectives, the ultimate strategic goal of developing a collaborative network of key leaders would be realized.

## The Challenge

The challenge to organize *successful* series of conferences to achieve the above goals was great indeed, if not mind-boggling. To our knowledge, no forum in the world existed which attempted to bring together the diversity of leaders that this program was intending to gather. Of course, there are international forums where leaders of government meet together. Meetings of the United Nations are examples of such forums. Though these international forums had worked well for some two decades after World War II, discussions at these forums have not been very productive during the last decade. In fact, the utility of many international agencies is being seriously questioned. In many of these international forums, conflict had become so intense and destructive that the United States, as well as several Western European countries have at various times withdrawn from some of these agencies, such as UNESCO and ILO.

There are also international forums and organizations where business leaders get together to discuss issues of mutual interest. Similarly, labor and media leaders meet in their own international forums. Yet, it is rare that leaders of labor, business and media join to consider complex issues in a collaborative mode. In fact, the relationship among these groups in the United States is characterized by one of strife, conflict, and mistrust (Nath, 1988). Japan, on the other hand, presents an exception to the rule because in that country leaders of government, business and labor do convene to plan national strategy. In fact, many writers have attributed the industrial strength of Japan to this unique national characteristic (Ouchi, 1984).

To sum up: No successful model or experience had been found

where leaders from many diverse backgrounds and nations were gathered to address strategic issues of shared interest, and to create common visions and strategies for world development. Thus, the challenge we faced was formidable. In this context, a very carefully selected planning group comprising of leaders of government, business, labor, academic institutions, media and international organizations was formed to move toward next steps.

## The Planning Committee

The first meeting of the planning committee was held in January 1982. This meeting was addressed by two of the senior members of the United Nations Development Programme. The gravity and the importance of the problem before the committee was stressed. The two speakers also pledged their support of the planning committee. Thus charged, the planning committee met in several brainstorming sessions. During these sessions, special attention was paid to the process issues; particularly, surfacing of conflicting viewpoints was encouraged.

It required almost a year to work through the content and process issues. Toward the end of the year, consensus emerged regarding the vision and objectives. At this point, a steering committee of five members was created to develop the action plan to implement the chosen objectives.

As the steering committee crystallized ideas about objectives and design of the conference, these were presented to the full planning committee for approval. We will now briefly describe the objectives as well as design of the first conference.

## Objectives of the First Partnerships Conference

A major purpose of the first partnerships conference was to bring together leaders of government, business, labor, media, academic institutions, and international organizations from developed and developing countries to identify strategic issues impacting on the relationship between developed and developing nations. In particular, it was expected that the conference would achieve the following objectives:

1. To examine problems confronting developing regions and nations.

2. To discuss the role of various stakeholders in the development process.
3. To identify areas of mutual collaboration between developed and developing nations.
4. To select the important strategic issues to be addressed in order to facilitate the process of development.
5. To suggest the next action steps.

Overall, the objective was to create a climate of openness and trust so that issues might be confronted clearly and discussed candidly.

## Design of the Conference

Three critical issues were considered in designing the conference. First, and probably the most critical, was the identification of participants. The second major issue was planning the content of the meeting and the third issue dealt with planning the process of the meeting.

**Selection of participants.** This tended to be the most difficult issue to deal with. It was decided early in the planning process that a most important aspect was to identify *appropriate leaders* from developing nations. At one level, it was necessary to seek representation from different parts of the developing world, that is, Asia, Latin America, Africa, and the Middle East. This was necessary to ensure that different viewpoints would be represented.

Strategic issues facing one set of developing countries may differ from another set of countries, depending upon the particular situation prevailing in a given country and/or region. For example, the issue of debt crisis was most critical for the Latin American countries, yet this was not an important issue for most countries of the Middle East. Also, issues facing newly industrialized countries are very different from issues facing African nations.

Though it was decided to seek representation from different regions of the world, it was also decided that each leader would be invited in his or her private capacity as a *statesperson*, rather than as a representative of a given country and/or region. This turned out to be a very crucial decision. The reasoning at the time was that, if a leader was invited as a representative of a given nation, the invitation would have to go through official channels. This may not only pose inordinate bureaucratic delays but someone other than the person being asked for may be sent to the conference. Since each participant came to the conference in his or her personal capacity as a leader with an important point of view, it was possible for each participant to express his or her candid opinions about various matters discussed at the conference. This candid exchange of views contributed greatly to the building of a climate of collaboration and mutual trust. In such a climate it was then possible to develop a common vision of the future, as well as commitment to this vision.

Having decided to invite leaders who had vision and long-term perspective, the next question was how to identify these people and persuade them to come to the conference. Multiple sources were utilized at this point. First, the United Nations network was tapped to develop a list of possible participants. Also, the International Trade Administration of the Commerce Department helped in identifying business leaders. In addition, media as well as labor members on the planning committee utilized their networks to identify labor and media participants. Also, academic contacts were used to generate an additional list of potential participants.

Finally, after long deliberation, it was decided that for the first conference non-U.S. participants would be matched with similar types of leaders from the United States.

**Program content of the conference.** Since the major content objective was to identify strategic issues that impact upon the relationship between developed and developing nations, it was decided by the planning committee that the content of the conference must reflect both the common vision as well as multiple perspectives. Two keynote addresses were planned; it was the purpose of these keynote addresses to articulate the vision. One of these keynote addresses was to be delivered by a leader from a developed country and the other by a leader from a developing country. In terms of multiple perspectives, three perspectives were planned: these included government, business, and international organization viewpoints.

**Process planning.** It was recognized early by the steering committee that a most critical aspect of the conference related to the creation of a climate of trust and openness so that various substantive issues might be productively discussed. Since participants were articulate high-level executives, it was decided to have a *dialogue* conference rather than a meeting where people gave speeches. As a result, most of the activity was designed to take place in small dialogue groups. These groups were organized according to the criterion that each group would have each type of viewpoint represented in the group. Also, moderators for each of the groups were selected for their sensitivity to the process issues. These moderators were distinguished people who had a major commitment to the vision of collaborative planning.

Since a recorder was also assigned to each group, the moderator was freed up primarily to set the climate and to make sure that the process would flow smoothly. The ultimate success of the conference must, therefore, be attributed importantly to the skill of the moderators who did an excellent job of establishing the appropriate climate in each of the groups so that issues could be dealt with openly and consensus achieved.

## Some Outcomes of the First Conference

The first conference was organized during October 1983. As indicated earlier, multiple lists of participants were generated and selections made. Almost all of the participants who were invited accepted. This, in itself, was seen as an early indication of potential success.

**The vision.** A keynote address for the conference was delivered by Prime Minister Edward Seaga of Jamaica. He most eloquently outlined the vision and called for joint action:

> There cannot be lasting recovery in the world economy if international trade is not resumed at a faster pace than is presently the case; and this means that the developing world must have access to additional credit, because it is from the developing world that expanded trade will be fueled fastest. . . .
>
> I have been saying for some time that the marketplace and the workplace of the developing world provide the key to recovery without inflation. The Third World has the markets needed to fuel the exports of the industrial nations and it has the workforce. Indeed the developing nations of the South today play as pivotal a role for U.S. jobs and profits as the U.S. plays for jobs and growth in the Third World. . . .
>
> The United States, as I know that an audience in Pittsburgh must be particularly well aware, is undergoing a painful process of adjustment to the shifting balances of its own industrial base. The American economy itself has only recently become significantly interdependent within the global marketplace. . . . This has been accompanied by the increasing participation of developing nations in the industrial marketplace, especially in those basic industries which involve the mass production of standardized goods, and words such as "deindustrialization" are heard more frequently nowadays. . . .
>
> Unfortunately, the reflex reaction has too often been the short-sighted one of protectionism, which will not, in the long run, help ease the fundamental transitions that are at work. . . .
>
> The multinationals have long been cast as the villains in the theatre of Third World development. They now have, I suggest, an un-

paralleled opportunity to change this image. They also unquestionably have the power—and the resources—to do so. . . . A "Multinationals for Development Initiative" is what I am here suggesting, and I take this opportunity to invite the multinational leadership to make its move in this direction by convening a conference in Jamaica, at an early date—to look at practical strategies to help us cross the next great frontier of mankind, together. (Nath, 1983, p. 11)

**Strategic issues.** At the content level, the conference identified four strategic issues which impact on the relationship between developed and developing nations. These were:

1.  The debt crisis
2.  Technology transfer from developed to developing nations
3.  Human resource development
4.  Legal and political environment.

Much discussion centered around the issue of comparative advantage of developed versus developing nations. It was felt by all participants that, if each nation can identify its niche, then it may be possible to work collaboratively so that all nations may benefit from each other. In this way, the goal of world development would be most fully realized. Another major theme that emerged was that development is not an activity confined only to *developing* nations. In fact, every place in the developing and developed nations is in the process of development.

**Climate at the conference.** The key meta-goal of the conference was to establish a relationship of collaboration and trust among participants. It was believed that such a climate would be conducive to candid discussion and development of a common vision. Writing in the Pittsburgh *Post Gazette* after the conference, Clarke Thomas (1983) sums up nicely the process outcomes of the conference.

> Some observations concerning the conference:
> First, there seemed to be a rare rapport among participants, with appreciation by Pittsburgh's and foreign guests alike for the opportunity to engage in dialogue and learn each other's views. There was a lack of the denunciatory rhetoric that so often mars international gatherings.
> A conclusion: If we are to have cooperation on our problems rather than confrontation, there needs to be a lot more such dialogue in this world of ours.

The desired climate was established at the conference. This, in turn, allowed difference of opinion to surface. A number of conflicting viewpoints were vigorously discussed. Since there was a family-like atmosphere, a problem-solving attitude prevailed throughout these discussions. *In OD terminology, the small dialogue groups sessions were indeed like focused team building sessions.* Conflicts were managed constructively resulting in successful outcomes.

The postconference responses of most participants emphasized the importance of dialogue groups and strongly recommended that this phase of the conference be further strengthened in the future.

**Debt crisis.** Since there was time to address in depth only one of the issues identified earlier, debt crisis was selected to be the issue. Many leaders had underlined the importance of this issue. For example, Farooq Sobhan, the chairman of the group of 77 countries, emphasized the urgency of this issue in the following words:

> For the developing nations this is the most difficult, desperate period since World War II. A recovery from the current world recession will help on commodity prices but won't resolve fundamental problems. . . .
>
> Debt, liquidity, trade, industrial development—all are linked to actions of the United States. For example, interest rates. The havoc that fluctuating exchange rates have played on our economies is enormous. Also, the rapid increases in protectionism in the developed world. A purpose of this conference should be to see how we can overcome some of these problems. This is not just a nightmare—many of us actually are experiencing this nightmare, with the situation desperate and getting worse. . . .
>
> There is a $100 billion shortfall in liquidity in the LDCs and the banks are beginning to cut back. That will create dangerous social problems. . . . Patchwork solutions won't do. The IMF is only aggravating the problems with the traditional medicine—cutting imports and so on. . . . (Nath, 1983, pp. 6–7)

Two major viewpoints about the issue emerged at the conference. The first was articulated by the representative of the International Monetary Fund. This viewpoint will be labeled primarily an *economic* viewpoint. A different perspective on the issue was presented by leaders of government from developing countries. This viewpoint would be labeled as a *political* viewpoint. A third viewpoint that *combined some aspects of the economic as well as political viewpoints* was put forth by a leading member of the financial community who also was minister of finance of a developing country. These three viewpoints, as well as varied nuances, were discussed in the dialogue groups. As a result of these discussions, a consensus emerged that creatively blended these viewpoints.

**Postmeeting evaluation.** At the conclusion of the meeting, it was the unanimous sentiment that the conference has been *very successful* in achieving all of its objectives. In postmeeting evaluation, many participants remarked that the conference far exceeded their expectations. In fact, deliberations during the conference were perceived to be so productive that many participants proposed holding such a conference every year.

## Second Partnerships Conference

Based on the successful outcome of the first conference, the evaluation group recommended that a second partnerships conference be organized in 1985. As in the case of the first conference, planning and steering committees were established. These committees were very similar in structure to the ones established initially.

These committees met several times. As a result of these meetings, it was decided to maintain the overall purpose as bringing together leaders of government, business, labor, media, academic institutions, and international organizations from developed and developing countries to discuss issues of mutual interest. The meta-goal of developing a network of committed leaders remained the same, as well as the process goal of establishing a climate of open sharing and mutual trust. However, several significant changes were made, both in the objectives as well as in design of the second conference. These changes will be described now.

**Objectives.** Unlike the first conference, which had rather broad open-ended objective of identifying strategic issues impacting on the relationship between developed and developing nations, the second conference was more *narrowly focused* on the twin topics of technology transfer and human resource development. In specific, the content objectives of the second conference were:

1. To examine the experience regarding technology transfer from developed to developing nations;
2. To discuss the relevance of emerging technologies for developing nations and regions;
3. To look at the human resource development issues particularly in regard to emerging technologies;

4. To examine the role of various institutions in facilitating the technology transfer and human resource development;
5. To suggest new institutional arrangements if necessary;
6. To consider the role of private initiative in the development process.

Overall, it was expected that the second conference would be more action-oriented and would, therefore, develop some concrete recommendations for implementing an action program. Whereas the first conference was primarily focused on the problems confronting developing nations, the focus of the second conference was on problems confronting developing and developed nations. As a result, it was decided to enlarge participation in the second conference to developed nations other than the United States.

**Design.** Three major changes were made in the design from the first to the second conference. First, the country representation from developed group was enlarged from United States only, to United States, Japan, and France. Also, a larger number of developing nations were represented at the second conference than the first. As a result, the second conference involved representatives from 25 nations, compared with 15 in the first conference.

Another design change related to the type of participants invited to the second conference. The first conference was heavily represented by leaders of financial institutions as well as government leaders. The second conference included leaders who were known for their expertise in technology transfer and human resource development. Also, the second conference represented a broader diversity of leaders of different types and from different countries.

The third and final design change involved strengthening the role of the small dialogue groups. For example, at the dinner time, participants also met in their respective small dialogue groups.

**Other aspects.** In the second conference, there was a greater involvement of the local Pittsburgh community. Several prominent members of the community were hosts to foreign guests at their homes. This hospitality was organized through the offices of the Pittsburgh Council for International Visitors and the United Nations Association of Pittsburgh.

**Some outcomes.** Like the first conference, the second conference proved highly successful in achieving its objectives. Outcome of the conference can be summarized in the following three emerging themes:

The first major theme that emerged from the conference was that investment in human capital is crucial to the development process. Pacific Rim countries have certainly demonstrated the importance of developing human resources in a free enterprise environment. Economic miracles can occur if individual initiative is encouraged and rewarded. The second theme was the recognition that new technologies are developing at a very fast rate, and there is an urgent need to develop an effective international mechanism which can facilitate the adaptation of these technologies to the local culture and environment of developing regions and nations. Third, the world has become an integrated marketplace and only those who think and act "globally" will survive. (Nath, 1985, p.1)

In addition to the above three themes, the two themes that emerged in the first conference were further reinforced by the second conference. First, there was consensus that development is a universal process. It occurs both in developed and developing nations. For example, development is occurring in Beijing, New Delhi, Pittsburgh, Paris, and Tokyo. Though the nature of technological transformation may vary from place to place, the process of transformation has common elements. Second, it was emphasized by the participants of the second conference that the key ingredient for successful management of transformation and development process is the partnership among government, business, labor, academic institutions, and media.

Finally, it was agreed that the next stage calls for a task force to specify a concrete proposal for evolving an effective international mechanism for the transfer of technology from developed to developing nations and regions.

## World Technology Center

In response to the recommendation of the second conference, a task force comprising of technology, management, and international experts was constituted to develop a proposal for an international mechanism for facilitating the transfer of relevant technologies from developed to developing regions and nations. The task force worked intensively for several months and developed a proposal for the establishment of a World Technology Center. The major purpose of the center would be to identify, adapt, and transfer emerging and other relevant technologies from developed to developing regions and nations. The center would also advise governments to establish the appropriate infrastructure (including human resources) so that developing regions and nations can effectively absorb the emerging technologies. The task force also identified several key emerging technologies and concrete projects based on these technologies.

## Istanbul Meeting

Ideas developed by the task force were presented at the round table organized by the United Nations in Istanbul in September 1985. The round table was attended by leaders of business and government, development experts, and representatives of international agencies. The idea of establishing a World Technology Center was endorsed by the round table. In particular, the round table suggested that human resource development aspects need to be emphasized.

## Beijing Conference

A high-level science policy conference on the topic of "Strategic Orientation of Science and Technology for Development" was organized by the National Research Council of China in collaboration with the U.N. system for financing science and technology. The conference was attended by distinguished scientists, corporate executives, and government representatives. The summary report of the conference was received by the prime minister of China in the Great Hall of the People's Republic in April 1986.

The idea of the World Technology Center was discussed in this conference and was unanimously endorsed by the delegates and presented to the prime minister. At this conference and in further discussion with Chinese Academy of Sciences, a number of concrete projects were also identified.

## Present Status

The World Technology Center is now being organized in collaboration with the United Nations Development Programme. The first major project of the center would be to design and operate a technology information network involving selected developed and developing nations. The network would be designed using state-of-the-art computer and communication technologies. A detailed feasibility study will be under way shortly. It is expected that a pilot test of the system will be initiated in the near future.

## SOME CONCLUDING REMARKS

The Organization Development movement started with a great promise. In the 1960s, emphasis was primarily at the individual level. Intervention strategies were primarily process-oriented. The focus was on "here and now." This led to a short-term perspective. As a result, participants achieved emotional high while attending workshops. Unfortunately, these effects didn't last long. In many cases, participants experienced a culture shock when they returned to their work environments. Thus transfer of learning from workshop to work situation was minimal. Though individuals may have benefited from the experience, it did little for their organizations.

The next phase in the development of the OD technology focused on team-level activities. Emphasis was placed on improving effectiveness of teams through team-building sessions. An attempt was made to integrate the content as well as process aspects; however, the emphasis continued to be placed a process issues (Heisler 1975; Porras & Berg 1978).

At the organization level, OD interventions have met with rather limited success. For example, Porras and Berg (1978) concluded that OD does not have an important impact on overall organizational processes, but instead impacts primarily on the individual. Research evidence also indicates that the most successful intervention strategy at the organization level has involved complex combination of several activities (e.g., process analysis, skill building, diagnosis, team building, intergroup, coaching/counseling and technostructural), with time spans in the 3-to-5-year range (Golembiewski, Proehl, & Sink, 1982).

As indicated earlier, the target of "Partnerships for Development" program was to intervene at the regional, national, and international levels. At these levels, there was no prior successful experiences to guide the development of intervention strategy. Though the final verdict is not yet in, the program so far has met with success beyond initial expectations. We will, therefore, reflect on some of the critical aspects of the program which might have led to its success.

### Critical Aspects of the Program

First, there was a focus on *both* content and process-level activities. Specific goals were set in both content and process areas and these goals were integrated. Thus, process goals facilitated achievement of content objectives. Achievement of process goals was ensured by careful selection of moderators with process and cross-cultural sensitivity. In fact, throughout the conference, very careful attention was paid to cross-culture issues. All staff involved in the program exhibited remarkable cross-cultural competence. This helped greatly in evolving mutual understanding and respect among participants, and between participants and staff.

A second unique aspect of the program was that the strategic focus was combined with an emphasis on "here and now." Though the issues discussed were strategic in nature; participants were encouraged to share their personal experiences and viewpoints about the issues; this led to very animated discussions. As a result, the level of motivation stayed exceptionally high throughout the conference. As indicated earlier, speeches were kept to a minimum. Therefore, everyone had ample time to participate and share views, facilitating networking among participants.

Third, an important aspect of the program was its focus on action. Even, in the first conference, where the primary objective was identification of strategic issues, it was emphasized that the ultimate objective of the program is to develop an action plan. This action focus helped to energize participants and staff. Thus, throughout discussions, there was a healthy flow of ideas from abstract to concrete.

Table 1 compares Partnerships for Development with traditional OD programs on several dimensions. As can be seen from the table, Partnerships for Development shares with OD programs humanistic

**TABLE 1. TRADITIONAL ORGANIZATIONAL DEVELOPMENT AND PARTNERSHIPS FOR DEVELOPMENT**

| Dimension | Traditional OD | Partnerships for Development |
|---|---|---|
| Level | Individual, team, organization | Regional, national, international |
| Time orientation | Short, medium term | Long term |
| Content-process | Primarily process | Primarily content |
| | Secondarily content | Secondarily process |
| Cross-cultural sensitivity | Usually not applicable | Most important |
| Participants | All levels | Top levels |
| Moderators (trainers) | Skilled in process | Skilled in content, process and cross-cultural sensitivity |
| Emphasis | Here and now | Strategic as well as here and now |
| Action focus | Yes | Yes |
| Values | Humanistic | Humanistic |

values as well as action focus. However, on several other critical dimensions, there are significant differences between traditional OD programs and Partnerships for Development program.

As indicated earlier, much earlier OD effort had focused on the micro-level. Now there is an urgent need to develop effective OD programs at the macro-level. We hope that the Partnerships for Development program, by providing an example of a successful application of OD technology to macro-macro-level phenomena, will encourage others in the field to develop additional programs to address significant issues at the regional, national, and international levels.

## REFERENCES

Bennis, W. (1984, August). The 4 competencies of leadership. *Training and Development Journal.*

Franklin, J. L. (1976). Characteristics of successful and unsuccessful organization development. *The Journal of Applied Behavioral Science, 12*(4), 471–492.

Golembiewski, R. T., Proehl, C. W., Jr., & Sink, D. (1982). Estimating the success of OD applications. *Training and Development Journal, 36* (4), 86–95.

Heisler, W. J. (1975, February). Patterns of OD in practice. *Business Horizon.*

Kilmann, R. H. (1984). *Beyond the quick fix: Managing five tracks to organizational success.* San Francisco, CA: Jossey–Bass.

Mitroff, I. I. (1983). *Stakeholders of the organizational mind.* San Francisco: Jossey–Bass.

Nath, R. (1983). *Highlights of the partnerships for development dialogue conference,* October 2–4. Pittsburgh, PA.

Nath, R. (1985). *Highlights of the second partnerships for development dialogue conference,* May 5–7. Pittsburgh, PA.

Nath, R. (Ed.). (1988). *Comparative management: Regional view,* Cambridge, MA: Ballinger.

Ouchi, W. G. (1984). *The M-form society: How American teamwork can recapture the competitive edge.* Reading, MA: Addison–Wesley.

Peters, T. J., & Waterman, R. H., Jr. (1982). *In search of excellence.* New York: Warner Books.

Porras, J. I., & Berg, P. O. (1978). The impact of organization development. *Academy of Management Review, 3,* 249–266.

Thomas, C. (1983, October 14). International cooperation is the key to a healthy global economy. Pittsburgh, *Post-Gazette.*

Tichy, N. M., & Devanna, M. A. (1986). *The transformational leader.* New York: Wiley.

# 11

# Ways to Different Organizations: OD, OT, or HSD? That is Not the Question

**Wolfgang Pilarz**
Vienna, Austria

Looking at the title, the reader may be confronted with various associations, suppositions, and questions to determine if it will be informative, useful, or entertaining to read on. What do you associate with it?

If you asked the question; "Why do we need different organizations at all?" then it is probable that you have an organizational understanding and experience which differs from the usual organizational and management theories. Or you may be in a state of mind where the maxim "more of the same" in dealing with social systems cannot be disturbed. You are lucky! In that case it is not worth reading any further; you will not miss anything.

It is a different matter if you ask questions like "What are the criteria for different organizations?" or "Could the organizations I deal with also be different?" or "What ways are possible?" or "Are there existing examples of such different organizations?" These and similar questions are referred to in the following.

## OUR PRESENT ORGANIZATIONS

In the field of organizational social sciences much has been done in the last 40 years. Fred Massarik et al. (1985) gives an interesting overview of this development and the change of focus of studies. The "practical" results have been various organizational handbooks, management skills, models for leadership, consulting styles, and so on, which have been spread by universities, by literature, by management training courses and by OD programs, and have found their way into organizations. Once these skills had been more or less willingly learned, attempts were made to apply them in practice. The impression could be gathered that managers and workers, consultants and scientists are always learning new vocabulary in the context of organizations but that common basic assumptions about how systems function have remained much the same. Constructs such as hierarchy, order, leadership, reports, function diagrams, goal orientation, motivational factors, rational decision-making processes, and control enjoy great popularity.

Activities carried out under these assumptions reinforce themselves in the manner of self-fulfilling prophecies. Once more it appears that the circle of "perception and action" has such a stabilizing effect that neither escape nor change is possible. We seem to be caught in the trap of the "more of the same" thinking, feeling, and doing. Outside observers may propose other explanations for organizational phenomena and believe that these could function differently but these arguments and concepts find little acceptance.

Why is this? There are often principally three impediments to a new organizational understanding.

First the individual can argue that nothing is achieved if only his particular assumptions about organizations are questioned. The collective relearning required is difficult to arrange.

This is where the diverse training and development programs come in. The history of management development (MD), organization development (OD), and, more recently, organizational transformation (OT), and human systems development (HSD) have been characterized by step-by-step enlargement of the circle of people involved, the themes selected and the methods employed. It was only 3 years ago that Adams (1984) claimed that it was too early to define OT because there was so much happening under this new rubric that a single author couldn't begin to capture the range of emerging ideas and technologies. He tries to define the limits thus: "OD is useful for helping a given organization (or unit within an organization) operate as effectively as it can, within the parameters of its charter. OT will help a given organization explore its purpose and charter in relation to the larger environment and facilitate the necessary fundamental realignments."

Massarik, Margulies and Tannenbaum (1983) established HSD as a new disciplinary designation and state:

> Our rationale for the choice flows, in part, from the substance of the human matrix, from the focus on values and related concerns with growth and development, from the holistic/systems perspective and from the growing awareness of the relevance of human experience. We realize that boundaries of disciplines cannot be established by fiat, but tentative delineation of such boundaries can furnish a basis for

reflection about a fields substance and about its direction. We may preliminarily think of HSD somewhat in line with the charts shown in Figure 1.

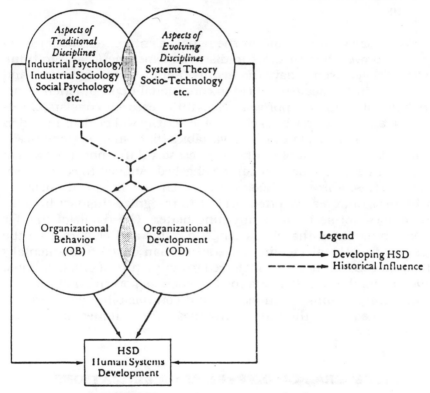

**FIGURE 1.** Charting human systems development.

Second it can be said that wherever there arc organizations they use similar rules of play. Yet, this need not be so. The examples to be discussed here are part of an attempt to overcome this hindrance of assuming that only a simple set of rules inevitably prevails.

Third another impediment is formed by the fact that the dominant understanding of organizations is tightly connected to the analytic-rationalistic orientation of the occidental world outlook. A fundamental relearning is therefore particularly difficult since this runs the risk of unloosing an avalanche of confusion in all areas of life.

The rationalistic orientation can be depicted in a series of steps:

1.  Characterize the situation in terms of identifiable objects with well-defined properties.

2. Find general rules that apply to situations in terms of those objects and properties.
3. Apply the rules logically to the situation of concern, drawing conclusions about what should be done (Winograd & Flores, 1986).

This arrangement is found in the usual scientific method successfully used over the centuries to discover, experiment, and to think scientifically. Even today, the acquisition of status, prestige, and resources in the academic field is conditional upon practicing this analytic-rationalistic approach. Scientific research consists of setting up situations in which observable activity will be determined in a clear way by a small number of variables that can be systematically manipulated, this simplicity being necessary if the modeling system is to make predictions that can be checked. Applied to complex social systems, these methods soon reach the limits of their capabilities. However, we often neglect to recognize this fact because there does not seem to be anything better. The result of this for theory building is that we attempt to refine and elaborate on the basis of traditional assumptions rather than create fundamentally different constructions. Transferred to our picture of organizations, this means that fundamental beliefs such as governability, understandability, stability, rationality, and controllability will never be relinquished. Only the intervening means, techniques, and methods may vary.

## TESSERA FOR DIFFERENT ORGANIZATIONS

Different organizations require new orientations and new basic assumptions. They require that we identify new organizational features and actions which increase our options in dealing with social systems. This is unavoidably the job of someone who is a member or a partner of organizations—in other words, everybody. It may be useful to adopt inspirations from others and to accept previously formulated concepts. But in the end every manager, consultant, or scientist must perform a concrete, personal activity and give it meaning.

The actor creates his or her own reality. By means of continually repeated actions and interpretations the actor turns his or her reality into something, apparently real, independent, and unalterable. One can also choose one's own reality which one knows exists through perception, thought, feeling, and by one's actions and which one therefore can change or reconstruct. The following tessera can only serve those who choose this second, self-determined version.

We are dealing here with conceptional indications which could help us to consciously construct alternative organizational realities. These constructional indications are comparable with tessera which differ from one another in color, shape, material, and surface-composition in that they belong neither to one logical category nor to a single scientific discipline. It doesn't matter that some are older than others, have been used or reproduced more often, or are refinements or developments of long-existing and well-known "raw materials."

These tessera alone do not build a picture. A designer is always required to create the mosaic.

The designer's previous experiences and sympathies, intuition and professional interests determine the way in which he or she selects the tessera and puts them together to form a picture. Later on, the chosen materials may be characteristic for the whole mosaic. But in order to call it a picture it would be necessary to establish meaningful relations between the parts. These relations may constitute patterns, ornaments, symbols, or representations. Human activities are responsible for the results of this creative process, even when they are unexpected. What a mosaic ultimately expresses depends on the way the spectator looks at it. If the observer focuses more on the analysis of the single tessera than on the composition of the relations, the unique quality of the work of art as a whole will remain hidden.

No two pictures are ever the same. However, they are related to one another because of the similarity of the materials used and can differ remarkably from the traditional mosaics of the old masters.

The following small selection of tessera should be understood in the manner outlined above and thereby encourage individual designing.

## ACCEPTING NONTRIVIALITY

It's becoming more and more usual for organizations to be described as complex systems (social, sociotechnical, economic, etc.). Complexity, understood as product of complicatedness and dynamic, leads necessarily to incompleteness in description and less unambiguous predictability (Probst, 1981). In spite of this insight we often create theories and actions as if it would be possible to exhaust complexity with an analytic-synthetic approach. In this, we develop explanatory models for organizations which are based on the concept of the Trivial Machine.

This classification of systems, by Heinz von Foerster (1985), in Trivial Machines (TM) and Nontrivial Machines (NTM) will be explained below.

Figure 2 shows the schematic representation of the TM, with the labels $x$, $y$, $f$, referring to input, output, and function of this machine respectively. This TM connects a certain input with a certain output without mistakes or change.

Because of the invariable relationship $f$ between input and output, the result $y$ can only vary by feeding different $x$. A certain output $y$ once observed for a given $x$ will be the same for the same $x$ given later. If a TM behaves in another way, we would say that the machine has been tampered with and is in need of repair.

So one can say that all TMs are:

• Predictable
• History independent
• Synthetically deterministic
• Analytically determinable

The inference scheme of trivial machines appear in many contexts and under most diverse names, for example:

| $x$ | $f$ | $y$ |
|---|---|---|
| input | function | output |
| stimulus | organism | response |
| cause | law of nature | effect |
| task | manager | action |

Nontrivial machines are profoundly different. They are provided with something like an inner voice or "a life of their own," which means that the machine's internal states (Z) codetermines its input—output relation. These internal states reinfluence themselves. But this special relationship and the way in which the input codetermines the subsequent internal state remains hidden from an

**FIGURE 2.** Trivial machine.

outside observer. Hence, the output of a NTM can neither be explained by the input nor by the present internal state alone. It is also a product of the machine's history. Figure 3 shows this arrangement as a machine within a machine:

One can say that all NTMs are:

- Analytically unpredictable
- History dependent
- Synthetically deterministic
- Analytically indeterminable

It is quite understandable that we are not very happy with NTM if we are interested in a simple construction of reality with a high probability of occurrence. To see the world as an accumulation of NTMs instead of TMs, is certainly the most adequate assumption, but not very common.

A number of consequences may arise especially in our understanding of social systems, for example, most of the organizational and management theories belong to the same type of explanation: to the trivial-machine scheme. They vary only by different assumptions and notations for the operator $f$.

An essential reason for this is that for many managers it is too painful and distressing to accept the events in organizations as neither predictable nor controllable. Anxiety regarding chaos and identity crises as leader would be provoked. For suppressing these unpleasantries, it is said that it is not worth formulating organizational theories in analogy to NTMs, because such beginnings won't bring certainty and control.

Nevertheless, it will be necessary to create new, communicable theories which can be used to further orientations for realistic organizational actions. Such theories will not try to discover Laws of

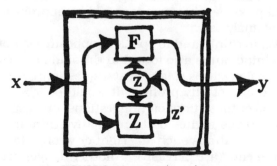

**FIGURE 3.** Nontrivial machine.

Social Nature but will try to point to the conventional and self-organizing character of human systems. Practical understanding, as a result of being embedded in a continuous action-process, will be seen as being more useful than artificial intellectualizing alone. The rediscovery and appreciation of intuition would be the outcome, thus allowing analytically separated conceptions such as individual experience, theory development, and concrete practice, to be brought closer together.

Paradoxically, the renouncement of domination, controllability, or manageability of organizations would bring more creative possibilities to systems and to their participants and would subsequently increase their number of choices. If we give up our desire for trivialization and standardization, the experienced variety of organizational realities could increase, and more attention would be paid to the uniqueness of organizations and to the individuality of their members.

A personal consequence and requirement at the same time, is to enjoy colorfulness, diversity, and surprises instead of fearing them.

## OVERCOMING DICHOTOMIES

It seems to be the most normal thing in the world to think in opposites. Even famous psychologists say that our thinking and our language could and would be meaningless without dichotomies. In his fundamentally interesting theory about personal constructs, Kelly (1955) states that human thinking creates systems of constructions which were used for the anticipation of events. These systems have been built on a variety of dichotomies. It is said that everyone has to live in such a system. Shades of gray can only arise out of deviations of a fundamental black and white scale. Advocates of this concept see a great advantage in this assumed structure of psychological processes because it would be appropriate for binary mathematical analysis.

To perceive, to think, and to speak in opposites is not only part of the common mind but is also found in the standard research methods of the social sciences. Many tests, questionnaires, and checklists are based on polarity profiles. It would be less harmful, if we were conscious of these implicit suggestions, one aspect being that the use of antonyms invites us to normative thinking. The transitions from classifications such as "right or wrong" to "good or bad" or "friend or enemy" are pervasive. Another danger arises when we believe that two different class elements should be primarily perceived and described within a dichotomy scheme. This presumption would lead to statements such as "Republicans are the opposite of Democrats."

Transferred to the field of organizations, it means that we have produced a lot of explanatory concepts which take dichotomous contradictions among different orientations for granted, as, for example, "concern for people versus concern for achievement" or "hierarchy versus chaos," or "capital versus work." It should not be denied that such differentiations could be useful, but for whom and when?

We should be aware that even distinct and essentially different things need not to be excluded automatically from each other, because in order to differentiate, it is not necessary to construct dichotomies. It would be sufficient to use contrasting backgrounds or to define boundaries. Hence, we are not dependent on a complementary color "green" for the perception of "red." It would be enough to develop contrasts such as "blue," "yellow," or "black." Skeptics may say, that the experience of "red" would not be the same with different backgrounds. Of course not! But the illusion is, to believe that we could experience something twice in exactly the same way. Overcoming this illusion an observer becomes open to qualitatively new aspects. For that reason the color "red" would not disappear—it becomes richer in facets.

A transition in this sense from "black and white seeing" to "color seeing" could overcome several blocking and restrictive assumptions about organizations.

## PROMOTING REDUNDANCIES

It is a characteristic feature of contemporary companies to practice a strict division of labor and functions. This is seen as a basic requirement for the efficiency of the organization and for the coordinated functioning of the system. According to the division of work, specialization of functions are promoted for rationalization and for the increase of expertise. As a logical consequence in this context, redundancies in organizations should be avoided because they are presumed to engender a waste of resources. They can also be made responsible for parallel work which can cause confusion and incompatible developments. This, it is argued should be avoided by means of the managerial function of coordination, which should also be able to guarantee integration. The separation of conceiving, organizing, planning, and controlling activities on the one hand, and their implementation on the other, seems to be conclusive and is supported by education and training. Indeed, these considerations are often used as an argument for the application of the hierarchical concept to industrial organizations.

Yet is it a crazy idea to promote redundancies in task-oriented social systems?

It would probably be easier to detect the positive sides of redundancies when we hear that redundancies are spoken of as functions and not as parts. In other words, it is not a prerequisite to build more of the same organizational elements, but to develop an holistic insight into the relationship between parts and a whole. In analogy to a hologram in each part, information, and function of the whole, should be saved in such a way that it is possible to reconstruct from each part, the whole picture. Such a holographic system is less troublesome and creates the capacity to self-organize. Redundancy in the functioning of the system is a potential that is, of course, not being used all the time, but it determines to a large extent the possibility of a system's capability to develop.

In the context of organizations, that would mean to overcome the discrepancy between specialization versus generalization and would enhance flexibility and the learning ability of a company. The level of alienated activities or processes could be reduced at the same time. This could be done by the implementation of multifunctional teams, highly autonomous small units, training with heterogeneous groups, low levels of institutionalization of work cycles, and decentralized availability of informations.

New technological possibilities can be used to support these processes. This tessera "promoting redundancies" can also be characterized as rejection of poorness and sterility in organizations and the estimation of diversity and the richness within it.

## USING DIFFERENT METAPHORS

Not only the analytical and rationalistic models of explanation are confronted with increasing criticism. There is a growing skepticism regarding digitalization in communication as well. Aspects of analogous communication, with vivid and metaphorical language, have become more highly esteemed, especially in connection with forming an organizational culture in which the importance of the language-in-use is often stressed.

Less applied is the well-known insight that the use of a certain metaphor can lead to a certain view of the world. In a way the metaphor is a construction for the conception of the world and it defines implicitly the range of actions. A shift in metaphor effects changes in the perceived possibilities and their meanings.

The use of different metaphors is also a suitable way for organizational analysis and for discovering new insights or possibilities. Morgan (1986) shows impressively that our conceptions of organizations are built on a very small number of images, which we take as self-evident.

> By using different metaphors to understand the complex and paradoxical character of organizational life, we are able to manage and design organizations in ways that we have not thought possible before. By building in the use of metaphors we have a means of enhancing our capacity for creative yet disciplined thought, in a way that allows us to grasp and deal with the many-sided character of organizational life and the increasing complexity of our world.

Beside the dominant mechanistic and biologistic analogies for organizations, Morgan explores less widespread metaphors such as organizations as brains, as psychic prisons, as cultures, as instruments of domination, as flux and transformation, and so on.

In addition to these, many other images can be constructed which create their own, specific insights. It is important not to forget that metaphors are always as-if suppositions which imply certain values and orientations, but no unalterable truth. Therefore it is always possible to reorientate oneself and to relearn. This kind of learning corresponds with the process that Argyris (1982) called double-loop learning, which leads in the sense of Watzlawick (1974) to second-order solutions. It means that the framework of a situation or a system becomes reinterpreted or modified.

But the new opportunity in the use of metaphors is not necessarily the substitution of one image for another which seems to be more practical. We would essentially progress, if we reach a status of flexibility in our thinking which allows us to grasp an organizational phenomenon simultaneously from the point of view of *various* metaphors. Only in this way may we appropriately address the complexity of the world. Meanwhile the search for the "best metaphor" is likely to go on in many academic and organization settings.

## SELF-EMPOWERMENT

It is not easy to give a short definition of the term "self-empowerment." But it should be clear that it doesn't mean that anything goes or everything is possible. Therefore it should not be understood as a new cloak for executives' desires to be omnipotent. Self-empowerment will express that, even if we have to accept that living systems cannot be dominated, there is no reason for inactivity or for feelings of helplessness. Self-empowerment includes the acquisition and acceptance of intuition and wisdom to work in accordance with, and not against, existing energies.

Self-empowerment is not intended in an egocentric way. The willingness to rouse one's own potentials within a perceived social system is strictly connected to the interest of supporting the empowerment of others, and this calls for a clear refusal of defensive thinking and obstructing actions. Transferred to organizations it requires a new understanding of leadership. It has to be formed by a strong generative orientation instead of aspiration for power. The creation of corresponding, supporting structures will then become obvious. Step by step this will lead to an elimination of a primarily hierarchical organizational concept. Differences in organizations can occur in a multitude of ways without being seen as expressions of power levels, or as symbols for domination or submission.

We can find the first signs in contemporary companies. Kiefer and Senge (1984), for example, found a number of innovative, successful organizations in which a fundamental reorientation takes place—the so-called "metanoic" organizations. This organizational concept stresses the importance of developing visions and values intuition as much as rationality.

## FAVORING SMALL, SUBJECTIVE THEORIES

In contrast to the efforts of some social scientists to elaborate general theories of social systems as completely as possible, this tessera speaks up for small and subjective theories.

First, it is recognized that no person, group, or organization can escape from its own subjective presumptions and constructions. Of course it is useful to become aware of one's peculiarity so that learning and an expansion of alternatives becomes possible. But it is an illusion to believe that it could be possible to become aware of *all* individual assumptions and actions, or to reach an assumptionless state.

If we accept this, it becomes less and less clear why we should search for intersubjective, general insights. Such a research process has the only consequence that the "discovered" regularities will reinforce the prevailing strong tendencies for unification. These kind of "insights" don't increase—they reduce the number of choices an organization has.

Second, it should be noted that often the range of a successful explanatory model is extended so far that its essential information is lost.

Even for theories and constructions the rule of thumb seems to be that "small is beautiful."

No secret should be made of the origin of most of these tessera nor where more can be found. We are talking here about the fundus in thought by the name of "radical constructivism," about the vast reservoir of systems theory and "cybernetics II," about the mythical creature of "evolutionary self-organization" and about the treasure chest of Heidegger's philosophy.

## 4 EXAMPLES FOR WAYS TO A NEW ORGANIZATIONAL UNDERSTANDING:

Searching for firms which have already taken some steps in the direction of new organizational understanding, it was possible to find some remarkable examples. The following representations are primarily based on self-descriptions and statements of exponents in order to make clear their subjective organizational theories and their conception of themselves. The selection of the four examples illustrates the wide range of starting points to develop a different organizational understanding and practice.

One can find other examples in this book. I would particularly refer to the representation of the Hanover Insurance Companies in the contribution of Peter Senge (this volume).

## W. L. GORE & ASSOCIATES

**Development.** Wilhelm L. Gore founded this firm in 1958, together with his wife, in order to explore the substance PTFE for insulating electronic cables. In 1969 his son Bob Gore, today president of the company, developed the world-renowned material GORE-TEX r, on which an exceptionally large product range is based.

The company currently has about 3,500 employees in 30 factories. Gore is represented in Europe with branches in West Germany, Scotland, France, Switzerland, the Netherlands, Belgium, Austria, Italy, Spain, Greece, and Sweden. Further factories are planned. In the last 15 years, growth rates for the company as a whole have consistently ranged between 18% and 32% per year.

Gore's products are in the fields of electronics (special cables), medicine (artificial limbs and arteries), membranes, seals, industrial filters etc. At the beginning there was doubtless a technical innovation; but the structure and philosophy of the organization show that this was neither a coincidence nor a short-lived wonder.

***Notable organizational features.*** In contrast to traditional hierarchies, Gore's organizational structure is a "grid." Within this interconnecting matrix, organization every employee communicates directly with his or her colleagues without going through other intermediaries.

Although the company cannot manage without superiors and subordinates, hierarchy and titles are avoided as far as possible. The leader of a group therefore does not receive his authority from above. His legitimacy comes from recognition by the staff. This complies with the concept of natural leadership and the informal organization becomes the structure. There are three types of sponsorship:

> The *initial sponsor,* who commits oneself to putting a new associate on the road to success. That could mean integrat-

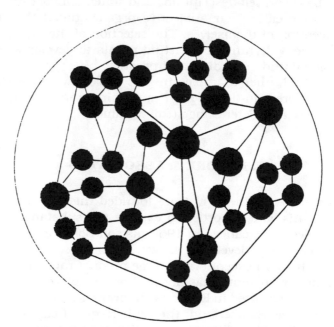

**FIGURE 4.** Gore's organizational structure.

ing him in the group or taking on an independent area of work.

The *advocate sponsor* is someone who speaks well of others, especially to people who appreciate the achievements.

Lastly there is the *compensation sponsor*, who is able to provide necessary rewards.

A further organizational feature which provides the individual with an overall picture is the limitation of the size of factories to between 150 and 200 employees. The quick reactions to developments in the market in the past is attributed to this self-restriction. This also helps to prevent bureaucratic tendencies.

Innovation is highly esteemed. The basic task of the intrapreneur is valued. Innovations are born of the problems and questions of the market place.

At Gore, the ability and willingness of the employees to act as intra- or entrepreneurs is considered to be an important factor in the success of a firm.

Intrapreneurship.   With their enthusiasm and stamina, these entrepreneurs within the firm (intrapreneurs) who have a personal vision (e.g., in solving a problem) are the origin and motor of the process of innovation. The intrapreneur derives motivation from self-affirmation and from recognition by his or her colleagues and customers, (as well as) from his financial interests in the company's success.

Stockownership.   For more than 10 years, every employee has been able to be a stockowner. In Germany, for example, each employee received, as a gift, 10% of his or her annual income in the form of Gore shares. In this way the employee participates in the economic results of one's activities in the firm, be these successes or failures. In addition to wages, the employee participates directly and long-term in the company's growth.

The combination of these two models results in a synergistic effect, which, in addition to material success, confirms the high personal effort as a meaningful and personally fulfilling activity.

**Orientation.**   The basis of trust and the particular atmosphere which have proven productive are created by four principles: freedom, fairness, self-commitment, and the waterline principle.

*Freedom* forms the basis of the company philosophy and means that every associate is given the freedom to grow in knowledge, skill, the scope of responsibility and the range of activities. Everyone will also help his fellow associates to grow.

This freedom is restricted by the *waterline principle*. This compares the firm with a ship and says that each member of the organization is asked to drill into the ship because otherwise nothing will happen. However caution is needed if he drills near the waterline. This is the case if the financial security of the firm, future opportunities or the company's reputation are threatened. If this happens, another person should be consulted. Who and how is not specified.

As a principle, *fairness* should not only apply between one another but also be practiced externally with customers and partners.

*Self-commitment* is the basis upon which intrapreneurship is built. Self-determination and orientation toward freedom are reinforced by voluntarily undertaking and fulfilling commitments.

As Bill Gore (president) puts it: "In our company people manage themselves. There is a fundamental difference between a commitment and an order."

## THE MONDRAGÓN COOPERATIVES

**Development.** Mondragón is a small town in the Basque region of Spain. It was here that, in 1943, a Jesuit priest founded a vocational school which was to become the starting point for the development of the Mondragón cooperative groups. The first graduates from the school went on to become engineers, and in 1954 founded the first cooperative, the ULGOR. They were able to raise the necessary capital, thanks to donations from friends and relatives, Basque drinking clubs, and the local authorities, and went into production making paraffin staves and later, ovens.

From humble beginnings—ULGOR had only 24 employees in 1956—the group has grown remarkably. Even before the end of the 1950s, the Fagor gas cooker factor, a foundry, the Arrasate engineering works and other cooperative societies were already in existence. At present the group comprises about 160 individual cooperatives, 88 of which are in industry, 7 in agriculture, 3 in the service sector, 1 in consumer goods, 44 in education, and 14 in housing development.

The group also has its own financial institution, the Caja Laboral Popular, an insurance institution and a research institution, both so-called "second-order cooperatives," to which other cooperatives belong. Mondragón currently has about 20,000 cooperative members, a turnover of more than a million U.S. dollars, and an export ratio of roughly 30%.

Since the early 1960s, the cooperatives have experienced dynamic rates of growth way above the average both for the industry and the region as a whole. However we care to measure this development— be it growth in turnover, net product, export ratio, employment or investment, or be it by productivity and profitability—it is clear that the cooperatives are as successful, more so than noncooperative enterprises in the Basque region. At the same time they have managed largely to avoid economic crises and to counteract the effects of national depression.

When compared on a regional basis, wages lie between 10% and 4% above comparative figures, although since the end of the 1970s the official rate of unemployment for the Basque region as a whole has been more than 20%. The cooperative group has actually managed to increase its labor force slightly, thus allowing the region to remain internationally competitive.

What is it then that has caused the type of growth not usually typical for cooperatives and what structures, processes, mechanisms, and philosophies exist to account for such continual success?

**Notable organizational features.** A striking feature of the group as a whole is its close networking. This is the result of special regional and historical conditions as well as several structural features.

The most important formal link is formed by the cooperative agreement. It was drawn up in 1960 by the founding members of the Caja Laboral Popular (CLP) and has to be signed by every cooperative which receives financial support and advice from the CLP. This agreement lays down mutual relations between cooperatives within the network and specifies cooperative principles. In signing the cooperative agreement, a cooperative also becomes a member of the bank's general meeting and is thus able to influence its decision making.

The CLP consists of a department responsible for all banking transactions (Division Bancaría) and a business department (Division Empresarial) which undertakes a series of integrated tasks:

*Promotion:* Setting up and development of new cooperative ventures which contribute to the development of structurally weak areas and sectors of the Basque region which were previously less developed.

*Advice:* Support of cooperative development through continual, close cooperation in technical, economic, and social matters and in administrative questions.

*Information:* Provision of precise information about individual cooperatives or groups and about the economic sector in which they are active. The aim of this is to maintain homogeneous administration.

A total of 110 employees in the business are responsible for carrying out diverse research and promotional activities, providing advisory services in the marketing, export, finance, legal, and technical fields and in inspecting the monthly reports of the cooperatives. If a cooperative should get into economic difficulties, the *area de intervención* intervenes directly and takes over the task of crisis management.

Further evidence of the close networking is to be found in the direct mergers which take place between cooperatives. The *grupos industriales* bring together cooperatives with identical or similar products in order to achieve advantages in buying, production, sales, and technology. The groups are thus able to combine export efforts and technology planning on the basis of investment plans within a business network.

The 12 *grupos sociales* are charged with the task of dividing the net surplus of the individual businesses equally among all members of the cooperative group. To this end, each business hands over its net surplus minus payments to the social and reserve funds. The aggregate surplus is then allocated on an equal basis to every cooperative member whose own business has incurred losses for that period. Where there are job losses within a particular enterprise, these must be compensated for by an equal number of new places in another enterprise of the same *grupo social* since dismissal of employees is not permitted. Other principles on which the *grupos* operate include preferential treatment for other group members in trade where products are of the same price and quality, avoiding open or hidden competition between members, and the setting up of social services.

The training and further education network makes an important contribution to the success of the Mondragón cooperative groups. The 44 teaching institutions offer extensive educational opportunities, ranging from kindergarten to university. The cooperative concept plays a central role in this system of education; students are not only taught about self-government, they also have the opportunity to take part in it from a very early stage; 1/3 of the school general meeting, which acts as its decision-making body, is comprised of the pupils themselves.

All members of a cooperative have a seat and a vote in the general meeting, which is held once or twice a year and is attended by about

80% of the workforce. Among other things, the general meeting is responsible for election and supervision of the board, decisions concerning capital supply, changing internal rules, and renewing the balance sheet. Board members are each elected for 4 years and half their number is replaced or reelected every 2 years. The board itself selects management, which undertakes leadership of the business for at least 4 years. Cooperative members elect representatives from each department for the Social Council, which represents "grass roots" interests *vis-à-vis* management. Other instruments include a management and a supervisory council.

The principle of identity stipulates that every employee is at the same time a member of the cooperative and that capital shares may only be owned by employees. Each new member is required to pay a membership fee equal to 1 year's earnings, for which the CLP makes credit available. A quarter of this donation is credited to the "collective account" as "lost investment" to make up for the efforts and achievements of members. The remaining individual credit bears a fixed rate of interest and can be increased or reduced by profit and loss distribution.

These regulations mean there is an influx of capital when new members join the cooperative. This is reinforced through the distribution of profits: 70% of profits are credited to the "individual account," 20% to the "collective account" for investment, reserves, social expenditure and covering losses and 10% to the Social Fund. If profits increase, individual credit may be reduced to 50% and collective increased to 40%.

Another characteristic feature of Mondragón is the very small difference in wage levels: Maximum income variation is in the ratio of 1 : 3. Quite apart from its ideological element, this egalitarian system of pay also has a cost-reducing effect and therefore promotes competitiveness. Compared on a regional scale, the lowest incomes are about 20% above comparative values, while the top income is about 40% below them.

**Orientation.** The establishment and growth of the collectives cannot be explained merely in terms of their internal structures. The Basque region has a long tradition of struggles for political and economic independence. The basic idea behind the cooperative and its system of self-government has been part of the Basque way of life for many years.

The Mondragón group not only has tradition on its side, it also has a clear orientation in which job creation is the primary objective. Any surplus tends therefore to be used as investment, for creating more jobs and for founding new cooperatives rather than in raising individual shares in profits. This does not always meet with approval, especially from younger members who are said, by older members, to think in an increasingly consumer-orientated way and to be therefore less concerned with observing the principle of solidarity (cf. Gubitzer, 1987). Nevertheless, until now, the Mondragón example has shown that it is possible to be successful by orientating toward the principles of cooperative self-government.

## The Democratic Principle

Eighty percent of members are in the general meeting. In spite of this, the distribution of competence levels within the enterprise means that proposals made at that meeting by workers are often not as sound as those put forward by management and are therefore less likely to succeed in practice.

The principle of solidarity is expressed at member level in the maximum wage ratio of 1 : 3 and in the objective of job creation. At cooperative level, solidarity is achieved through the foundation of cooperative groups. Redistribution of profits and losses within these groups reduces individual risk.

The principle of identity requires that every member pays a capital contribution which he or she may not withdraw during the term of membership. This means capital can be neutralized to a certain extent and that members cannot join purely in order to take up a financial interest in the cooperative.

## BUSINESS ASSOCIATION "AKTION DRITTER WEG"

***Development.*** The *Aktion Dritter Weg* has its root in two societal phenomena which reached their high point in Europe in 1968; the German student movement and the "Prague Spring." These led to the organization of a series of international conferences at the International Cultural Center in Achberg on Lake Constance.

The meetings were attended by people with the most varied outlooks, yet with one thing in common—they had all been looking into practical altenatives to the existing system in East and West, and together they developed a number of basic principles. In order to test their model in practice, the business association *Dritter Weg* (Third way) was founded in 1977.

Within 10 years, 19 smaller enterprises came into being in West Germany and Switzerland. These enterprises operate in various fields; types of business range from a publishing firm, to a wool and silk producer, a natural products firm, to agriculture, a tea room, a cultural center, and a consultancy to a computer hardware and software manufacturer. Turnover of businesses within the association is about 9 million DM. In addition to the business association itself there is a member organization and a nonprofit trust organization. The member organization offers sympathizers the opportunity to support the association, while the trust plays a major role in neutralizing available capital. (This will be discussed in detail later.)

**Notable Organizational Features.** Businesses can only be set up within the framework of the *Aktion Dritter Weg* if they agree to incorporate the following basic features:

An employee's function and performance are not related to income in concrete terms. He or she undertakes to use one's abilities within the job and receives an income according to one's needs. This decoupling of individual performance and income is justified on the ground that the complexity of the system of production makes it impossible to determine an individual's contribution. This means there can also be no objective procedure for rewarding human work.

In practice, income determination under the "third way" system occurs either:

1. By means of a private agreement oriented toward the performance possibility of the enterprise and the requirements of the individual; or
2. In the form of a fixed outline agreement according to social parameters.

A maximum income which is determined by the AGM applies to all employees.

The businesses within the organization are neither private property nor cooperative forms of collective property. Capital and the means of production are given in trust to firms but are the property of the nonprofit-making trust organization. Budgetary planning for the association as a whole occurs at an annual conference for this purpose, which is attended by workers from the various firms. The trust, or bodies selected by it, perform purely executive functions and provide business communities with capital in the form of operating funds. The business communities themselves operate autonomously and also decide independently what proportion of those funds are to be used for investment and what proportion for further nonprofit-making purposes by the trust.

Instead of hierarchical company structures there is a principle of cooperative consultation and decision making by all members. Every employee of a firm is involved in making essential decisions concerning worker's rights on an equal basis. Fixing and changing working conditions, business perspectives and income distribution and the election of delegates and authorized agent therefore occurs in company meetings.

A fundamental idea of the *Aktion Dritter Weg* involves linking up businesses which produce surpluses to nonprofit-making institutions for social and educational purposes. The business association thereby performs certain governance functions by carrying out cultural, educational, and research work. The transfer of financial means from "surplus" to subsidized companies is decided at quarterly delegate meetings. In practice this leads to an active interest in and a high level of information about the other firms in the association, despite the fact that they operate in different fields and have specific and varied business cultures.

**Orientation.** The *Aktion Dritter Weg* focuses primarily on Rudolf Steiner's concept of the three divisions within the social organism. The *Dritter Weg* is not only considered essential but also the one free, democratic socialism of self-government. As far as possible, economic, state, and cultural functions are to be carried out on a decentralized basis through the association of autonomous enterprises.

Theoretical models also refer to long-term social renewal. Results of research, the practical experience of the association and political commitment toward more direct popular legislation—these are the three pillars by which it is hoped to bring about the 'transformation of the social organism'. As Michael Bader (manager of the Institute for Developmental Research) puts it: "Our main aim is to achieve clarity about target perspectives but what we lack above all are the right ideas for changing our society. Clarity is our first priority, conceptually speaking; it acts as the starting point for social restructuring."

Further, this model of social renewal is based on Steiner's anthroposophic image of human beings. Three basic human impulses are seen as basic:

1.  Self-determined behavior: Once present-day people have gotten rid of their fears, resignation, and discouragement, they then have the need not only to carry out instruction but also to act in a self-responsible manner, using their own understanding of the meaning of one's actions. This freedom impulse must be

observed in all areas of social life and in particular in the workplace.
2. Democratic voting: Present-day people obviously want to have a say in things which are equally binding for everybody. It is here that the democratic impulse is to be seen, and this can also be applied to the world of work.
3. Solidarity in sharing: More and more people now feel a strong need for solidarity and sharing with those who live on life's darker side. This basic impulse of brotherliness can be taken to mean standing-by and helping one another without expecting anything in return.

Observing these basic impulses in view of worldwide interdependency the "law of integrals" should lead to behavior in keeping with human worth and one's relation to the cosmos.

## WOMEN'S WORLD BANKING

***Development.*** Credit and female entrepreneurship are the two areas in which Women's World Banking (WWB) is active. The initiative for WWB was taken at the 1975 United Nations International Women's Conference in Mexico. At that conference the limited access of women to credit (institutions) was identified as a main drawback to participation in economic life. A number of women working in large financial institutions took up the challenge to design an organizational structure which should become an institutional solution to women's apparent limited access to capital sources.

The idea of a women's bank was rejected, for it would imply being forced to compete with other commercial banks. The alternative which emerged was the design of a credit-granting mechanism because the founders believed an intermediary, financial situation to be best suited to work in cooperation with other commercial banks and local financial institutions.

Through the years the objectives of WWB came to be:

- To help create an environment in which women have equal access to the benefits of the formal economy.
- To build local support bases with individual countries that can continue to identify and respond through their own resources to the specific needs of women entrepreneurs in that nation.
- To establish a network of women throughout the world that en-

ables them to share experiences and knowledge with each other
and with those women yet to enter the marketplace.
- To expand and strengthen the network of women who participate
  in financial decision making in their economies.
- To create mechanisms which provide access to credit, capital,
  information, technologies, and markets.

In order to realize these aims, WWB structured itself in the form of
an international network. It was thereby possible to set up an organization and 32 national divisions (local affiliates) in every conti-
nent and a joint capital fund of $5 million within 11 years.

In this way, credit has been made available to 3,000 women since
1981. Technical and managerial assistance now is also frequently
offered to female entrepreneurs.

The loan guarantee program is the crux of WWB's development
strategy for leveraging financial institutions to help women obtain
loans. Relationships are established on the local level between WWB
affiliates and lending institutions. It is on this level that careful
applicant screening and program modifications take place. While
50% of the loan guarantee is provided through the WWB capital
fund, 25% is insured by the local WWB affiliate, with the remaining
25% guaranteed through the local bank.

Loan recipients and selected projects must meet the standards
established by WWB. These include:

- Evident potential for business development and employment
  generation;
- A viable business venture for which capital is needed in order to
  expand operations and maximize potential;
- Lack of access to other capital;
- Ability and willingness to learn basic management principles and
  technical applications necessary to ensure project success.

The local committee is solely responsible for deciding when to grant
a loan. The group of women entrepreneurs who receive support from
WWB consist roughly of: self-employed women, women starting
their own small business, women who own or operate existing businesses and groups of women working together in projects or enterprises. The activities of the affiliates are as well rural as urban
based.

**Notable organizational features.** WWB chose to present its
organizational structure by the metaphor of a wheel. The development strategy of WWB revolves around the *capital fund.* The fund

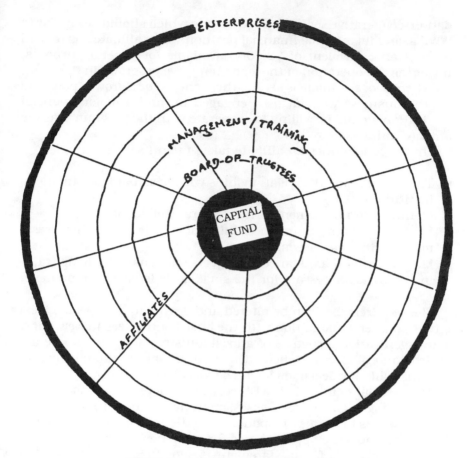

**FIGURE 5.** WWB's organizational structure.

was established through grants from international agencies, governments, and individuals and through the sale of debentures. The capital fund is intended to support WWB's operations with its interest earnings and to collaterize guarantees to local affiliates.

The capital fund is managed by the *board of trustees* which resides in New York, where also the headquarters of WWB is to be found. WWB/NY helps affiliates to establish themselves and to find international grant and soft loan funding, provides guarantees to support lines of credit from local commercial banks for affiliates and coordinates interaffiliates' coordination and communication.

Women in any country can set up a *local affiliate*. Each affiliate is required to conform with certain criteria set out by WWB/NY. Those criteria regard its legal status (i.e., cooperation, association, foundation, cooperative society), its objectives which should be similar to WWB's, and its minimal financial position. Each affiliate has to hold at least an equivalent of $20,000 available for general purposes, including the operation of the loan guarantee program. In the country where a local affiliate is set up, there should be a growth potential for the business women to be engaged in, and a major financial institution should be willing to cooperate with the program that the affiliate initiates.

The responsibilities an affiliate takes upon itself are:

- The establishment of relationships with local banks or financial institutions;
- Identification of women entreprencurs eligible for loans;
- Screening of applicants on viability of business and the assessment of financial needs;
- Monitoring and assistance to projects, such as organizing training activities necessary for the small-scale female entrepreneur.

The requirements can be altered and geared to the specific local situation after consultation with the board of trustees in New York. The organization structure of a local affiliate should be, above all, suited to local circumstances. Once an affiliate is established, all responsibility for decisions lie at the local level.

An essential element in WWB's continued development is the process of self-assessment. Self-assessment has been a mechanism for WWB affiliates to be more responsible, better informed and prepared to develop and seize opportunities for women entrepreneurs.

Each year a pro forma statement is sent to all affiliates asking them to review their yearly performance, develop goals and program priorities, and establish resource requirements and budgeting. It is an ongoing exercise in self-auditing and self-learning. It also engenders the development of new strategies, policies, procedures and a business plan for the following year.

**Orientation.** Not only the spirit of foundation and the self-organization practiced show a consequent alignment toward efforts of emancipation. The criteria for the selection of investment projects also imply considerable differences unusual in the trade.

WWB will attempt to avoid investments in companies considered to be negligent in the following areas of concern:

- Discrimination in employment, promotion, and training practices on the basis of sex, race, religion, color, national origin, marital status, or age.

- Excessive reliance on military projects.
- Foreign investments which support governments whose policies inhibit political and economic rights of any substantial social group.
- Pollution and/or destruction of the environment.
- Fraudulent marketing practices and/or the production of harmful goods and services.

## SUMMARY

What can we conclude from the above descriptions and hints? They could perhaps help in turning around the everyday assumptions about change and stability in organizations. That would mean that the question is no longer "is planned change possible and which ways are useful?" but rather "do I still need to consider organizations to be stable or do I allow myself to reconstruct and act in new ways?"

Obviously it is also possible to filter out common features from these examples: that is not at all difficult since features such as "dismantling of hierarchies," "networking of independent units," "confidence in individual initiative," "clear value-orientation," "use of varied metaphors," "openness," and so on, clearly emerge.

Exploring these common features further could obstruct the view of what is really essential. It would reinforce the impression that there really are such things as recepies, instruments and "right ways" to different, better, and more human organizations. It is equally impossible to have objective limits when an organization has begun to change or has already done so. It is nice to know that with the setting-up of the first cooperative in 1954, the foundations of the Mondragón-system were laid; or that the rebirth of Hanover Insurance was introduced by John Adams in 1969; or that the business association *Aktion Dritter Weg* was set up in 1977. These dates can no doubt be viewed as the birth of or transition to a new system. Perhaps it would also be useful—in the sense of this chapter—if other possible "punctuations" were considered. For example, if the germ cell for 'Mondragón' is located in the vocational school which was founded in 1943 or in the Basque cooperative attempts of the 1920s? (Tries at self-government were defeated during the Spanish Civil War. The collective experiences at that time possibly encouraged the later re-establishment of the autonomous firms.)

In the case of *Aktion Dritter Weg* we could discover, for example, that at least one member company—Compact Computer Systeme

**FIGURE 6.** And what does your mosaic of different organizations look like?

GmbH—has been founded 8 years earlier or that many of the founding members of the business association had already theoretical and practical experience of self-government and self-organization during the German student movement. From similar aspects, further interesting factors are to be found in the Hanover Insurance, WWB, and Gore descriptions which made them prime examples of ways to different organizations.

There is one thing that cannot be replaced by tessera or case examples: Everyone must create his own picture of ways to different organizations.

## REFERENCES

Adams, J. D. (1984). *Transforming work. A collection of organizational transformation.* Alexandria, VA: Miles River Press.

Adams, J. D. (1986). *Transforming leadership: From vision to results.* Alexandria, VA: Miles River Press.

Argyris, C. (1982). *Reasoning, learning and action: Individual and organizational.* San Francisco, CA: Jossey-Bass.

Argyris, C., & Schön, D. A. (1978). *Organizational learning: A theory of action perspective.* Reading, MA: Addison-Wesley.

Ashby, W. R. (1956). *An introduction to cybernetics.* London: Chapman & Hall.

Bader, M. (1986). *Criteria for self-management. Keeping work and income apart.* Unpublished manuscript, Goppingen, FRD.

Bateson, G. (1984). *Geist und natur. Eine notwendige Einheit.* Frankfurt: Suhrkamp.

Beer, S. (1966). *Decision and control.* London: Wiley.

de Bono, (1985). *Conflicts: A better way to resolve them.* London: Harrap.

*Caja Laboral Popular.* The Mondragon Experiment.

*Contraste.* (1983, January). *Zeitung für Selbstverwaltung, 10.*

Daft, R. L., & Weick, K. E. (1984). Toward a model of organizations as interpretation systems. *Academy of Management Review, 9*(2), 284–295.

Daft, R. L., & Wiginton, J. C. (1979). Language and organization. *Academy of Management Review, 4*(2), 179–191.

Dekker, H. (1987). *Credit and female entrepreneurship: The approach of women's world banking.* Netherlands: Free University of Amsterdam.

Dörner, D. (1976). *Problemlösen als Informationsverarbeitung.* Stuttgart: Kohlhammer.

Elias, N. (1983). *Engagement und Distanzierung.* Frankfurt: Suhrkamp.

Feyerabend, P. (1983). *Wider den Methodenzwang.* Frankfurt: Suhrkamp.

Flecker, J., Gubitzer, L., & Tödtling, F. (1984). Betriebliche Selbstverwaltung und eigenständige Regionalentwicklung am Beispiel der Genossenschaften von Mondragón. *Wirtschaft und Gesellschaft, 4.*

Flick, & Klein, G. (1987, January). Tonbandprotokoll des Vortages im Rahmen des "OT Symposiums". *Schloss Hernstein.*

Foerster, H., von. (1985). *Sicht und Einsicht.* Wiesbaden: Vieweg.

Glaserfeld, E., von. (1985). Konstruktion der Wirklichkeit und des Begriffs der Objektivität. In H. Gumin & A. Mohler (Eds.), *Einführung in den Konstruktivismus.* Munich, West Germany.

Gubitzer, L. (1987, January). Mondragón. Tonbandprotokoll eines Vortrages im Rahmen des "OT Symposiums". *Schloss Hernstein.*

Hampden-Turner, C. (1983). *Modelle des Menschen. Ein Handbuch des menschlichen Bewusstseins.* Weinheim: Beltz.

Hedberg, B. L. T. (1981). How organizations learn and unlearn. In P. Nystrom & W. H. Starbuck (Eds.), *Handbook of organizational design.* New York: McGraw-Hill.

Heil, P. M. (1981). *Sozialwissenschaft als Theorie selbstreferentieller Systeme.* Frankfurt: Campus.

Heil, P. M. (1984). Towards a theory of social systems: Self-organization and self-maintenance, self-reference and syn-reference. In H. Ulrich & G. J. B. Probst (Eds.), *Self-organization and management of social systems.* Heidelberg: Springer.

Jantsch, E. (1975a). *Design for evolution: Self-organization and planning in the life of human systems.* New York: Braziller.

Jantsch, E. (1975b). *Design for evolution.* New York: Braziller.

Jantsch, E. (1979). *Die Selbstorganisation des Universums.* Munich: Hanser.

Kelly, G. A. (1955). *The Psychology of personal constructs.* New York: W. W. Norton.

Kiefer, C., & Senge, P. (1984). Metanoic organizations. *Organizational dynamics.* New York: Springer.

Klein, E. (1986, November). Die Aufgabe eines Personalkoordinators (W. L. Gore ed.). Interview in Putzbrunn, Munich.

Löbl, E. (1975). *Wirtschaft am Wendepunkt.* Cologne: Achberg.

Luhmann, N. (1984). Soziale systeme. *Grundriss einer allgemeinen Theorie.* Frankfurt: Suhrkamp.

Malik, F. (1984). *Strategie des Managements komplexer Systeme. Ein Beitrag zur Management-Kybernetik evolutionärer Systeme.* Stuttgart: Hauft.

Massarik, F. (1983). Seeking essence in executive mind: A phenomenological view. *The functioning of the executive mind.* San Francisco, CA: Jossey-Bass.

Maturana, H. R. (1985). *Erkennen: Die Organisation und Verkörperung von Wirklichkeit.* Wiesbaden: Braunschweig.

Maturana, H. R., & Varela, F. J. (1987). *Der Baum der Erkenntnis.* Munich: Bern.

Miller, E. J., & Rice, A. K. (1973). *Systems of organization. The control of task and the sentinent boundaries.* London: Tavistock.

Morgan, G. (1986). *Images of organization.* Beverly Hills, CA: Sage.

Nystrom, P. C., & Starbuck, W. H. (1984). To avoid organizational crises, unlearn. *Organizational dynamics*, pp. 53–65.

Piaget, J. (1973). *Einfürung in die genetische Erkenntnistheorie*. Frankfurt.

Prigogine, I. (1985). *Vom Sein zum Werden. Zeit und Komplexitat in den Naturwissenschaften*. Munich: Piper.

Probst, G. J. B. (1981). *Gesetzeshypothesen als Basis für Gestaltungs- und Lenkungsregeln im Management*. Bern: Haupt.

Riedl, R. (1985). *Evolution und Erkenntnis. Antworten auf Fragen aus unserer Zeit*. Zurich: Piper.

Saake, R. (1986). Aktion Dritter Weg. Ein Modellversuch. In M. V. Limbacher (Ed.), *Projekt Antroposophie. Denn das Leben verlangt eine Verwandlung unseres Denkens*. Hamburg.

Senge, P. M. (1985). *System dynamics, mental models and the development of management intuition*. Cambridge, MA: System Dynamics Group, MIT Press.

Smith, G. L., & Tippet, B. A. (1985). *Evaluation of women's world banking*. USAID report. International Science and Technology Institute, Inc., MA.

Spencer, B. G. (1969). *Laws of form*. London.

Steiner, R. (1977). *Geisteswissenschaft und Soziale Frage*. Dornach.

Stichting WWB Nederland. (1986). *Overview of the Stichting to promote WWB*. Utrecht.

Tannenbaum, R., Marguilies, N., & Massarik, F. (1985). *Human Systems Development*. San Francisco, CA: Jossey-Bass.

Touraine, A. (1977). *The self-production of society*. Chicago: University of Chicago Press.

Trist, E. L., Higgin, G. W., Murray, H., & Pollack, A. B. (1963). *Organizational choice*. London: Tavistock.

Ulrich, H., & Probst, G. J. B. (Eds.). (1984). *Self-organization and management of social systems*. Heidelgerg: Springer.

van Haagen-Baas, M. (1987, January). *Women's world banking. Fallbeispiel fur Organisationen im Wandel*. Prasentationspapier im Rahmen des "OT Symposiums" in Schloss Hernstein.

Ven, A. van der, & Joyce, W. F. (1981). *Perspectives on organizational design and behavior*. New York: Leicht veranderte Ausgabe von Trist.

Videointerview mit Mitgliedern der Aktion 3. (1986, September). *Weg in Goppingen*.

Walsh, M. (1986). Women's role in management and industrialization. *RVB Research Papers*, 7. Netherlands: Delft.

Watzlawick, P. (Ed.). (1985). *Die erfundene Wirklichkeit. Wie wissen wir was wir zu wissen glauben?* Munich.

Watzlawick, P., Weakland, J. H., & Fisch, R. (1974). Lösungen. *Zur Theorie und Praxis menschlichen Handelns*. Bern: Huber.

Weisbord, M. R. (1987). *The productive community. How people find dignity and meaning in the workplace*. San Francisco, CA: Josscy-Bass.

Westerlund, G., & Sjöstrand, S. E. (1981). *Organisationsmythen.* Stuttgart: Klett-Cotta.

Winograd, T., & Flores, F. (1986). *Understanding computers and cognition: A new foundation for design.* Norwood, NJ: Ablex.

Women's World Bank. (1985). *Annual report,* New York.

# 12

# Catalyzing Systems Thinking within Organizations*

**Peter M. Senge**
*Sloan School of Management, MIT*

Managers live in a world that is dynamic and highly interconnected, where causality is typically nonobvious, and where obvious solutions often result in more harm than good. The characteristic ways of approaching problems, especially in most management teams, assume that the world is static (that a one-time intervention will result in a one-time change), that problems are separable, that causality is relatively straightforward, and that obvious solutions, given sufficient commitment and energy, will produce predictable improvements. This mismatch, between the nature of reality and the predominant ways of thinking about reality, lies at the heart of why organizations do not learn effectively.

Over the past several years, we have been involved in a variety of experiments that focused on designing learning processes to enhance quality of thinking in management teams.[1] We have been especially interested in learning processes that improve the operating policies and strategies in running a business. Lying behind every strategy is a worldview or "mental model," a set of assumptions about the organization, its products, its customers, and its competitors. An effective learning process starts with bringing those assumptions into the open. Then, we help managers in conceptualizing how forces within and outside the organization interact to

---

* I am indebted to the many colleagues involved in the research reported herein, especially to Nathan Forrester, who collaborated in the case study, and Jennifer Kemeny and Barry Richmond, with whom I have collaborated on similar projects. However, I am solely responsible for the views expressed in this chapter.

[1] This research is part of the Program in Systems Thinking and Organizational Learning. The purpose of the program is to work in partnership with a group of corporations to explore the tools, process, and organizational conditions for developing systems thinking. The corporations involved in the program include Analog Devices Inc., Apple Computer, Ford, Hanover Insurance, Herman Miller, Polaroid, Shell International, and Trammell Crow.

shape business conditions, eventually developing simulations and games so that managers can recreate the dynamics as these interactions play out over time. The intended outcomes of such learning processes are improved mental models, better strategies and operating policies, and explicit theories of business dynamics that can stimulate learning throughout an organization.

Research into managerial learning processes fills an important void in current efforts to improve organizational effectiveness. In recent years, many organizations have worked to clarify their missions, visions, and values. Many have attempted to reorganize into leaner, more locally controlled and market-responsive structures. Yet, all too often the core operating (as opposed to espoused) policies that control organizational behavior have remained unchanged. The reason for this lack of change is that the thinking that lies behind such policies has remained unchanged. Learning processes such as those described below are a powerful complement to clarifying mission, vision, and values because they lead to a rethinking of how business policies and strategies must be altered to achieve new desired results. They are also essential to consistent and harmonious actions across diverse, locally controlled business units. Take away such learning processes, and I believe that sincere efforts to instill new management practices will often lead to frustration and cynicism rather than to fundamental and lasting improvements.

This research also addresses important questions in strategic management, especially in implementing new strategies that break with traditional habits, norms, and assumptions. Here, too, I believe that the problem often lies with failing to recognize the importance of prevailing mental models. New strategies are the outgrowth of new world views. The more profound the change in strategy, the deeper must be the change in thinking. *In fact, one can argue that evolving the mental models of managers is the fundamental task of strategic management:*

> The choice of individual courses of action is only part of the manager's or policymaker's need. More important is the need to achieve insight into the nature of the complexity (being addressed) and to formulate concepts and world views for coping with it. (Mason & Mitroff, 1981, p. 16)
> Strategies are the product of a worldview . . . the basis for success or failure is the microcosm of the decision makers: their inner model of reality, their set of assumptions that structure their understanding of the unfolding business environment and the factors critical to success. . . .When the world changes, managers need to share some common view of the new world. (Wack, 1985, p. 89, 150)

Learning processes that will have the most enduring benefit for an organization will influence not only *what* managers think but their predominant *ways of thinking,* helping to evolve more systemic, dynamic worldviews. This means not only changing the *content* of shared mental models, but the *organizing principles* of such models. Organization development professionals have long advocated a systems perspective on organizational change. Likewise, a recent strategic management text begins by calling for a more dynamic perspective and criticizing. "The essentially static nature of . . . earlier work . . . (which neglected) time, second order effects and feedback loops . . . the ingredients for the insightful analysis that was needed to move the field of strategy its next step forward (Lorange, Scott Morton, & Ghoshal, 1986, p. xviii).

The challenge now lies in moving from theory to practice. What is needed are specific tools and replicable processes for helping managers rethink their world. The research presented in this chapter offers one step in this direction. A general three-step process for organizing a "systems thinking learning process" is presented. A case study then illustrates how the process might be carried out, some of the existing tools that can be used, and the types of insights and changes that can result. After examining this particular case, we will step back and reflect on some basic questions concerning how to make the organizational "soil" more fertile for systems thinking, how to improve the "seeds" (specific learning processes) trying to take root in that soil, and the potential of such learning processes in developing more effective organizations.

## CREATING SYSTEMS THINKING LEARNING PROCESSES

The purpose of a systems thinking learning process is to help managers to (1) see through the superficial symptoms into the underlying causes of problems, (2) reorganize perceptions into a clearer, more coherent picture of business dynamics that can be more effectively communicated, and (3) create tools that can accelerate the learning of others.

We have experimented with many alternative processes to catalyze systems thinking within management teams, but all can be broken down into three basic stages.[2]

---

[2] The following description makes no effort to provide detailed directions for carrying out a systems thinking learning process. For a more detailed description see B. Richmond, "The Strategic Forum," High Performance Systems, Inc., Lyme, NH.

- Mapping mental models
- Challenging mental models
- Improving mental models

I believe that these stages represent a generic learning sequence applicable to both the individual and the group.

The particular tools utilized in this research draw on the "system dynamics" methodology developed originally at MIT (Forrester, 1961; Roberts, 1978). The system dynamics approach involves developing feedback models to show how current policies and structure influence behavior in complex human and social systems. The method has been applied to understand corporate, urban, regional, national, and global policy issues. Frequently it has shown how pressing problems were being exacerbated by the very managerial policies intended to solve them. Such policies tend to produce "better for worse behavior," relieving symptoms in the short run only to leave underlying stresses unaltered or even worse in the long run (Forrester, 1971; Meadows, 1982).

The chief limitation in past applications of tools such as system dynamics is that the models are constructed by expert consultants, who then attempt to explain their operation to managers. Even when this process results in improved decisions, it rarely alters the way managers think. By contrast, this research attempts to develop an explicit learning process aimed at evolving the mental models of managers. In this process we try to make the managers the "model builders" to a far greater extent than in most prior work.

### Mapping Mental Models

Mapping mental models involves making explicit the present set of guiding ideas in managing the business. This includes the management team's initial strategic objectives and strategies—the team's espoused goals and the means they assume necessary for attaining these goals. The mapping phase also involves helping the team represent, or "map," managers' views of "the system" they are trying to manage.

The learning process starts with current objectives and strategies because these provide an initial glimpse of the prevailing mental models guiding management of the business. Strategic objectives reflect what people currently think is achievable in particular time frames. Strategies reveal assumed areas of high leverage in attaining objectives. As the learning process unfolds, both assumptions will be challenged, so it is important that they be made explicit at the outset.

It is also important at this stage to get people talking about their doubts and perceived issues or problems with the current strategy. One problem with the typical statements of strategic objectives and strategies is that they suppress the variation in viewpoint that is normally present in a management team. Airing doubts and reservations surfaces differing views. Often, minority views reflect important aspects of the system that are neglected in the strategy. Yet, team members are often reticent about bringing perceived problems into the open, especially those that have been discussed in the past, because they don't want to be viewed as "negative."

Doubts and criticisms of the strategy may be brought to the surface by simply getting the group to identify major business issues or potential barriers or problems they foresee. Another technique that we have found especially useful for airing unexpressed reservations and doubts is to have the team prepare several possible scenarios. One scenario, the one closest to most teams' espoused view of the world, should be a "high success" scenario. Such a scenario traces out over time what will happen as their strategy unfolds "according to plan." Then, the team members are asked to prepare individually or in small groups a "failure" or, if that is too disconcerting, a "low success" scenario. Presenting their failure scenarios inevitably turns out to be a rich source of data about business assumptions that may not be evident in the official strategy. From a process standpoint, this exercise also allows joint acknowledgment of fears and uncertainty that clears the air for subsequent inquiry.

We have used several tools to begin helping a team to map the interdependencies that characterize their business world. One especially useful approach has been the construction of a "big picture" diagram that maps the primary physical *flows* of materials, labor, customers, and products, and identifies the major *policies* that control these flows. Such a map provides a context for discussing the team's strategy and beginning to draw out some of the assumptions behind the strategy (Figure 1 shows an example).[3] Another mapping tool is the "policy structure diagram." This diagram focuses on a particular policy, such as hiring or capital investment, and facilitates a discussion of the goals, types of information, pressures, and constraints that affect how this particular decision is actually made (see Figure 2). The policy structure diagram leads to a "microlevel"

---

[3] See Richmond (1987) for a discussion on how to develop and use "big picture" diagrams.

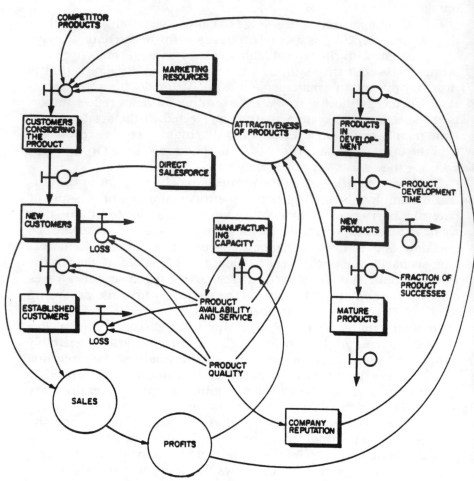

**FIGURE 1. A Typical "Big Picture" Diagram**

The "big picture" lays out the primary physical flows of materials, labor, customers, and products and identifies the major policies that control these flows. The purpose of such a diagram is to create an initial visual backdrop for discussing a team's present strategy.

The example shown here depicts (1) the flow of developing new customers and the way company resources (manufacturing capacity, direct salesforce and marketing) influence customer development, and (2) the flow of new product development as influenced by profits, product development time, and the fraction of product successes. This diagram helps to interrelate policies for investment in manufacturing capacity, new products, salesforce, and marketing.

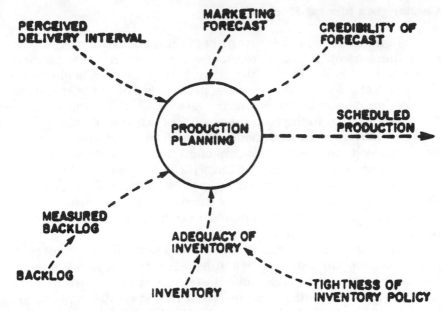

**FIGURE 2. A Typical Policy Structure Diagram**

The policy structure diagram focuses on a single decision area. The purpose of such a diagram is to help managers reflect on the information inputs to a decision, and the goals, pressures, and constraints that influence how this decision *is actually made* in the firm. The policy structure diagram helps to ground discussions of strategy in the operating realities of the business and identify potentially important issues in how new strategies might be operationalized.

The example shown here, showing the types of information that influence production planning, would focus a discussion on how production schedules are actually set, and how production policy may or may not be consistent with overall strategic objectives like customer service, cost ratios, and abilities to serve growing or changing markets.

discussion that complements the "macro" discussion stimulated by the "big picture."[4]

In the initial mapping stage, there is no intent to expose short-comings or to explore poorly defined areas in prevailing mental models. The objectives are simply to make prevailing assumptions more explicit and to begin to engage the managers in a dialogue around their current worldviews. Problems with current mental models become evident as the systems thinking process continues.

---

[4] Policy structure diagrams are discussed at length in J. D. W. Morecroft (1984).

## Challenging Mental Models

Challenging mental models means beginning to reveal internal contradictions, inconsistencies, or incompletenesses in prevailing mental models. This is the juncture when team members begin to see
that the real purposes of a learning process is not to figure out the
system "out there" but to examine more deeply the world we carry
"in here," that is, to improve the quality of our own thinking.

The challenge to mental models arises from examining assumptions in a systemic light. Managers often have accurate perceptions
of the pieces of the systems within which they operate, but fail to
appreciate what happens when the pieces interact. We may assert
that "when A and B interact C is the outcome," yet discover that
when A and B are built into a model according to our specifications
the outcome is different from C.

In this stage, participants are introduced to the discipline of computer modeling through constructing and exercising simple simulation models that begin to examine the feasibility of the current strategy. The type of questions addressed at this stage are "Can we get
there from here?" and "Are our strategic objectives internally consistent over the target time period?" We often call the models constructed in this stage "reality check" or "consistency check" models
because they are aimed at discerning glaring inconsistencies or
overlooked dynamics that will obviously bear on the success of the
team's strategy.

The challenging mental models stage is delicate because for the
first time in the learning process the managers' assumptions will be
called into question. This has several important implications. If
trust and openness in the group are not well established, individuals may be threatened and react defensively. Defensive reactions
may be sophisticated and difficult to recognize, such as "This is all
quite clear," or "Yes, I understand." Or, the defensive reactions may
take the form of attacks on the models or the modeling process. For
this reason, we often find it useful to do some preliminary work with
the team members on recognizing defensive routines and assuming
responsibility for dealing with one's own felt threat in a learning
situation.[5]

It is important also that the team members have a high level of
ownership of the simulation models used. A good "reality check"

---

[5] There are several approaches for helping individuals in work team settings to
improve their capacity for inquiry and learning. See, for example, Argyris (1982),
Dyer (1987), and Schein (1969).

model is simple: The managers participating in the process should be able to construct the model themselves in a short period of time.[6] This means that the model will be built up from pieces that are well understood. Simplicity also dictates that the model contain few feedback processes. Multiple feedback effects, which account for much of the surprising behavior of complex systems, appear to be largely unrecognized in most managers' mental models. But, the model must be complex enough to yield new insights. Typically, an effective reality check model will have one or two feedback relations that have gone unrecognized or unappreciated in the present strategy.

## Improving Mental Models

Improving mental models means the ongoing, open-ended process of explicating, testing, and revising managerial assumptions. In this stage, the team members are creating new constructs and worldviews, and assessing the consistency of their own policies and behavior in the light of new understandings.

In this stage, the team is drawn into a conceptualizing process to expand the simple reality check models and identify a variety of potentially important feedback dynamics. We often call this the "closing the loops" phase because more and more of the feedback dynamics of the real system are examined.

This stage is inherently open-ended and can continue for a considerable period of time. The key to its success lies in identifying what system dynamicists call "dynamic hypotheses." A dynamic hypothesis explains a particular problematical pattern of behavior in terms of specific feedback interactions. At this stage, the group begins to develop and test its own theories of the dynamics crucial to their business.

Improving mental models also involves testing the effects of changes in policy and structure. Alternative policies may come from initiatives previously under consideration by the management team. As the learning process progresses, new initiatives and interventions are identified and tested. The important feature of the process is the *discipline* imposed by the modeling process. New initiatives must be translated into specific changes in policy and

---

6 This requires a modeling software that non-technical managers can understand very easily. The software used in this research is called STELLA and allows construction of dynamic simulation models at a screen of a personal computer with advanced graphics capabilities. It is available from High Performance Systems, Inc., Lyme, NH.

structure, and the effects must be tested and understood. None of this *guarantees* that the models constructed by the team predict what would occur if the initiative were implemented. But, it does guarantee that the assumptions behind a new strategy or policy initiative will be explicit and well thought out, and that they will be subject to continued testing and improvement.

Eventually, putting new ideas and policies into practice will require that many in the organization become part of the learning process. This may be done through case studies, management games, or other learning tools based on insights developed by the management team. Whatever the tools, the basic stages of mapping, challenging, and improving mental models remain intact.

It is also important to keep in mind that the full benefits of an effective learning process may occur only over a considerable period of time. New conceptual perspectives are assimilated gradually, often stimulated by ongoing processes of dialogue and debate among managers. Eventually, new perspectives lead to new perceptions. New actions may come relatively quickly or await new circumstances conducive to new actions. As will be illustrated below, one consequence is that it may be difficult to trace the precise evolution of new ideas and new policies that might have germinated in a systems thinking learning process. The formal process is best thought of as catalyzing a larger, more diverse organizational learning process, gently nudging managers toward seeing their world in a more systemic and dynamic way.

## A CASE STUDY: CLAIMS MANAGEMENT AT HANOVER INSURANCE

The following case description is synthesized from a series of working sessions that occurred over about a year. There were more than 20 working sessions, averaging 2 hours each, involving the vice president for claims and two who reported to him directly. A large number of issues were explored; those that are reported here provide a good example of the style and content of the sessions.

### Background

The Hanover Insurance Companies were purchased by State Mutual in 1969 with the intent of expanding State Mutual's business into property and liability lines in the Northeast and Midwest. At the time of purchase, Hanover was at the bottom of its industry. Financial performance was extremely poor. Morale and commitment were low. Management lacked a clear direction for improvement. Jack Adam was brought in from State Mutual to be president of Hanover with a mandate to do whatever was necessary to make the company competitive. Adam, along with his eventual successor William O'Brien, saw the organization as an opportunity to try out new ideas that he had been developing throughout a career in the insurance industry, but which were difficult to implement in successful businesses with little motivation to change. Clearly, if ever fundamental change were needed, it was at Hanover.

Over the ensuing 15 years, Adam and O'Brien developed a business philosophy rooted in the core values of openness, localness, and merit. Openness meant an environment of honesty, forthrightness, and inquiry. Openness demanded of managers that they recognize their own defensiveness and games playing when confronted with embarrassing or threatening situations. Openness was intended as the antidote to the internal politics that dominate most large corporations. Localness meant that no decision should ever be made at a higher level than absolutely necessary. Localness implied a relatively flat organization with local business units—in this case, local offices and regional branches—with the resources to exercise general management responsibilities. Merit meant an environment where "conclusions, decisions, and rewards focus on the attainment of the organization's purpose and vision in a way that is consistent with its values." For Adam and O'Brien, merit meant that business decisions should be based on all pertinent facts and information and on managers' continual willingness to test decisions with others.

Adam and O'Brien found that not all of Hanover's managers were prepared for the new ground rules. During the first several years, turnover among Hanover's more traditional managers ran high. But, eventually, a fairly high level of commitment to the core values developed throughout the organization. Management seminars based on the core values became established. Sessions at the national and local levels focused on applying the values to business issues. Eventually, skill development programs around openness and mentoring were established for all levels of management. In parallel to the work on core values, Adam and O'Brien wrote and talked extensively with Hanover's managers about the organization's basic mission and purpose.

While a philosophy to work by was being established, the organization's reporting structure was being gradually streamlined and its business direction clarified. Eventually, a level of regional management was eliminated altogether and replaced with "internal boards" designed to make local managers able to function as autonomous general managers. Out of the work on purpose and mission, an overarching business vision eventually emerged. This vision was one of unquestioned superiority in the property and liability industry, a vision that would have had no credibility in 1969. But, by the end of the 1970s, Hanover was consistently in the upper half of its industry.

Today, Hanover's profitability consistently ranks in the upper quarter of the property and liability industry. Over the past 10 years the company has grown 50% faster than the industry as a whole. Moreover, many in the organization espouse the view that business success is linked to the development of a more open, creative work environment.

Interest in systems thinking at Hanover is an outgrowth of continuing efforts to develop management skills commensurate with the overall management philosophy. Beginning in 1982, a 1-week program, "Thinking about Thinking," was established to introduce managers at all levels to subtle thinking habits which compromise openness and inquiry. The program, taught by a retired philosophy professor from the University of New Hampshire, helps managers to appreciate how desires for simplistic explanations and quick-fix solutions are rooted in reductionistic scientific philosophies underlying much modern education. The program also provides an introduction to systems thinking as an alternative scientific philosophy, one which emphasizes interconnectedness and continuous change.

Thus, there was already interest in systems thinking within Hanover when the company joined our research program at MIT. It was decided that a logical starting place for a systems thinking learning process would be in claims management. There was a widely shared feeling that dollar settlements on claims, at Hanover and throughout the property and liability industry, were significantly in excess of fair and just settlements. Moreover, improved settlement processes might have considerable leverage on overall business performance, since claims settlements constitute more than 60% of total corporate expenditures.

But, there were also reasons to question if Hanover could do much to improve its claims performance. Many felt that the causes for excessive settlement costs lay outside Hanover's control. Competitors were having the same or worse difficulties. The prevailing attitude throughout the industry was that rising settlement costs were due to erosion in ethical standards throughout society, accompanied by aggressive lawyers and increased willingness to litigate. If Hanover had any leverage, some thought, it may lay only in overriding its values of openness and localness with more vigorous national cost controls, to pressure adjusters toward lower settlements. Obviously, such an approach was disdained by the claims management.

## Getting Started: What is the Strategy? The Current Mental Models

At the first meeting of the claims management team, the team provided an initial statement of strategic objectives, strategies, and perceived barriers facing the organization. Given Hanover's emphasis on vision and values, it was not surprising that the claims management team began with a very clear idea of its vision and how it wanted to see the basic values of the larger organization operate within the claims organization. Moreover, the group appeared to have a high level of openness and mutual trust, reflecting several years of working together in an environment that places a premium on these characteristics.

In their vision statement, the management team stated their intent to be pre-eminent among claims organizations in the insurance industry. Their vision was summarized in the phrase "fair, fast, and friendly." They wanted to provide fair settlements of customers' claims, prompt attention to new claims, and to treat customers well. They discussed at length their image of the ideal claims adjuster: one who is capable of conducting thorough professional investigations, has excellent communication skills, keeps neat and complete file records, and is able to educate claimants regarding the fair value of their claims, while at the same time being able to detect those with the slightest fraudulent inclinations. We joked a little about the claims adjuster who "walks on water," but it was clear that the group held very high expectations for the types of adjusters they sought to attract and develop within Hanover.

This initial statement of strategic objectives identified 10 different measures of performance, including productivity measures such as the "production ratio" (number of claims settled relative to new incoming claims), as well as subtler objectives such as quality investigation and "vigorous oversight of litigation." The team then elaborated 12 different strategies to accomplish its strategic objectives. Three quarters of the strategies were concerned with developing adjuster capacity and litigation management. As it turned out, this reflected a shared assumption that building a corps of outstanding adjusters and improving litigation management were keys to achieving their strategic objectives.

When asked to discuss the barriers and problems they perceived with their strategy, the vice president began to talk about what the team called the "balls in the air" problem, the challenge of simultaneously keeping many performance standards on target, like a juggler. Their experience had been that, whenever emphasis was increased on a particular objective, such as settlement size, progress on that objective was accomplished at the expense of backsliding on some other objectives. The team also saw barriers to success being that investigations needed to be more thorough, adjusters were too concerned with not looking bad, adjuster turnover was high (although it was falling), service was inconsistent, and prestige of adjusters within Hanover and the entire industry was low. They were also concerned that their attorneys were not taking enough litigated cases to trial and that responsibility for litigation management was too diffuse.

The initial discussion of the current strategy illustrated what we are coming to see as two general characteristics of nonsystemic thinking—formulating strategic objectives and strategies at the same level of abstraction and ignoring interconnections among strategic objectives. "Strategies" are often simply subobjectives, which it is assumed are necessary to accomplish in order to achieve the overarching strategic objectives. For example, at Hanover the strategies "hire better people" and "increase field experience and exposure of adjusters" are subobjectives assumed important to accomplish the strategic objective of "building adjuster capacity." As they are commonly expressed, strategies lack operational depth. They fail to explain why present difficulties arose and fail to provide a clear picture of what will actually have to happen in order for strategic objectives to be achieved.

The other problem with common formulations of strategic objectives and strategies is that they are "laundry lists." The 12 strategies stated by the Hanover team ignored the interdependencies among different strategies. In fact, one of the reasons for beginning a learning process with listing elements of the current strategy is to create a record of the *form* as well as the substance of the current mental models guiding the business. The "strategy laundry list" suggests an image of a business as a set of separate processes and problems to be resolved by separate and distinct initiatives. In fact, our experience is that managers are keenly aware of interdependencies. But, they lack a *language* for expressing and examining how different problems are interrelated and how different strategic initiatives will interact.

To begin piecing together some of the elements in the strategic puzzle a simplified "Big Picture" diagram was produced to summarize the discussions of strategic objectives, strategies, and possible barriers (Figure 3). The diagram highlighted major dimensions of the claims management system as they saw it: the adjusting process, including litigation and subrogation (retrieving payment from other insurers), adjuster capacity, including hiring and training, and the interaction of capacity and the adjusting process. The diagram served as a way to summarize the discussion of strategies by pointing to the different parts of the "claims system" those strategies were intended to influence.

Out of this dialogue the team decided what specific issues it wanted to examine more deeply. The team decided that the first step was to look more closely at the nature of adjuster capacity, and that we would eventually return to the more complex questions of how capacity interacted with the adjusting process.

## Initial Reality Check Models: Challenging the Mental Models

The first reality check model focused on building adjuster capacity. Discussions had revealed that the number of adjusters has been expanding at about a 30% annual rate for several years to keep pace with rapid growth in claims. Such high personnel growth rates invariably stress alignment and productivity. The first strategic objective stated was "maintain 100% production ratio (claims settled relative to incoming claims). So, continuing high growth in incoming claims suggested continued high growth in new hires.

The model distinguished new adjusters from experienced adjusters (see Figure 4). Initially, the team made a simple assumption that new adjusters were 30% as effective as experienced adjusters. We also asked the team to estimate how long it took to develop an experienced adjuster and the average time an experienced adjuster stays in that position. Once these numerical assumptions were established by the team, it became possible to examine how overall "effective adjuster capacity" would be affected by different growth rates in adjuster hiring.

The simple adjuster capacity model quickly showed the difference between overall growth in numbers of adjusters and growth in effective adjuster capacity. In particular, the more rapidly new adjusters are hired, the greater the difference between numbers of total ad-

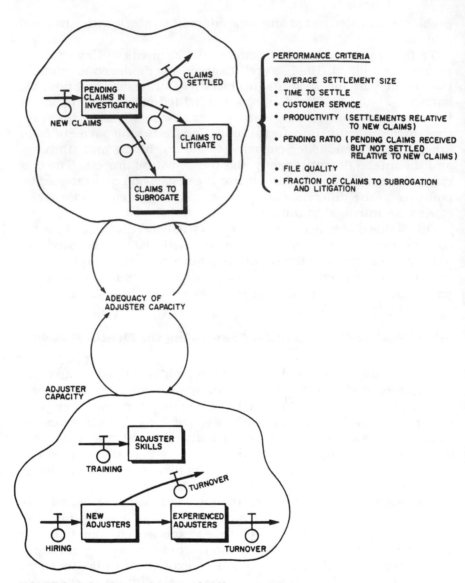

**FIGURE 3. A Big Picture Diagram for Claims Management**

The big picture for claims management highlighted the adjusting process, adjuster capacity, and their interaction through the adequacy of adjuster capacity. If adjuster capacity is inadequate, claims may build up in pending, average settlement size may increase, or other performance criteria may erode. If adjuster capacity is in surplus, costs are too high and work habits may deteriorate. Adjuster capacity is continually changing (through hiring, turnover, and training) in response to pressures from the adequacy of adjuster capacity.

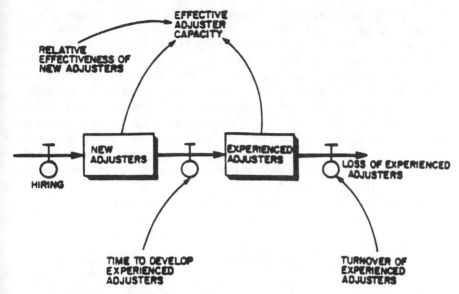

**FIGURE 4. Initial Reality Check Model**

The first reality check model distinguished new adjusters from experienced adjusters. When simulated, it showed that the more rapidly new adjusters are hired, the greater the proportion of new adjusters in the total adjuster pool. At high rates of hiring, as Hanover had experienced in recent years, effective adjuster capacity grew more slowly than total numbers of adjusters.

justers and effective adjuster capacity. The reason lies in the different effectiveness levels of new adjusters and experienced adjusters. The more rapidly new adjusters are hired, the larger the proportion of new adjusters relative to experienced adjusters, and consequently, the slower the growth in adjuster capacity.

The model began to raise questions regarding whether desired growth in adjuster capacity could be achieved merely through hiring new adjusters. This immediately led to a discussion of subtler aspects of developing experienced adjusters, a subject of deep concern to all members of the team. The need for improved training was discussed, as was the high turnover in experienced adjusters. The possibility that internal organization within claims offices might impede the development of new adjusters was also discussed. Clearly, the adjuster capacity model illuminated fundamental difficulties in building capacity.

But the most important insight from the adjuster capacity model came when one of the team members criticized the way the initial model lumped new adjusters and experienced adjusters into "effective adjuster capacity." He pointed out that there is no one single adjuster capacity, but different types of capacity for dealing with different types of claims. After discussing these criticisms, we decided to distinguish "simple claims capacity" from "complex claims capacity." While this distinction clearly oversimplified the many types of claims, it helped to differentiate the type of work assigned typically to new adjusters from that assigned to experienced adjusters. The team agreed that almost all complex claims were handled by experienced adjusters. Conversely, new adjusters dealt primarily with simple claims. This led to a revised model that linked "simple claims capacity" and "complex claims capacity" to the respective types of adjusters (see Figure 5).

We then simulated the revised adjuster capacity model with his-

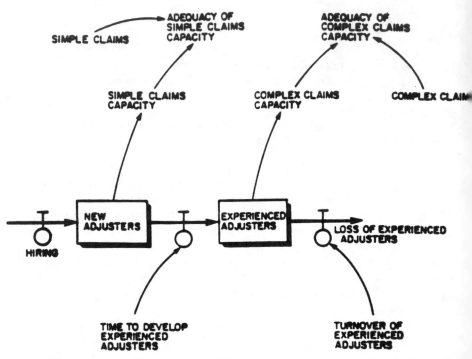

**FIGURE 5. Revised Reality Check Model**

The initial reality check model was revised to further distinguish capacity for adjusting simple claims from capacity for adjusting complex claims. The resulting model revealed a connection between rapid growth and difficulties dealing with complex claims. When total numbers of adjusters are being expanded rapidly, complex claims capacity expands more slowly than simple claims capacity because of disproportionate numbers of new adjusters.

torical rates of adjuster hiring and incoming claims. The team estimated the number of new adjusters hired per year over the past several years and the number of incoming claims, broken down into simple claims and complex claims. The resulting simulations showed consistently inadequate complex claims capacity. That is, the number of complex claims grew more rapidly than the capacity to handle complex claims. Inadequate complex claims capacity persisted for a variety of assumptions regarding hires, claims, and time to develop experienced adjusters. At this point, the team member who had originally suggested the model revision, proclaimed, "This is exactly what we have experienced; we are losing money because of inadequate capacity to deal with complex claims."

The ensuing discussion led to a refined statement of the original problem that motivated our project, perceived overpayment on settlements. Reflecting on the dynamics of the revised capacity model, the team felt strongly that much of the overpayment came from inability to deal with complex claims. In light of the fact that adjusters had been expanding at 30% per year over the past 3–5 years, it now became clear that the rapid personnel growth led inevitably to a disproportionate influx of new adjusters, relatively fewer experienced adjusters, and problems in handling complex claims.

The adjuster capacity models illustrate the benefits of simple reality check models. First, these simple models allow the managers themselves quickly to become part of the modeling process. In fact, a change in the initial model that led to important new insights was proposed by a team member, not by the technical facilitators. Second, the simple reality check models provided new perspectives on the group's strategic objectives. As a result of working with the adjuster capacity models, the group came to appreciate the subtleties in building adjuster capacity, especially when overall rates of growth are high. From this point onward, whenever capacity problems were discussed, there was a shared awareness that growing capacity and hiring new adjusters were not synonymous.

Lastly, the team discovered how its policies might be contributing to its strategic problems. Prior to this, the claims managers appreciated intellectually the systems precept that the "system produces its own behavior." But, seeing how their rapid hiring may have exacerbated overpayments on complex claims truly captured their interest and planted the first seed in developing a systems perspective on claims management.

Seeing how present policies may be contributing to present problems can be threatening. The mental models lying behind present policies are called into question. The adjuster capacity models were successful tools for challenging mental models because they were simple and understood by the managers involved, and because they were subject to being manipulated by the managers themselves. They succeeded in introducing the claims managers to dynamic models as learning tools.

## Closing the Loops: Improving Mental Models

Through simple reality check models (of which there were others in addition to the adjuster capacity models) the team learned to apply the modeling discipline to examine pieces of the claims system. This naturally led to the desire to begin putting the pieces together to examine policy alternatives within the entire adjuster capacity-claims adjusting system. Variables that had been defined as external in the simpler models, such as pending claims to adjust, were to become part of the "system."

The simple adjuster capacity models had sensitized the team members to the possibility that adjuster capacity was inadequate. This led to revealing questions such as "Are there ways in which the system compensates for inadequate capacity so as to mask the need for developing additional capacity?" and "What are the signals that indicate that capacity is adequate when in fact it might not be?"

Discussions over several meetings focused on interactions among adjuster capacity, claims adjusting, and performance standards. Several preliminary models were developed during these discussions. Finally, a hypothesis began to emerge.

The key to the hypothesis lay in distinguishing two classes of performance measures: "*production standards*" and "*fuzzy standards.*" Production standards are measures such as "production ratio" and "pending ratio," which indicate whether current claims pending are being settled at a rate commensurate with the inflow of new incoming claims. The production standards are relatively easy to measure, are understood by everyone in the business, and send out clear immediate warning signals when they become out of balance. The fuzzy standards include quality of investigation, file quality, effective oversight of litigation and subrogation, and service quality. The fuzzy standards are difficult to measure. Though there is widespread appreciation that the fuzzy standards are important, the team felt that there is usually considerable uncertainty as to how well a claims office is doing on the "fuzzies." Because they are easier to measure, the team felt that there were natural pressures to manage by the production measures. As the vice-president put it, "In this business there are lots of ways to look good without being good."

Building a formal model helped the team develop a more explicit and complete description of its hypothesis. The model was constructed through a series of group discussions, then put into an exercise that allowed each member to work with it individually. The model is easiest to explain in three stags: pending claims and the production measures, pressures to add adjuster capacity, and pressures to adjust fuzzy standards.

Figure 6 shows the way the *production standards* are related to the backlog of pending claims and the flow of new incoming claims and settlements. There are three basic production standards: production ratio (settlements relative to incoming claims), pending ratio (number of pending claims relative to incoming claims), and the average settlement time (ratio of pending claims to settlements). All measure the extent to which the current rate of settlements is in balance with the volume of new incoming claims. For example, if settlements are less than new claims, production ratio is less than 100%, the stock of pending claims will be rising, and, thus, the pending ratio and average settlement time will be rising.

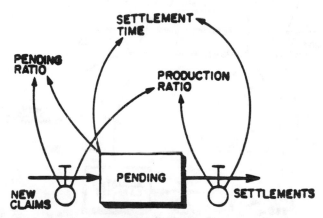

**FIGURE 6. Interrelating Capacity and Performance**
Step 1: Defining the Production Standards
    The first step in developing models to interrelate adjuster capacity and overall adjusting performance was defining the "production standards," the measures used to monitor whether the claims workflow was being handled. The three production standards, production ratio (settlements relative to new incoming claims), pending ratio (pending claims relative to new claims), and average settlement time, are measured in all claims offices and branches and comprise information central to the "scorecard" used for evaluating performance.

Figure 7 shows how pressure from the production measures are related to *adjuster capacity.* If the number of new incoming claims increased relative to settlements, pending claims would grow and pressure on existing claims capacity would build. In the terms of the model in Figure 7, staffing needs would increase, sending a signal to boost hiring of new adjusters. If hiring resulted in increased adjuster capacity commensurate with the increased staffing need, settlements would rise to match the increase in new claims and restore the production standards (typically, Hanover seeks to keep production ratio at 100%, pending ratio at about 2 months' worth of claims and average settlement time at 2 months).

But the above scenario presumes that adjuster capacity adjusts

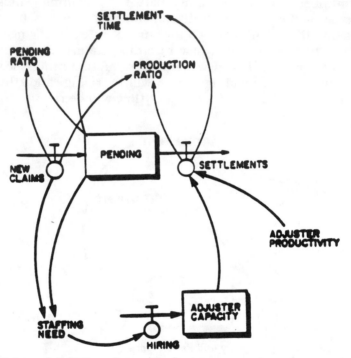

**FIGURE 7. Interrelating Capacity and Performance**
**Step 2: Relating Workload and Adjuster Capacity**
Perceived need for staffing changes are geared to the volume of new claims and to pending claims. For example, if pending builds over time, there is a perceived need for more adjusters, and vice versa. Changes in hiring and adjuster capacity, in turn, alter the number of claims settled ("settlements"). The feedback process shown in the diagram indicates that, if pending increases, adjuster capacity will increase in order to increase settlements and bring pending back into balance.

fully to match the increased volume of incoming claims. There are many reasons why this might not happen. First is the natural caution in bringing on new adjuster capacity which represents a significant cost commitment. Second are the delays in locating, hiring, and training new adjusters. Third is the intrinsic difficulty in building experienced adjuster capacity to match high rates of claims growth, as discussed above. For all of these reasons, it is unlikely that significant increases in incoming claims can be met fully by increased adjuster capacity in the short run.

The alternative to building capacity to match growth in incoming claims is to increase the productivity of existing claims adjusters. How do adjusters manage to settle a larger volume of claims per adjuster per month? Primarily, through spending less time on each individual claim. Herein lies the connection to the fuzzy standards. The team felt that there is strong pressure to maintain the production standards in Hanover. But, if this cannot be done through rapid increases in adjuster capacity, it must be accomplished by letting fuzzy standards slide, so that individual claims can be settled more quickly. As one team member pointed out, "The quickest way to eliminate a growing pending pool is to simply call each claimant, ask them what they think their claim is worth, and put the check in the mail."

The response of *fuzzy standards* to capacity pressure (staffing need relative to actual adjuster capacity) is shown in Figure 8. If capacity pressure leads to lowering fuzzy standards, such as quality of investigation, individual claims are settled more quickly, adjuster productivity increases, the rate of settlements increases and production measures are restored.

When production standards, fuzzy standards, and adjuster capacity interact, the outcome for quality and settlement size depends on the relative strengths of the different response mechanisms in the capacity-adjusting system. Three possible outcomes are summarized in Figure 9a, 9b, and 9c. In all three cases shown, there is an increase in new incoming claims beyond initial adjuster capacity. The increase in incoming claims occurs at month 6. The immediate consequence of the increase in incoming claims in all three cases is for the production measures to worsen: production ratio (settlements/incoming claims) declines, and settlement time and pending ratio increase.[7]

The three outcomes differ in how adjusters and fuzzy standards

---

[7] The pending ratio dips for the first month because new incoming claims increase suddenly in the test, while pending claims build gradually.

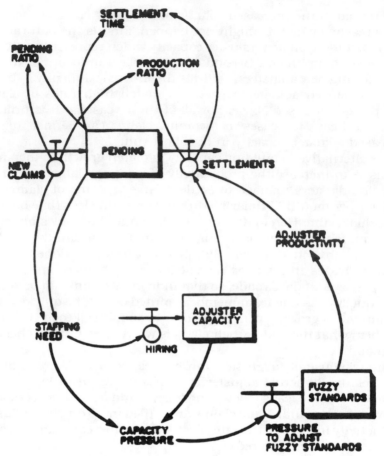

**FIGURE 8. Interrelating Capacity and Performance**
   **Step 3: Relating Workload and Fuzzy Standards**
   If increased staffing need is not met fully by increased adjuster capacity, capacity pressure builds, leading to pressure to adjust fuzzy standards. Reduced fuzzy standards, such as lower quality of investigation or poorer file quality, means that claims are settled more quickly and adjuster productivity increases. Thus, changes in fuzzy standards and adjuster productivity comprise another feedback process that can bring settlements into balance with new claims and pending claims.

respond to the increase in claims. In the first case, increased new claims and pending claims is met fully by hiring adjusters. There is no change in the fuzzy standards. In the second case, increased new claims leads to lowering of fuzzy standards. There is no hiring of adjusters. In the third case, a combination of hiring and lowering of fuzzy standards occurs.

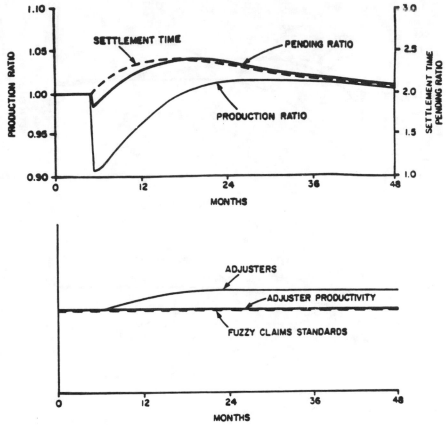

**FIGURE 9a.** Simulation of Capacity-Performance Model With One-Time Increase in Incoming Claims

Case 1: Fuzzy Standards Remain Fixed while Adjuster Hiring Responds to Capacity Pressures

Incoming claims increase at month 6 leading to imbalance in production standards: production ratio is depressed and pending ratio and settlement time begin to climb. Eventually, increased adjusters leads to increased settlements, rebalancing production ratio. Eventually, pending ratio and settlement time are restored as the build-up in pending is reduced.

In the first case (Figure 9a), rising number of adjusters eventually increases settlements and restores the production measures. Production ratio gradually returns to 100%, and pending ratio and settlement time eventually return to their original values. Note that production ratio is below 100% for about 12 months, during which time the pending ratio and average settlement time are rising be-

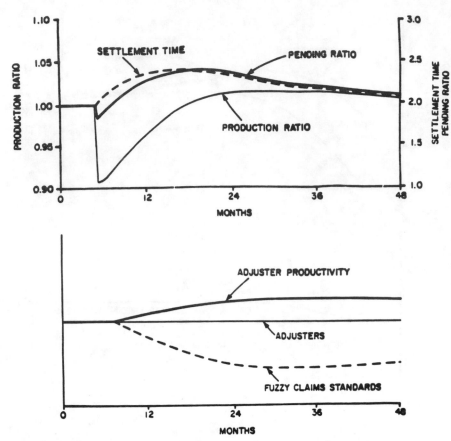

**FIGURE 9b. Simulation of Capacity-Performance Model With One-Time Increase in Incoming Claims**
**Case 2: Fuzzy Standards Adjust but Adjusters Remain Constant**
The response of the production measures is almost identical to Case 1. But, re-balancing of production measures is accomplished through erosion of fuzzy standards, with numbers of adjusters held constant. Comparing FIGUREs 9a and 9b shows that there is no way to tell from the production measures whether adjusters expand or fuzzy standards erode in response to an increase in incoming claims.

cause settlements are below new claims and pending claims are increasing. (Production ratio is subsequently greater than 100% for many months in order to reduce the high pending ratio.) The time lag in adjusting production ratio is due to the delay in bringing new adjusters onboard. This delay could be longer or shorter, depending on how quickly new adjusters could be hired and trained. The significant point is that, if increased adjuster capacity bears the full bur-

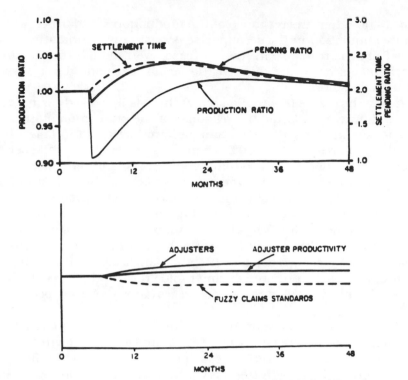

**FIGURE 9c. Simulation of Capacity-Performance Model With One-Time Increase in Incoming Claims**

**Case 3: Fuzzy Standards and Adjusters Respond to Capacity Pressure**

Once again, production measures show imbalance and gradual correction after increase in new claims. Combined response of standards and adjusters means that number of adjusters does not have to increase as much as when standards remained fixed (case 1). Likewise, standards do not fall as far as in the case when adjusters remained fixed (case 2).

den for boosting the rate of settlements, there will be significant periods of time when production standards are not being met.

In the second case (Figure 9b), production ratio also gradually increases and pending ratio and settlement time are eventually restored. In the second case, there is no increase in adjuster capacity. Production ratio increases due to rising adjuster productivity. As in the first case, there are significant delays in restoring the production standards. For example, production ratio takes almost 15 months to be restored to 100% after the increase in new claims. The delays could be longer or shorter, depending on how quickly fuzzy standards decline and adjuster productivity increases. It is important to note that the response of the production standards over the entire simulation in the second case is qualitatively undistinguishable from the response in the first case, even though the response mechanisms are quite different (lowering fuzzy standards versus hiring adjusters).

In the third case (Figure 9c), when there is increased hiring *and* lowered fuzzy standards, the response of the production standards is once again the same. For example, production ratio falls, then eventually is restored to 100%, then rises above 100% while settlements exceed new claims so that pending ratio and settlement time can be restored. The adjustment mechanism in this case involves increased adjuster capacity and increased adjuster productivity.

The third case is undoubtedly the most realistic. The team felt that simultaneous increases in the number of adjusters (which are measurable) and erosion of fuzzy standards (which are not measurable) probably occurred often. If the organization is under nearly continual capacity pressure during rapid growth, which seems to be true, these two adjustment processes are probably occurring continually.

To test what would happen with a realistic input in new claims, the model was simulated with new incoming claims growth at their historic rate (30% average increase per year) with random fluctuations around the growth trend (10% standard deviation, matching historic month-by-month fluctuations). In Figure 10, changes in adjuster capacity and fuzzy standards are occurring concurrently. The result is that production standards, such as production ratio, fluctuate about reasonably acceptable levels (Figure 10a), while number of adjusters grows and fuzzy standards steadily erode (Figure 10b). For the claims team, the consequences of the steady erosion in fuzzy standards were clear—declining investigation quality, rising average settlement size, and increasing losses in litigation, exactly what had been experienced over the past several years.

The significant managerial point illustrated by the above simulations is that it is impossible to tell *how* settlements and claims volume are being kept in balance by merely monitoring the production standards. In all cases, the production standards are continually being restored toward their nominal values. An important insight brought out by the model is that the production standards simply do *not* reveal the specific nature of how settlements and incoming claims are brought back into balance. Production standards can be controlled by increased capacity, lowered fuzzy standards, or a combination of the two. With the simulations it was now possible

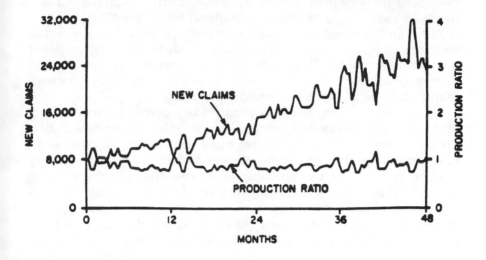

Figure 10a

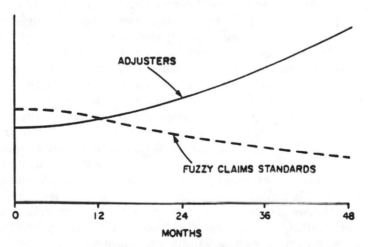

Figure 10b

**FIGURE 10. Simulation of Capacity-Performance Model with Rising Claims Volume**
A steadily rising, randomly varying volume of new claims leads the model to show steady erosion in fuzzy claims standards, while adjusters are expanding. Eroding standards seem to be a basic mode for the capacity-performance model, since they can be stimulated with a variety of inputs. Note that the measurable performance indices, like production ratio, remain within normal ranges (production ratio = 1), giving no indication of the erosion in standards.

to explain the vice-president's earlier statement, "In this business, there are many ways to look good without being good."

The claims management team spent several hours in a series of meetings developing and working with workload-capacity models of the sort illustrated in Figures 8–10. Some were less complex. Some were more complex. All dealt with the basic trade-offs between maintaining fuzzy standards and building capacity.

What emerged from these meetings was a deeper understanding of the systemic forces that can bias the organization toward undercapacity, even while adjusters are being added rapidly. The workload-capacity models, along with the earlier simple adjuster capacity models, resulted in the growing awareness that (1) the existing claims management system revolves around performance indexes that can lead managers to underestimate consistently the capacity needed and (2) even when hiring is aggressive, achieving growth in claims capacity commensurate with high standards of quality may be difficult.

In one follow-up discussion after the team members had worked individually with a model-based exercise in which capacity-management and fuzzy standards interacted, several interesting observations were made. There was some discussion of how claims managers can know whether or not they have inadequate capacity. Normal production standards can be extremely misleading. If fuzzy standards have eroded, capacity could be seriously deficient and yet production standards would give no indication of inadequate capacity. In fact, as one team member observed, the usefulness of the production standards is itself linked to the fuzzy standards. "The production standards *are* valid indicators of how well we are doing," she said, "*if* the fuzzy standards are not allowed to erode. Only when the 'fuzzies' are being met does the production ratio correctly indicate if we have enough adjuster capacity."

Another observation was that eroding fuzzy standards leads to subtle redefinitions of "simple" and "complex" claims. When there is persisting capacity pressure, simple and complex claims tend to be redefined to fit the type of capacity available. Since experienced adjusters are usually in short supply, complex claims get treated as if they were simple, by assigning them to inexperienced adjusters. The result is poor investigation and overpayment on claims that should receive careful investigation.

The vice-president made an observation that was especially striking. He said, "As I think about the implications of this exercise, it becomes obvious to me that we may have half the number of adjusters that we should have. You must realize that that is a crazy thing to say. We already have a lower case load per adjuster than almost all of our competitors. What the model gives us is a different basis against which to evaluate our business. Normally, you can only compare yourself to your competitors. Without these models, people here would think that I had lost my mind if I proposed that we should double our number of adjusters."

By the same token the group was concerned that no "model" become the authority. They felt that it was extremely important for others in the claims organization to build up their own models from scratch. *What had made the process useful for the team was conceptualizing and analyzing the models themselves and, in the process, coming to their own understanding.* We would need to find ways to facilitate similar experiences for others within the organization.

## Broadening the Learning Process and Action Steps

The learning process summarized above took place over a 6-month period. In the 6 months following, a wide range of related issues was explored by the team. Rather than attempt to summarize these discussions, an illustration of the types of action steps being taken and the ways that other managers are being drawn into the learning process is given.

One potentially important organizational change being examined is the creation of a "claims processing center," where simple claims warranting little investigation and adjusting can be handled separately from more complex claims. For the members of the claims management team, the rationale for the "processing center" is to speed up handling of simple claims *and* improve the environment for quality investigation and resolution of more complex claims. They feel that the present atmosphere in claims offices is contrary to maintaining high quality standards, in part, because "processable claims" are continually mixed with "adjustable claims." As a result, there are no clear, consistently applied set of quality standards that adjusters can internalize and exert pressure on one another to maintain.

The way that the team has approached the processing center idea has been instructive of bringing the systems thinking process to bear on possible action steps. First, like most good management teams, the claims management team has a "bias toward action." They are eager to translate new insights into tangible results. And, as for many senior management teams, reorganization is an attractive channel for action. However, instead of rushing out and implementing the reorganization, the claims team has spent considerable time examining their own and others' mental models regarding how a processing center might actually work. The team members individually developed "high success" and "low success" scenarios of what might happen once the processing center was implemented. The effects of introducing a processing center were also simulated in the workload-capacity models.

It has now become clear that success of the "processing center" idea, like so many reorganizations, will depend on the operating policies followed by claims managers in the new structure. In particular, how will adjuster capacity decisions respond to the new conditions created by the new structure?

For example, in one simulation test, the number of new incoming claims to be adjusted was suddenly reduced to simulate the effect of introducing a processing center that siphons off a fraction of "processable claims" from the overall claims load. The expectation was that with less new claims to handle claims adjusters would have more time to do a quality job adjusting the claims they had. This is exactly what happened, in the short term. Fuzzy standards went up for several months. Then, however, fuzzy standards came down once again. Why? Because with fewer claims to adjust, production standards indicated excess adjuster capacity. Hiring was less than adjuster turnover, and the adjuster level declined. The end result was fewer adjusters and only slightly higher fuzzy standards, an outcome that matched some of the "low success" scenarios the team members had developed.

Examining the claims processing center has underscored the importance of broadening the learning process beyond the claims management team. Hanover's espoused "localness" means that staffing and quality policies are controlled by claims managers throughout the company. These managers will need to develop shared understandings of the dynamics of capacity and fuzzy standards.

Current work is focused on developing a "claims management learning laboratory." The learning laboratory will be a place where managers can come for dialogue and debate regarding key issues they face, stimulated by a variety of learning tools, such as the models discussed above.

One tool for the learning laboratory will be a "claims game" now being developed by the management team. The intent of this game will be to have claims managers discover for themselves the fundamental pitfalls and leverage points in managing capacity growth, settlements, and investigation quality. The game will present information on production standards, average settlement size, and other variables by which claims managers make decisions. The player-managers will have to decide each month how many new adjusters to hire, and whether to exert additional pressure on production standards and investigation quality. Players will compete against one another to see who can minimize cumulative cost, including settlement costs and operating expenses, over a 4-year period.

Initial tests of the game with the management team indicate that, even after analyzing the issues over a year via big picture maps, scenarios, and simulation models, the role-playing experience provided by the game produces powerful new learnings. New learnings occur because the game requires the learner to *take actions*. Action taking can reveal illuminating discrepancies between espoused views based on abstract understandings and actual behavior.[8]

## CASE SUMMARY

The above case illustrates how a systems thinking learning process can enhance the quality of thinking in a management team. Over the course of our working sessions, team members have developed a richer, more explicit view of the system in which they are managing. I hope the above snapshots illustrate that this view has evolved toward being more systemic, dynamic, and testable. They have identified specific shortcomings in operating policies and strategies. They have initiated new policies and strategies, and perhaps more important, developed a powerful respect for explicating and testing mental models as the stepping stone to better policies and strategies.

In addition, the process has produced concrete new tools that have the potential to catalyze learning in the larger claims organization. Producing new learning tools for the larger organization means that the learning process will not stop with a small group of top managers. If new insights and strategies are generated only in the top management team, the result will be a top-down change process that is unlikely to enlist the genuine commitment of managers not involved in the learning process. The efforts of the Hanover team to

---

[8] Brunner emphasized that mental growth proceeds along three fundamental dimensions: *abstract-symbolic, iconic, and enactive* (see Bruner, 1966). The game playing process brings the enactive mode of learning to the abstract and iconic modes created by simulation analysis and feedback loop conceptualization. Insights from game playing also relate to Argyris' and Schon's distinction of "espoused theories" and "theories in use" (see Argyris & Schon, 1978).

design new learning tools like the claims game is a good example of the emerging role of leadership as "managers of organizational learning."

Much remains to be done, both to aid and study the learning process as it unfolds. Present research is focused on studying the Claims Learning Laboratory, especially to develop methods to measure shifts in mental models more rigorously, and to better understand relationships between mental models, operating policies, and individual behavior. The microcosm of learning in specific groups of managers needs to be related to the macrocosm of learning in the entire organization. And, experiences at Hanover need to be compared with similar learning experiments in other companies to understand the roles played by an organization's culture, business setting, and leadership.

## CHALLENGES IN DEVELOPING SYSTEMS THINKING

I have met few advocates for short-term atomistic thinking. Most managers believe their business could benefit from a more long-term wholistic perspective on policy and strategy. Individuals with general management responsibilities typically espouse the greatest interest in understanding how policies in one functional area interact with policies in other areas, and how actions that are beneficial in the short run can be counterproductive in the long run. Why, then, is systems thinking the exception rather than the norm in most of our corporations?

There appear to be two fundamental difficulties in developing systems thinking within organizations. The first is that few managers and consultants are trained in the necessary skills and that few tools have been available to accelerate skill development. The second is that the systems perspective is threatening for managers in most organizations. Even when individuals or groups achieve new systemic insights, they may find the implications of those insights incompatible with the goals, rewards and pressures of the larger systems within which actions must be taken.

Future success in extending the type of work done at Hanover into other organizations will depend on better understanding of the organizational conditions that can encourage, recognize, and reward systems thinking and further improvements in the tools and processes that can stimulate systems thinking. We call these the challenges "enriching the soil" and "improving the seeds" so that people's innate aptitude for systems thinking can grow in an organizational setting.

## "Enriching the Soil:" Organizational Environments Conducive to Systems Thinking

The environment for new ways of thinking can be thought of in terms of a "macro-environment" and a "micro-environment." By macro-environment, I mean the attitudes, values, and guiding ideas that prevail in the organization as a whole. By micro-environment, I mean the skills, habits, and norms operative in a working team.

***Why is systems thinking threatening in organizations?*** Despite rhetoric to the contrary, our experiences have repeatedly shown that systems thinking is threatening in an organizational setting. It is threatening *politically,* because it cuts across traditional boundaries of managerial accountability. It is threatening *intellectually,* because it demands a substantial investment of time and energy to rethink implicit mental models from a more explicit, conceptual vantage point. It is threatening *strategically,* because it continually calls into question uncertain longer-term consequences of actions whose short-term gains are more predictable. And, it can be threatening *philosophically,* because it is predicated on a world view, which is foreign to many, that our actions are continually creating our reality, often in ways we don't appreciate. In an organizational setting, the implication—that our problems arise because of, not despite, the actions we have taken to solve them—can be contrary to established ways of defining problems and developing solutions.[9]

When confronted with situations that are threatening, people tend to react defensively. One effective defensive reaction is to advocate taking a longer-term wholistic perspective, but making no serious efforts to develop that perspective. Another is to assert that systems thinking already exists. Another is to delegate the activity to the strategic planning or operations research staff, so that line managers can avoid the learning process itself.

***Guiding ideas.*** How can an organizational environment overcome or displace the threats inherent in the systems perspective? One starting point is nurturing guiding ideas (values, beliefs, viewpoints) conducive to systems thinking.

In a recent meeting of the CEOs of the organizations participating

---

9 B. Richmond also argues that there are fundamental impediments to systems thinking at the individual level concerning the way we experience reality as a series of short-term events, construct internalized frames of reference oriented toward things and events, and have been evolutionarily programmed to react to external threats to our survival (see B. Richmond, "Systems Thinking: Four Key Questions" Lyme NH, High Performance Systems Inc.).

in our research program, one of the participants asked, "What are the key 'intellectual concepts' that prepare an organization's members for systems thinking?" The ensuing discussion was exploratory. Not everyone agreed on every point. But, all agreed on the importance of the question. Below are some of the ideas that emerged.

*Vision* and *spirit* were felt to be essential so that self-interest would not predominate. If self-interest is paramount, individuals are unable to see beyond, to what is best for the larger enterprise. If what is best for the enterprise is not in view, the fundamental rationale for systems thinking disappears.

*Openness* is necessary to break through gamesplaying and internal politics. Openness starts with rehabilitating the individual's capacity to inquire, to be curious, to be aware of his or her own internal deceptions and biases. Challenging the views of others in a way that promotes trust and joint inquiry requires that individuals continually challenge their own ideas.· In most organizations individuals do not perceive that it is safe to expose their own doubts, uncertainties, and misunderstandings.

*Localness* is the antidote to referring decisions "upstairs." Localness distributes responsibility for systems thinking among a large number of managers who must balance short-term and long-term benefits and evaluate how actions taken in one part of their systems will affect others. Localness also dictates that senior management reconceive its role as managing organizational learning processes, so that shared visions and mental models can bring coherency to actions of diverse local decisionmakers.

*Handling complexity* and *change* must become recognized as management's ongoing job. The complexity doesn't go away, and it does not yield to simplistic solutions. Change is the only constant and dictates continuous ongoing learning.

*Converging* and *diverging problems* need to be distinguished to understand where "linear" versus "process" thinking is necessary. Converging problems have *solutions*. Diverging problems have no simple solutions. Diverging problems pose *tradeoffs* between conflicting objectives and require choices. In a well-designed organization, senior managers deal primarily with diverging problems.

Understanding the *limits to reductionistic thinking* is the antidote to managers' fatal tendency to think they have "the answer." Reductionistic thinking causes diverging problems to be mistaken as converging, leading to a search for solutions rather than new perspectives. The resulting "solutions" typically lead to improvement in the short run only, if at all, and frequently exacerbate underlying problems. Organizations reinforce reductionistic thinking by making managers feel that it is their job to have *the answer*.

It is important that guiding ideas such as those above not be seen as new "answers" to be inoculated into the organization. Rather, there must be, in the words of Bill O'Brien, president of Hanover Insurance, a "birthing process." Our limited experience suggests that the birthing process requires many years and that it is unlikely to succeed if there is only one leader, regardless of his or her position, who assumes responsibility for the change process. In all successful cases we know where new guiding ideas have been assimilated into an organization there existed a genuine partnership among two or more leaders, each of whom assumed full responsibility for success.

***Conditions for learning in management teams.*** Some of our most discouraging experiences have come from settings where, in retrospect, the management team was either comprised of the wrong people or the team was unprepared for the demands of a learning process focused on improving mental models.

The overall lesson we have drawn is that the systems thinking learning process should be seen as part of the larger process of developing an effective management team. This leads to an expanded view of team building to include developing shared mental models and ways of thinking about business strategy and policy. But, it also suggests that there may be conditions in a team's development that must be met before the systems thinking process is likely to succeed.

The task, then, is to identify conditions that appear to be important for a successful learning process and consider how these conditions can be recognized and nurtured in real settings.

The first condition for learning is that assembled team needs to be a group of people who have the power to act and who need one another to act. Actions are always based on assumptions. When action is required, the fundamental learning questions are "What are the assumptions underlying our current actions?" and, "Can we improve these assumptions so as to act more effectively?" In such a context, managers can evaluate for themselves whether or not the learning process clarifies and improves the assumptions underlying their actions. They can assess the "value added" of the process.

Second, the management team must be truly motivated to learn. This means, among other things, that team members must not feel that they already understand everything they need to understand in order to manage successfully. Nothing impedes learning as much as the belief that one already has all the answers. In potential learning situations, there is always a calculation of expected costs and benefits that must be made. Unless the participating managers believe that the possible benefits of new understandings justify the time and effort that will be required, the likelihood for a successful learning process is low.

Third, the team needs to have established some basic norms of open and honest exchange. People must feel free to talk about what is important to them, their own assumptions, and their own perceptions of others' assumptions. People must feel free to "question the party line." They must feel free to challenge one another's assumptions. They must have some skills in doing so in a way that promotes a spirit of genuine inquiry and mutual learning. While openness is almost always espoused, it has been our experience that in many management teams members are reticent to expose their own ignorance or challenge the ignorance of other team members.

For example, in one unsuccessful learning process experiment, the participants never generated much enthusiasm for the possibility of new insights. One of the two most senior executives participating frequently expressed the view that he didn't see how such models could reveal new insights, since the inputs were primarily managers' own assumptions. He was not interested in making assumptions explicit or in discovering internal inconsistencies in operating assumptions. He repeatedly found conclusions to be "obvious." The more junior members exuded an air of "we don't have any real problems, except difficulty in getting people to execute our intended strategies." In private, the junior managers said that they did indeed have doubts regarding some of the company's policies, but they didn't feel it was possible to discuss their doubts publicly in the team. In such a situation, little could be accomplished by the group as a whole, unless team members were willing to examine their own process of interacting, which neither they nor we were prepared to do.

We are finding that the first and second conditions, team composition and willingness to learn, can be assessed to some degree by more careful interviewing and screening before commencing a formal learning process. In more recent experiments, two and sometimes three rounds of interviews with prospective participants have helped to appreciate the team's present level of development, identify important elements of prevailing mental models, and assess the team members' motivation.[10] The interview process also serves to involve members individually or in small groups in developing initial "big picture" diagrams and "reality check models."

The third condition, openness and honesty, cannot always be

---

[10] Richmond (1987a) describes in detail a recommended series of interviews in advance of formal group meetings.

detected prior to convening the team. Here, I believe, future work must explore how the team modeling approach described above can be integrated with methods to build managers' skills in group inquiry. For example, initial experiments with a case analysis methodology developed by Argyris have proven very effective at helping team members recognize and discuss opinions and attributions otherwise kept private (Argyris, 1982; Argyris, Putnam, & Smith, 1985). This seems a positive step in the direction of opening people to examine undisclosed, and perhaps unrecognized, mental models. But, there is much to learn in integrating systems modeling and methods for improving group learning processes.

## Improving the "Seeds:" Processes and Tools for Systems Thinking

*Improving understanding of mental models.* The systems perspective may provide a useful framework for organizing assumptions contained within managers' mental models. The perspective suggests that there are three fundamentally different kinds of assumptions within mental models (see Figure 11).[11] First, there are assumptions about system "behavior," the patterns of change that have happened, are happening, and that might happen in the future. Second, there are assumptions about system "structure," the pressures, goals, and constraints influencing decisions and how different variables interact with one another. Third, there are assumptions about the expected effects of changes in policy. This third class of assumptions links structure and behavior.

Assumptions about behavior are generally the least controversial. Nonetheless, sometimes managers simply do not know basic data regarding their business. In such circumstances, the construction of formal models brings to the surface inadequacies in basic business data and forces managers to make explicit their operating assumptions regarding business conditions.

Assumptions about policies and structure concern how decisions are made and the basic physical processes and information flows that connect different parts of the business. We find that managers typically have a rich store of information regarding the structures within which they have many years of experience. They can often describe operating policies with a fairly high level of consistency.

---

[11] This view of assumptions within mental models is adapted from one presented originally by J. Forrester (1980).

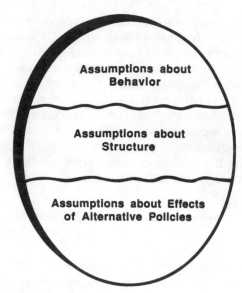

**FIGURE 11. Strata of our Mental Models**

Our mental models contain several layers of assumptions. Included in assumptions about behavior are assumptions about present conditions and about the patterns of change, such as, "Our problem is low quality but it is getting better." Included in assumptions about structure are our beliefs about basic interdependencies, such as "If demand falls, there is pressure to reduce inventories." Included in assumptions about the effects of alternative policies are expectations and beliefs about the consequences of changes in policy and strategy, such as "We can build market share by reducing price." Of the three types of assumptions, assumptions about the effects of alternative policies are most central to strategic management. They are also the most questionable.

They also can agree fairly quickly on the major structural interdependencies between the pieces.

In general, the most important and questionable assumptions concern how alternative policies will influence future behavior. In dealing with a complex system, people may have excellent understanding of the individual pieces of the system and how they are interrelated and yet consistently misjudge the dynamic behavior as the pieces interact and how that behavior would be altered by new policies. *Yet*, it is exactly this set of assumptions that underlies the design of new managerial policies. Consequently, clarifying the links from structure to behavior and the likely effects of alternative policies is where tools such as system dynamics have their greatest leverage.

For example, the claims managers at Hanover had little difficulty describing the basic processes of hiring and training new adjusters and the personnel policies operating in this part of the system. But, they were surprised initially when those same processes and policies resulted in persistent undercapacity for complex claims given historical growth in hiring.

In another session the subject was litigation management. The claims managers had been advocating a tougher stand and taking more cases through to be tried to verdict, rather than settled out of court. In fact, the vice-president was preparing a speech on the subject. The team constructed a reality check model of cases in litigation, those settled in court and out of court, and the respective costs. The team had no difficulty conceptualizing the interrelationships in the model. But, when simulated, the model showed that, for any range of assumptions the team could supply for likely fraction of cases won, costs of winning and losing, and overhead and legal costs, the more cases tried to verdict, the greater the total financial cost to Hanover. Initially, this came as a considerable surprise. Eventually, the team came to conclude that taking poorly investigated cases through to verdict would only increase Hanover's losses and lawyers' earnings. Only when investigation quality was improved, would tougher litigation management yield benefits. The vice-president rewrote his speech.

What these examples suggest is that, by and large, operating mental models are often quite simple from a dynamic viewpoint. The system dynamics models used in the above examples contained 10–15 variables and 2–5 feedback processes. Yet, they yielded outcomes that were initially surprising to a group of highly competent and experienced managers. Moreover, we have seen similar results frequently with simple reality check models. This suggests that managers' mental models used in forming expected outcomes from alternative policies may focus on only a small number of variables and recognize few, if any, feedback processes.[12] Is this so typically or only rarely? Is it true predominantly in situations where experience is weak or also where experience and competence judged by peers is high? These will be important questions in future learning experiments.

***Improving representations of mental models.*** More effort must be put into developing orderly procedures for clarifying managers' prevailing assumptions and feeding this information back to

---

[12] Recent experimental studies have shown that people consistently misperceive feedback processes in moderately complex simulation games (Sterman, 1987).

them. Presently, we have experimented with three distinct approaches to exposing assumptions at the outset of a learning process: stating the current vision, strategic objectives, strategies, and perceived barriers or difficulties; the "big picture" diagram; and constructing alternative scenarios. Each has been helpful, but a more systematic, consistently applied methodology for mapping mental models would, undoubtedly, have great advantages.

Applying the three-level framework described above might help in organizing information regarding mental models. For example, managers might be asked to identify in advance the major patterns of future behavior (or scenarios) they judge of most interest. They might also be asked to identify the principal variables and major interconnections that characterize the business as a system (i.e., the "big picture"). They might also be asked to state their recommended changes in policy and structure and why they expect such changes to produce more desired behavior. Collecting this data systematically in advance would (1) allow for comparisons of different individual's assumptions when the group meetings commence and (2) provide a record for each individual to reflect upon as a learning process unfolds. The collection and analysis of these data would also be an effective way to involve internal consultants who are not expert systems modelers in designing a learning process.

***Measuring success.*** A theme running throughout our experiments has been to view learning as involving two fundamental dimensions: understanding and action. In our minds it is counterproductive to ignore either. To say that someone has a new "understanding," when his or her behavior remains unchanged, implies that the understanding is passive. Whitehead decried the fixation of Western education on "inert knowledge":

> In training a child to activity of thought, above all things we must beware of what I will call "inert ideas"—that is to say, ideas that are merely received into the mind without being utilised, or tested, or thrown into fresh combinations. . . Ideas which are not utilised are positively harmful. (Whitehead, 1957, pp. 1–2, 4)

Conversely, new actions divorced from serious inquiry and rethinking are apt to be short-lived. New actions not linked to new understandings create no foundation for continued learning in the future. This is one of the pitfalls of the traditional consulting mode that may induce managers to take new decisions and actions but in no way leaves them better prepared for coping with new problems in the future.

However, our view of learning as involving understanding and action makes the assessment of progress difficult. A learning process is unlike a traditional modeling project, were success might be judged by an insightful model, or a model that fits historical data, or a model that leads to new decisions. A learning process focused on policy and strategy is unlike other group processes, whose success might be judged by participants' feelings of increased clarity, openness, and candor. A learning process focused on understanding and action cannot even be evaluated on the basis of espoused insights, since there is no guarantee that the insights will produce new, more effective behavior.

*Ultimately, the only valid criterion for evaluating a systems thinking learning process is the organization's enhanced capability over the long term to create the results desired by its members.* Assessing success requires ascertaining whether new, more effective policies are being implemented and whether new shared understandings are being assimilated in the organization. Clearly, such assessment is exceedingly difficult.

On an interim basis, success must be evaluated by a variety of means. There are the subjective assessments by the managers involved that they are perceiving the business more clearly, recognizing the shortcomings of particular policies, and seeing possibilities for more effective structures and policies. New policies and structures can be evaluated for their consistency with espoused understandings and for their apparent success. Obviously, such assessments are inevitably subjective. Moreover, the effects of any new policy are always confounded by a multiplicity of concurrent internal and external changes—reality never presents laboratory test conditions where changes in a system can be tried one at a time.

One interesting new approach to measuring the effect of a learning process is through simulation gaming. Simulation games provide a way of measuring behavior under controlled conditions. That is, in a game situation believed to replicate certain features of the managers' world, what behavioral rules do participants follow? Statistical analysis of game protocols can reveal implicit decision rules of players (see Sterman, 1987). This might prove a powerful means of identifying gaps between "espoused theories" and "theories in use," and measuring whether people's behavior actually changes as a result of a learning process. As noted above, analysis of behavior in simulation games is now under way at Hanover.

**_Improving the available tools._** The learning process experiments conducted over the past 2 years would not have been possible without the software STELLA, which allows the construction of dynamic simulation models at the screen of a personal computer. With this new tool, it has become possible to involve managers in the modeling process for the first time.

But STELLA still requires the skills of an expert system dynamics model-builder to build well-formulated and carefully tested models. What STELLA currently lacks is the heuristics used by experienced modelers in model construction and testing. As these become integrated into the software, it will become increasingly a general purpose systems modeling tool for the nonexpert. Although a true general purpose nonexpert's modeling tool is probably 10 years away, upcoming improvements may allow people with less and less formal training to build better and better models. If this happens, one of the chief barriers to wider availability of systems thinking learning processes will diminish.

Another type of tool that may be closer to our grasp are special purpose learning tools. A special purpose learning tool would be designed to facilitate learning around a specific set of issues, unlike STELLA which is equally applicable to modeling any (societal, corporate, biological, physical) type of dynamic system. Management games such as the Hanover claims game are special purpose learning tools. It would be relatively straightforward to convert the Hanover game into a claims management game applicable to any insurance company. Other existing system dynamics games include a production-distribution game, which shows how industrial systems can self-generate cycles, a sales game, a product life-cycle management game, a growth and capacity management game, a macroeconomic game, and a national resource management game (see Sterman, 1987a; Sterman & Meadows, 1985; Meadows, 1985).

Another type of special purpose learning tool is the "computerized case study," which combines a traditional case analysis with system models to analyze the general policy and strategy issues posed by the case. The computerized case study is designed for an individual rather than a group, but could be used in a group setting. It takes the form of a diskette for a personal computer. After reading the case, the learner(s) is given several general questions regarding what lessons should be drawn from the case, reflects on his or her own assumptions, then is assisted through simulation models and games to analyze the case more rigorously. The computerized case combines the power of a well-selected and well-researched case to reveal managerial lessons and the rigor of systems modeling to draw out those lessons (Graham, Morecroft, Senge, & Sterman, 1989).

## BUILDING MORE EFFECTIVE ORGANIZATIONS

It was stated at the outset that systems thinking and learning processes designed to develop such thinking could contribute to building more effective organizations. In closing, I would like to point to several specific ways in which I believe this can happen.

### "Visioning" and Systems Thinking

In recent years, management teams, especially top management teams, have engaged with increasing regularity in diverse forms of "visioning processes," designed to clarify the team's objectives in light of its members' sense of organizational mission and core values. Visioning processes are as diverse as the consultants and consulting companies that specialize in their facilitation. Some emphasize "mission statements," others "corporate visions" or "value statements." Almost all attempt to relate mission and vision to strategy and strategic objectives. But, despite differences, visioning processes share certain fundamental premises: first, that a key function of leadership is establishing a clear and compelling direction; second, that objectives arrived at by a team working collectively are more likely to engender commitment than those arrived at by executives working unilaterally; third, that objectives seen as consistent with an individual's personal sense of purpose will make that individual happier and more productive.[13]

I believe that both the visioning process and the systems thinking process suffer when they are not coupled. Without shared understanding of the predominant forces shaping change, the visioning process lacks grounding. Without a clear and compelling picture of the results truly desired by the team, the systems thinking process lacks direction and motivation.

Systems thinking learning processes counter what I find to be the greatest weakness of visioning processes: manager's perception that

---

[13] The role of visioning in organizational development is discussed in Vail (1982), and in Kiefer and Stroh (1984).

the team's articulated visions and objectives are naïve, or, even worse, hypocritical. I believe that the skepticism often felt by managers toward visioning is rooted in uncertainty about the forces shaping change. If they can gain greater clarity about those forces, it has always been my experience that people feel empowered in influencing the future.

An episode in the Hanover claims project illustrated the way systems thinking can enrich visioning. Several months into the process, after considerable time examining why adjuster capacity tends toward inadequate levels of experience and why "fuzzy standards" for investigation and customer service erode, the group spontaneously began to describe their ideal claims office. They discussed how there would be a team atmosphere in which seasoned and relatively inexperienced adjusters would work closely together. Young adjusters would get to work on complex and challenging claims, and would develop judgment through mentoring relationships and work cooperatively with experienced adjusters. Team members would continually assist in and review one another's investigations to maintain the team commitment to investigation quality. People would work hard but have enough time to conduct thorough investigations and treat claimants as individuals with unique problems and needs.

The management team's vision of its ideal claims office was especially interesting in contrast to their original visions for the claims organization articulated in our first meeting. This latter vision had an operational depth missing in the original visions. While very much in line with the original visions of excellence and elevating Hanover's reputation among customers and in the industry, the latter vision suggested how the broad-brush vision might be accomplished operationally. Consequently, the latter statement of vision was more compelling. One had the feeling, as the managers talked, that you could literally see how such a claims office would function.

Just as systems thinking enriches visioning, so too can visioning make systems thinking more effective. In fact, in my experience, *the systems thinking process is unlikely to result in important and lasting changes in the absence of a strong sense of purpose and vision.*

One reason concerns people's willingness to change. A systemic examination almost always shows the need for fundamental shifts in current operating policies. Systems modelers have traditionally adopted a "rationalist" stance as regards change—namely, that if people only understood why current policies were counterproductive, they would surely change those policies. But, there is much evidence to suggest that people often prefer the status quo over fundamental changes in actions and policies. Change is always threatening. It always involves a degree of risk. Many management teams would prefer to achieve moderate levels of success following established policies and procedures than to undertake significant changes.

Genuine vision creates the willingness and ability to change. Vision dislodges people from their commitment to the status quo. The fundamental characteristic of vision is that an individual truly cares more about something that doesn't exist than what currently does exist. When such a shift occurs authentically, attachment to the present is reduced and there is a new openness to alternative courses of action.[14]

Such vision also established a second critical condition for systems thinking to take root, a focus on the long term. For years, consultants and analysts advocating a systems perspective have tried to convince managers through rational argument that current policies should be changed to achieve greater long-term success. In my experience such arguments almost always fail to produce new, longer-term behavior. The visionary perspective suggests a different approach. It suggests that people will focus on the long term when there is a result they care about deeply, which can only be achieved over the long term. In the presence of a genuine vision, the future is *valued* in a manner that doesn't occur otherwise.

I don't mean to suggest that vision and systems thinking are *all* that's needed to produce changes in individual and organizational behavior. Rather, my point is that a clear picture of a desired future and a deep understanding of the systemic forces shaping change constitute the necessary foundation for creating new behavior in the future—that is, for redesigning the policies, structures, reward systems, and organization processes that can make change possible.

**Theory-Based Strategy**

Midway through the learning process at Hanover, the claims vice-president observed that the company may have half the adjust capacity it needs to achieve its goals of quality investigation and cus-

---

[14] Neurobiologists are beginning to supply one explanation for the connection between vision and action through establishing that perception is highly selective based on "the future options" that an individual has set in advance. When new options are established, an individual can literally "see" new aspects of their reality (see Irgvar, 1985).

tomer service at the current volume of claims. As reported above, he was particularly taken aback by this realization because the company already employed more adjusters per claim volume than most of its competitors.

This story illustrates the potential of developing an explicit theory of dynamics as a new basis for strategy and policy. The two sources of ideas underlying most organization's strategy and policy are its traditions and the practices of its competitors. A third, distinctly weaker influence is new concepts based on management research. The systems thinking learning process offers a new alternative. As illustrated above, through developing and testing dynamic models, a management team can forge a dynamic theory of its business that synthesizes the experience and perspectives of its members. The strengths of this theory are that it is internally consistent and it is comprised of explicit assumptions. Internal consistency and explicitness do not guarantee that the theory is correct. But, they do provide a clear basis for policy choices and a foundation for continued testing and improvement of operating assumptions.

If a series of learning processes such as described above could be carried on over a period of time within an organization, the result would be a growing body of theory of the organization's critical dynamics. The organization would, in effect, be building a "library" of formal models developed by its own managers to describe the dynamics characteristic of its internal processes, its market, and its interaction with competitors. The library of basic models would continually evolve as old theories were revised and new ones developed. But, at any point in time, there would be a clear body of current theory and management principles from which managers could draw.

Such a library would have many important uses within the learning organization. First, dynamic models developed and tested against past experience could dramatically accelerate training new managers. Secondly, such models could be a reference for framing new problems and a jumping off point for helping managers conceptualize new dynamics. Last, such a library of basic models would represent a unique form of institutional memory, a *public* body of knowledge that would help make operating policies more understandable, defensible, and less arbitrary, just as publicly stated visions, values, and strategic objectives serve to make strategies more understandable.

### Training a New Type of Professional

Lastly, it is unlikely that systems thinking learning processes will become widely available until there is a sufficient supply of professionals capable of designing and facilitating such processes. I will label this new type of professional as a systems thinking learning consultant. But the skill profile might very well fit a new type of manager as well.

The range of skills such professionals will need includes the skills of "process consultants," system thinking model-builders, and a fair amount of the skills of a general management or strategic planning consultant. Such a professional must be adept at group facilitation, especially in the areas of visioning, openness, group inquiry, and defusing defensive routines. Such a professional must be able to conceptualize, formulate, analyze, and test systems models of corporate behavior. And, such a professional must have a keen appreciation of the content and context of a wide range of basic management issues.

Few people today possess the skill profile of the systems thinking learning consultant. But, the elements for a curriculum for training such a professional do, by and large, exist. The task is to pull these elements into a coherent whole and begin the training process. Twenty years ago, much less was known about training the systems thinking model builder or the process consultant. Hopefully, the considerable contribution this new type of professional could make will call forth effort and resources adequate to the task.

## REFERENCES

Argyris, C. (1982). *Reasoning, learning and action.* San Francisco, CA: Jossey-Bass

Argyris, C., & Schon, D. (1978). *Organizational learning: A theory of action and perspective.* Reading, MA: Addison-Wesley.

Argyris, C., Putnam, R., & Smith, D. (1985). *Action science.* San Francisco, CA: Jossey-Bass.

Bruner, J. S. (1966). *Toward a theory of instruction.* Cambridge, MA: Harvard University Press.

Dyer, W. G. (1987). *Team building: Issues and alternatives* (2nd ed.). Reading, MA: Addison-Wesley.

Forrester, J. W. (1961). *Industrial dynamics.* Cambridge, MA: MIT Press.

Forrester, J. W. (1971, January). Counterintuitive behavior of social systems. *Technology Review, 73,* 3.

Graham, A. K., Morecroft, J. D. W., Senge, P., & Sterman, J. (1989). *The computerized case study. A new tool for management education* (Working paper). Cambridge, MA: Sloan School of Management, MIT.

Kiefer, C., & Stroh, P. (1984). A new paradigm for developing organizations. In J. Adams (Ed.), *Transforming work.* Alexandria, VA: Miles River Press.

Irgvar, D. H. (1985). Memory of the future: An essay on the temporal organization of conscious awareness. *Human Neurobiology,* p. 4.

Lorange, P., Scott Morton, M., & Ghoshal, S. (1986). *Strategic control systems.* St. Paul, MN: West Publishing.

Mason, R., & Mitroff, I. (1981). *Challenging strategic planning assumptions.* New York: Wiley and Sons.

Meadows, D. H. (1982, Summer). Whole earth models and systems. *Co-Evolution Quarterly, 20.*

Meadows, D. (1985). Strategem 1: A resource planning game. *Environmental Education Report and Newsletter, 13*(2).

Morecroft, J. D. W. (1984). Strategy support models. *Strategic Management Journal, 5,* 215–229.

Richmond, B. (1987). *Systems thinking: Four key questions.* Lyme, NH: High Performance Systems Inc.

Roberts, E. B. (1978). *Managerial applications of system dynamics.* Cambridge, MA: MIT Press.

Schein, E. H. (1969). *Process consultation: Its role in organization development.* Reading, MA: Addison-Wesley.

Sterman, J. (1987). *Modeling managerial behavior: Misperceptions of feedback in a dynamic decision making environment* (Working paper, WP 1933-87). Cambridge, MA: Sloan School of Management, MIT.

Sterman, J. (in press). Testing behavioral simulation models by direct experiment. *Management Science.*

Sterman, J., & Meadows, D. (1985, June). Strategem 2: A microcomputer simulation game of the Kondratiev cycle. *Simulation Games, 16,* 2.

Vail, P. (1982). The purposing of high performing systems. *Organizational Dynamics, 23.*

Wack, P. (1985, September–October). Scenarios: Uncharted waters ahead. *Harvard Business Review, 73.*

Wack, P. (1985, November–December). Scenarios: Shooting the rapids. *Harvard Business Review, 139.*

Whitehead, A. N. (1957). *The aims of education and other essays.* New York: Macmillan.

# 13

# Organization Development Efforts by "Self-Confirming" Task Groups: A Japanese Case*

**Hiroko Kobayashi**
*Continuing Education Center,*
*Tokorozawa, Japan*

The rapid economic growth of Japanese industries, which has been watched with keen interest throughout the world, owes much to the enthusiastic organization development efforts, not only by large corporations but also by small and medium-sized enterprises. For example, at the annual OD convention held by Sanno Institute of Business Administration and Management, numerous presentations of OD efforts and their results have been reported by various small as well as large companies, (Sanno Institute, 1979, 1985, 1986). I have been involved directly in such efforts in the process of consultation to Japanese corporations, (Kobayashi & Kobayashi, 1986).

As far as Japanese OD is concerned, various methods and techniques, such as role training, team building, data feedback, KJ method, and QC circle have been adaptively adopted, according to organizational needs and situations. Regardless of differences of methods, either in training style or problem-solving style, OD is usually developed on the basis of activities by small groups which vary in level of structure, (Kuniya & Kobayashi, 1974/75; Umezawa, 1977).

The present writer has consulted with and developed such small groups in the form of "self-confirming" task groups. The self-confirming task group is a living group whose characteristics are therapeutic and educational, as described later. Such groups are able to

* Listening to Professor Massarik's presentation, the author shared his ideas completely (Tannenbaum, Margulies, & Massarik, 1985). His comments supported me and encouraged me. This is directly connected to my motivation to write this chapter. In conclusion, I would like to express my appreciation for his clear and warm guidance. (Grateful acknowledgement also is made of the advice and counsel of Professor William M. Elder, Osaka Women's Junior College.

judge the surrounding conditions in which they live and to decide spontaneously regarding their chosen directions.[1]

In this chapter, I would like to focus on the following two facets:

1.  The fact that the factors which have effects on the process of self-confirming task group—such as the attitude of the president, the consciousness of the participant employees, and especially the consultant's stance and characteristics of her approach—are closely related to the process and outcomes of the development of the group.
2.  The relationship between the development process of self-confirming task group and the desired effects; in other word, how does the self-confirming task group make participants change their consciousness and arouse their awareness of role responsibility, finally changing the underlying organizational climate and problem-solving style?

This chapter describes experiences during a 1-year period (May 1985–May 1986) in OD efforts by a Japanese enterprise (S&SK). Because similar process and outcomes observed in other companies under the consultation by the present writer and others, this case was regarded as a fairly typical example of OD efforts in Japanese companies.

## PROCESS OF OD

The 1-year OD effort could be divided into four stages:

1.  Diagnosis stage—November 1984–April 1985
2.  Intervention and action stage—May 1985–April 1986
3.  Evaluation stage—April–May 1986
4.  Process-maintenance and transition stage—June 1986–January 1987

### The Enterprise Studied and Its Principal Situation at the Time of Introducing OD

S&SK is a producer and distributor of silver drawing products and flat-square stainless steel. By 1986 the capital of S and SK com-

---

[1] In a book edited by Bennis, Schein, Steel, and Berlew (1968, Part 2) self-confirming, consisting of two major processes of self-evaluation and self-definition, is the basis for interpersonal relationships.

panies was 20 million yen and 60 million yen respectively; sales amounted to 2 billion and 465 million yen; the number of employees of S company, the sales division of S&SK, is 25, while for SK company, the manufacturing division, the employee number is 103. S&SK has 9 executives and 17 division and section managers.

The percentages of those with less than 10 years and those with more than 15 years are large. In terms of age, older employees are in the majority. With the exception of blue-collar workers at the plant, all the salespersons, engineers at manufacturing division and section managers are college or university graduates. Their level of technology and engineering competence is high.

S company was established in 1955 as a dealer stocking and distributing general steel products. In 1966 it expanded to silver drawing of steel materials and established the manufacturing division, SK company, independent of the sales division. Although it enjoyed a monopolistic period as a founder of such a business, the appearance of competitors and excessive investment resulted in severe financial problems. In hard times characterized by major workforce reduction, and so on, the company embarked on a program of reconstruction. At that point S&SK welcomed the current top management of its principal lender, a bank, to its management.

Due to the strength of yen, depression and consecutive drastic changes in sales, the current situation in S&SK has come to be still more severe. It has to cope with problems such as decreasing volume of orders, exchange losses (it takes 4 months from receiving orders to shipment), excessive inventory; repeated demands for bargaining, necessity of severe cost reduction, and quality problems in the manufacturing division. (quality control requirements led to the introduction of QCs—Quality Circle programs.)

As a long-term strategy, development of new technology and new products was clearly called for. Re-evaluation of iron itself as a basic raw material and careful consideration of future prospects of new materials (titanium, Si-steel) became an urgent agenda. As to management, S&SK is committed to the synergy of human harmony (*hito no wa*) in the organization and "to devote oneself to and transcend the individual and serve to the community" (Goethe).

S&SK's organization chart is as follows:

In 1982 the current president transferred to S&SK from the lending bank. In May 1984, 5 to 6 months after taking the post, he was enthusiastic about "making this company excellent." As a means, he considers introducing TQCs and a morale survey for the managers at the factory level. Before realizing these ideas, the following approach develops:

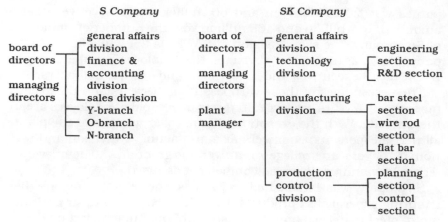

**FIGURE 1.** Organization chart.

In May 1983, mutual feedback of problems by 15 sales managers and 3 factory managers was carried out by means of mutual image exchange. In January 1984, a 2-day residential meeting was held spontaneously by managers. They discussed desirable actions to be taken by S&SK managers and steps needed to make profit. In May 1984, the managers met again, and identified and confirmed the problems they experienced at that moment, as follows:

- The productivity of the factory. How to upgrade the inside management of the factory: problems of quality, time limit of delivery, and cost control; evaluation of the human resources at the factory; quality and capability.
- How to cope with the conflicts between the sales division and the manufacturing division.

Although these problems were recognized by the president as well as the other managers, no concrete actions had been taken. One of the reasons for this inaction might be traced to the president's hesitancy in dealing with the relatively unfamiliar environment of the factory. Further, S company and SK company were at odds with each other, and therefore their relationship was rather like that of "rivals." In leader–subordinate relations, a top-down system was rather strong at SK company. On the contrary, at S company members were so familiar among themselves as to call each other by nicknames such as *goro-chan* and *yama-chan.* On the other hand, some scapegoating also was seen at S company.

## Initiating OD Efforts

In April–October 1984, exchanges of views regarding the current situation of the company proceeded at several meetings and in memoranda. We visited the factory in order to grasp the real problems that the president wished to resolve by means of the consultation—his motives and background—and indeed whether needs for consultation were to be found, not only in the president's own view but also in the company as a whole. In December 1984–January 1985 identification of problems and coordination of planning consultative action went forward. The board of directors decided, in April 1985, to start training in fiscal 1985, and expressed such desires as follow: to include management, human relations, problem solving in the workplace as the content of training; starting in May 1985, to have 3-hour meetings every month focused on executive training; to have 3-hour meetings once a month focused on managers' training.

The president's choice of OD rested on his previous career as training manager. Accordingly, as initial focus he chose intuitively the human side of the enterprise, more than the creation of new products. However, he spoke reminiscently after 1 year, when this OD efforts had concluded, that, as he saw it, in training task groups for problem solving, both the technical and human problems of the company had been successfully addressed.

## Steps in Training and Process Intervention

Tracing back the 1-year training process by problem-solving task groups, we can identify the following phases:

Step 1: Grasping the existing circumstances of the firm and reconfirming the problems to be considered.

Step 2: Specifying and sharing the tasks/problems to be solved.

Step 3: Planning the concrete action plan for improvement.

Step 4: Putting the plan into practice.

Step 5: Reviewing and evaluating planned actions.

Step 6: Planning the next plan and enhancing motivation to carry it out.

Steps of the training and points in process intervention are summarized as follows:

## Step 1.

*First training for managers* (May 11, 1985)

1. Grasping the present situation, both positive and negative, of the firm. Examining ways of feeling and perceiving.

    A.   To facilitate disclosure of own real feelings (*honne*) as much as possible, in free talking.

    B.   To become aware of and change the differences and disagreements among themselves, and to develop empathy for similarities without feeling at risk.

*First training for executives* (May 16, 1985)

1.  Grasping the current situation, inside and outside the firm, including review of the past and projection of the future.

2.  Deeper recognition and understanding of role.

    A.   To avoid concealing positions, and to express, as individual executives, on their own responsibility, what they think and what they feel.

    B.   To accept each other in how they think and feel without regard to whether or not they are "right."

    C.   To verify logically and emotionally the validity of their opinions through collection of relevant data, and to modify actions accordingly.

*Second training for managers* (June 8, 1985)

1.  Reconfirming the present situation; considering common, special, and sequential problems.

2.  Narrowing the problems, as seen by the managers.

    A.   To realize the necessity of confirming and modifying their ideas and feelings by relating to those of their colleagues, rather than being confined exclusively to their subjective understanding.

    B.   To obtain a factually based understanding of their issues.

    C.   To become aware of both task functions and process in groups.

    D.   To deepen understanding of managerial role problems; to emphasize that they, as managers of S&SK, should deal with the problems of the workplace and the whole company as their own problems.

## Step 2.

*Second training for executives* (July 15, 1985)

1.  Reconfirming the present situation.

    A.   To get new information and to learn how to collect information through interaction among participants.

    B.   To get beyond concern for their own personal face (*mentsu*) and examine openly the problems and orientation of the company.

    C.   To realize that the common problems of the company are their own personal problems.

*Third training for managers* (July 13, 1985)

1. Confirming with each other definition of the problems.
2. Determine the issues that they have to confront as managers, and form an action plan.
   A. To collect information actively about the problems to be handled and to examine them from various dimensions.
   B. To look carefully at the attitudes of managers in grappling with problems.
   C. To ask them to form concrete and practical action plans: what, how, and when.

*Fourth training for managers* (August 3, 1985)
1. Identifying and sharing the content and scope of the problems to be dealt with.
2. Narrowing down and sharing the matters to be improved.
   A. To recognize the variety and extent of the problems that both one's own and other sections have, and to deepen understanding of the relationship among sections.
   B. Not only to understand the matters to be improved by managers but also to discuss how they can collaborate in problem solving.

*Third training for executives* (August 12, 1985)
1. Narrowing and sharing the issues to be improved. Each executive considered the direction to be taken: policy, strategy, middle- and long-range plans, and problems to be solved. After that they shared their understanding of the main problems to be solved in the areas for which they are responsible.
   A. To identify the issues which S&SK needs to confront, without calling to account past actions or concentrating on the difficulty of the problem-solving process.
   B. To deepen understanding of the necessity for interaction and collaboration between their department and others.

## Step 3.
*Fifth training for managers* (September 7, 1985)
1. Examining the concrete action plan for improvement.
2. Beginning action for improvement.
   A. To create supportive and collaborative relationships among managerial groups.
   B. To have conviction that action will be supported and accepted by colleagues.

*Fourth training for executives* (September 14, 1985)
1. Connecting the training for managers with the training for executives.
2. Beginning action for improvement.
   A. To deepen understanding of the connection between the

issues discussed in the group and job situations to avoid isolation from on-the-job matters.

B.   Understanding on-the-job matters helps one take the concerns of others as one's own problems and deepen one's role consciousness and sense of responsibility.

C.   To gain confidence from their subordinates that the top management is reliable.

D.   To become able to carry out his tasks on the job on his own initiative, without waiting for training. Each executive becomes able to decide and solve on his own authority and responsibility. For example, redesigning of work systems is in progress at the factory.

**Step 4.**
(September 1985–November 1985)

Executives have come to understand on-the-job situations in the training so they know what they need to do now, and they can lead their subordinates as needed. One-on-one guidance, aimed at changing awareness of jobs, has been done among managers and between managers and their subordinates.

Some sales sections talked about stock, overtime work, transport costs, control of purchasing and dispatch, rationalization of packing, and sales promotion as an action plan for improvement. As a result, they reduced stock by about 10 million yen during 2 months from September.

In the production sections, managers talked with their subordinates about establishing a production control system. With mutual consensus to "do first of all what can be done," the following basic items were considered:

1.   To arrange production schedule by thinking ahead at least 3 months.
2.   To control and observe strictly the date of delivery.
3.   To establish the criteria for deciding whether or not to accept orders with low return or in small lots when the production process is not full.

In order to do the above, managers led workers to write precise daily reports. By so doing, workers grasped the existing situation and improved issues. This resulted in clarifying in detail the weight, number, hours, unit cost, and so on, in each process of production. Several kinds of training were carried out through this kind of action.

## Step 5.

*Fifth and sixth training for executives and sixth training for managers* (November 15, 1985; December 16, 1985; December 28–29, 1985, in residence)

1. Reviewing the progress that has been made by the above-mentioned actions.
2. Comparative review of the problems that have occurred in the execution of the plan.
3. Revising plans for improvement and discussing how to deal with them from now on.
    A. To review the actions for improvement, and to evaluate and share the joy of successful actions. Also to point out honestly needed modifications.
    B. To broaden the grasp of existing situation in the firm.
    C. To agree to continue further development of the plan.

(At the end of the training, the president expressed his feeling that executives had achieved a stronger sense of unity.)

*Seventh training for executives* (February 14–15, 1986, in residence)

1. Reviewing whether strategy, sales and production systems, and indirect/administrative sections had functioned appropriately during this term.
2. Free discussion about what was necessary for the next plan; focus ideas for making the next plan.
3. Clarifying the role of executives. Clarifying the role of the board of executives and the role of each executive in order to strengthen the basis for forming future policy, business plans, and strategy.
    A. It seems too early to review this consultation fully, but it was felt that this was needed in order to move into action planning for the next term.
    B. More emphasis was placed on how they would carry out the future plan than on why they hadn't carried out past plans.
    C. Detailed look at the role of managers, as a real implementalizer of the plan, and expectations toward them in the area of strategic planning.
    D. To talk about their everyday concerns in order to form a common basis of thought and sense of unity.
    E. To deepen consciousness of themselves as executives and to identify the role to be performed.

## Step 6.

*Eighth training for executives* (March 14–15, 1986)

1. Designing a draft of the next plan and examining its content.
   A. All executives should feel responsibility for participating fully in the next phase of the program.
   B. Should their own ideas openly and should listen carefully to others' ideas.
   C. Not only grasp the direction of the company including next policy and plan, but also its implementation.

*Seventh training for managers* (March 28–29, 1986, in residence)

1. Report on the progress of second action plan for improvement (planned in December 1985).
2. Understanding the future problems and identifying the role to be taken in this problem solving.
3. Feedback of the above-mentioned report to the board of executives.
   A. To expect each manager to behave spontaneously.
   B. To understand his own role based on his own awareness of the problems at hand.

*Ninth and Tenth training for executives* (April 15, 1986; April 24, 1986)

1. Forming the next plan: basic policies of management, orders and production planning, and equipment investment.
2. "A feedback letter" to each manager summing up executives' expectations of them.
   A. Make a plan with concrete content.
   B. Deepen exchange between executives and managers, and listen carefully to opinions offered from managers.
   C. Write "a letter from executives" giving attention to managers' career development.

*Eighth training for managers* (April 24, 1986; May 9, 1986)

1. Forming a concrete action plan for the next term.
2. Coordinating it with superiors and receiving their approval.
3. Drawing up the "job implementation program."
4. Sending a letter from executives to managers and distributing a memo on a development/training plan to subordinates.
   A. A work implementation program is useful to check the progress of daily work.
   B. Each plan is well known, agreed to and supported not only by the person himself but also by one's superiors, colleagues, and subordinates.
   C. Doing this gives each manager a sense of fulfillment that he is useful and accepted in the company, and satisfaction with achievement.

## Phases in the Group Process

Our above description has focused on problem-solving process. Now we would move to the developmental phases of group process. A "self-confirming" task group is characterized by the fact that it lays emphasis on problem solving as a task group as well as on interpersonal and group process in terms of self-confirmation.[2]

The course of group development during 1 year was as follows:
Groping stage (May–July 1985)

- What members have usually felt at the workplace became a topic of conversation.
- There was little interaction and conversation among them, rather they were explaining things to the consultants.
- The group was directed by some "strong men" who took leadership.
- They were searching for their points of contact and groping for directions.

Experimental stage (August–September, 1985)

- They began to feel the common ground which motivated their behavior.
- The atmosphere developed in which they were conscious of themselves moving and trying new actions.

---

[2] There are many researches about phases in problem-solving groups. In the study reported by Bales and Strodbeck (1951), groups change from emphasis on orientation to problems of evaluation and finally to problem of control. Fisher (1970) identified four developmental phases in task-oriented groups: orientation, conflict, emergence, and reinforcement. Compared with this, developmental phases in sensitivity-training groups are different. Bennis and Shepard (1956) and Bennis (1964) clarified six phases: phase 1 dependence authority relations—subphase 1 dependence-flight, subphase 2 counterdependence-fight, subphase 3 resolution-catharsis; phase 2 interdependence-personal relations—subphase 4 enchantment-flight, subphase 5 disenchantment-fight, subphase 6 consensual validation. It is common knowledge that Rogers (1970) found 15 concrete patterns in the developmental process of encounter groups. Saji, Ishigouka, and Agari (1977) analyzed similar developmental phases of group process. Sarri and Galinski (1985) extracted 7 phases (origin, formative, intermediate 1, revision, intermediate 2, maturation, and termination phases) in the group development of social group work by using three dimensions of social organization of the group: activities, tasks and operative process of the group, and the culture of the group.

- They confirmed their interface on the job and developed a feeling that they could do this task together.
- The sales section was lagging behind the production department.

Activity stage (October–December, 1985)

- Exchange of ideas among managers and their subordinates as well as among executives and managers has been made on their own initiative in the process of carrying out the plan for improvement.
- Cooperative and supportive relationships have been created in the group.
- Not only certain "strong men" attracted attention but also the members who had been noticed took a leading role. Shared leadership appeared in the group. Leadership role changed with different situations.
- Some members were excited and stimulated by expression of opinions of others.
- Transition from a feeling of "it is useless to try" to a real feeling of "it is possible to do" began to appear.
- However, executives did not yet have a sense of unity.
- Disharmony remained between sales and production departments.

Permeation stage (January–March, 1986)

- Each person tried new changes on the job, a number of "buds" and "stirring" for improvement appeared.
- As a result, there were positive opinions expressed about how to grasp facts, how to make collaborative relationships, and how to lead and advise.
- Opinions about the future of the company were expressed actively. It was stated that they had never discussed the company's future this broadly and deeply. Members expressed the hope that this session could lead to the next step.
- An atmosphere of self-examination has appeared. People have come to feel keenly the limited scope of their information and poverty of their ideas, and the necessity for intellectual innovation.

Transition stage to steady progress (April–May, 1986)

- Role consciousness of executives and managers have been clearly established.
- They talked frankly about the problems and what to do about them, relating this to their own experiences. They came to accept each other as their own colleagues, and a sense of security of being accepted by the group developed.
- They had a consciousness of the severity of their own true value being examined.

## Points of Consultation Through the Whole Process of OD Efforts

A training program of 1 year was not predetermined, but was planned contingently as the occasion demanded. We had training sessions in residence in one case, or in another case over 1–2-month periods at the workplace, according to needs.

However, the following points were taken into consideration throughout the consultation:

1. To grasp accurately the existing situation in each session (to recognize problems to be improved by looking squarely at the situation, not just complaining about it). Identifying problems.
2. By presenting and discussing the problems seen by each member through the training, to identify more clearly the problems as well as to recognize deeply the common problems to be confronted. Sharing of problems.
3. To take charge of the problems to be handled in connection with one's own role, to recognize each other's problems, and to implement the plan to solve these problems. Taking roles and grappling with problem solving.
4. The action research (Kobayashi, 1984) followed a process of examination and confirmation both at training sessions and OJT at the workplace. Process involves a repetitive series of attempts such as a sequence of training: (1) hometask (trial and fact finding at the workplace), (2) training, (3) hometask. Connecting training with workplace and job. The results of the above-mentioned process also permeated into actual daily work, and stabilized in the organization and systems of the workplace to become a "movement" for problem solving.
5. The process of OD lifts up individual, interpersonal, and job

problems and motivates for their solution. In the process of OD the task is primarily to squeeze out the pus, accumulated for long, concerning what management and control of the organization have be done. The members of the organization feel the sore inbearable and want to keep it under cover, if possible. Especially top management often feels keenly its lack of power to manage. He or she tries to accept deeply these facts as facts. And starting from these facts, he or she strive for leading the organization. Accordingly, making a success of OD, he have careful consideration for their severe suffering in the organization. This is determined by the strength of top management's decision to change. This is the reason the first issue is to move top management and that it is said that "OD can not start until top management says yes."

In a case of S&SK the promoter of OD was the president. When the author launched on the consultation, the first step was to confirm strongly the "president's decision to change." The attitude of this president made it possible to accept the facts as facts and brought about awareness of the possibility of future development. His "awareness" in the process that "his subordinates were worthy of trust" became a source of great deal of energy necessary for OD efforts. The consultant's role is to facilitate decision, and confirm the strength of decision, and further to give assistance and support when asked throughout the process, so to give effective leadership.

## EVALUATION OF OD EFFORTS

After the year's training we assessed the outcome of OD efforts by means of a questionnaire on training results and changes in organizational climate. This research aimed at grasping the present situation (May 1986) of the organization, next to compare this situation with the conditions of a year previously, and finally to find out the problems to be solved in the future, identify desirable goals for the future and to be useful in implementing action for improvement.

The subjects totaled 75. They included 9 executives (participants in the training), 17 managers (participants in the training), 26 subsection chiefs, leaders, and subleaders, and 23 employees.

The questionnaire was distributed after training for executives and managers, and collected at the end of May 1986. Concerning four dimensions of organizational climate—goal orientation, effectiveness, willingness, identification—a questionnaire of 28 items with a 7-point scale was prepared. These items are collected and analyzed for each dimensions. In addition to these items, a section for free answers was provided, data collected, and its contents arranged into six clusters.

## Behavioral and Attitudinal Changes

All participants felt training to be useful for themselves and workplace. However, 66.7% of executives felt it to be very useful for themselves, 41.2% of managers felt so. For problem solving of the workplace, 77.8% of executives felt it to be very useful, 35.3% of managers reported they felt so. Impact of the training was more remarked in executives than in managers, and in managers of S company (50% for both themselves and workplace) than in those of SK company (26.8% for themselves and 14.3% for workplace).

We arranged contents of free answers about training outcome into six clusters, as shown in Table 1.

Remarkable results are found in "perception of present situation, clarification of policy and goals," "willingness to act and enhancement of work," and "interaction and feeling of identification." But "new understanding of role" is limited to self-perception. It does not appear in actual daily work nor is it recognized by colleagues.

## Changes in Organizational Climate

Generally speaking, assessment of data is as follows (see Table 2). Compared with the situation a year previously, an overall positive change of 0.73 was seen. Positive changes were seen in "goal-orientation" (0.84) and "effectiveness" (0.82) in the four dimensions. Items showing most remarkable change were "to judge what is important and engage in the necessary tasks" (1.23) and "vision and policy of the company are clear" (1.03). Further, positive changes showed in "there is an atmosphere of improving work methods, not limited to past ways of working" (1.01), "there is an atmosphere of future possibility and hope to proceed in a positive manner" (0.99), "middle and long term goals are distinct" (0.97).

About the present situation: High score items are "there is an atmosphere of future possibility and hope to proceed in a positive manner" (2.72), "vision and policy are definite" (2.95), "There is an atmosphere of improving work methods, not limited to past ways of working" (2.96). To the contrary, lower score items are "people live

TABLE 1.   DIFFERENCES IN CONTENT CATEGORY BY PERCEPTIONS FOR ONESELF AND THE WORKPLACE

| | Executives | | | Managers | | | |
|---|---|---|---|---|---|---|---|
| | Perception by Themselves | | Perception by Managers | Perception by Themselves | | Perception by Executives | |
| | a | b | | a | b | | Total |
| Perception of present situation, clarification of policy and goals | 3 | 10 | 12(*4) | 4 | 8 | | 37(*4) |
| New understanding of role | 4 | | | 9 | | | 13 |
| Interaction and feeling of identification | | | | 7 | 10 | 7 | 24 |
| Learned new way of perceiving | 4 | | | 3 | 3 | | 10 |
| Willingness to act and enhancement of work | 6 | 6 | 6(*2) | 6 | 5 | 5 | 34(*2) |
| Recognition of importance of learning and education | 1 | | 1 | 3 | 1 | 5 | 11 |

Number: frequency of answer to each content.
*: negative and desirable responses.
a: for oneself; b: for the workplace.

comfortably and work relaxed" (4.36), "people have no anxiety and fear about the prospects of job and security of livelihood" (4.21), "employment and education of persons capable of coping with technological innovation is being done" (4.09), "right persons were assigned to the right post and people work with pleasure and pride at their own job" (4.09). Considerable difference was seen in response to "people live comfortably and work relaxed" and "people have no anxiety and fear about the prospects of job and security of livelihood."

## Comprehensive Evaluation of OD Efforts

In considering the results of the above research on training effectiveness and organizational climate and of the later progress of S&SK, the OD effort can be generally evaluated as follows:

## TABLE 2. ORGANIZATIONAL CLIMATE

| | Average[A] | SD | Average[B] | SD | B-A | T |
|---|---|---|---|---|---|---|
| **(A) Goal orientation** | | | | | | |
| 1. Clear vision and policy | 2.95 | | 4.03 | | 1.08 | 5.43*** |
| | | 1.17 | | 1.24 | | |
| 2. Clear long- and middle-term image of own department | 3.20 | | 4.16 | | 0.97 | 4.45*** |
| | | 1.21 | | 1.41 | | |
| 3. To choose alternatives by examining all possible conditions | 3.22 | | 3.88 | | 0.65 | 2.92*** |
| | | 1.27 | | 1.42 | | |
| 4. To act positively feeling possibility and hope | 2.72 | | 3.71 | | 0.99 | 4.56*** |
| | | 1.22 | | 1.39 | | |
| 5. To employ/educate personnel to cope with tech. innovation | 4.09 | | 4.93 | | 0.84 | 3.60*** |
| | | 1.51 | | 1.31 | | |
| 6. Tasks/goals of div./sect. attractive and worth doing | 3.17 | | 3.93 | | 0.76 | 3.68*** |
| | | 1.31 | | 1.17 | | |
| 7. To think from a long-term/comprehensive standpoint | 3.86 | | 4.42 | | 0.56 | 2.43** |
| | | 1.48 | | 1.30 | | |
| | 3.32 | 1.39 | 4.15 | 1.38 | 0.84 | 9.74*** |
| **(B) Effectiveness** | | | | | | |
| 1. To understand policy/tasks of one's own div./sect. | 3.26 | | 4.13 | | 0.87 | 3.63*** |
| | | 1.46 | | 1.38 | | |
| 2. To share role/job appropriate to each position | 3.57 | | 4.28 | | 0.72 | 3.03** |
| | | 1.42 | | 1.43 | | |
| 3. Managers recognize/work at their role | 3.30 | | 4.05 | | 0.75 | 3.18** |
| | | 1.53 | | 1.32 | | |
| 4. Delegated appropriate role and job, using ability fully | 3.24 | | 3.97 | | 0.74 | 3.48*** |
| | | 1.30 | | 1.26 | | |
| 5. To judge what is important, engage in the necessary tasks | 3.07 | | 4.30 | | 1.23 | 5.75*** |
| | | 1.23 | | 1.35 | | |
| 6. To communicate with related sect., work effectively | 3.71 | | 4.44 | | 0.73 | 3.44*** |
| | | 1.33 | | 1.25 | | |
| 7. Trust/assistance among headquarters, factory, branches | 3.50 | | 4.21 | | 0.71 | 3.31*** |
| | | 1.25 | | 1.32 | | |
| | 3.38 | 1.38 | 4.20 | 1.34 | 0.82 | 9.67*** |

(continued)

**TABLE 2** (*Continued*)

|  | Average$^A$ | SD | Average$^B$ | SD | B-A | T |
|---|---|---|---|---|---|---|
| **(C) Willingness** | | | | | | |
| 1. Reserves of energy in company, can use as needed | 3.51 | 1.36 | 4.00 | 1.47 | 0.49 | 2.07 |
| 2. To put right person in right place, work with joy/pride | 4.09 | 1.51 | 4.49 | 1.47 | 0.40 | 1.61 |
| 3. To absorb actively new tech./knowledge | 3.13 | 1.38 | 4.01 | 1.26 | 0.88 | 4.03*** |
| 4. To improve work methods, not limited to past ways of working | 2.96 | 1.40 | 3.97 | 1.26 | 1.01 | 4.56*** |
| 5. To propose/offer opinions positively | 3.59 | 1.52 | 4.46 | 1.24 | 0.88 | 3.79*** |
| 6. Superiors take responsibility for subordinates' actions | 3.01 | 1.51 | 3.54 | 1.38 | 0.53 | 2.20 |
| 7. To live comfortably/work relaxed | 4.36 | 1.64 | 4.68 | 1.54 | 0.31 | 1.17 |
|  | 3.52 | 1.56 | 4.16 | 1.43 | 0.64 | 6.86*** |
| **(D) Identification** | | | | | | |
| 1. To behave for one's team, not just for own interests | 3.04 | 1.36 | 3.74 | 1.24 | 0.70 | 3.23** |
| 2. To be friendly, joining hands together | 3.32 | 1.53 | 3.88 | 1.49 | 0.56 | 2.25 |
| 3. To have interest in policy/achievement, a sense of unity | 3.27 | 1.55 | 4.12 | 1.50 | 0.85 | 3.28** |
| 4. To talk frankly, understandably, useful for prob solving | 3.64 | 1.37 | 4.47 | 1.22 | 0.83 | 3.83*** |
| 5. To express opinions frankly without reserve/hesitation | 3.21 | 1.48 | 3.85 | 1.49 | 0.64 | 2.59** |
| 6. Managers adopt subordinates' ideas/opinions | 3.27 | 1.52 | 3.91 | 1.36 | 0.65 | 2.68** |
| 7. Not to have anxiety/fear on future of job/security of livelihood | 4.21 | 1.67 | 4.32 | 1.62 | 0.10 | 0.38 |
|  | 3.42 | 1.55 | 4.04 | 1.45 | 0.62 | 6.60*** |
| TOTAL | 3.41 | 1.47 | 4.14 | 1.40 | 0.73 | 16.29*** |

(A = Present Situation, B = One Year Ago)　$n = 76$
***$p < .001$
**$p < .01$

1. Recognition of the current situation, clarification of policy and goals:
   Management policy put in order. All members were able to move forward toward the goals spontaneously, deliberately, and positively.
2. Willing attitude and enhancement of work level:
   The actual condition of the workplace became clear and a willing work attitude was enhanced. People could express frankly their opinion. Operational conditions of machinery and hours of operation could be grasped exactly, so it became easy to map out a schedule of operation.
3. Interaction and feeling of identification:
   It was felt that policy and strategy were planned and implemented by all members. They could influence each other through mutual confrontation. Communication between executives and managers became better and they began to collaborate with each other. Interaction between sales department and factory has been effected and a sense of identification was attained.
4. New awareness of role:
   A new understanding of roles induced responsible action.
5. Problems remaining:
   There are overall unresolved problems such as comfort, stabilization of job and livelihood, and employment and development of human resources. The differences of perception are found between participants and nonparticipants (below the subsection chief), especially in respect to collaboration among related departments, frank disclosure, and recognition of managerial role (see Table 3).
6. Launching the cycle of problem-solving action:
   For the first time, the policy of the company was presented in written manner as the next term plan. A program of investment in plant equipment, long needed, was made, and carried out, and resulted in reduction of production process and cost.

After training, improvement of daily work continued using training as a lever.

## FUNDAMENTAL ATTITUDE AND CHARACTERISTICS OF APPROACH ADOPTED BY A CONSULTANT

We have described OD efforts and its outcome during 1 year at a Japanese small and medium-sized enterprise. Next we will describe the basic way of thinking and type of approach which the writer

**TABLE 3. ORGANIZATIONAL CLIMATE BY STATUS**

| Number | Executive 9 Average | SD | Manager 17 Average | SD | Chief/Leader 26 Average | SD | Worker 23 Average | SD | Total 75 Average | SD |
|---|---|---|---|---|---|---|---|---|---|---|
| **(A) Goal orientation** | | | | | | | | | | |
| 1. Clear vision and policy | 2.22 | 0.63 | 2.71 | 0.96 | 3.15 | 1.23 | 3.17 | 1.27 | 2.95 | 1.18 |
| 2. Clear long- and middle-term image of own department | 2.44 | 0.68 | 2.71 | 0.75 | 3.65 | 1.24 | 3.39 | 1.34 | 3.21 | 1.21 |
| 3. To choose alternatives by examining all possible conditions | 2.56 | 0.83 | 3.00 | 0.91 | 3.46 | 1.25 | 3.39 | 1.55 | 3.23 | 1.28 |
| 4. To act positively feeling possibility and hope | 2.78 | 1.13 | 2.59 | 0.69 | 2.46 | 1.08 | 3.09 | 1.59 | 2.72 | 1.23 |
| 5. To employ/educate personnel to cope with tech. innovation | 3.11 | 1.52 | 3.76 | 0.88 | 4.38 | 1.71 | 4.35 | 1.43 | 4.08 | 1.51 |
| 6. Tasks/goals of div./sect. attractive and worth doing | 2.33 | 0.82 | 2.94 | 0.80 | 3.35 | 1.47 | 3.43 | 1.38 | 3.16 | 1.30 |
| 7. To think from a long-term/ comprehensive standpoint | 3.00 | 1.15 | 3.41 | 0.91 | 4.27 | 1.56 | 4.00 | 1.62 | 3.84 | 1.48 |
| | 2.63 | 1.06 | 3.02 | 0.93 | 3.53 | 1.51 | 3.55 | 1.52 | 3.31 | 1.39 |
| **(B) Effectiveness** | | | | | | | | | | |
| 1. To understand policy/tasks of one's own div./sect. | 2.44 | 0.68 | 2.65 | 0.76 | 3.85 | 1.56 | 3.39 | 1.66 | 3.27 | 1.47 |
| 2. To share role/job appropriate to each position | 3.11 | 0.57 | 3.53 | 0.92 | 3.58 | 1.64 | 3.74 | 1.65 | 3.56 | 1.43 |

| | | | | | | | | | | |
|---|---|---|---|---|---|---|---|---|---|---|
| 3. | Managers recognize/work at their role | 2.67 | 1.05 | 3.00 | 1.08 | 3.19 | 1.64 | 3.91 | 1.67 | 3.31 | 1.54 |
| 4. | Delegated appropriate role and job, using ability fully | 3.22 | 1.03 | 3.29 | 0.89 | 3.04 | 1.29 | 3.39 | 1.61 | 3.23 | 1.30 |
| 5. | To judge what is important, engage in the necessary tasks | 2.55 | 0.96 | 2.71 | 0.57 | 3.42 | 1.47 | 3.09 | 1.25 | 3.05 | 1.23 |
| 6. | To communicate with related sect., work effectively | 3.00 | 1.05 | 3.18 | 0.92 | 4.08 | 1.62 | 3.91 | 0.97 | 3.69 | 1.31 |
| 7. | Trust/assistance among head-quarters, factory, branches | 3.11 | .074 | 3.29 | 0.82 | 3.54 | 1.41 | 3.83 | 1.46 | 3.52 | 1.27 |
| | | 2.87 | 0.93 | 3.09 | 0.92 | 3.53 | 1.56 | 3.61 | 1.52 | 3.37 | 1.38 |

(C) Willingness

| | | | | | | | | | | |
|---|---|---|---|---|---|---|---|---|---|---|
| 1. | Reserves of energy in company, can use as needed | 2.44 | 1.07 | 4.06 | 1.26 | 3.69 | 1.17 | 3.35 | 1.49 | 3.52 | 1.37 |
| 2. | To put right person in right place, work with joy/pride | 3.44 | 1.26 | 4.06 | 1.16 | 4.54 | 1.65 | 3.87 | 1.57 | 4.09 | 1.52 |
| 3. | To absorb actively new tech./knowledge | 2.78 | 0.92 | 2.53 | 0.78 | 3.68 | 1.49 | 3.13 | 1.54 | 3.14 | 1.39 |
| 4. | To improve work methods, not limited to past ways of working | 2.56 | 0.83 | 2.50 | 0.94 | 3.00 | 1.49 | 3.41 | 1.61 | 2.96 | 1.41 |
| 5. | To propose/offer opinions positively | 3.00 | 1.05 | 3.19 | 0.88 | 3.77 | 1.76 | 3.78 | 1.61 | 3.55 | 1.52 |
| 6. | Superiors take responsibility for subordinates' actions | 2.44 | 1.17 | 3.06 | 1.21 | 3.08 | 1.64 | 3.22 | 1.67 | 3.04 | 1.53 |

(continued)

**TABLE 3** (Continued)

| Number | Executive | | Manager | | Chief/Leader | | Worker | | Total | |
|---|---|---|---|---|---|---|---|---|---|---|
| | Average | SD | Average | SD | Average | SD | Average | SD | Average | SD |
| 7. To live comfortably/work relaxed | 3.22 | 1.03 | 3.94 | 0.87 | 4.88 | 1.86 | 4.59 | 1.56 | 4.37 | 1.59 |
| | 2.84 | 1.12 | 3.34 | 1.21 | .380 | 1.72 | 3.62 | 1.65 | 3.52 | 1.56 |
| (D) Identification | | | | | | | | | | |
| 1. To behave for one's team, not just for own interests | 2.33 | 0.67 | 2.94 | 0.73 | 3.15 | 1.56 | 3.26 | 1.59 | 3.04 | 1.37 |
| 2. To be friendly, joining hands together | 2.22 | 0.63 | 2.88 | 0.76 | 3.81 | 1.47 | 3.57 | 1.93 | 3.33 | 1.53 |
| 3. To have interest in policy/achievement, a sense of unity | 2.89 | 1.20 | 2.69 | 0.58 | 3.23 | 1.55 | 3.91 | 1.93 | 3.27 | 1.56 |
| 4. To talk frankly, understandably, useful for prob solving | 3.22 | 0.92 | 3.24 | 0.64 | 3.81 | 1.66 | 3.96 | 1.46 | 3.65 | 1.38 |
| 5. To express opinions frankly without reserve/hesitation | 2.33 | 0.94 | 2.88 | 0.76 | 3.15 | 1.56 | 3.87 | 1.70 | 3.21 | 1.49 |
| 6. Managers adopt subordinates' ideas/opinions | 2.56 | 0.83 | 3.00 | 0.79 | 3.31 | 1.56 | 3.70 | 1.83 | 3.27 | 1.50 |
| 7. Not to have anxiety/fear on future of job/security of livelihood | 3.44 | 1.57 | 4.00 | 0.97 | 4.69 | 1.88 | 4.09 | 1.74 | 4.20 | 1.68 |
| | 2.71 | 1.10 | 3.09 | 0.86 | 3.59 | 1.69 | 3.76 | 1.77 | 3.43 | 1.55 |
| TOTAL | 2.77 | 1.06 | 3.14 | 1.00 | 3.61 | 1.63 | 3.63 | 1.62 | 3.41 | 1.48 |

adopted in conducting consultation. We called the central group in consultation "self-confirming" task group, and defined its characteristics as decision making and management. "To be participative" is fundamental in conducting our consultation.

Points that we are always concerned about are as follows:

- Each member can participate in decision making.
- A doesn't exploit B, and C is not sacrificed for D.
- Decisions are made openly and are understood by all (even though every person may not always agree).
- To be respected as human beings (to have an opportunity to grow) and to become conscious of responsibility for others.
- To establish a mutually helping relationship, that is, how can I help someone gain energy? To build a relationship of "codevelopment/growth" of supporting and of being supported. This means that one is pleased with mutual growth.

When the author expressed her opinions and pointed out problems in the group in order to facilitate the realization of these things, she kept in mind the following points:

- To speak concretely and clearly about what is occurring here and now (what was expressed and not expressed, feeling and attitude of speaker, feelings of other members as receiver of the message, and problems they are feeling).
- All members should feel ownership in discussions. This implies mutual understanding, seeking a common orientation, moving on to the next step, hints for problem solution, motivation for collaboration and helping relations.

Differences among OD activities and consultation are discussed as national and racial differences. "Participative management" seems to succeed easily in Japan, because it is said that most Japanese have the psychological mechanism to behave according to "ethics of the field" (*ba no rinri*). It is "ethics of the field" that causes Japanese to participate in trips for employees and year-end parties, because those events are carried out by all members. There is difference from European "ethics of the individual" (*ko no rinri*) which emphasizes self-assertion (Kawai, 1982, 1984). In Japan participation itself has significance. There is no self-assertion strong enough to destroy total harmony. Attacks on self-centeredness function as an adequate restraint to maintain the total balance. A leader of an organization in Western countries where self-assertion is strong seems to use his power to hold together and lead the organization. In contrast, a Japanese leader (*cho*) maintains harmony of the whole as a go-between and organizer rather than a leader and is careful not to lose the total harmony (*wa*).

However, a system in which the locus of responsibility is not clearly, such as organizational management based on this "field," has operated better than one might expect in the higher growth periods when all things ran smoothly, but in the present time of crisis (high yen recession, decline in exports, diminution of management resources, cost reduction, decrease in personnel, etc.) this system suddenly reveals all inefficiency.

In the present situation of Japanese enterprises, the important thing is not to talk about differences in consultation among nations and which way to choose, but to integrate both ethics of field and of individual by taking account of both ethics. One always emphasizes on importance of communication when doing OD in Japan. It is very important to verbalize and become conscious of things that are difficult to say, which means integrating both individual and field ethics, in order to create "vitality with mutual consent" in the organizations. Actions to stimulate participants "to become conscious of" seem to be indispensable for the process of consultation.

We continue to describe the characteristics of our approach to consultation by following its process:

*Situation 1:*   Members are able to share information, identify problems, and share in problems (everyone having an opportunity to express himself).

*Situation 2:*   Problem solving becomes the task of the group as a whole, and possible alternatives for solution are groped for ("possible" also means that alternatives are accepted in the group). In the process of sharing information, its evaluation and selection, and strategy formation are worked on as a joint effort.

*Situation 3:*   Alternative methods are, tacitly understood, chosen, determined, and accepted in the field.

*Situation 4:*   Decision making is prone to end at the above step, but it is important here to verbalize the solution alternatives that have been chosen and to make decision making explicit (In many cases the consultant points out this necessity).

*Situation 5:*   The next step is to clarify different roles for problem solving and to help each become conscious of one's own responsibility. In addition, on one's own responsibility, each person forms an action plan to fulfill his or her own role, and these are mutually understood. Each plan becomes more realistic through mutual concern, advice, collaboration, assistance, and coordination. (There are many steps taken in the form of Off-JT to further the above and relate it directly to daily work.)

Situation 6: There is follow-up on how the action plans are implemented in connection with changes in the existing managerial organization as a whole or specific workplaces. (There are actually many training programs that will be carried out after 6 months or 1 year.)

## CLIENT'S IMPRESSIONS AND COMMENTS ON OD EFFORTS

### What the Client Obtained from One Year of OD Efforts:

1. "Training" combined smoothly with "field/daily work," so it did not feel unnatural. Agenda, problems to be dealt with, or issues presented in the training program have been assimilated by members, and often appear in different kinds of conferences (such as sales promotion and production) and meetings for information sharing and arrangement. Because members all have readiness in these matters, they participate more deeply in meetings and conferences. It seems to be the same in informal situations.

Issues discussed in the training and results examined by teams in the training did not stop with presentations at the training, but are now being carried out before our eyes at the factory (e.g., equipment investment program). This fact is very significant. Members felt that "we thought up and created the plans by ourselves and carried them out," not at the direction of top management. Members have good reason for expressing a positive response.

2. Members begin to appeal step by step to the top about the organizational system and management. There are such phenomena as an executive's awakening from "hibernation", direct appeal of managers to top, quick responses of plant managers to top.

3. Each member now has more definite action goals in the workplace. This was their first experience with this kind of training. Mutual feedback that has occurred spontaneously among members in the group work has stimulated them to understand each other's role, and action goals to be achieved by each have stood out in sharp relief. The so-called "love letter from executives" had a very strong impact on managers. (Reactions to this letter

were "I had no idea people saw me that way", and "They've hit a sore point." This led to serious self-examination and search for new behavior.)

## Present Situation and Problems to be Solved

As mentioned earlier, S&SK had many external difficulties and a lot of old internal problems, so that it was pitching and rolling violently and was in a tight corner. However, whenever it confronted problems, it experienced an unexpected energy for working on solutions welling up from inside. In this sense, now it has an excellent chance to change the organizational culture.

Problems to be solved were as follows:

1. Not accustomed to timely communication of information. Norms inhibit awareness of this, so organizational flow of information is not good.
2. The way of organizational decision making is premodern, which results in "leaving things to others" or "procrastination."
3. How to reduce perceptual differences between managers who participated in the training, and subsection chiefs who did not.
4. It is hoped that managers' approaches to the board of executives will consist of frank opinions and proposals, not at random but in systematized form.

## How to Further These Collective Efforts:

1. Follow up of the training:
   Managers reply to executives about how they understand and are dealing with the so-called "love letter". Concerning the "job implementation program" presented after the training ended, reviews of progress in meeting the goals and means to strengthen future actions need to be considered. Executives also need to review their own "job implementation program".
2. In connection with team building of *shoku-cho* (first line supervisor), chief and blue-collar worker:
   Concerning this, cost reduction and prevention of defects are now the most critical issues at the factory. A zero-defect movement was announced and was to start in September 1986. It is necessary to manage this movement carefully.

3.  In the future development of the OD program the following mea-
    sures should be considered:
    To have regular conferences composed of managers like a junior
    board of management and to exchange ideas to participate in
    actual decision making with the board of executives (in order to
    rejuvenate the organization, to introduce fresh ideas into strat-
    egy formation, and select and educate executive candidates).
    Next to develop family training or team building.

## CONCLUDING NOTE

The case described in this chapter was presented at the fifth meeting (September 24, 1986) of the Continuing Education Center over
which the author presides. Professor Fred Massarik (Anderson
Graduate School of Management, UCLA) then visiting Japan, joined
in the discussion. We want to conclude this chapter by recounting
this discussion.

In response to the question asked by participants about characteristics of Japanese consultation, the president of S&SK expressed
his opinion that it was a soft technique, but this was sometime
more severe, because one had to confront the other at a deeper and
more fundamental dimension. Professor Massarik also pointed out
many similarities between consultation in Japan and in the U.S.A.,
based on his own experience. He noted his impression that there are
more differences among particular enterprises than among nations.
The author agrees with him in this respect.

Professor Massarik continued as follows:

*   In the U.S. situational leadership, TA, Gestalt therapy, and such
    are declining as interventions. At this time, people are beginning
    to stress the importance of strategic and holistic thinking.
*   Todays' OD effort appropriately emphasizes *process* in team
    building rather than technique. Balance of technology and
    human relations is important; the idea of attending to the "whole
    gestalt" is increasingly important.
*   It is often noted that human individuality is alienated by the
    organization. In response, development of purposeful balance be-
    tween the technical and human sides constitutes the central
    challenge.
*   With respect to the relationship of technical progress to human
    sensitivity, while organizations change when people are function-

ing fully and while human feelings of joy and satisfaction are a key source of energy, the creative design of new organization forms will prove to be a major thrust in the 1990s.

## REFERENCES

Bales, R. F., & Strodbeck, F. L. (1951). Phases in group problem solving. *Journal of Abnormal and Social Psychology, 46,* 485–495.

Bennis, W. G. (1964). Patterns and vicissitudes in T-group development. In L. P. Bradford et al. (Eds.), *T-group Theory and Laboratory Methods* (pp. 248–278). New York: Wiley.

Bennis, W. G., & Shepard, H. A. (1956). A theory of group development. *Human Relations, 9,* 415–437.

Bennis, W. G., Schein, E. H., Steele, F. I., & Berlew, D. E. (Eds.). (1968). *Interpersonal dynamics* (rev. ed.). Homewood, IL: Dorsey Press.

Fisher, B. A. (1970). Decision emergence: Phase in group decision-making. *Speech Monographs, 21,* 53–66.

Kawai, H. (1984). *Japanese and identity—Eye of a psychotherapist.* Tokyo: Sogen-sha.

Kawai, H. (1982). *Depths in Japanese Balance Structure.* Tokyo: Chuo-koron-sha.

Kobayashi, K., & Kobayashi, H. (1986). *Organization development efforts in Japanese corporations after the economic crises.* Document LEST 86–1, Aix-en-Provence: Laboratories d'Economie et de Sociologie du Travail, CNRS.

Kobayashi, K. (1984). *Action research note.* Bulletin, Department of Social Relations, Toyo University, 22(1):5–22.

Kuniya, N., & Kobayashi, K. (1974–1975). Current trends in organization development in Japan. *Interpersonal Development, 5,* 136–155.

Rogers, C. (1970). *On encounter groups.* New York: Harper & Row.

Saji, M., Ishigouoka, Y., & Agari, I. (Eds.). (1977). *Group Approach.* Tokyo: Seishi-shobo, 1977.

Sanno Institute of Business Administration and Management (1978, 1985, 1986). *OD Conference Report.* Tokyo-Sanno IBAM.

Sarri, S. M., & Glinski, M. L. (1985). A conceptual framework for group development. In M. Sundel et. al. (Eds.), *Individual changes through small groups* (2nd ed., pp. 70–86). New York: Free Press.

Tannenbaum, R., Margulies, N., & Massarik, F. (1985). *Human Systems Development.* San Francisco: Jossey–Bass.

Umezawa, T. (Ed.). (1977). *Japanese organization development—Its development and Cases.* Tokyo: Diamond Co.

# part four

# Trends and Time Lines in the OD Profession

# 14

# Organizational Change and Development: Core Practitioner Competencies and Future Trends

*Jane L. Esper*

I became involved in this research with the desire to get out of my office at Ford Aerospace (where I was an internal organizational development consultant) and out of my classroom at University of Southern California (where I was completing an MBA). I wanted to find out what was really happening in the field of Organizational Development. The project was modeled after a similar experience in my senior year at the University of Michigan which focused on practitioners in training and development.

What I hoped to gain from this project was a broader view of Organizational Development and an up-to-date understanding of what individuals in the field were doing. I also wanted to get a sense of how unique the work at Ford was in terms of a large-scale change effort. I was well versed in what was happening at Ford and had lots of ideas about that change process, but I did not have a sense of the larger field. Finally, I also wanted to get some input to a decision I had been considering regarding work for the doctorate with an OD emphasis.

Regarding an approach to this project: it was clear to me that I had to get out and talk to key people though I was not quite sure about just what I wanted to talk to them about. In a sense the real catalyst to my effort was Ken Shepherd's dissertation at UCLA. He had undertaken a comprehensive look at the Organizational Development field and at core competencies required of practitioners. I decided to continue to look at the issue of core competencies and also to try to get a sense of where the field as a whole was going. I wanted to get a macro, big picture sense of such core competencies and of future trends.

Two individuals who were additional catalysts to my efforts early on were Tom Cummings, my adviser at the University of the Southern California, and Kathy Dannemiller, a colleague and mentor in Ann Arbor, Michigan. As I expressed my interest to get out and talk with key individuals in OD, Tom and Kathy started by suggesting a "starter" list of people.

My experience was one of "network explosion." In sending out some initial letters requesting interviews, I found an incredible openness, a willingness to share, a pervasive warmth.

The early interviews were very rough. It was only as I got past the initial interviews that I began to gain some clarity and smoothness. People I talked to at the outset probably really wondered what I was up to. By the fifth interview I was beginning to settle in on a set of interview questions that I could feel comfortable with. The questions focused on two issues: first, core competencies required of all Organizational Development practitioners regardless of specialization, and second, a look at the future of the field to identify emerging trends and key issues.

I started the interviews with an introduction of myself and a brief description of my work at Ford Aerospace. Then I introduced the project and the two major issues that I wanted to look at. What I did next was to get the person I was talking to, to describe briefly his or her background. I then addressed the first question around core competencies: "What do you see as the core competencies required of all Organizational Development practitioners regardless of specialization? What competencies are essential for a practitioner in the field today?" As the interview started to wind down I would ask: "What competency do you see as most missing in practitioners today?"

Then the interview moved on to the second issue: a look at the field's future. I would ask: "When you take a forward look at the field what do you see as emerging trends and key issues? What is happening in the field today that's new and exciting, and promising for the future? What do you see when you take that look ahead?"

On both issues I probed, perhaps relentlessly, for specifics so that the broad generalizations might quickly evolve into tight, more coherent ideas. Many times I asked "What does that mean? How so? What would be an example? Say more—I'm not clear." I closed each interview by explaining how I would use the data and agreeing to send a copy of the completed report to each person interviewed.

What was important to me in the interviews was to ask open-ended questions and let the individuals talk about what was most important to them, what they cared about most. It turned out that I was asking questions which people had a lot to say about. Regarding core competencies there seems to be a mutual concern in the field today about the competencies of practitioners, the professional training available to practitioners and, at least on the West Coast the issue of accreditation. Regarding future trends, people had a lot to say about what is missing in the field and where the field should be going.

Starting each interview I mentally prepared myself to "hear everyone's truth as truth" and not allow myself to "argue with the data." I remember a friend's description of a "Cartesian thinker" as one who hears an idea as something to be challenged and argued. I recognize a bit of that in myself. Thus, the mental preparation for each interview was important. It was a time to hear their "truth as truth."

The interviews were a tremendous opportunity for me. My greatest learning comes from dialogue, listening, observing and synthesizing. The diversity of perspectives was a delight to me. The excitement came in seeing the underlying similarities that join the diversity of perspectives into a coherent whole.*

What follows is a reprise of 31 interviews with the following individuals listed in the order in which the interviews were conducted. Also shown is the abbreviation or name of the individual who had referred me to the person interviewed; in the "Referred By" column TC stands for Tom Cummings, KD stands for Kathy Dannemiller, and JE is used when I was able to contact the individual directly.

| | INTERVIEWEE | DATE (1987) | REFERRED BY |
|---|---|---|---|
| 1. | Newt Margulies, University of California, Irvine; dean, Graduate School of Management | 2/25 | JE |
| 2. | Tony Raia, University of California, Los Angeles; Anderson Graduate School of Management | 3/2 | TC and Newt Margulies |
| 3. | Lou Davis, University of California, Los Angeles; | 3/2 | TC |

---

* I want to express a warm thank you to the individuals who gave so generously of their time, either in person or over the phone, in these interviews. I hope I do justice to the richness of ideas and to the depth of thought that I encountered. Special thanks to Project Advisor Tom Cummings for the flexibility and free rein he gave me and for the link he provided to many of the individuals I was later able to interview. Special thanks also to Kathy Dannemiller, my mentor and friend, who has shared so much of her wisdom with me. Many times throughout this effort as I attempted to piece together what I was hearing, I would weave the pieces into a whole with a phrase, thought or idea I had learned from Kathy.

|     | | | |
| --- | --- | --- | --- |
|     | Anderson Graduate School of Management | | |
| 4. | Fred Massarik, University of California, Los Angeles; Anderson Graduate School of Management | 3/3 | TC and Newt Margulies |
| 5. | Alan Glassman, Cal State, Northridge | 3/4 | TC |
| 6. | Frank Friedlander, Palo Alto, Calif. | 3/6 | KD |
| 7. | Jerry Harvey, George Washington University | 3/10 | KD |
| 8. | Will McWhinney, Fielding Institute, CA | 3/10 | TC |
| 9. | Warren Schmidt, University of Southern California, School of Public Administration | 3/11 | TC |
| 10. | Richard Beckhard, New York City | 3/12 | Warren Schmidt |
| 11. | Jay Galbraith, University of Southern California, Center for Effective Organizations | 3/11 | JE |
| 12. | Alex Norman, University of California, Los Angeles, School of Social Welfare | 3/17 | Newt Margulies |
| 13. | Sam Shirley, TRW, director of human resources | 3/19 | Newt Margulies, Tony Raia |
| 14. | Peter Vail, George Washington University | 3/23 | KD |
| 15. | Mike Beer, Harvard Graduate Business School | 3/23 | TC |
| 16. | Charlie Seashore, American University, NTL, Washington, D.C. | 3/28 | KD |
| 17. | Edie Seashore, American University, NTL, Washington, D.C. | 3/28 | KD |
| 18. | Michael Maccoby, Washington, D.C. | 3/28 | TC |

| 19. | Dave Nadler, New York City, Delta Consulting Group | 3/31 | TC |
| 20. | Warner Burke, Columbia University | 3/31 | KD |
| 21. | Peter Block, New York City, Design Learning, Inc. | 3/31 | KD |
| 22. | Neil Clapp, New York City | 3/31 | KD |
| 23. | Debbie Cornwall, Harbridge House, Boston | 4/1 | Nancy Badore |
| 24. | Dan Isenberg, Harvard Graduate Business School | 4/1 | Gary Jusela |
| 25. | Barbara Toefler, Harvard Graduate Business School | 4/1 | Gary Jusela |
| 26. | Bill Torbert, Boston College, dean, Business School | 4/3 | Gary Jusela |
| 27. | Bob Miles, Harvard | 4/3 | TC |
| 28. | Bob Mueller, Detroit, private consultant | 4/6 | JE |
| 29. | John Turner, Detroit, Ford Motor Company | 4/6 | KD |
| 30. | Bruce Bond, Detroit, Ford Motor Company | 4/6 | KD |
| 31. | Jim Eckstein, Detroit, Ford Motor Company | 4/7 | KD |

## *I. CORE COMPETENCIES*

It is important to begin a discussion of core competencies with some framing provided by two individuals I interviewed. There was real concern expressed about trying to "box in" people with a prescriptive description of the competencies required of a practitioner. A "recipe" approach to effectiveness is not at all consistent with drawing upon individual uniqueness and strengths to accommodating the complexity that exists within organizations today. Two quotes capture this framing:

You can't disconnect competency from the person. The statement of competency has to be influenced by whom we're talking to. It's an abstraction to think that competencies exist independent of the person. Especially competencies with an interpersonal or conceptual component are heavily influenced by the values, life history and style of the person. People molding themselves into competencies just won't work.

You can't slice competencies into small segments . . . you have to work with the larger system, you need generic skills to respond to complex changing situations.

The message in a discussion about competencies is that there are some general attributes and core skills that are essential and yet they need to be taken with the flexibility to accommodate the uniqueness of the individual practitioner and the complexity of the client system. Core competencies that emerged from the interview data exist at three levels:

- Competencies regarding the practitioner in relation with *self*.
- Competencies regarding the practitioner in relation with the *client*.
- Competencies regarding the practitioner in relation with the *client system*.

## Core Competencies Regarding the Practitioner in Relation with Self

One set of competencies deals with the organizational change practitioner as an individual. Seven distinct competencies or attributes are included within this set. They are:

- A strong knowledge of self and values regarding what one stands for.
- An ability to keep oneself healthy.
- A strong ego, i.e., an internal reward system.
- An ability to be client centered, i.e., present and not needy.
- An ability to laugh and not take oneself too seriously.
- An ability to live with ambiguity and questions.
- An ability to ask for help and broaden our resource base.

*Strong sense of self and personal values.* An important theme that emerged in the interviews had to do with a strong sense of who we are, what we stand for and what values we bring into a client system. This was described a number of ways:

> It's about being in touch, being alive, living what I believe, being accountable, being deeply committed to living out what I talk about, living my life with courage and humility. . . . It has to do with who you are and ability to make a contract with the client. It is higher than the conceptual skills; it is fundamental therapeutic skills of empathy, confrontation, unconditional positive support, love and regard.

> Underneath the theory and the concepts and the frameworks is still the person and the personal challenge to understand and live out your values. Life itself is a lab and we are the students.

> The best organizational development consultants are people who are very centered and authentic and able to be themselves.

> The first formal exposure I had to this job (internal Organizational Consultant) was the most naked I ever felt. I never got so in touch with myself. The job required it. It requires the real examination of self.

> It has to do with understanding self. The socialization, values and behaviors and to be able to change those and mature and go beyond. It's being in touch with ourselves.

> It's essential to have a set of conscious beliefs to live by regardless of situations.

Regarding what one individual saw most missing in the field:

> People don't know themselves, they don't want to. They don't do introspective things.

A significant theme that is expressed in these quotes is a need to have a strong sense of who we are and the values we believe in, and to present that self and these values to the client system without compromise.

**An ability to stay healthy.** Linked closely to having a strong sense of self and what one stands for is an ability to keep oneself healthy. This theme was captured in quotes as these:

> I am most competent in the role when I am most 'centered' about myself. . . . What I do is go to a group as a participant every few years to get myself straightened out.

> One needs the ability to manage one's own anxiety. . . . We need to manage our own anxiety, otherwise we become part of the organization's anxiety.

One aspect of staying healthy as an organization change practitioner relates to a real commitment to change and to an "optimism around change and potentiality." A number of individuals spoke of the need to be interested truly in helping organizations and in making these organizations better places to be.

**A strong ego.** Another theme focused on the presence of a strong ego; or what a number of people described as a sound internal reward system. This is best captured by one individual who said an organizational change practitioner needs to be:

> A secure person who doesn't plan to have needs met while working, who has an internal reward system, who doesn't rely on a lot of positive feedback. It's contrary to a lot of organizational development people. In systems change you have even more anonymity. You don't see the results of efforts as you do in small groups. I have a personal philosophy about an inverse correlation between my effectiveness and who knows about it.

Others talked in terms of being "internally controlled" and not bringing their own needs for recognition and reward into the client system.

**Being client centered, "present and not needy".** Another personal competency relates to an ability to stay client centered, to be "present and not needy" in the client system. "Not needy" referred to not bringing your own agenda, expectations, goals, or "right answers" to the organization. This "present and not needy" theme was expressed a number of different ways:

> Being free of wanting anything in particular to happen.

> I've seen trainers get in trouble working their agenda. The "red flag" is coming in with a preconceived notion of how they (the client) should be.

> Ability to be aware of when you're working your agenda, i.e., your ego, your needs, not the clients.

> It's important not to feel that you need that job. You keep yourself free to be yourself. You better be able to put your full attention where the client is.

> The ability to listen is absolutely key. When you go into a system there is so much you don't know. Particularly if you've come off a successful situation you're tempted to fit the client system with what you know. It's really important to listen and not take charge. It's the client's problem; the client has to live with it. You're there to be helpful.

An ability to listen clearly and really hear.

The red flag is when I catch myself saying "if I were CEO what would I do."

Being "present and not needy" is really about giving up *control* and meeting the client system where it is. It is about not imposing your sense of how things should be or filtering the data to fit your own biases and perceptions.

It is also about *objectivity*. You are not there to solve the client's problem unilaterally, but rather to work with clients to help them resolve their own issues. The control is in the client's court and real change has to originate there, not with the consultant. It's about being client-centered; being able to be present totally to the client and to focus on the client's needs. It links back to our responsibility to keep ourselves healthy so we are not working out our personal issue/problems/needs with the client.

***An ability to laugh.*** Another personal competency has to do with the ability to laugh and not take ourselves too seriously. This was expressed a number of ways:

> (In response to what do you see as missing:)
> Laughter: the ability to enjoy on-the-job; not taking things too seriously; it has to be a Buddhist laugh, we're laughing at ourselves.

> Being able to say "boy I really blew that one."

> You're in trouble if you're called the expert and you believe it.

> We are dealing with behavior; we'll foul up and when we do, we better be willing to admit it. It ties into credibility. Don't allow yourself to set yourself up as in infallible expert. Too many in the field set themselves up as perfect.

***Living with ambiguity and questions.*** The willingness to laugh and not take ourselves too seriously closely ties to an ability to tolerate ambiguity and to live with unresolved questions. The complex turbulent situations practitioners find themselves in are not conducive to clear answers. Our job is to ask good questions. The complexity that organizations are faced with today is more characterized by paradoxes and questions than black-and-white answers. This was described a number of ways:

> I've given up on answers, only better questions. I was brought up to know answers. Now, I'm here to develop better questions and opportunities.

You need a real tolerance for ambiguity. I see more power in question than answers. You have to see how much you don't know.

What you know isn't as important as what you don't know. You have to be able to keep learning.

You don't solve paradoxes, you set up coping mechanisms.

**Asking for help.** Part of dealing with the complexity and ambiguity is being able to ask for help. It requires knowing what we do not know and opening ourselves to help from outside. This notion was expressed by a number of individuals who talked about creating consulting *teams*, pulling in *shadows*, creating *support groups*, and broadening our resource base:

You have to know when you need help and when to get yourself a *shadow*.

She knew when she didn't know and pulled me in as a *shadow* to learn about organizational design.

You can't know it all . . . . we need to team up.

It's very important for people to be able to establish support groups; a safe place to share dreams and frustrations; to know who you are and what you want. Most of us have learned to be afraid to be confused, uncertain or wrong. Today if the step is wrong it's okay; I move forward and I'm smarter now. We need to help people find those stable places. It helps them make better judgments and move with greater confidence when they do move.

Another response to the complexity and ambiguity that is a reality today is to broaden our resource base:

You have to look beyond the core of where you go for knowledge. . . . Sometimes the disciplines on the fringes are the ones on the leading edge. Otherwise we are too focused. We have to test.

(Spoken by an internal who brings in externals to work with):

When you lead in a discipline that is how you think, you don't entertain new ideas. You have to reach out, lift out, open your mind. You have to talk with leading experts; you have to examine how those people network, to whom they are connected, where their new ideas are coming from.

The turbulent environments that organizations exist in today create many complexities that have to be dealt with. "Having all the answers" is not realistic. Rather, today's complexities call for the ability to ask the right questions and to pull together the appropriate, needed resources. That might mean the formation of a consulting team or partnership, including key individuals from inside the organization.

Today's conditions call for an ability to say, "I don't know," to frame the questions, and to find ways for dealing with the "white water" we live in today—the turbulence driven by a high rate of unpredictable social and technological change which presents us with very few clear answers and lots of questions. We, as organizational development practitioners, have to get used to that and then help our clients ask the questions and bring the resources together to resolve them. The client is most likely feeling overwhelmed, anxious, and not as in control as they are used to or would like to be. Our role is to help figure out how the client is going to deal with the complex changing environment in which they live.

## Core Competencies Regarding the Practitioner in Relation with the Client

The first set of competencies that evolved from the interviews have to do with the practitioner as an individual and included:

A strong sense of self and personal values;

An ability to stay healthy;

A strong ego and an internal reward system;

An ability to be present and not needy which is really about control and being client centered;

An ability to laugh and not take ourselves too seriously or get set up as the expert;

A tolerance for ambiguity and questions that are a reality in the 'permanent white water';

An ability to ask for help and stay open to new ideas.

The second set of competencies addresses the relationship of practitioner with client, and includes:

An ability to develop rapport and trust with the client.

An empathy and sensitivity to see the world from client's eyes.

An ability to give feedback "side by side."

A gutsiness "to speak the unspeakable" and to take tough stands, balanced with a sense of timing.

***Rapport and trust.*** The importance of the rapport with the client and trust was raised in almost every interview:

> It's about good conversations with clients regarding the affairs of the organization, a conversation not interview. It's an ability to act in such a way that the client talks freely and then respond (to the client) so that the client feels trusted, confident, understood. In American business today most mid- and upper-managers don't expect to have serious relationships in the organization. Deep friendship and rapport are not part of job. It's important for the consultant to remember that the client doesn't have the same expectation. It's one more role-to-role relationship. It's the capacity of consultant to move from an initial starting condition to a deeper more authentic rapport.

> Relationship skills: How to blend into territory, not being seen as so different they (the consultant) engender resistance yet still maintain a unique way of thinking, having the capacity to confront and knowing when to confront, how to confront at the right time and still blend in.

> How to tune in to the client: how to speak the language, not 14-syllable words, how to play golf, knowing how to know people, tuning in to where people are and feeling comfortable.

> Can have lots of skills without caring . . . mechanistic and cold. Need to build rapport. Today I see consultants who don't build the rapport and trust needed for change . . . it's almost the old skills from NTL years, caring, wanting to help, and being sensitive. Otherwise, it can be very mechanistic.

> Have to inspire trust and confidence, the client feels good when the consultant is around.

> We believe the delivery mechanism is the relationship, the relationship on the project is the fundamental element . . . need to build, maintain, and leverage the relationship.

> All these things contribute to developing trust with the client, it's the essential ingredient, if you have that you are in good shape, if not, you can only be of limited help.

> Serious Organizational Development work can't get done without that chemistry/rapport, especially if just below the surface is anxiousness, fear, depression, anger.

> We're dealing with people who really know where some bodies are buried, we have to develop the rapport to deal with that.

Part of the rapport and trust has to do with the alignment, congruity, fit between the consultant and the client:

Best consultants are kind of fatalistic regarding the chemistry between themselves and the client. We'll find we can work together or we can't. So be it. It's contrary to working hard to build relationship regardless of chemistry.

The first conversation is around values. If we agree on values I don't worry.

A good fit with the client system, understanding underlying values, the nature of the system, value consistency, have to have a relationship.

The rapport with the client was recognized as the foundation of any change effort. Part of the rapport was described as enthusiasm:

Enthusiasm . . . need to energize the client. Client feels better when consultant is around, interested and willing to try new things, . . . it's a sheer upbeat quality.

Energy and enthusiasm are my two most effective tools. People believe I believe in what I do.

Have to have some sense of drama . . . we need to move, to energize. . . . I get people to look from another view.

**Empathy and sensitivity.** The second competency regarding the relationship between the practitioner and the client is the empathy and sensitivity to see the world through the client's eyes.

Really effective Organizational Development consultants have to put themselves in the manager's role; how can I help this executive cope with forces to move change forward. It involves less and less "techniquey" things . . . requires really learning to immerse in the organization, to see the dynamics and forces in the organization.

To be able to *empathize*—to understand their problems and how they view them, without identifying yourself with it or getting wrapped up—it's balancing, understanding and empathy with objectivity—you just have to feel the balance.

Some of the old things . . . being accepting of people, understanding how the world looks from their eyes. The ability to internalize what people are feeling. I have to be able to become you, really feel what you feel.

Regarding what's most missing in practitioners today: sensitivity, plain old-fashioned sensitivity.

A number of people talked about empathy in terms of the death and rebirth cycle that change represents to an individual and an organization.

> It's painful when we have to change, change represents giving up the old way of work and moving on to a rebirth of something new.

> No one thinks about what resistance to change is. It is seen or rationalized as a political concept. Actually, it's anaclitic depression caused when the support system is removed.

> We need to ask "do I know how to help people maintain self-esteem in time of change?"

***Giving feedback.*** Part of rapport and empathy is an ability to give feedback to the client. One person described this with a story:

> You have to find a balance between honesty and frankness, being straight with people but at the same time balance that with a sensitivity to the level of information they can accept. For example, I worked with a company with a new president who came in overwhelmed with "In Search of Excellence" and MBWA. Being decisive really stuck with him. He would go around talking with people, hearing a lot of nifty ideas and he would say, "That sounds great! Go do it!" It created chaos in the organization. Underlings were taking projects on of the president, and their boss was out of the loop. How do you confront the president? You have to determine the degree to which he can take feedback. He needs support but also he has to stop this behavior. You have to cushion. You have to protect his ego. It's the ability to give difficult feedback.

Another individual described giving feedback side-to-side rather than confrontation feedback. "If you don't experience me as trying to change you, then anything can be talked about."

***A gutsiness.*** Another competency in the consultant–client relationship is captured in the word "gutsy." This was described as "a willingness to speak the unspeakable," "to recognize the dead moose in the center of the floor," "to determine what's not being talked about and getting all the stored up stuff out in the open and talked about." Gutsiness also was described as taking tough stands:

> You have to be gutsy, risk taking. You can't always agree with the client but you can't put your goal ahead of his.

> Have to have courage to tell people, show people, areas they don't want to talk about and see.

Able to be strong and take tough stands on unpopular issues. It's not easy.

The gutsiness to talk about what's not being talked about, to stand up to controversial issues has to be balanced with a sense of timing, that is, the notion that "you can't bend the river." Some things just aren't going to change and we need the wisdom to know when to stop trying.

## Core Competencies Regarding the Practitioner in Relation with the Client System

The third set of competencies is centered around the practitioner role within the client system. These competencies include:

A need to know what is happening in the environment of the organization, what's pushing on the organization.

A deep understanding of the client organization as a *system*.

The organizational change practitioner's role as a "reflective practitioner" in the client system.

An ability to be flexible and to meet the client system where it is, as opposed to being "tool and technique" driven.

Recognition of the client as change agent.

The political skills to create the acceptance and commitment to move change forward.

***The environment of the organization.*** One of the significant themes addresses the practitioner's need to know what is happening in the environment of the organization, knowing the business issues, the key success factors, the market place; talking in the client's language, not Organizational Development jargon; knowing how to get committed customers; knowing where a client's pain is coming from, whether it is an inability to compete on cost and quality, technological changes or government regulation. Our effort as Organizational Development practitioner cannot be an end in itself but needs to make sense within the context of the organization and its environment. Organizational Development has to be linked to the core business issues. Individuals in the interviews expressed this a number of different ways:

It's critical to be able to understand the business/task environment of the organization. You have to be able to diagnose with insiders what the key success factors are. . . . Then have to be able to translate the external reality to what the organization needs to do well. I see organizational development's role as helping the organization develop a better fit with the environment.

You need a much more business-policy perspective, not just an organizational development perspective.

You have to understand the nature of the business, see the critical linkages, and then design the structure and the processes to match.

An ability to understand the business they are working in, see self as part of the business system, become more like the general manager.

You have to historically know what's going on in the world in which the client is embedded.

I have to know the business. I don't get anywhere if I'm insensitive to their business. Organizational Development people fail because they have not been a value-added as perceived by the line organization.

An antenna has to be out about what's happening in the world, with society, what are the external factors and the implications (for the organization).

Organizational Development practitioners have to work within the context of the strategy of the business and within the long range plan.

It was clear from the interviews that a practitioner has to have a clear understanding of what's happening in the environment of the organization. Organizational Development interventions have to make sense in the context of the organization's strategic business issues.

***The client organization as system.*** The second theme that emerged in the practitioner's relationship with the client system was the need to have a deep understanding of the client organization *as a system.* It's the ability to see the interconnectedness of all the parts of the client system and not becoming immersed in one piece without seeing the impact on the whole. This was described a number of ways:

We're moving toward a wholistic understanding of organizations. . . . I see it as demanding a systemic understanding.

You have to have a systems perspective and see the interconnectedness of the parts that locks in stability. You can't just work with individuals or groups unless you do so in relation with larger environmental changes. You need to work with the next level up and in parallel levels. Working with Department A alone would sub-optimize the organization. You have to think of the larger system. Everything is locked into everything else.

What I do is help an organization become healthy and successful. I act on behalf of the organization. It's system's view. I confront the individual client on the narrow way he may be seeing the organization. You have to keep all the stakeholders in mind. You have to understand the business and then understand the system elements to make the organization competitive. The 7S model is helpful (Identify strategy, structure, systems, staff, skills, style and shared values within an organization).

One individual described a different view of systems when he said:

You have to have systems understanding. Systems aren't necessarily real large and complex. They could be you and me. Systems thinking and perception are the key skills. The system will tell you what the intervention is, (should be). It's helpful to have some standard interventions but they're so basic, anyone can learn them. It pays to understand the basic macro-elements of the field, otherwise you would be rearranging the deck chairs when the Titanic is sinking. You have to see the larger environment, competition, vertical and horizontal integration, the reality of Federal regulation. You don't have to know much and be an expert but you need the basic language of the field.

We're just beginning to understand systems theory. . . . It's the notion that the behavior of each member of the system is not independent. It's ridiculous to talk blame and reward, it's not problem solving—it's system change, not what caused it but rather what will fix it.

Developing a deep understanding of the client organization as a system has to include creating a vision of the future. The creation of a preferred future creates energy to move forward toward an improved future state. This was described by an individual who said:

The diagnostic process has to lead toward a future state. Organizations need to move forward. They have to know where they're going. Vision has to come from the diagnostic process.

Given a more intellectual work force and a more mobile work force, we have to create a vision of the "mechanoic" organization—a purposeful, healthier organization driven by goals, not control, with the emphasis on what people can become, not how to force (people) fit.

The competency required of the Organization Development practitioner is to see the organization as a system with interconnected parts. Understanding the client organization as a system has to include developing a preferred vision of the organization's future.

***The reflective practitioner.*** Another competency deals with the practitioner's role as "*reflective* practitioner." This involves an ability to sit down and "think" with the client. A depth of thought is required today to make sense out of the complexity and paradoxes that organizations are faced with. As reflective practitioners our role is to help the organization develop "fresh eyes," new paradigms, new ways of thinking, to respond to complexity and turbulence. Our role is that of catalyst, to push the client out of old ways and into new ways of thinking, and to broaden perspective. People described this a number of different ways:

> One of the aspects of the consulting role is to serve as conceptual therapist. This role is to help the organization develop fresh eyes in how they look at self, the organization and how they make sense out of complexity and paradoxes. You, as consultant can provide eyes and models to the client system for seeing how they can see the world.

> So few are willing to sit with the client and think; the client doesn't expect it and consultants aren't geared up for it. You have to think with the client regarding the turbulence and where we'll be in five years. It's most essential. When the folks at Ford think about the next oil crisis they need an organizational practitioner in the room to prevent "group think."

> You have to know how to think and to get the client system to learn to think.

In response to "What do you see as most missing?":

> An absence of thought, an emphasis on techniques and skills, and not on thoughtful ways of acting.

> I don't think they (consultants) think about it. The client pays me to think about the organization and what's needed. I might spend two hours playing through everything that happened. Why? What does it mean? I don't think people put in that kind of time.

Our role as reflective practitioners also requires us to bring a long-range perspective to an organization:

> A good Organizational Development consultant has a natural nose for the way the world is going, a 5-year perspective. One of the chief perspectives an organizational consultant can provide is a longer view

over time. For example, companies pretending that AIDS won't affect them. . . . The organizational consultant has to fantasize regarding 40 percent of the company population with AIDS in 5 to 10 years. . . . The perspective of time and the ability to fantasize the impact of trends on organizations is a very important organizational consultant contribution. Organizational practitioners need to become much more futuristic regarding demographics, social trends, technology, economics, the environment and politics. We have to see the trends and how they will impact the organization's performance.

***Flexibility, meeting the client system where it is.*** Another competency regarding the practitioner's relationship with the client system is a *flexibility* to bring to our understanding of a client system. Flexibility is meeting the client system where it is right now. One individual described it as:

> If you are really true to the profession you are ahead of the organization, yet you have to meet the organization where it is. You have to come with a great design and start where the organization is today.

Another described it as:

> You need to take the client systems where (they are) now, not be predictive (but) focus on the here and now.

One individual described her approach in the client system when she said:

> I don't come in with a package model. I come in with lots of ideas without representing any particular school of thought. I'm very responsive to the needs of the institution. I'm a good listener.

These descriptions captured what a number of people were talking about when they said that we have to be flexible in the client system and to start where that client system is right now.

Flexibility also means balancing theory and practice, that is, the ideal with the real world. One individual described this as:

> You have to manage the tension between a normative view (the ideal of what the organization needs to be) and the situational reality of the client system . . . its a tradeoff between ideals and reality.

> You need to combine theory and practice, i.e., the conceptual framework with the ability to use it. Many colleagues are on one side or the other. You have to balance.

The ability to meet a client system where it is today and the ability to balance theory and practice link closely to a concern that a number of individuals raised about the *mechanization* of the field today, and a recognition that the field is becoming tool-and-technique driven. One individual described this when he said:

> Organizational development is more necessary than ever. I'm not sure the profession is geared up. It's so commercial. Consultants are trying to make financial careers out of organizational development. More and more have gone to independently operated businesses.

This raised an interesting issue, namely that with the commercialization of the field, younger practitioners have an incentive to master a few techniques and then use these consistently. The goal to make a career in Organizational Development seems to reduce the willingness to take risks and to try new approaches. This was captured by one individual when he said:

> You need flexibility in how you make sense out of the field. The field is still technology and technique driven. We're very mechanistic. The alternative is a generalist. . . . You need a real familiarity and comfort with a wide range of interventions. What young consultants do is get comfortable with limited intervention and then force-fit it.

We need to know the tools and the techniques and some standard intervention: "you need depth in your bag of tricks." But the tools and techniques are not an end in themselves to be force-fit. We have to tailor the techniques to meet the unique needs of the client system. The concern about the "mechanization" at the field was referred to as a "hammer-and-nail approach" to Organizational Development—"if all I have is a hammer everything tends to look like a nail."

Tailoring the tools and techniques to meet actual needs will become more and more important in the future, given the complexity and turbulence that organizations are continually faced with. At the time that we need to be more flexible and responsive to the unique complex needs of each organization, we find countervailing trends: we are becoming more tool-and-technique driven by the commercialization of the field, and yet the future calls for individuality, flexibility, and responsiveness.

**The client as change agent.** The next theme concerns how we define our role as a change practitioner. A number of individuals talked about the need to recognize the client as a change agent, as the owner and driver of the change process. The organizational change practitioner shows up but for a brief period, yet the change process within the organization is an ongoing, long-term effort energized by the individuals inside the client system. Our role as OD practitioners is to support that change process and to internalize it within the organization. Our role is to empower the people inside the organization to move the change forward. We can make a significant contribution with our process knowledge and content expertise, in context of our awareness of the business environment of the organization, but we are not center stage. We need to be client-centered and to recognize that the change process has to originate in and be implemented by the client system.

This idea was referred to as the *"Blip Theory"* of Organizational Development. We as practitioners are really just a "blip" in the life of an organization. We show up for awhile but then we leave, and whatever change process is under way is going to continue after we're gone. For, as humbling as this notion is, it is a realistic and grounded view of our role as change practitioners. We are not the change *makers* or visible stars. We have a service role, a support role, we are catalysts, a guides, a stage managers, but we are not the intrinsic focus of the change process. Individuals that I talked with described this as follows:

> Consultants come in and do something in a limited time frame. Organizations don't change that way. The consultant is a blip on the organization, not the major event.

> Our challenge is to go into an organization and see the impact of forces on that organization that we have nothing to do with, and support the organization in making sense out of those forces and move toward a preferred state for itself.

> Really effective organizational development consultants have to put themselves in a manager's role and ask "How can I help this executive cope with forces to move change forward?" The key element is *helping* this executive move change forward. The executive is the change agent, not we as practitioners.

> We do large-scale organizational change as facilitators, not as the change agent. Organizations aren't changed by consultants, but by external forces and by the manager's response. Consultants don't create change, external events do, like Japan and the dollar.

> You have to let the organization set where it wants to go, not you. When my values don't match I get out. I'm not the determiner of where the organization goes.

The ability to align the practitioner's value with that of the organization's makes it easier for the practitioner to support the client as the change agent and as driver of change. It becomes much more difficult for the practitioner to support the client if the practitioner's values are not aligned with the values of the organization. One individual described this in these words: "We cannot be the owner of the change. We can influence the change and take pride without being the sole owner." Our goal as organizational change practitioners is to work ourselves out of a job and to transfer the organizational change skills to the real leaders of change inside the organization. This applies equally to the internal and to the external practitioner. The external practitioner has the extra task of transferring the skills to the internal practitioner so that the latter in turn can more effectively support the organization's managers in moving the change forward. The "internal" and "external" have to work together to imbue key others with the knowledge and skills to make the change process happen.

***Political skills.*** Finally, in our role as organizational change practitioners in relationship with a client system, we have to recognize the politics of the organization and to develop our own political skills. We need to move beyond the naïve perspective of "politics as a dirty word" to an awareness of politics as a reality in every organization. We need to develop our own political skills—the ability to build acceptance and commitment to a change process. If we cannot build acceptance and commitment in the whole organization to the change, we have nothing in the end except a good plan. Political skills are about creating alignment within an organization to make change happen. The practitioner has to be a political, not in an Machiavellian sense, but rather in terms of evolving acceptance and commitment, to build alliances and consensus, so that the entire organization may become involved in the change process at hand.

One individual described the dynamics of the politics of change when he said:

> You have to know where the power is in the organization, see the driving and restraining forces and how to get the resisting forces involved. In dealing with power you have to recognize power as duality, a paradoxical thing. It's naïve to think that if everyone participates it will all work out. All change efforts have a coercive element. You have to know how much power the leader has, and then leverage it to push the change through. . . . You have to manage the forces. . . . Our role is in helping managers deal with the dynamics of change and politics, to help managers think through the process of making change happen.

A number of individuals described political skills in these terms:

> In some situations you have to recognize multiple sources of power. You have to manage the process to bring people together on consensus.

> You have to understand the nature of commitment. If you assume the organization is a transforming thing where individuals are involved in a change effort, you need commitment to get from here to there.

> An ability to be strategic, knowing how to get change going in a political sense, not just knowing the mechanisms.

> You need political skills especially in a system's view of an organization.

> You don't control politics. You have to manage them. People are still incredibly naïve about politics. . . . Corporate politics are the most important and get the least attention. I don't know where you get it (a political sense) but by living, getting burned and surviving and looking back.

> I see a naïveté regarding organizational politics. . . . There's lots of organizational people who think politics is a dirty word. . . . There are a number of practitioners not aware that organizational politics have impact on what they do into an organization. . . . Organizational development will move in from the periphery to the center of the organization if we can deal with politics. Then we can facilitate the organization's strategic planning process. . . . The flip side worst-case is that we don't work well within the politics. Then we will be on the periphery (of the organization).

Our role as organizational change practitioners requires political skills, i.e., an ability to create acceptance and commitment to a change process. Our role is to see the client as change agent and driver of the change process and define our role as internalizing the change process inside the organization.

## Fundamental Core Competencies

Core competencies for the organizational change practitioner thus exist at three levels:

> Practitioner in relation with self;
> Practitioner in relation with client; and
> Practitioner in relation with client system.

Underlying all those are some fundamental competencies that simply have to be there. It would be difficult to call ourselves Organizational Development practitioners without them. The following discussion is not meant to be comprehensive but rather seeks to create a flavor of the practitioner's repertoire. The following fundamentals were raised in the interviews:

*Process skills* are essential. The organizational development field is a "process for improving process"; "our unique product as organizational development practitioners is process." The process skills have to be there to complement a content expertise and an awareness of an organization's environment. Fundamental process skills include an understanding of the dynamics at the individual, group, and organizational level.

We have to understand the *change process* and the nature of resistance—how change happens in organizations. We have to understand fundamentally *management theory* and how organizations work. We need to have the *diagnosis* models and techniques to understand the uniqueness of the management team and of the organization that is our client system.

We need the *conceptual ability* to make sense of the complexities and ambiguities we encounter in an organization. We need sound *communication skills;* an ability to really listen and to articulate our perception. Finally, we need an understanding of the *consulting process* as it develops in an organization context.

## II. A WATERSHED TIME

The Organizational Development field seems to be in a watershed period. It's a time of transition. A "from/to" theme emerged in the interviews. The field which started in the 1960s, seems to be wrestling with an identity crisis and upheaval, characteristics of adolescence. As one person put it:

> Theories will have to be extraordinarily different. Looking at an organizational development text book is like a chemist looking at alchemy. We have a few beginning chemists out there. We need whole new ways of thinking.

This view was most evidenced by a number of individuals who said that they never used the term "organizational development," and who wished the name would just go away. It almost seems to be an embarrassment or an unwillingness to be associated with the term, which evokes "softy," "touchy feeling" images.

The field is growing up to respond to the needs of organizations today. The changes in the Organizational Development field mirror the changes that organizations have faced since the 1960s, as described in "Megatrends," "Future Shock," and "Third Wave." The turbulence, rapid unpredictable change and resultant complexities that organizations are forced to deal with today are reflected in the organizational development field. "Permanent white water" is everywhere.

Our challenge as a field is to move *from* the soft touchy/feeling image of our early phases to respond *to* the complex needs of organizations today. This "from/to" theme was loud and clear in the interviews:

| FROM | TO |
|---|---|
| 1. Relatively stable environments where a model of unfreeze/change/refreeze made sense | Environments characterized by "permanent white water" with constant unpredictable change where "refreezing" is impossible, or at least inappropriate |

Frozen workplace is a temporary phenomenon. Today change goes more like a bullet train than a melting iceberg.

One has to recognize change is constant. Unfreeze/change/refreeze is nonsense. It's much more dynamic.

This whole business of rate of change . . . the trouble is the rate of change . . . is an *enormous* rate of change.

| | |
|---|---|
| 2. In stable environments you have problems to be solved with clear answers | In "permanent white water" you have:<br>(a) multiple stakeholders and conflicting needs<br>(b) paradoxes to be coped with, i.e., productivity versus QWL, competition versus collaboration |
| 3. A micro-perspective with focus on the individual | A macro-perspective with focus on the system |

At first the unit of analysis was the individual. Today it is the system and the system's environment and subsystems.

The field is more "macro" now. We've moved from, "if you change enough individuals the organization will change" to large-scale change across the organization.

We've moved to a macro-perspective from an interpersonal perspective.

| *From* | *To* |
|---|---|
| 4. Solely *process skills*—a softy, touchy/feeling image of organizational development; *Goal*: Human values; *Location*: Organizational Development at the periphery of the organization | *Process skills to compliment a content expertise* and an awareness of business issues and environment of the organization; *Goal:* Organizational effectiveness: a fit between the organization and its environent; alignment among the organzation's strategy, structure, systems, etc; a productive community that values the integrity and dignity of the individual; *Location:* Organizational Development efforts *mainstreamed* in the organization and *linked to core business issues.* |

We're getting away from too much touchy/feeling. That's good news.

We were 'value drivers' for years. We created human values . . . broadened today to include organizational effectiveness.

We still are messing around in the middle of the organization with administering fine-tuning. . . . We're not addressing the strategic issues.

| | |
|---|---|
| 5. Organizational Development as an end in itself; tool-and-technique driven | Organizational Development as a means to an end of organizational effectiveness; see organizations as complex systems with interconnected parts, use tools and techniques in the context of organization's unique needs. |

6. Organizational Development as problem-solving interventions; developmental change

Organizational Development as creation of preferred future; transformational change; movement toward a preferred future

The Organizational Development field has grown beyond its early years, and is now wrestling with identity crisis and transition. The growing pains in the field are intensified by the constant change and turbulence that is characteristic of the "permanent white water" we're navigating in. Our challenge as professionals is to come through this watershed time, to live through a stormy adolescence without losing our identity and cohesiveness as a professional community.

## III. FUTURE TRENDS

In the interviews I asked each individual to take a forward look at the field and to describe key issues and trends that would impact our role as organizational change practitioners. Two sets of trends were manifest: the first was trends impacting the organizations we serve, and the second trends within the Organizational Development field itself.

### Future Trends Impacting Organizations

*Global Markets.* The key trend impacting organizations is the internationalization of the marketplace. It is clear that we are shifting to a global economy and the United States is challenged to find innovative ways to respond to global competition:

> International competition is a major issue for this country. We can't emulate Japan, we have to be global in our thinking and find unique new ways (to compete).

> Internationalization of everything. Boundaries are increasingly blurred. We need to learn to think internationally, not nationally. So who cares if automobiles are made in Japan.

> Internationalization—we're continuing to emerge to a global economy driven by transportation, communication, labor cost advantages . . . it's present in all markets.

We can't compete in cost or quality. It has to be technological and innovative.

There's a growing emphasis on entrepreneurship where the organization supports somebody or a group developing a new idea under the protection of an umbrella, like they were starting their own new business—the press to be innovative is so strong.

**Hi-tech/Hi-touch.** Many individuals talked about the fundamental impact technology will continue to have on organizations and a need to develop a "hi-tech/hi-touch" balance to ease the transition many organizations will experience.

More and more organizations will see technological changes. Service sectors will be fundamentally impacted by technology. Xerox and AT&T say the big issue of technological change is not capacity. Capacity is here today for almost anything we can dream of. The next big change is in organizations and behavior. Organizational development practitioners have to be prepared to help. The way work is organized will alter radically.

There's lots of organizational development work given the impact and pervasiveness of the computer. Voice-activated capability is around the corner . . . main frames will be on the wrist. The power and flexibility of the combination is breathtaking and presents unbelievable change in organizations. Could lead to dissolution of organizations as we know them.

Information technology and the impact on the people side are becoming much more integrated. For example, departments of the future are showing up with information people, organizational development people and future planners. Information people know they need help. Organizational development people are more scared of the machines.

Continuing issues of integrating manufacturing strategy and human tools . . . with Cad-Cam technique. The two communities tend to be separate.

We'll see some real changes in how to use tools and technology with office and advanced manufacturing management system.

There's more focus on a shift from bureaucratic industry (the big brain runs everything) to techno/service organizations with jobs fragmented, control down at the next level, focus on the customer where everyone has a customer.

Most of our management concepts developed for an industrial society—how to use an organization's machines to turn out products now; we're more interested in training people to use their heads—it's a different set of competencies. We need more attention to psychology—all this interest in organizational cultures and values—the same time we want people to use their heads, they have to know the values of the organization and the stakeholder's needs—the soft stuff at the periphery is becoming more important.

Other trends include the blending of the public and private sector, changing values and ethics, and the impact of AIDS.

### *Blending of public & private sectors.*

The boundaries are blurring between government, business and not-for-profit centers. We can't afford finger pointing anymore. We require the mobilization of resources among the three.

Highest growth area is government; the catalyst is the threat of contracting government work out; more cost conscious now. The government environment has changed dramatically in the last 5 years.

Narrowing gap between public and private sector. We've looked too long at business as concerned with economics and at the civil sector concerned with social welfare. More and more we have to look at both. For example, child care was traditionally the responsibility of the civic sector. More and more private sector is providing child care.

### *Values & ethics.*

I see a big change in values in the next 30 years with working women and children of two-career families.

Significant shift in society regarding the nature of the psychological contract between employer and employee. Loyalty is changing . . . profound effect . . . all these mergers and acquisitions, layoffs, down-sizing. Organizational development people are now confronted with the value/ethics of how people are treated. We have to understand how the psychological contract is changing.

Ethics and values . . . when change wasn't as constant as it is today, everything could be done by routine, by values. Now the values that are part of how the organization operates are open to change. We have to help define values. Ethics is a conflict in competing claims, it's about trying to figure out what's right given multiple not single stakeholders.

### *Impact of AIDS.*

The organization will be impacted by the plague of AIDS—it will wipe out large groups of people—we're not doing anything with managers to train them to deal with this kind of crisis.

Global competition, the impact of technology, the blending of the public and private sector, changing values and the rise of ethical issues, the impact of AIDS, are trends that will impact organizations in the future. Our role as Organizational Development practitioners is to understand these and other future trends and to help the management team respond effectively.

## Future Trends within the Organizational Development Profession

In addition to environmental trends expected to impact organizations in the future, numerous trends were discussed regarding the future of the Organizational Development profession as such. The environmental trends impacting organizations are mirrored in the trends within the Organizational Development profession. These trends include:

- A focus on strategic/systems thinking and large scale system-wide change.
- A focus on top management/leadership development and the manager as "moral agent".
- A deepening of the level at which change happens.
- A fundamentally different way to see our role and purpose in organizations.
- The emerging role of internal Organizational Development consultants, both in human resources and in line organizations.
- A need to develop richer theories of how organizations change.

### Strategic/Systems Thinking and Large Scale System Change

The competitive pressures and environmental changes organizations are facing today present a challenge to the Organizational Development practitioner to respond to the strategic needs of the organization. Competitive pressures and rapid change are forcing corporations to identify their strategies for focusing resources on their competitive advantages. No longer can companies compete on all fronts. Strategy serves to focus resources by identifying "what business we're in" and "what competitive advantage we can compete with." The Organizational Development practitioner is challenged to deal with the strategic issues of an organization to help create a fit between the organization and its environment.

Strategy also serves to create alignment among internal systems and processes of the organization. Dealing with strategic issues requires an ability to see the organization as a system with interconnected parts:

What's at the leading edge? The skill to *integrate several components* of a change effort; strategic planning, structural design, organizational life, and careers.

I see people starting to think in terms of *system*. What I do affects any other part. Don't change the subsystem. Now with change you have to see how the pieces interact. No one person can see all the pieces . . . Have to get the right players together.

I hope it is an elimination of the field at least as a word . . . if the only purpose of Organizational Development is to make people better and the organization is peripheral, it's not good—the client is an organization as a *system* with people.

Second new issue in addition to large scale system-wide change is the question of strategy. It's scary how many Organizational Development people cannot talk *business strategy*. We have to be competent regarding the strategy and the language of business—finance, markets— being able to talk and understand ROA.

Future competency: to be able to know and participate in real *strategic planning*. It may not suit the touchy feely stuff but it suits the client.

Organizational Development still has not faced up to *strategic needs*. Still messing at mid-level with administrative fine tuning.

A focus on strategic issues and organizations as whole systems closely linked to what some individuals described as large-scale system-wide change:

Regarding state of the art practice in Organizational Development: There are two content areas. One is large system change: organizations as system; look at strategy, structure, culture and leadership in large scale change. Two is process: small group and interpersonal process, individual behavior. I see large-scale change span the two areas . . . need the ability to work at two levels,—large system and individual/small group level.

Regarding large system change: Still don't understand how large organizations go through change. Large-scale change is much more complex (than incremental or transitional change). It's not clear where you're going, it's strategy change.

It involves moving one hundred thousand people. Just making transition management bigger is not enough. It's frame-bending change with still some continuity.

The question of how you influence entire organizations is really unknown.

One area where large-scale change is most evident relates to the proliferation of the mergers and acquisitions, and joint ventures of the mid- and late-1980s. The restructuring often fails because of implementation issues, not because of faulty strategy. The strategy driving the restructuring is often clear. What's missing are the internal structure and systems, to implement and sustain the restructuring. Merging organizational cultures and dealing with the human resource issues are often neglected in a restructuring driven by product and financial decisions. It's this internal lack of congruence that most often causes the large-scale restructuring efforts to fail.

The challenge to the Organizational Development practitioner is to work with the client to address strategic issues, to create a fit with the external environment as well as the internal congruence within the organizational system. Given the strategic direction, does the organizations structure fit? Are the management and information systems in place to support the strategy? How are the human resources issues being addressed? Is there a cultural fit across merging entities? These are the questions we have to deal with if we're going to be a part of the large scale system-wide changes currently in progress.

### Top Management/Leadership Development and Manager As Moral Agent

Responding to strategic issues and large-scale change requires an ability to deal effectively at the executive level in the organization. An emerging trend within the Organizational Development field points toward top management and leadership development.

Organizational Development needs to facilitate top management thinking. It's much needed. Organizational Development people are often timid, ignorant of business problem, not competent to think of business problem, unable to adjust an Organizational Development style to issues that really count. Top managers are extremely competitive and not easy to consult to. Organizational Development consultants who are good are self-assured aggressive people.

We do a marvelous job in developing managers and an incredibly poor job in the development of leaders.

Our challenge as Organizational Development practitioners is to develop an effective rapport with top management and support their leadership role in dealing with strategic issues and the organization as a whole system.

The constant change that is now characteristic calls for a new role of the manager—as moral agent. Basic values and ethical beliefs once taken as given are now open to change. Ethical dilemmas abound. Our role as Organizational Development practitioners is to recognize the manager's role in ethics and as moral agent and begin to talk about the moral and ethic implications of actions and decisions inside an organization. We need to work with top management to "set a course for the restoration of decency. The moral climate has to be an objective of change and development."

## Deepening the Level at Which Change Takes Place

Another trend within the Organizational Development field is toward a deepening of the level at which change takes place. People talked about this in terms of working with culture, drawing energy from a collective unconsciousness, changing context, breaking history, transforming versus developing:

We have to make changes much more fundamental than behavior. We have to work deeply with culture, can't make change within existing system.

There's a sudden influx of cultural stuff. I use explicit work with myths as a fundamental element of understanding contemporary organizations. . . myths are the collective social unconsciousness. . . . I go to anthropology to understand the myths of the source cultures.

Imaging workshops have suddenly take off with OT [Organizational Transformation], huge growth—flash, then serious work will continue—OT emerged from those who saw a spiritual content to any social interaction—in organizations there is hopefully a shared spirit—get people collected around spirit—you can free up a lot of energy—not necessarily useful or good—how do you get at the shared spirit?; deep futuring, fantasy, re-mythicizing, meditation, chants—most people in the field don't know the difference between spirit that takes over—company hype vs. spirit that emanates from self—an internal spirit—there's a slight difference—it's a danger of takeover.

A whole movement about breaking history . . . what would break the current history? How can we internalize that incentive to be different as opposed to reacting to an outside push? What would change the context? If the context is there anything can happen.

You need to understand the nature of the workforce and how development (improving something) is different from transforming; (a change in the shape of things. For example, Kodak, going back to "square one," fundamental change in the shape of the beast, changing everything).

I hope leading ideas go toward deep understanding of complex systems phenomenology . . . more thoroughness, not the quick once-over (packages). It is a countervailing trend. Phenomenology is out of philosophy. The issue is to deeply enter another's world for mutual exploration as a team, discovery about system and each other. It's a way to enter another's experience world.

Regarding Organizational Development's role in testing assumptions, our own and the organization's:

Can't by definition easily see implicit assumptions; it's tricky because the assumptions underlying behavior are not explicit. How do you mesh different implicit assumptions? Extremely frightening to deal with unfavorable assumptions. It's why the apparent resistance to change exists. To test assumptions is to challenge how one makes sense of the world.

## A Fundamentally Different Way to See Our Role and Purpose in Organizations

Rapid unpredictable change presents us with an opportunity to rethink our role as Organizational Development practitioners and the process of creating change within an organization. The constant change organizations are faced with today makes it virtually impossible for any one person to know the "right" answer, make sure decisions, accurately anticipate the consequences of an action, or predict the likelihood of an external event. This kind of uncertainty calls for a synergistic approach to management. Any one person is not smart enough to get a clear reading in today's turbulence. It takes the synergy of a team to manage the dynamics and paradoxes of constant change.

Our role as "expert," or the client role as expert has to be complemented today with the synergy that comes from multiple perspectives. Our responsibility to have the "right" answers has to be balanced with a responsibility to ask the right questions. It's a process of decentralization, a process of broad-based involvement. Maybe our job isn't so much to have answers and ask questions as it is to structure a way for the organization to pose its own questions, to develop its own answers, and to draw its own lessons learned. Maybe our job is to get the whole system in a room together (were this possible!) and use our expertise to help all involved make sense out of the prevailing turbulence. In such times the synergy of multiple perspectives is essential and sole reliance on a single expert is fraught with danger.

Marv Weisbord described a fundamentally different role and purpose for Organizational Development practitioners in his Third-Wave article in the December 1987 *Organization Dynamics.* He described the role of the Organizational Development practitioner as:

1. Assessing the potential for change; is there a committed leader?, is there an incentive to be different, i.e., pain in the organization, or in its environment?; is there energy to move change forward?
2. Getting the whole system in a room to broaden perspective and gain a common picture of what's happening.
3. Focusing on the future and creating a preferred vision of what we can be.
4. Structuring tasks that utilize the diverse perspectives and expertise across the system, creating an environment for learning *as a system.*

Beckhard's model for change was:

$$D \times V \times F > R$$

or Dissatisfaction × Vision × First Steps must be present to overcome the Resistance to change. Weisbord adds Leadership to the model, and basic assumptions that:

> Broadening perspective and creating synergy across the system are essential to making sense out of constant change and moving toward a preferred future. The effort has to involve the wisdom of the whole system.
>
> Creating an environment for learning is essential to success in "permanent white water," where questions are as legitimate as answers, and where creativity and innovation are rewarded.

This Third Wave model of Organizational Development serves an invaluable dual purpose. First, to ensure greater organizational effectiveness in time of constant change by drawing up the collective wisdom of the whole organization. Second, to create dignity and meaning for individuals by creating opportunities to understand and resolve issues that impact them. And to create community by bringing people together in synergistic effort.

This approach in no way advocates just a process expertise on the part of the Organizational Development practitioner. More than ever before the Organizational Development practitioner has to understand the business issues and the environmental influences the organization is faced with. The Organizational Development practitioner brings a process expertise, a business knowledge, as well as unique content expertise to the client system. But neither the practitioner nor the client can afford to get set up as *the* expert. Rapid change demands the synergy and collective wisdom of the whole system.

### The Internal Organizational Development Consultant

Another trend within the Organizational Development profession focuses on the roles of Human Resources professionals and the line managers as change agents.
Regarding line management as change agent:

> Most change is brought about by continuous effort. We have to free up the system to be self-renewing, not dependent on outside help to kick it into gear. Line management and the Organizational Development outside person are like two overlapping circles. We're still at the basic education stage of the line manager. It's an incredible virgin world out there. Flip charts and pen still pretty cutting edge, we don't have to worry about "beaming up Scotty."

> More and more the role of the external is to develop the internal in the organizations in which they work.

> Spoken by an internal Organizational Development person who brings in a lot of external consultants:
> I have a strong preference for consultants who work with me, not their own program.

> We will work more with internals; we'll shift in our usage to more work with internals.

Regarding the changes of Human Resources professionals and their role as change agent:

> Human Resources has to be a risktaker. Human Resources is responsible for the effectiveness of the organization, the guardian of management process. I want to see Human Resources people take more leadership. Senior Human Resources generalists need to see how the organization is functioning and be able to suggest improvements . . . bottom line is Human Resources as initiators . . . Human Resources (HR) has to speak the manager's language and be effective management coaches. . . . It's a whole new role.

> HR needs a real understanding of strategy and market place and what the strategy process looks like. Human Resources has to be a guideline in strategic thinking. I see Human Resources bring people together but not guide. I see a disconnect between Human Resources and planning. Planning people are writing procedures. Human Resources is worried about the people. They're not together.

> The risk of true Human Resources specialists is that they are divorced from real business issues.

> The Human Resources organization needs to be proactive, the line looks to Human Resources for a model . . . top management is the client; if we're not in touch with operations we can't serve top management.

> I believe there is a need for Human Resources people to have credibility to say "the emperor has no clothes." It takes a willingness to be in touch in your own organization—not tolerating ineffectiveness inside Human Resources. Human Resources needs to live in a glass house . . . Human Resources as the model for the organization.

## Need for Richer Theories of How Organizations Develop

The final trend addresses the need for more coherent theories and substantive knowledge of how organizations change and develop:

> We don't have theories of Organizational Development. We have normative ideas . . . not integrated into coherent theory. We can get a lot better. There are recurring problems in organizations. We need to provide better macro-theory on how organizations evolve, the agendas encountered at different stages. We need to understand patterns . . . not well developed.

> Some (Organizational Development) practitioners do well with process without enough substance. This field needs more knowledge. Key

knowledge areas are: socio-tech; strategic issues, What business are we in?, business competition, behaviors for success, areas for real cost saving, understanding motivation of different people. People with process without content and vice versa can go astray.

## SUMMARY

The purpose of this research project was to identify core competencies of the Organizational Development practitioner and future trends in the field. The project included 31 interviews with practitioners and researchers in the field. Four areas of core competencies, a description of a "watershed period" for the field, future trends impacting organizations and corresponding trends impacting the organizational development profession were identified from the interview data.

## REFERENCES

Bennis, W. (1985). *Leaders—The strategy for taking charge.* New York: Harper and Row.

Block, P. (1987). *The empowered manager.* San Francisco, CA: Jossey-Bass.

Schon, D. A. (1987). *Educating the reflective practitioner.* San Francisco, CA: Jossey-Bass.

Tannenbaum, R., Margulies, N., & Massarik, F. (1985). *Human systems development.* San Francisco, CA: Jossey-Bass.

Weisbord, M. (1987). The Third Wave. *Organizational Dynamics,* Winter.

# 15

# Organization Development in the 1980s*

**Marshall Sashkin**
*U.S. Department of Education*

**W. Warner Burke**
*Teachers College, Columbia University*

The term Organization Development (OD) was not used prior to about 1960. One early attempt to review the new field was made by Clark and Krone (1972) in their paper, "Toward an Overall View of Organizational Development in the Early Seventies." They defined an "open systems" framework emphasizing adaptive change by managers in response to environmental changes and pressures. Managers would need new skills in attending to the environment and anticipating impact on the organization through "open systems planning" (Jayaram, 1978). The insights they developed would then be used to modify organizational structures and processes through "open systems redesign" (Krone, 1974). This framework, often in an expanded variation, remains at the heart of most concepts of Organization Development, up to and including the present review.

Since Clark and Krone, OD has developed into a widely known field of applied research and practice. OD aims involve improving both organizational performance *and* the "quality of work life" experienced by organization members. These aims are attained by applying knowledge about people in organizations, derived from the social and behavioral sciences (Burke, 1982, 1987). Although there exists a body of OD research and practice reports, it would be difficult to argue that OD is a coherent discipline. There is no single theory that encompasses most of the research and practice; nor is

* The views expressed in this article are those of the authors and do not necessarily represent the policies of the Office of Educational Research and Improvement or the U.S. Department of Education. We wish to thank Jerry Hunt and John Blair for their extensive assistance in revising this chapter, as well as for their endurance and apparently inexhaustible patience. We also want to acknowledge the helpful, detailed comments provided by two anonymous reviewers and the assistance of Barry Macy and Randall Schuler. Address all correspondence to Marshall Sashkin, 8706 Nightingale Drive, Seabrook, MD 20706.

there a code of ethics among practitioners to which most or all would subscribe, although some of us have attempted to address issues of ethics (e.g., Burke, 1982; Frankel, 1986; Golembiewski, 1979; Walton & Warwick, 1973; and White & Wooten, 1986). Indeed, even a definition must remain relatively general if it is to receive widespread acceptance among scholars and practitioners. Yet, as a field, OD is researched, criticized, summarized, and reviewed.

In the first section of our review we identify two critical, parallel issues that underlie OD theory and practice. The first is the focus on changes in organizational *structures,* (including task structure and technology) versus changes in the ways people *behave* with and toward one another. Parallel to this first critical issue is a focus on "bottom-line" or performance and profit indicators versus a concern with "humanistic" outcomes, centering on the needs, desires, and general satisfaction of organization members. We shall see how these two parallel sets of contrapuntal themes, summarized in Table 1, are the overt and hidden aspects of a framework for integrating OD theory and practice in the 1980s.

To begin exploring this matter we turn, in the next section, to a more detailed examination of OD in the decade of the 1980s. Our review of the OD literature leads us to discuss four key research issues. On the basis of this research-focused literature review, we derive a set of ongoing trends of the 1980s. These trends are summarized in three key conclusions offered about OD in the 1980s. In conclusion, we speculate about OD from the 1980s into the 21st century, offering three scenarios and some suggestions for choosing among them.

In sum, we will in this review show how OD has developed to the present state of the art, define (to a degree) just what that state is, and suggest—at least tentatively—where the field might be heading.

## PAST ANNUAL REVIEWS

The first *Annual Review* article on OD was prepared by Friedlander and Brown (1974), who argued that attempts to develop OD theory had generally failed, due to an all but total focus on tying research to theory. This early theory was divorced from practice and therefore relatively useless for informing and guiding practice. Friedlander and Brown called for a "theory of practice, which emerges from practice data and is of the practice situation, not merely about it" (p. 336).

Friedlander and Brown identified two basic OD approaches. The

### TABLE 1. COMPETING OD APPROACHES AND VALUES

| OD Approaches | OD Values |
| --- | --- |
| Change the design and structure of work | Improve performance and profit, "bottom-line" measures |
| OR | OR |
| Change behavioral processes in organizations (that is, the way people work together) | Improve quality of work life of organization members, especially those at mid and lower levels |

first, which they called the "Human-Processual" approach, centered on people and the organizational processes based in people's behavior and focused on fulfillment of human needs and values. The second, which they labeled the "Technostructural" approach, centered on technology and the manner in which technology affects organizational structures and focused on task accomplishment aims (improved performance). Finally, Friedlander and Brown observed that "the human-processual and technostructural change approaches converge at the interface of the organizational process and structure" (p. 315). They illustrated this in Figure 1.

The framework developed by Friedlander and Brown helps one to understand what OD is all about and why OD may or may not be successful. That is, they defined the human-processual aspect of OD as including survey feedback, several forms of group development

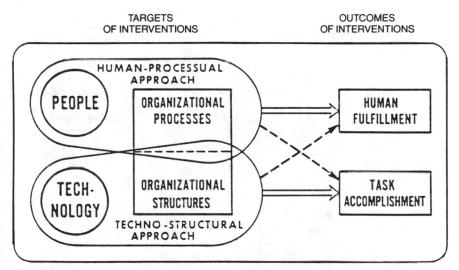

**FIGURE 1.** Approaches to organization development. Reproduced, with permission, from the *Annual Review of Psychology*, Vol. 25. © 1974 by Annual Reviews, Inc.

(team building) interventions, and intergroup development activities, and concluded that though such OD activities typically affect people's attitudes, there is rarely any substantial effect on either stable behavioral processes or on performance outcomes. In contrast, the technostructural approach, consisting of sociotechnical systems (STS) interventions, job design, and job enrichment, was seen as having substantial effects on performance. The overlap between the two OD approaches, as shown in Figure 1, suggests conflict rather than complementarity. It has been the work of the past decade to turn this conflict into an integrative model by linking these approaches and value outcomes, as shown in Figure 2.

In their review of comparative OD studies and comprehensive case reports, Friedlander and Brown characterized successful OD as

1. Instigated by both external and internal pressures;
2. Actively supported by top management;
3. Involving many people at many organizational levels;
4. Requiring much shared decision making throughout the organization;
5. Long-term (several years) in perspective;
6. Hard to evaluate in terms of clear quantitative outcomes.

The second *Annual Review* article, by Alderfer (1977), provided a detailed descriptive picture of OD research and practice in the late

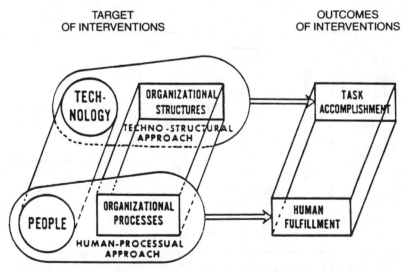

**FIGURE 2.** Linking organization development approaches.

1970s. He observed that, by the end of the 1970s, OD was being applied to a wide range of organizational settings in addition to the business/industry situations so typical of early OD efforts. Schools, hospitals, and even communities and countries were engaging in OD activities. At the same time, the standard OD interventions—team building, survey feedback, and structural change—were being refined. OD practitioners involved in team-building activities, for example, no longer typically assumed that everyone on the team shared the same goals prior to the intervention. Indeed, developing a common goals framework became an early focus and an integral part of team building. And research was getting much better, through new instruments, new methods, new foci, and new concepts. Such research, however, continued to be driven by academic theory rather than being focused on practice concerns, as called for by Friedlander and Brown.

The third published *Annual Review* article (Faucheux, Amado, & Laurent, 1982), gives us a widely divergent and fascinating (though hard to integrate) European view of OD. The authors think of Europe as "north" ("Anglo-Saxon") versus "south" ("Latin") rather than, as typical in the United States, "east" versus "west." Structural and especially sociotechnical themes are said to characterize Northern European/Anglo-Saxon OD (including Scandinavia, the Low Countries, and perhaps Germany, but excluding Great Britain!). In "Latin" Europe (France and Italy are the only countries mentioned) dominant OD approaches are identified as Marxist-oriented social-movement-based OD and neo-Freudian psychoanalytical frameworks. Brazil is given as an example of a "Latin bureaucracy" in which North American and Anglo-Saxon OD does not work, period. It is not clear where Great Britain fits, as the source of both sociotechnical *and* neo-Freudian OD concepts and approaches!

Faucheux et al. (1982) are most interesting when they give insights on OD in North America, insights that illuminate the blind areas that American OD has: for example, our heavy task orientation as opposed to trying "to deal with the social intricacies of human collectivities" (p. 353) more characteristic of the Latin countries of Europe. Their insights about OD in North America are summarized as follows:

> The field of planned change, which has been commensurate with OD in the U.S. for nearly 20 years, is now undergoing a very significant transformation. It may not be an exaggeration to see in the sociotechnical system approach a new paradigm. (p. 365)

The most recent annual review, by Beer and Walton (1987) is in part an effort to incorporate OD into the realm of general and human resource management, rather than an exploration of OD as a unique field of organizational inquiry and practice. The present approach is similar to that of Beer and Walton in its attempt to provide a broad overview of the field and where it is headed, including—but not limited to—research findings. The present approach differs, however, in that we view OD as remaining a distinct field of study and action rather than as becoming incorporated as an aspect of general management.

Implicit in the difference between the present review and the approach taken by Beer and Walton is the issue of values. Earlier we noted that OD has two aims, one being directed toward improved organizational performance and the other centering on improvements in the "human condition" within organizations (Table 1). This is an explicit factor in the Friedlander and Brown (1974) review, is reflected in the Alderfer (1977) review, and is a major overt and covert theme in the review by Faucheux et al. (1982). "Traditional" OD values center on the importance of people, and of their roles in organizations. An OD approach to organizational improvement must include both a "people" as well as a "performance" focus (Tannenbaum & Davis, 1969). Beer and Walton (1987), however, caution OD practitioners that the latter value—performance—must become predominant, with the former—concern for people—kept in the background as a long-run strategic vision but not as an operational part of OD. Thus, one might see Beer and Walton's position as an attempt to integrate the conflicting aspects of OD by eliminating some of them, by coopting OD into the broader management domain, and by relinquishing an overt concern for improving the "quality of work life" of organization members. We prefer to reemphasize the importance of both OD aims, improving organization members' quality of work life, *and* improving bottom-line performance outcomes. Making this issue explicit leads us to consider the question of whether OD is distinct from what has been called "Quality of Work Life."

## QUALITY OF WORK LIFE

The concept of quality of work life (QWL) has become increasingly popular as defining an area for study by social scientists as well as an arena for social action and organizational change. However, QWL remains a somewhat vague, fuzzy construct. What exactly *is* QWL?

Is it OD? Various definitions have been offered since the term was first used in the late 1960s. Even though most people would see QWL as a part of, if not the same as OD, Carlson (1980) defined QWL so broadly that it subsumed OD, rather than vice versa.

The only empirical effort to define QWL, through a factor analytical study (Taylor, 1978), yielded a single predominant factor that could not be clearly interpreted. Perhaps the most clear and comprehensive analysis is offered by Nadler and Lawler (1983), who identify four different major definitions of QWL over the time period 1969–1980. The earliest definition used QWL as a variable, specifically as workers' reactions to the work, expressed in terms of satisfaction. Soon, however, QWL came to be seen as a particular organizational improvement approach involving labor–management cooperation. In many applications during this period, from about 1969 to 1975, performance and productivity improvements were explicitly excluded as QWL aims, in part to reassure workers and unions that this was not simply another management ploy to get more productivity out of labor at no cost. The third definition, common through the mid-1970s, identified QWL with the specific changes and methods that were often involved: teams, autonomous groups, job enrichment, and sociotechnical change. Finally, beginning in the mid- to late-1970s, QWL came to be seen by many as a social movement, and it is, indeed, in this context and incarnation that it was identified by Faucheux et al. (1982) as perhaps being the successor to OD. Of course, in this final definition QWL focuses on just one of the two pairs of OD aims and values (as defined in Table 1) and is therefore clearly *not* the same as OD, in our view. But the issue can, perhaps, best be expressed as one of viewpoint.

Seashore (1973) suggested that QWL can best be thought of as a set of three umbrella constructs. In each of these three constructs specific variables can be defined, but they change across the three situations. The three umbrellas are really viewpoints: the viewpoint of workers, of managers (or the organization as a whole), and of society. Table 2 presents an illustrative set of variables, listed within each viewpoint category.

Thus, a "quality" work life may mean different things to different people in different roles, or to the same person in different roles; that is, as an employee of a university—a professor—one may be concerned with how one's role as a teacher fits with one's role as a member of a profession—a researcher or scholar—and with one's other professional role as a private consultant. The dean of the college, however, is concerned with the quality of students that faculty can attract and with the number of students in a class. But consider

**TABLE 2.   QUALITY OF WORK LIFE VARIABLES: 3 PERSPECTIVES**

| Worker | Organization | Society |
|---|---|---|
| health | productivity | effect on propensity toward deviant behavior |
| security | absenteeism | contribution toward "full" employment |
| job satisfaction | turnover | facilitation of positive intergenerational socialization processes |
| personal growth | quality of production | impact on older citizenry (direct and indirect, current and future) |
| adequate income | development of promotable employees | |

that the professor is also a private citizen. As such, one may be concerned about how the university professor is contributing to solving the problems of socializing young adults to the traditional norms and values of society and work.

Even more troublesome, different people in the same role may have discrepant views of QWL, not merely on the basis of different personal values but as a result of different abilities and aptitudes. The same assembly job may be very low in quality from the viewpoint of a bright, intellectually gifted college graduate, moderate in quality to an "average" worker with a high school education, but high in quality to a mildly retarded individual. For one person, growth and satisfaction may mean very different things than for another.

Faucheux et al. (1982) agree most with Nadler and Lawler's (1983) fourth definition of QWL as a social movement and seem to consider QWL identical to OD. But this is actually just the reverse side of the position taken by Beer and Walton (1987), who drop the workers' and societal viewpoints and accept only the organizational perspective. In contrast, Faucheux et al. see OD as QWL for workers and society, but not for managers of the organization. The definition of OD used here makes it clear that OD is both more and less than QWL. OD, in the present view, does not include the social movement/societal viewpoint identified by Nadler and Lawler and by Seashore, but does incorporate both workers' QWL as well as QWL from an organizational viewpoint.

The confusion introduced by the varying and sometimes conflicting definitions and views of QWL is not, in our view, random noise. Rather, this confusion represents the playing out of the conflict between bottom-line and humanistic values in OD. Seashore's analysis suggests to us that both of these value positions are legitimate and that neither can be labeled true or false. It therefore seems to us to be of great importance that OD incorporate both of these value premises, not through continual conflict but in much the same way that technology and social structure are "jointly optimized" in the sociotechnical systems approach. This is what we have tried to illustrate in Table 2.

## OD LITERATURE IN THE 1980S

More comprehensive reviews of the OD research literature prior to 1980 are provided in the *Annual Reviews* and in an exhaustive overview by Macy (1986a), on which we will comment later. As our aim was to examine OD trends and directions, our in-depth survey of the literature was confined to publications of the 1980s. Sources included both academic and popular literature but centered on the PsychInfo data base, the past several years of the *Journal of Applied Behavioral Science* and *Group & Organization Studies*, and OD Division papers and presentations at the national Academy of Management meetings.

The PsychInfo data base search yielded 210 items, of which about half were actually OD articles that included some empirical data (even if case study in nature). This was a surprisingly low number of reports for a 4-1/2-year period (1981–1985), considering that the data base includes quite a few nonmainstream journals (such as *Leadership and Organization Development* and *Management Education and Development*). Of the 84 reports that could clearly be called OD, the largest number were published in *Training and Development Journal* but few of these, if any, included empirical data. Of the remainder, 21 appeared in *G & OS*, 17 in *JABS*, and 6 in the next most-cited source, *Human Relations*. Perhaps encouraging, from an OD researcher's perspective, is evidence that the data base failed to capture a substantial number of OD reports. Examination of the contents of the 1983 and 1984 volumes of *JABS*, all of which were supposedly in the PsychInfo data base, identified 25 (of a total of 67) articles that were, on closer examination, clearly OD research. Thus, crude extrapolation suggests that the true number of OD research reports may be about 2-1/2 times that indicated by the PsychInfo data base search. In real numbers, this means that over the 1981–1985 time span there were perhaps 500 published OD-related articles, with about 250 of these representing data based research reports.

In reviewing the OD literature up to 1980, Spier, Sashkin, Jones, and Goodstein (1980) identified 717 OD references for the decade of the 1970s, 207 for the 1960s, 31 for the 1950s, and just 7 for the period up to 1950. With these figures as a baseline for comparison, the very great increase in OD reports from 1950 to 1970 was not maintained through the first half of the 1980s. From about 3 reports per year in the 1950s, 21 per year in the 1960s, and 72 per year in the 1970s, the average remains about 75 per year in the 1980s. Stability also appears in the number of papers and symposia submitted to the Academy's OD Division for 1984–1986, with about 40–50 papers and 15–20 symposia. Overall, evidence from several sources suggests that the dramatic rise in OD research through the 1960s and 1970s has, in the 1980s, stabilized.

Until now we have considered only numbers and totals. Content categorization of OD research adds considerably to our understanding of the field. Such an examination identified four major categories. Unsurprisingly, the two outstanding ones center on *research issues*—that is, problems and methods (by far the most common topic)—and *theory* (with somewhat greater than half the number of citations as research methods); these results are unexceptional.

More interesting were the major research issues to appear in the literature; we shall briefly review these in the next section. As for the development of OD theory, the relative frequency of citations may be misleading. Some, for example, limit their theoretical contribution to the use of the word *theory* in the article title. In a three-page article in *Training and Development Journal,* for example, Weisbord (1985) defines *team effectiveness theory* as the use of teams and team-building activities to introduce change. Other contributions seek to reconnect with some of the writing basic to OD. An example is provided by Mendenhall and Oddou (1983) in their paper, "The Integrative Approach to OD: McGregor Revisited." Still others hark back to fundamental OD theories and approaches of the 1960s and 1970s. Sashkin, Burke, Lawrence, and Pasmore (1985), for example, sought to highlight three "neglected" OD approaches (Walton's, 1969, third-party consultation; Lawrence & Lorsch's, 1969, contingency theory; and the sociotechnical systems approach of Pasmore & Sherwood, 1978). We find no real coherence among the various theoretical contributions of the 1980s that would lead us to think that the field of OD is approaching a theoretical synthesis.

Turning to topics with fewer numbers of citations, we find two more that have enough items to be worth noting. The first is team building. This is hardly surprising; by the 1980s team building has become a standard item in the tool kit of just about every OD practitioner; the paper by Weisbord (1985), cited earlier, is one demonstration of this fact. Indeed, Friedlander and Schott (1981), along with Weisbord (1985) consider teams to be a primary vehicle for organizational change. Murrell and Valsan (1985), for example, report on the use of team building in Egypt, and Eden (1985) provides a "true field experiment" on the effects of team building, followed up by a more strongly supportive "quasiexperiment" (Eden, 1986b). And Fiedler, Bell, Chemers, and Patrick (1984) describe an OD program to increase mine productivity and safety that, though based on team building, does not even use the term in the report's title, an indication of just how deeply embedded team building has become as a foundation stone of OD practice.

The second of these two remaining categories is unexpected. It contains reports and studies dealing with organizational cultures and change. This is a topic that we do not find in the reviews of the 1970s. Organizational culture also appeared as the single most common theme of papers and symposia at the 1985 Academy of Management OD Division meetings (followed by research methods, sociotechnical systems, and team building). However, with rare exception (e.g., see Wilkins & Ouchi, 1983), such reports lack empirical referents, let alone research data. That is, we find much in the way of concept and discussion, focused on the pragmatic (Ernest, 1985) as well as the more academic (Kilmann, Saxton, & Serpa, 1985), but little indeed that could be termed empirical research. Most of the references in this category are symposium presentations, papers in nonacademic (or nonresearch) magazines and journals (such as *Personnel Administrator*), nonrefereed publications (such as chapters in annual "research" volumes; e.g., Trice & Beyer, 1986) or books. In fact, two of the most widely recognized OD practitioners in the United States, Warren Bennis and Edgar Schein, have both produced recent books dealing with organizational culture (Bennis & Nanus, 1985; Schein, 1985). We will return to this new focus on culture.

In the PsychoInfo citations there were three additional topics that received some mention. These were survey feedback, OD in schools, and ethics. The first two can be seen as continuations (with reduced emphases) of earlier OD trends (e.g., see Gavin [1984, 1985] and Fullan, Miles, & Taylor [1981]). The third topic, OD values and ethics (e.g., Frankel, 1986), may represent an attempt to deal directly with the value conflict issues we identified earlier (see Table 1 and Figure 1), issues that have long been central to OD. Another possibility is that the values/ethics issue has come to the fore in OD as a result of its emphasis in general, across Academy of Management divisions.

Still another explanation might be that an ethical code is seen as an important aspect of the professionalization of OD, as an area of application and practice, just as in the fields of medicine or law (White & Wooten, 1986).

Having characterized the nature of the OD literature, we must look a bit more closely at what it tells us with regard to our current knowledge of OD. This will highlight the means by which the themes identified in Table 1, task versus process OD aims and people-centered versus performance-centered OD values, have approached the integrated state illustrated in Figure 2.

## OD RESEARCH: ISSUES AND ANSWERS

Topical trends in the OD literature provide leads as to where the field is going, and we shall shortly engage in some detailed speculation in that regard. However, before looking at what we might expect during the remainder of this decade and on into the next century, we should take a close and critical look at the status of OD research knowledge. What do we really know? What are the key research problems, and their solutions, if any? We identified four themes in the OD research literature, and we shall review each one in some detail.

*Issue 1: How good is the research?* Beginning in the late 1970s, various scholars began to examine the net findings of OD research, concentrating on whether consistent improvements as a consequence of OD activities could in fact be demonstrated (e.g., Franklin, 1976; Morrison, 1978; Porras & Berg, 1978b; White & Mitchell, 1976). They quickly, however, began to be concerned with the quality of OD research (Porras & Berg, 1978a), with some reviewers (Terpstra, 1981, 1982) concluding that much OD research shows unrealistic positive outcomes, due to weak, nonrigorous research designs that make it easy for researchers to find what they are—consciously or unconsciously—looking for. This debate over the quality of OD research raged on until quite recently, when an exceptionally careful review by Woodman and Wayne (1985) reported finding *no* relationship between research rigor and positive research findings. Indeed, tracking OD research in the early 1980s, Nicholas (1982) and Nicholas and Katz (1985) find evidence that the quality of OD research has been consistently improving over time. Although some argue that the final word is not yet in, most scholars seem willing to conclude that general positive biases on the part of OD researchers using weak research designs have not been the primary source—and are probably not a significant cause—of positive OD research findings. Developments with respect to the second research issue, however, may make superfluous much of the concern and argument around OD research quality.

***Issue 2: What are the true effects of OD interventions?*** Perhaps the most exciting new methodological innovation in the social sciences in this decade has been a set of methods called "meta-analysis" (Glass, McGaw, & Smith, 1982; Hunter, Schmidt, & Jackson, 1982). This approach makes use of certain quantitative data that can be gleaned from some research reports. These data are used to determine the true effects of experimental treatments, across research studies. It is important to realize that meta-analysis goes far beyond traditional integrative research reviews, whether qualitative or quantitative, allowing the strongest and clearest conclusions possible about the actual effects of specific actions.

The first meta-analysis of direct relevance to OD effects was performed by Guzzo, Jette, and Katzell (1985). Examining outcomes across more than 70 research studies, these researchers were able to assess the relative effect of several types of OD intervention. Their results were quite encouraging, showing that job design, participative management, sociotechnical systems interventions, and other OD actions all had quite positive effects on performance (output, turnover, absenteeism, and disruptions), ranging from an average improvement of one-quarter to one-half a standard deviation. This provides further, strong evidence that OD effects do not depend primarily on poorly designed or controlled research.

A more narrowly focused review of the effects of autonomy and participative decision making (Spector, 1986), which included a number of OD efforts as well as some noninterventional studies, corroborates some of the results reported by Guzzo et al. Spector found that high levels of autonomy and participation designed into the job were associated with high satisfaction, commitment, involvement, performance, and motivation, and with low levels of physical symptoms of ill health, emotional distress, role stress, absenteeism, turnover intent, and actual turnover.

A recent, massive review of some 800 work improvement and productivity efforts by Macy (1986a) draws generally positive conclusions with respect to both performance and worker satisfaction. However, a meta-analysis by Macy, Izumi, Hurts, and Norton (1986) of the 56 studies that included the required statistical information confirmed only the productivity effects; effects of workers' self-perceived quality of work life were almost uniformly *negative*. Macy (1986b) suggests that these odd results may be due to the performance pressures placed on workers by certain effective OD "action levers" (such as the use of work teams or new work structures). With respect to performance criteria, however, the results of this meta-analysis are quite consistent with earlier reviews of OD, both traditional and meta-analytic. There is little doubt that, when applied properly, OD has substantial positive effects in terms of performance measures.

**Issue 3: What is really changing?** A longstanding problem has centered on the question of what really changes as a result of OD interventions. It is probable that every OD practitioner has completed a project that to all appearances was quite successful—even taking into account the sort of bias one would expect when the consultant rates his or her own work. Yet, the clients report that the situation is *worse,* not better! Golembiewski, Billingsley, and Yeager (1976) sought to explain this unsettling paradox. They defined three types of change. *Alpha* change is "true" change, a change in measured attitudes and behavior that can be shown to result from an OD intervention. *Beta* change occurs when measurement scales themselves change, in the minds of organization members. For example, what had before the OD intervention seemed to be a pretty good climate might afterward be viewed as rather poor in comparison with a newly recognized ideal. And this might be the case even though the OD intervention really *improved* the situation! Thus, the outcome might appear to be little or no change, or even to be negative, although the "true" result is a positive change. This true result is, however, detectable only if the shift in organization members' internal measurement scales can be identified and taken into account. The third type of change, *gamma* change, makes quantitative OD effects almost impossible to demonstrate because the basic dimensions, the very ways in which organization members see the organization, have been changed as a result of OD activities.

There has been a modest amount of research over the decade since Golembiewski et al. (1976) published their paper on types of change, most of it dealing with how to detect the different types (e.g., Armenakis & Zmud, 1979; Lindell & Drexler, 1980; Van de Vliert, Huismans & Stok, 1985; Zmud & Armenakis, 1978). Oddly enough, despite general acceptance of the concepts defined by Golembiewski et al., and recognition of their import (their original paper won the 1976 McGregor Award), almost no OD research appears that takes type of change into account unless the researchers are explicitly studying how to measure one or more of the three types of change. This may be due to the difficulty in applying the concepts, in actually trying to identify and take into account the type of change. The primary effect of this work may be to raise the awareness of OD practitioners and to help them explain why they may feel rotten even though objective indicators say that things are getting better.

**Issue 4: Is what you want what you get?** More than a decade ago King (1971, 1974) showed that the "pygmalion" or self-fulfilling prophecy (Merton, 1948) effect identified by Rosenthal (1966, 1976) applied to OD as well as to the classroom. Rosenthal's most striking illustration of the effects produced by researchers' expectations was obtained in elementary school classrooms. Twenty percent of children in each of 18 schools were *randomly* labeled as students "who would show unusual academic development during the coming school year." At the end of the school year, those who were "academic bloomers" were found to have substantially greater IQ gains compared with others in their class. Similarly, King (1971) found that when supervisors expected hard-core unemployed trainees to learn and perform well, the trainees did so; when the supervisors' expectations were for poor learning and performance, then that too was the result. Later King (1974) found that an OD intervention proved effective, in terms of "hard" performance criteria, when those involved were led (by the experimenter) to expect it to, whereas the same intervention failed when organization members were led not to expect strong positive results. None of these findings implies that expectations alone can improve performance; teachers worked differently with the academic bloomers than with those not so labeled, and organization members took a different approach to the OD intervention they expected to work than to the same intervention when they were led not to expect it to work. Thus, expectations are not magic and cannot in and of themselves produce the desired effects. Expectations may, however, be a *necessary* (but not sufficient) condition of OD effectiveness. This is the argument developed by Eden (1984, 1986a) and his associates (Eden & Ravid, 1982; Eden & Shani, 1982).

This issue, which, at first glance, may seem to benefit OD practice, also presents some serious problems. Expectation or experimenter effects are considered highly undesirable threats to the validity of research. Thus, as a scientist the OD practitioner is confronted with a double bind: Using expectation effects may be necessary if the OD effort is to have the desired positive impact, but doing so may invalidate the worth of the OD activity as research!

*Summary.* OD research has, by the mid-1980s, shed quite a bit of light on the effects and effectiveness of OD. We are also in the position of understanding far more clearly than ever the key research problems in OD. Solutions are another matter. Although few today are willing to argue that OD has no real effects, there remains considerable uncertainty over how properly to measure these effects. And it may well be that effective OD is actually inconsistent with rigorous research, as some have argued (see Argyris, Putnam, & Smith, 1985). Further OD research is needed to determine whether effective OD interventions can be combined with rigorous research. Rosenthal's (1976) work suggests this is possible *if* the researcher-practitioner's expectations are taken into account as part of the research design.

We suggest that the clear research demonstration of positive OD impacts owes much to the integration of task structure and behavioral process-based OD approaches and of people-centered with profit-centered OD values. The work on types of change shows an increasingly sophisticated appreciation of the true interdependence of structure and process in OD. The newest theme, concerning the effects of expectations, may be another way of showing that the two value sets in Table 1 can be integrated if that is what we choose to expect. Future research should examine new ways of integrating or combining structural OD interventions with OD activities centered in behavioral processes (Sashkin, in press). Multivariate research is needed on the combined and interactive aspects of these two factors, which have all too often been treated only independently.

## TRENDS IN ORGANIZATION DEVELOPMENT

Some years ago, Friedlander (1976) likened OD to an adolescent going through the maturing process in the context of a strange and complex family situation, a *ménage à trois*. It is now more than a decade since he used that metaphor, and in that time OD has passed through adolescence about as successfully as most adolescents do. That is to say, the field is alive and kicking, has learned a trade, has attained modest success at it, and hopes for grand successes in the future. New relationships have taken the place of the nuclear family. One might even say that arising out of a sort of *ménage à trois*, OD has formed a new one, with culture and with sociotechnical systems (STS), as a means of dealing with deep and abiding value conflicts. Moreover, OD may be courting the strategy domain as well. Before going too far with this tempting metaphor, we should consider for a moment the trends and prospects for OD today in the late 1980s.

*Trend 1: Systematic structure-process integration.* Throughout our review we have observed increasing evidence of a marriage between task focus and process skills, not just at the level of a specific "micro-intervention" like a team-building meeting or a problem-solving session centered on survey feedback data, but at the larger, system level. We believe that this structure-process integration (shown in Figure 2), which was hinted at in the early review by Friedlander and Brown (1974), has developed over the past decade and has come to characterize OD practice in the 1980s. Effective OD practitioners in the 1980s use (and teach) process skills not to make people feel better about their work, one another, or the organization, but to help people learn to solve problems and get their work done more effectively. Furthermore, OD practitioners take a larger, more systemic perspective, focusing on organizational issues such as strategic planning, reward systems, management structures, and information systems; no longer is the OD focus solely on teams, interpersonal issues, and training. The broadened perspective of OD, we should note, incorporates rather than excludes these "micro-issues."

Perhaps a key to the sort of task-process integration we refer to can be seen in the STS approach, which has come into much greater use in the early 1980s (see Walton, 1985). STS provides strong support for task-process integration, since it explicitly aims to "jointly optimize" the technical and social structures of the organization. And there is convincing evidence (Guzzo et al., 1985; Macy et al., 1986) that the STS approach has strong positive effects on productivity and performance. We expect the implementation of "new work structures," as Walton (1985) terms this sort of change, to proceed at an increasingly rapid rate over the remainder of this century. Effective attention to an integration of the task and process aspects of OD provides resolution to one of the two critical themes in OD that we identified at the beginning of this review.

**Trend 2: Culture by design: Integrating value perspectives.** Consistent with the sort of larger scale, system approach just described is the recent salience of organizational culture. Indeed, OD practitioners often find that their clients use the term *culture* before they do, even quoting Deal and Kennedy (1982) to them! The concept of culture has become more clear and has attained general acceptance due to its importance for understanding how to manage, lead, and change large and complex systems. Senior managers in many corporations are aware, as was not true a decade ago, that significant changes in organizational mission and strategy will produce great frustration, if not outright failure, unless concomitant consideration is given to modifying the organization's culture such that norms and values support the change (see Schein, 1985). Thoughtful strategy development is becoming a common aspect of

OD (Eadie & Steinbacher, 1985). Such strategic designs are carried out by designing the organization's culture, a process often simply called "managing change," which has become a catchword for OD as applied to designing organizational cultures. Lest all this begin to sound rather abstract, recognize that the aim is to build a culture that values productivity, performance, and bottom-line outcome measures, a culture of "excellence" (Peters & Waterman, 1982).

Such cultures can only be developed through leadership, and for this reason leadership has come to the forefront as a critical issue at the organizational level. We refer not to the sort of academic models of leadership that actually deal with the practice of lower and mid-level supervisory management (Blake & Mouton, 1978; Fiedler, 1967; Hersey & Blanchard, 1982; Stogdill & Coons, 1957; see Yukl, 1981, for a comprehensive overview). Rather, we refer to top-level, organizational leadership (Sashkin & Fulmer, in press) of the sort that transforms organizations (Burns, 1978; Tichy & Devanna, 1986) by empowering organization members (Burke, 1986). The importance of top management for successful OD is not, of course, a new concept; nor are we really speaking of a new sort of role for the CEO. This sort of executive leadership is precisely what top-level management has always been about (e.g., see Mintzberg, 1973). The change is in conscious direction of the leadership process to attain concrete changes in organizational culture (see Schein, 1985).

We have asserted that these culture-building efforts by top-level leaders aim to incorporate organizational values of excellent performance into the culture. This takes care of the bottom-line value position of organizational management, but how is this integrated with the people-centered value position of OD, focused as it is on the quality of work life from the point of view of lower-level organization members? We have hinted at how, when we mentioned empowering employees (Burke, 1986). Such empowerment is a critical part of a broad strategy of management that is commonly referred to as participation.

Participation in management, employee involvement, and related sorts of activities—hallmarks of OD practice and values—are more in evidence today than ever before (Hoerr, Pollock, & Whiteside, 1986; Walton, 1985). The efficacy of participative management and its positive bottom-line effects have received empirical research support (e.g., see Miller & Monge, 1986) and the participative approach has been increasingly advocated (Sashkin, 1982, 1984, 1986).

Others, however, have pointed out that though evidence abounds that participative ways of managing pay off, at the bottom line as well as in terms of other performance indicators, the process is often resisted, especially at higher levels of management (Saporito, 1986). Saporito quotes one executive as stating that the delegating of decisions took the fun out of managing. Others appear resistant due to contradictory values (e.g., Locke, Schweiger, & Latham, 1986), even to the point of denying the positive effects of participation.

Without a greater understanding of executives' needs for power, of the dynamics of power and politics in organizations, and of the values underlying different managerial approaches, the OD emphasis on creating participative organizational cultures through top-level leadership might prove to be more of a fad than an enduring approach for building people-centered values—particularly a lower-level employee quality of work life viewpoint—into organizational cultures.

Participation encourages human development needs centered on autonomy and control of one's own actions (Argyris, 1957). It provides for satisfaction of the need for achievement and closure (McClelland & Burnham, 1976; Sashkin, 1982, 1984). And when applied in a group context (e.g., Likert, 1967) and in conjunction with a sociotechnical systems approach, participation provides for satisfaction of the need for work-relevant interpersonal contacts (Mayo, 1933; McClelland, 1955). Thus, we come full circle, finding that effective integration of the conflicting value perspectives of management and workers is best accomplished in the context of effective integration of task and process foci, as was illustrated at the beginning of this review (see Figures 1 and 2). The sociotechnical approach (Pasmore & Sherwood, 1978), when combined with the development of a culture-by-design, can together serve to integrate the longstanding overt and covert conflicts in OD.

In sum, these first two critical trends suggest that OD practice may be resolving the structure versus process issue while dealing with the performance versus people concern. These ends are achieved by combining an STS design approach with a focus on changing organizational culture through executive leadership.

***Trend 3: Managing conflict.*** Conflict resolution and effectiveness in lateral relations have long been acknowledged as important for organizational effectiveness, and conflict management has been a basic element of OD since the 1960s (Walton, 1969, 1987). It appears to us that managing conflict is becoming even more of a focus in OD practice. There are at least three factors behind this. First, there is the tendency toward more decentralized authority structures and flatter hierarchies. In such circumstances getting the work done effectively depends more on influence skills and less on the exercise of power as a function of position of status (Kanter,

1984). Second, we see a continuing emphasis on collaborative approaches to labor–management relations and a continuing move away from the classic adversarial model (Shirom, 1983). OD is an important factor in this move. Finally, the incredible increase in organizational mergers and acquisitions in the 1980s has created many more settings in which serious conflicts are bound to occur and in which achieving some degree of smooth working relationship—if not total integration—is critical. In sum, managing conflict is a major OD trend that is likely to increase in scope in the future.

***Trend 4: Better research.*** As we saw from our review of OD research, there is much greater sophistication today about research in general and its relation to OD in particular. Critical issues and problems are far better and more clearly defined than was true a decade ago and, more important, OD practitioners are aware of those issues to a much greater degree than was true in the past. It may, however, be that awareness and understanding is as far as we can go, with respect to resolving some of the research problems (in particular, in reference to the fourth issue identified earlier), in order to have greater, more positive, and more lasting OD effects, not just to control or correct for these problems while doing "good research." Thus, we may see OD practitioners making active use of expectation effects and beta change, rather than correcting research designs for these "artifacts." Indeed, some might say that practitioners will merely have new labels for (and perhaps a better understanding of) what they would do anyway.

In sum OD research is more sophisticated, more methodologically sound, than ever. We are approaching some real syntheses of research findings, and this trend will continue as more and better meta-analyses are carried out. And OD practitioners are learning how to use experimenter effects and other research artifacts to the benefit of OD efforts in organizations.

***Trend 5: Improved theory?*** We are much less certain of this trend than we are of the others; perhaps it reflects our hopes more than it does reality. Our hope is that the increased interest in meta-analysis may indicate an increase in efforts at integrating not just various sets of research studies but in doing so in a way that results in good OD theory. Indeed, we hope to be seen as an example of this; it would be foolish to assert that the integration arguments just reviewed are proven fact, that they are anything other than hypotheses based on a careful review of OD research and practice.

It is our belief that OD professionals today recognize clearly—and more than they did a decade ago—that no strong integrative theory of OD exists. We have broad macrotheories of change, such as that developed by Lippitt and his associates almost 30 years ago (Lippitt, Watson, & Westley, 1958). And we have narrow, small-scale "mid-range" theories (see chap. 2 in Burke, 1982). Still, we lack a widely accepted theory of organizational change through OD, and none seems to be on the horizon. We can only suggest and hope that the integrations and advances discussed here may eventually address this lack, too, moving us toward completion of the OD theory statement developed by Friedlander and Brown (1974).

## SUMMARY: ORGANIZATION DEVELOPMENT IN THE 1980S

We see three major conclusions about OD in the 1980s. First, the casual observer as well as the practitioner finds much less strangeness in the field and a much greater sense of respectability for organization development. Many OD interventions are so standard, such as off-site meetings or team building sessions, as to be familiar to any experienced manager. Rarely does one see the use of T-groups or encounter groups. And though OD research is not welcomed in the traditional research publications, there are respectable outlets and even an occasional article in the *Academy of Management Journal* and the *Journal of Applied Psychology*.

Second, there has been an effective integration, resolving the long-standing conflict between structural OD concerns and behavioral process issues as the focus of OD activities. At the microlevel this is seen most clearly with respect to team building (DeMeuse & Liebowitz, 1981). In the 1980s, team building rarely (if ever) consists of open-ended examination of interpersonal relations. Team building interventions today typically have a clear task focus; process is a way of improving how the team accomplishes its tasks, not an end in itself. On the macrolevel, the sociotechnical systems approach seems to be serving as a vehicle for integrating these same task structure and behavioral process concerns. Moreover, the emphases on reward systems, management information systems, structures and strategies indicate that OD professionals have broadened their perspectives. In these ways, the "human processual" and "technostructural" cores of OD identified by Friedlander and Brown (1974) are being effectively connected.

Third, there is a greater focus on organizational culture, not from a pure process viewpoint but from the sort of structural perspective commonly used by organizational sociologists such as Talcott Parsons (1960). Such an approach makes clear how values affect critical organizational functions. When combined with the sort of perspectives on leadership common to sociologists such as Selznick (1957) or Perrow (1979) but unfamiliar to most of those in the field of "organizational behavior," this cultural perspective suggests some interesting new directions for OD practice. More important, it suggests that leaders act to create cultures that integrate the two value perspectives—organizational bottom-line and humanistic quality of employee work life—that have long been the source of covert conflict in OD theory and practice. Future OD research should focus on empirical and experimental measurement of cultural OD interventions and their effects, including especially effects on values that concern both performance and people.

## Implications for Practitioners

In the 1960s and well into the 1970s, OD practitioners had to fight constantly such stereotypes as "group grope," "flaky, soft" orientations toward human behavior, and beliefs such as "If people feel better, performance will be better." This strangeness about OD, as we have noted, is all but gone. In fact, the problem today may be not being different enough. The system may have co-opted us. In other words, what we face today are serious questions of values and ethics. In the face of (a) companies being bought and sold more rapidly than ever before, and (b) activities such as downsizing, undoubtedly a significant change is under way in the nature of the psychological contract between employee and employer. Loyalty to one's employer may be a thing of the past. What constitutes commitment in the workplace may be considerably different in the 1990s. What is fair treatment of employees today? Do we practitioners support the organization from which our salary comes or the individual being considered for outplacement? Who is our client? Although we in OD have always been confronted with the conflict of the individual versus the organization, what is unprecedented is how deep this issue has become. Never before have we had to face so squarely our own beliefs, values, and ethical standards. It is far more than merely espousing Theory Y. Understanding ourselves more thoroughly and determining what stances we wish to take and under what circumstances are more important than ever.

Organizational culture is here to stay; the notion is not a passing fad. OD practitioners must immerse themselves in understanding the concept, in ways of assessing organizational culture, and in ways of changing it. There are at least two major practice areas for OD consultants. One concerns the alignment of strategy and culture. When top management decides to change the organization's strategy without a commensurate plan to modify the culture accordingly, the new strategic thrust is likely never to materialize. The second OD practice area is the alignment of two cultures as a consequence of acquisitions/mergers or a significant reorganization. "But that's not the way we do things" is the often heard retort. OD practitioners must help the two cultures find a third, new one that is acceptable to and effective for both.

There are no doubt additional implications. In any case, for the 1980s and at least into the early 1990s, the two mentioned above seem to us to be at the top of the list.

## Organization Development in the Future

Popular yet astute observers of current and future shifts in organizational effectiveness have their differences but also reflect common ground. Consider Naisbett and Aburdene's *Re-Inventing the Corporation* (1985), Rosabeth Kanter's *The Change Masters* (1984), and the latest thinking of Tom Peters (1987). They all agree that effective organizations in the future

1. Will be flatter structurally, and organizational members will "network" more to get work done and to communicate.
2. Will involve organizational members more in decisions they are expected to implement.
3. Will be more people oriented.

If these observers are no more than half correct, OD practitioners will have plenty of work and articles like this one will continue to be written.

OD, however, is still a field in transition, as one of us wrote more than a decade ago (Burke, 1976). Even though certain principles have been delineated (e.g., change involves unfreezing, intervention, and refreezing), and most agree that OD practice follows an action research model, OD nevertheless is comparatively young. OD is no longer an adolescent, but neither is it a mature adult. So, the future is still a prediction, not a foregone conclusion. Thus, we shall provide three possible scenarios for the future, giving you, the reader, choice and involvement—in the OD fashion.

***First scenario:*** OD is stagnating, retrenching, and collapsing inward upon itself. Having ultimately failed to demonstrate clear and convincing bottom line effects, and with evidence that even positive attitudinal effects are ephemeral, OD as it was known from the 1970s to the 1980s is well on the way to being no more. The few real contributions, in terms of specific, focused "intervention" activities will become—indeed, *have* become—part of the normal functioning of a good personnel department ("human resources" department, for anyone new to the game), as well as standard elements of the management consultant's tool kit. Of course, organizations do change, and help with the problems of change is certain to be a continuing need. Such help is likely, in the future, to be more structural and technical than process- or attitude-focused. Although it is unlikely, it may be that some aspect of OD as we know it will ultimately emerge, like a phoenix, from the ashes of its own demise.

**Second scenario:** To all appearances, OD is healthy and stable, entering a period of slow but steady and productive growth in which the primary task is refinement and consolidation. OD practitioners realize that they cannot work miracles, but have also come to understand better that their effort can make a difference. Some of the most generally useful bits and pieces of OD practice have become widely integrated into organizational life. The very notion of the work group or team, and of team building, has become accepted and commonplace, and it is worth noting that this was not the case 20 years ago, nor is the case in much of the industrialized world outside the United States (including Japan, as both authors were surprised to discover personally). There is now strong evidence that OD can and does make a difference and that effects are not dependent on poor research designs or chance. Although without a common theory of OD, practitioners have shown that they know what they are doing. Finally, there has been major progress in integrating structural and process-centered change interventions that may eventually lead to even stronger OD effects. In sum, OD is no longer as exciting as when it was a new and radical approach to creating change in organizations, but it has demonstrated strength, substance, and persistence.

**Third scenario:** OD is moving in new, exciting directions—structure, culture, and leadership. It is about to become in fact what it has always hoped to be, a true and viable strategy for improving whole organizations, in terms of both human needs of organization members and bottom line results. At the same time, OD is seen to be based in approaches and techniques that have been proven effective for solving organizational problems so that they stay solved and for making significant improvements in "organizational life." OD remains, as it has been for some time, the leading edge of applied behavioral science. Furthermore, and more to the point, organization culture will be the OD focus of the late 1980s and of the 1990s. This will be true on a large scale, in terms of the sort of cross-cultural value differences explored in depth by Hofstede (1980), as well as on the scale of the organization, in terms of specific OD interventions, as detailed in articles such as Jaeger's (1984, 1986). But the real key to changing culture, as implied already, is not the sort of micro-OD intervention approach, like team building, that we are familiar with. As has now been recognized more appropriately, the key is in leadership, specifically the leadership of the chief executive officer. This is the focus advocated and explored for many years by Argyris (1973), who even takes the position that it is the values expressed through the actions of the CEO that ultimately drive OD.

Some of the most current culture-changing OD work (e.g., Frohman & Sashkin, 1985) has involved a CEO and top executive team in analyzing the organization's value base, acting to make changes through a general corporate philosophy, and then carrying out that philosophy in terms of policies, programs, and personal actions. Thus, in the late 1980s and through the 1990s, the structural focus that has since the late 1970s become a stronger and more important element of OD will continue to drive major OD activities. We will continue to learn to use task-process integration and sociotechnical systems approaches to design and change organizational cultures in order to integrate the organizational value of performance and productivity with organization members' value of a high quality work life.

## A Choice

Which of the above scenarios is it likely to be? We have already rejected the first, at least as a likely option, yet it cannot be completely ruled out. Without a coherent theory of OD practice and of change, the field is vulnerable, and there remains the possibility that OD will eventually become so fragmented as to have no coherence as a discipline. Thus, though not the most likely outcome, the first scenario is feasible. Still, it seems far more likely that even under the worst of circumstances OD will continue to exist as an identifiable field of research and practice. And those scholars and practitioners with some vision will be studying sociotechnical systems and culture, along with organizational leadership.

But what about a choice between the second and third scenarios? One of us predicts the second, but hopes for the third. The other hopes for no worse than the second while predicting the third. Perhaps the first is a realist and the second an idealist, if not a cockeyed optimist. In any case, we indeed agree that OD is alive and well in 1987, and all indications are that it will continue to thrive well past the millennium.

## REFERENCES

Alderfer, C. P. (1977). Organization development. In M. R. Rosenzweig & L. W. Porter (Eds.), *Annual Review of Psychology* (pp. 197–223). Palo Alto, CA: Annual Reviews, Inc.

Argyris, C. (1957). *Personality and organization.* New York: Harper & Row.

Argyris, C. (1973). The CEO's behavior: Key to organizational development. *Harvard Business Review, 51*(2), 55–64.

Argyris, C., Putnam, R., & Smith, D. M. (1985). *Action science.* San Francisco: Jossey–Bass.

Armenakis, A. A., & Zmud, R. (1979). Interpreting the measurement of change in organizational research. *Personnel Psychology, 32,* 709–723.

Bass, B. M. (1985). *Leadership and performance beyond expectations.* New York: Free Press.

Beer, M., & Walton, A. E. (1987). Organization development. In M. R. Rosenzweig & L. W. Porter (Eds.), *Annual Review of Psychology* (pp. 339–367). Palo Alto, CA: Annual Reviews, Inc.

Bennis, W. G., & Nanus, B. (1985). *Leaders.* New York: Harper & Row.

Blake, R. R., & Mouton, J. S. (1978). *The new managerial grid.* Houston: Gulf.

Burke, W. W. (1976). Organization development in transition. *Journal of Applied Behavioral Science, 12*(1), 22–43.

Burke, W. W. (1982). *Organization development: Principles and practices.* Boston: Little, Brown.

Burke, W. W. (1986). Leadership as empowering others. In S. Srivastva & Associates (Eds.), *Executive power* (pp. 51–77). San Francisco: Jossey–Bass.

Burke, W. W. (1987). *Organization development: A normative view.* Reading, MA: Addison–Wesley.

Burke, W. W., Clark, L. P., & Koopman, C. (1984). Improve your OD project's chances for success. *Training and Development Journal, 38*(8), 62–68.

Burns, J. McG. (1978). *Leadership.* New York: Harper & Row.

Carlson, H. C. (1980). A model of quality of work life as a developmental process. In W. W. Burke & L. D. Goodstein (Eds.), *Trends and issues in OD: Current theory and practice* (pp. 83–123). San Diego: University Associates.

Clark, J. V., & Krone, C. G. (1972). Toward an overall view of organizational development in the early seventies. In J. M. Thomas & W. G. Bennis (Eds.), *The management of change and conflict* (pp. 284–303). Middlesex, England: Penguin Books.

Deal, T. E., & Kennedy, A. A. (1982). *Corporate cultures: The rites and rituals of corporate life.* Reading, MA: Addison–Wesley.

DeMeuse, K. P., & Liebowitz, S. J. (1981). An empirical analysis of team-building research. *Group & Organization Studies, 6,* 357–378.

Eadie, D. C., & Steinbacher, R. (1985). Strategic agenda management: A marriage of organizational development and strategic planning. *Public Administration Review, 45,* 424–430.

Eden, D. (1984). Self-fulfilling prophecy as a management tool: Harnessing Pygmalion. *Academy of Management Review, 9,* 64–73.

Eden, D. (1985). Team development: A true field experiment at three levels of rigor. *Journal of Applied Psychology, 70,* 94–100.

Eden, D. (1986a). OD and self-fulfilling prophecy: Boosting productivity by raising expectations. *Journal of Applied Behavioral Science, 22,* 1–13.

Eden, D. (1986b). Team development: Quasi-experimental confirmation among combat companies. *Group & Organization Studies, 11,* 133–146.

Eden, D., & Ravid, G. (1982). Pygmalion vs. self-expectancy: Effects of instructor and self-expectancy on trainee performance. *Organizational Behavior and Human Performance, 30,* 351–364.

Eden, D., & Shani, A. B. (1982). Pygmalion goes to boot camp: Expectancy, leadership, and trainee performance. *Journal of Applied Psychology, 67,* 194–199.

Ernest, R. C. (1985). Corporate cultures and effective planning. *Personnel Administrator, 30*(3), 49–60.

Faucheux, C., Amado, G., & Laurent, A. (1982). Organizational development and change. In M. R. Rosenzweig & L. W. Porter (Eds.), *Annual Review of Psychology* (pp. 343–370). Palo Alto, CA: Annual Reviews, Inc.

Fiedler, F. E. (1967). *A theory of leadership effectiveness.* New York: McGraw–Hill.

Fiedler, F. E., Bell, C. H., Jr., Chemers, M. M. & Patrick, D. (1984). Increasing mine productivity and safety through management training and organization development: A comparative study. *Basic and Applied Social Psychology, 5,* 1–18.

Frankel, M. S. (1986). Values and ethics in organization development: The case of confidentiality. *Organization Development Journal, 4*(2), 14–20.

Franklin, J. L. (1976). Characteristics of successful and unsuccessful organization development. *Journal of Applied Behavioral Science, 12,* 471–492.

Friedlander, F. (1976). OD reaches adolescence: An exploration of its underlying values. *Journal of Applied Behavioral Science, 12,* 7–21.

Friedlander, F., & Brown, L. D. (1974). Organization development. In M. R. Rosenzweig & L. W. Porter (Eds.), *Annual Review of Psychology* (pp. 313–341). Palo Alto, CA: Annual Reviews, Inc.

Friedlander, F., & Schott, B. (1981). The use of task groups and task forces in organizational change. In R. Payne & C. Cooper (Eds.), *Groups at work* (pp. 191–218). London: Wiley.

Frohman, M. A., & Sashkin, M. (1985, August). *Achieving organizational excellence: Development and implementation of a top management mind set.* Paper presented at the annual meeting of the Academy of Management, Organization Development Division, San Diego.

Fullan, M., Miles, M. B., & Taylor, G. (1981). *Organization development in schools: The state of the art.* Washington, DC: U.S. Government Printing Office.

Gavin, J. F. (1984). Survey feedback: The perspectives of science and practice. *Group & Organization Studies, 9,* 29–70.

Gavin, J. F. (1985). Observations from a long-term survey-guided consultation with a mining company. *Journal of Applied Behavioral Science, 21,* 201–220.

Glass, G. V., McGaw, B., & Smith, M. L. (1982). *Meta-analysis in social research.* Beverly Hills, CA: Sage.

Golembiewski, R. T. (1979). *Approaches to planned change.* New York: Marcel Dekker.

Golembiewski, R. T., Billingsley, K., & Yeager, S. (1976). Measuring change and persistence in human affairs. *Journal of Applied Behavioral Science, 12,* 133–157.

Guzzo, R. A., Jette, R. D., & Katzell, R. A. (1985). The effects of psychologically based intervention programs on worker productivity: A meta-analysis. *Personnel Psychology, 38,* 275–291.

Hersey, P., & Blanchard, K. H. (1982). *Management of organizational behavior* (4th ed.). Englewood Cliffs, NJ: Prentice–Hall.

Hoerr, J., Pollock, M. A., & Whiteside, D. E. (1986, September 29). Management discovers the human side of automation. *Business Week,* pp. 70–75.

Hofstede, G. (1980). Motivation, leadership, and organization. *Organizational Dynamics, 9*(1), 42–62.

Hunter, J. F., Schmidt, F. L., & Jackson, G. B. (1982). *Meta-analysis: Cumulating research findings across studies.* Beverly Hills, CA: Sage.

Jaeger, A. M. (1984). The appropriateness of organization development outside North America. *International Studies of Management and Organization, 14,*(1), 23–35.

Jaeger, A. M. (1986). Organization development and national culture. *Academy of Management Review, 11,* 178–190.

Jayaram, G. K. (1978). Open systems planning. In W. A. Pasmore & J. J.

Sherwood (Eds.), *Sociotechnical systems: A sourcebook* (pp. 28–38). San Diego: University Associates.

Kanter, R. M. (1984). *The change masters: Innovation for productivity in the American corporation.* New York: Simon & Schuster.

Kilmann, R. H., Saxton, M. J., & Serpa, R. (1985). *Gaining control of the corporate culture.* San Francisco: Jossey–Bass.

King, A. S. (1971). Self-fulfilling prophecies in training the hard-core: Supervisors' expectations and the underprivileged workers' performance. *Social Science Quarterly, 52,* 369–378.

King, A. S. (1974). Expectation effects in organizational change. *Administrative Science Quarterly, 19,* 221–230.

Krone, G. G. (1974). Open systems redesign. In J. Adams (Ed.), *New technologies in organization development: 2* (pp. 364–391). San Diego: University Associates.

Lawrence, P. R., & Lorsch, J. W. (1969). *Organization and environment.* Homewood, IL: Irwin.

Likert, R. (1967). *The human organization.* New York: McGraw–Hill.

Lindell, M. K., & Drexler, J. A., Jr. (1980). Equivocality of factor incongruence as an indicator of type of change in OD interventions. *Academy of Management Review, 10,* 269–274.

Lippitt, R. O., Watson, J., & Westley, B. (1958). *The dynamics of planned change.* New York: Harcourt, Brace, & World.

Locke, E. A., Schweiger, D. M., & Latham, G. P. (1986). Participation in decision making: When should it be used? *Organizational Dynamics, 14*(3), 65–79.

McClelland, D. C. (Ed.). (1955). *Studies in motivation.* New York: Appleton–Century–Crofts.

McClelland, D. C., & Burnham, D. (1976). Power is the great motivator. *Harvard Business Review, 54*(2), 100–110.

Macy, B. A. (1986a, August). *An assessment of United States work improvement and productivity efforts: 1970–1985.* Paper presented at the National Academy of Management meetings, Chicago.

Macy, B. A. (1986b). Personal communication.

Macy, B. A., Izumi, H., Hurts, C. C. M., & Norton, L. W. (1986, August). *Meta-analysis of United States empirical organizational change and work innovation field experiments.* Paper presented at the National Academy of Management meetings, Chicago.

Mayo, E. (1933). *The human problems of an industrial civilization.* New York: Macmillan.

Mendenhall, M., & Oddou, G. (1983). The integrative approach to OD: McGregor revisited. *Group & Organization Studies, 8,* 291–301.

Merton, R. K. (1948). The self-fulfilling prophecy. *Antioch Review, 8,* 193–210.

Miller, K. I., & Monge, P. R. (1986). Participation, satisfaction, and productivity: A meta-analytic review. *Academy of Management Journal, 29,* 727–753.

Mintzberg, H. (1973). *The nature of managerial work.* Englewood Cliffs, NJ: Prentice–Hall.

Morrison, P. (1978). Evaluation in OD: A review and assessment. *Group & Organization Studies, 3,* 42–70.

Murrell, K. L., & Valsan, E. H. (1985). A team building workshop as an OD intervention in Egypt. *Leadership & Organization Development, 6* (2), 11–16.

Nadler, D. A., & Lawler, E. E. III (1983). Quality of work life: Perceptions and directions. *Organizational Dynamics, 11*(3), 20–30.

Naisbett, J., & Aburdene, P. (1985). *Re-inventing the corporation.* New York: Warner Books.

Nicholas, J. M. (1982). The comparative impact of organization development interventions on hard criteria measures. *Academy of Management Review, 9,* 531–543.

Nicholas, J. M., & Katz, M. (1985). Research methods and reporting practices in organization development: A review and some guidelines. *Academy of Management Review, 10,* 737–749.

Parsons, T. (1960). *Structure and process in modern societies.* New York: Free Press.

Pasmore, W. A., & Sherwood, J. J. (Eds.). (1978). *Sociotechnical systems: A sourcebook.* San Diego: University Associates.

Perrow, C. (1979). *Complex organizations* (2nd Ed.). Glenview, IL: Scott, Foresman.

Peters, T. J. (1987). A world turned upside down. *Academy of Management Executive, 1*(3), 231–241.

Peters, T. J., & Waterman, R. H. Jr. (1982). *In search of excellence: Lessons from America's best-run companies.* New York: Harper & Row.

Porras, J. I., & Berg, P. O. (1978a). Evaluation methodology in organization development: An analytical critique. *Journal of Applied Behavioral Science, 14,* 151–173.

Porras, J. I., & Berg, P. O. (1978b). The impact of organization development. *Academy of Management Review, 3,* 249–266.

Rosenthal, R. (1966). *Experimenter effects in behavioral research.* New York: Appleton–Century–Crofts.

Rosenthal, R. (1976). *Experimenter effects in behavioral research* (enlarged ed.). New York: Irvington.

Saporito, B. (1986). The revolt against "working smarter." *Fortune, 114*(2), 58–65.

Sashkin, M. (1982). *A manager's guide to participative management.* New York: American Management Association.

Sashkin, M. (1984). Participative management is an ethical imperative. *Organizational Dynamics, 12*(4), 4–22.

Sashkin, M. (1986). Participative management remains an ethical imperative. *Organizational Dynamics, 14*(4), 62–75.

Sashkin, M. (in press). Content and process in OD intervention: The message from research. *Organization Development Journal.*

Sashkin, M., Burke, R. J., Lawrence, P. R., & Pasmore, W. A. (1985). *OD approaches: Analysis and application. Training and Development Journal, 39*(2), 44–50.

Sashkin, M., & Fulmer, R. M. (1988). Toward an organizational leadership theory. In J. G. Hunt, B. R. Baliga, H. P. Dachler, & C. A. Schriesheim (Eds.), *Emerging leadership vistas.* (pp. 51–65). Lexington, MA: Lexington Books.

Schein, E. H. (1985). *Organizational culture and leadership.* San Francisco: Jossey–Bass.

Seashore, S. E. (1973). Personal communication.

Selznick, P. (1957). *Leadership in administration.* Evanston, IL: Row, Peterson.

Shirom, A. (1983). Toward a theory of organization development interventions in unionized work settings. *Human Relations, 36,* 743–764.

Spector, P. E. (1986). Perceived control by employees: A meta-analysis of studies concerning autonomy and participation at work. *Human Relations, 11,* 1005–1016.

Spier, M. S., Sashkin, M., Jones, J. E., & Goodstein, L. D. (1980). Predictions and projections for the decade: Trends and issues in organization development. In W. W. Burke & L. D. Goodstein (Eds.), *Trends and issues in OD* (pp. 12–37). San Diego: University Associates.

Stodgill, R. M., & Coons, A. E. (Eds.). (1957). *Leader behavior: Its description and measurement.* Columbus, OH: Bureau of Business Research, Ohio State University.

Tannenbaum, R., & Davis, S. A. (1969). Values, man, and organizations. *Industrial Management Review, 10*(2), 67–86.

Taylor, J. C. (1978). An empirical examination of the dimensions of quality of working life. *Omega, 6*(1), 1–8.

Terpstra, D. E. (1981). Relationship between methodological rigor and reported outcomes in organizational development evaluation research. *Journal of Applied Psychology, 66,* 541–543.

Terpstra, D. E. (1982). Evaluating selected organization development interventions: The state of the art. *Group & Organization Studies, 7,* 402–417.

Tichy, N. M., & Devanna, M. A. (1986). *The transformational leader.* New York: Wiley.

Trice, H. M., & Beyer, J. M. (1986). Charisma and its routinization in two social movement organizations. In B. M. Staw & L. L. Cummings (Eds.), *Research in organizational behavior* (Vol. 8. pp. 113–164). Greenwich, CT: JAI Press.

Van de Vliert, E., Huismans, S. E., & Stok, J. J. (1985). The criterion approach to unraveling beta and alpha change. *Academy of Management Review, 10,* 269–274.

Walton, R. E. (1969). *Interpersonal peacemaking: Confrontations and third-party consultation.* Reading, MA: Addison–Wesley.

Walton, R. E. (1985). From control to commitment in the workplace. *Harvard Business Review, 63*(2), 76–84.

Walton, R. E. (1987). *Managing conflict.* Reading, MA: Addison–Wesley.

Walton, R. E., & Warwick, D. P. (1973). The ethics of organization development. *Journal of Applied Behavioral Science, 9*, 681–698.

Weisbord, M. (1985). Team effectiveness theory. *Training and Development Journal, 39*(1), 27–29.

White, S., & Mitchell, T. (1976). Organization development: A review of research content and research design. *Academy of Management Review, 1*, 57–73.

White, L.P., & Wooten, K. C. (1986). *Professional ethics and practices in organizational development.* New York: Praeger.

Wilkins, A. L., & Ouchi, W. G. (1983). Efficient cultures: Exploring the relationship between culture and organizational performance. *Administrative Science Quarterly, 28*, 468–481.

Zmud, R., & Armenakis, A. A. (1978). Understanding the measurement of change. *Academy of Management Review, 3*, 661–669.

# An End-of-the-Eighties Retrospective: A Commentary Appended to Organization Development in the 1980s

Marshall Sashkin
W. Warner Burke

It was in 1985 that we began work on this overview of OD in the 1980s. Thus, it is worth a brief, short-term, retrospective analysis as the decade draws to a close. We see no major differences in our original conclusions, but then it would be unlikely to find any at this time; after all, it is not that long ago that we wrote the original paper. We do, however, see some changes in emphasis that are worth mentioning.

Our first two trends, structure-process integration and culture by design, might be better expressed as the micro (task design) and macro (organization design) aspects of the same basic issue: redesigning organizations. A key issue we failed to raise in this regard is that of choice versus chance, that is, the nature of work is changing, at least in postindustrial societies, from an individual to a team focus (as we noted earlier) as well as from simpler to more complex technologies. This is true even at the lowest levels; package delivery services must, for example, now screen delivery personnel, ensuring that they can operate the miniaturized computer link devices that permit the organization to track packages in the system.

Organizations can deal with these changes the same way that changes have, for the most part, been dealt with in the past: with indifference and by making minor modifications or, as Lindblom (1959) put it, "muddling through." Of course, such an "incremental" change strategy is how the United States became involved in Vietnam and how the Soviet Union got mired down in Afghanistan. If we simply leave things to work themselves out, they will indeed do so. The outcome may, however, not be much to our liking.

Alternatively, executives can choose to take an active role in redesigning organizations and work processes within them. Such choices may be rare, but are not nonexistent. In 1988, for example,

347

as a way to build traditional quality back into the process of manufacturing cars, Volvo began to advertise how teams are used to assemble whole subassemblies of automobiles. However, back when Volvo first experimented with this major organizational and work redesign program, the first plant was designed so that it could easily be changed back to the traditional assembly-line approach, just in case the program failed. We must learn how to approach such changes in ways that build in an escape but do not, by so doing, inculcate expectations of failure (King, 1974).

This brings us back to the issue of leadership; that is, the decision to take control over and try to design organizational cultures—and change—can only be made by top-level leaders. We can, as noted above, leave these processes to chance; the "population ecology" approach shows that some organizations will survive and others won't, depending on how well they adapt to and fit their new environments. But if we elect to try to control and design organizational change, we will need leaders who are capable of being what Bennis and Nanus (1985) call "social architects"; that is, such leaders must understand organizational culture and how to design and change it (Schein, 1985).

Having observed that the single critical role of organizational leaders may be in creating culture, Schein (1985) goes on to suggest that such a task may be impossible for most top executives. Unfortunately, both the required understanding and the necessary skills seem to be uncommon. Thus, simple logic suggests that a critical prerequisite for organization development may be executive development, not in terms of traditional management training and development but as a means of producing competent social architects. In some ways this is not unlike the approach advocated for some time by Argyris (1970, 1971, 1976; Argyris & Schon, 1974). Argyris has been criticized by some (e.g., Sashkin, 1977) for an unproductive overemphasis on the chief executive as a necessary first step in organization development. He may, however, have been correct—but a generation ahead of the field!

Thus, we come to the limits of our vision. The 1990s may be the period during which organization development and (a new sort of) management development are reconnected. Such a prospect raises mixed feelings in one who spent serious effort in "decoupling" the two (Burke, 1971)! Such sensations aside, both authors have been engaged in developing new approaches to identifying and training leaders who can design organizational cultures (Burke, 1988; Sashkin, 1986). It is much too soon to speculate on the ultimate success or failure of such efforts, but it is encouraging that others in our field seem to be working on the same issues (e.g., Kouzes & Posner, 1987). If we succeed in learning how to develop effective organizational leaders, and in improving organizational effectiveness through their OD efforts, then the coming century may very well be the first in which humans successfully shape their social environments in consciously chosen ways that are designed to enhance human and organizational effectiveness.

## REFERENCES

Argyris, C. (1970). *Intervention theory and method.* Reading, MA: Addison-Wesley.

Argyris, C. (1971). *Management and organization development.* New York: McGraw–Hill.

Argyris, C. (1976). *Increasing leadership effectiveness.* San Francisco: Jossey–Bass.

Argyris, C., & Schon, D. A. (1974). *Theory in practice.* San Francisco: Jossey–Bass.

Bennis, W. G., & Nanus, B. (1985). *Leaders.* New York: Harper & Row.

Burke, W. W. (1971). A comparison of management development and organization development. *Journal of Applied Behavioral Science, 7,* 569–579.

Burke, W. W. (1988). *Leadership report* (2nd ed.). Pelham, NY: Burke Associates.

King, A. S. (1974). Expectation effects in organizational change. *Administrative Science Quarterly, 19,* 221–230.

Kouzes, J., & Posner, B. Z. (1987). *The leadership challenge.* San Francisco: Jossey–Bass.

Lindblom, C. E. (1959). The science of "muddling through." *Public Administration Review, 19* (spring), 79–88.

Sashkin, M. (1977). Review of Argryis' "Increasing Leadership Effectiveness." *Personnel Psychology, 30,* 273–280.

Sashkin, M. (1988). The visionary leader: A new theory of organizational leadership. In J. A. Conger & R. N. Kanungo (Eds.), *Charismatic leadership in management.* San Francisco: Jossey–Bass.

Schein, E. H. (1985). *Organizational culture and leadership.* San Francisco: Jossey–Bass.

# Author Index

# Subject Index